The
Development
of Affect

Genesis of Behavior

Series Editors: **MICHAEL LEWIS**

*The Infant Laboratory, Institute for Research in Human Development
Educational Testing Service, Princeton, New Jersey*

and **LEONARD A. ROSENBLUM**

*State University of New York, Downstate Medical Center
Brooklyn, New York*

Volume 1　　**The Development of Affect**
Edited by **MICHAEL LEWIS** *and* **LEONARD A. ROSENBLUM**

The Development of Affect

Edited by

MICHAEL LEWIS

The Infant Laboratory
Institute for Research in Human Development
Educational Testing Service
Princeton, New Jersey

and

LEONARD A. ROSENBLUM

State University of New York
Downstate Medical Center
Brooklyn, New York

PLENUM PRESS · NEW YORK AND LONDON

Library of Congress Cataloging in Publication Data

Main entry under title:

The Development of affect.

(Genesis of behavior; v. 1)
"Derived] from papers presented and discussed at a conference ... held under the auspices and with the support of Educational Testing Service in Priceton, New Jersey."
Includes indexes.
1. Emotions in children — Congresses. 2. Affect (Psychology) — Congresses. 3. Developmental psychology — Congresses. I. Lewis, Michael, 1937-(Jan. 10)-   II. Rosenblum, Leonard A. III. Series.
BF723.E6D43   152.4   77-19209
ISBN 0-306-34341-X

© 1978 Plenum Press, New York
A Divsiion of Plenum Publishing Corporation
227 West 17th Street, New York, N.Y. 10011

Printed in the United States of America

Contributors

JEANNE BROOKS, *The Infant Laboratory, Institute for Research in Human Development, Educational Testing Service, Princeton, New Jersey*

JOSEPH J. CAMPOS, *University of Denver, Denver, Colorado*

DANTE CICCHETTI, *Department of Psychology and Social Relations, Harvard University, Cambridge, Massachusetts*

THÉRÈSE GOUIN DÉCARIE, *Université de Montréal, Montreal, Quebec, Canada*

ROBERT N. EMDE, *University of Colorado Medical School, Denver, Colorado*

HARRY F. HARLOW, *University of Arizona, Tucson, Arizona*

JEANNETTE HAVILAND, *The Infant Laboratory, Institute for Research in Human Development, Educational Testing Service, Princeton, New Jersey*

CHARLOTTE HENDERSON, *University of Denver, Denver, Colorado*

SUSAN HIATT, *University of Denver, Denver, Colorado*

MARTIN L. HOFFMAN, *University of Michigan, Ann Arbor, Michigan*

CARROLL E. IZARD, *University of Delaware, Newark, Delaware*

JEROME KAGAN, *Harvard University, Cambridge, Massachusetts*

EVA L. KATZ, *University of Colorado Medical School, Denver, Colorado*

DAVID H. KLIGMAN, *University of Colorado Medical School, Denver, Colorado*

MICHAEL LEWIS, *The Infant Laboratory, Institute for Research in Human Development, Educational Testing Service, Princeton, New Jersey*

CLARA MEARS, *University of Arizona, Tucson, Arizona*

v

HARRIET OSTER, *Human Interaction Laboratory, University of California, San Francisco, California*

SALLY PROVENCE, *Child Study Center, Yale University, New Haven, Connecticut*

DOUGLAS RAMSAY, *University of Denver, Denver, Colorado*

JAMES H. REICH, *University of Colorado Medical School, Denver, Colorado*

LEONARD A. ROSENBLUM, *State University of New York, Downstate Medical Center, Brooklyn, New York*

CAROLYN SAARNI, *New York University, New York, New York*

L. ALAN SROUFE, *Institute of Child Development, University of Minnesota, Minneapolis, Minnesota*

MARK D. STARR, *Educational Testing Service, Princeton, New Jersey*

MARILYN SVEJDA, *University of Denver, Denver, Colorado*

JUDITH K. THORPE, *University of Colorado Medical School, Denver, Colorado*

TED D. WADE, *University of Colorado Medical School, Denver, Colorado*

Preface

How are we to understand the complex forces that shape human behavior? A variety of diverse perspectives, drawing upon studies of human behavioral ontogeny, as well as humanity's evolutionary heritage seem to provide the best likelihood of success. It is in the attempt to synthesize such potentially disparate approaches to human development into an integrated whole that we undertake this series on the *Genesis of Behavior*.

In many respects, the incredible burgeoning of research in child development over the last decade or two seems like a thousand lines of inquiry spreading outward in an incoherent starburst of effort. The need exists to provide, on an ongoing basis, an arena of discourse within which the threads of continuity between those diverse lines of research on human development can be woven into a fabric of meaning and understanding. Scientists, scholars, and those who attempt to translate their efforts into the practical realities of the care and guidance of infants and children are the audience that we seek to reach. Each requires the opportunity to see—to the degree that our knowledge in given areas permits—various aspects of development in a coherent, integrated fashion. It is hoped that this series—by bringing together research on infant biology; developing infant capacities; animal models, the impact of social, cultural, and familial forces on development, and the distorted products of such forces under certain circumstances—will serve these important social and scientific needs.

This series, *Genesis of Behavior*, is the successor to a previous series of volumes by us entitled *Origins of Behavior*. As in the past, it is our intention that each volume in this series will deal with a single topic that has broad significance for our understanding of human development. Into its focus on a specific area, each volume will bring both empirical and theoretical perspectives and analysis at the many levels of investigation necessary to a balanced appreciation of the complexity of the problem at hand. Thus, each volume will consider the confluence of the genetic, physiological, and neurophysiological factors that influence the individual infant and the dyadic, familial, and societal contexts within which development occurs. Moreover, each volume will bring together the vantage points provided by studies of human infants and pertinent aspects of animal behavior, with particular emphasis on nonhuman primates.

Just as this series will draw upon the special expertise and view-points of workers in many disciplines, it is our hope that the product of these labors will speak to the needs and interests of a diverse audience, including physiologists, ethologists, sociologists, psychologists, pedia-tricians, obstetricians, and clinicians and scientists in many related fields. As in years past, we hold to our original objectives in this series of volumes to provide both stimulation and guidance to all among us who are concerned with humans, their past, their present, and their future.

The present volume, the first in the series *Genesis of Behavior*, represents the concerted attempt to awaken interest in, focus atten-tion on, and motivate others to study the development of affect. While the history of psychology attests to the interest in affect, until recently relatively little attention or effort has been given to the inquiry into affective development. Thus, in the last two decades, a plethora of studies on cognitive and perceptual development have appeared while affective development has been almost ignored. Given our commitment to the integration of diverse categories of human behavior into a balanced and holistic approach to development, such an absence of material appears unwarranted and potentially dangerous for the con-struction of models of growth, development, and change. With the emergence of new technologies, as in facial measurement or measure-ment of autonomic nervous system responsivity, and the growth of our knowledge about the perceptual and cognitive development of the growing child, it would appear that there now exists a significant set of tools and theoretical perspectives to allow us to undertake the explora-tion of the development of a significant category of human behavior that is still relatively unexplored: affective growth and development.

The structure of the volume is such that the reader will be able to find information on general issues in the study of affect, the measure-ment of affect, the relationship of affect to cognition and the develop-ment of self, and, from a clinical perspective, individual differences in affect development and affective dysfunction, particularly as it appears in Down's syndrome infants. These various perspectives within the domain of affect provide an integrated framework in which to view the meaning and development of affect.

The chapters in this volume derive from papers presented and discussed at a conference on affect development held under the auspices and with the support of Educational Testing Service in Princeton, New Jersey. The participants in the conference were Clara Mears Harlow, Harry F. Harlow, Joseph J. Campos, Harriet Oster, Jeannette Haviland, Jeanne Brooks, Michael Lewis, Robert Emde, Dante Cicchetti, Jerome Kagan, Leonard A. Rosenblum, Thérèse Gouin Décarie, Sally Provence, Martin Hoffman, Carroll Izard, Allen Wiesenfeld, and Carolyn Saarni.

Michael Lewis
Princeton, New Jersey

Leonard A. Rosenblum
Brooklyn, New York

Contents

Introduction: Issues in Affect Development

MICHAEL LEWIS AND LEONARD A. ROSENBLUM   1

1   *On Emotion and Its Development: A Working Paper*

JEROME KAGAN   11

2   *Facial Expression and Affect Development*

HARRIET OSTER   43

3   *Hearts and Faces: A Study in the Measurement of Emotion*

MICHAEL LEWIS, JEANNE BROOKS, AND JEANNETTE HAVILAND   77

4   *Emotional Expression in Infancy: I. Initial Studies of Social Signaling and an Emergent Model*

ROBERT N. EMDE, DAVID H. KLIGMAN, JAMES H. REICH, AND TED D. WADE   125

5   *The Emergence of Fear on the Visual Cliff*

JOSEPH J. CAMPOS, SUSAN HIATT, DOUGLAS RAMSAY, CHARLOTTE HENDERSON, AND MARILYN SVEJDA   149

6   *Affect Development and Cognition in a Piagetian Context*

THÉRÈSE GOUIN DÉCARIE   183

xi

7 Self-Knowledge and Emotional Development
MICHAEL LEWIS AND JEANNE BROOKS   205

8 Toward a Theory of Empathic Arousal and Development
MARTIN L. HOFFMAN   227

9 The Nature of Complex, Unlearned Responses
HARRY F. HARLOW AND CLARA MEARS   257

10 Affective Maturation and the Mother–Infant Relationship
LEONARD A. ROSENBLUM   275

11 A Clinician's View of Affect Development in Infancy
SALLY PROVENCE   293

12 An Organizational View of Affect: Illustration from the Study of Down's Syndrome Infants
DANTE CICCHETTI AND L. ALAN SROUFE   309

13 Emotional Expression in Infancy: II. Early Deviations in Down's Syndrome
ROBERT N. EMDE, EVA L. KATZ, AND JUDITH K. THORPE   351

14 Cognitive and Communicative Features of Emotional Experience, or Do You Show What You Think You Feel?
CAROLYN SAARNI   361

15 Prior State, Transition Reactions, and the Expression of Emotion
MARK D. STARR   377

16 On the Ontogenesis of Emotions and Emotion–Cognition Relationships in Infancy
CARROLL E. IZARD   389

Author Index   415

Subject Index   423

Introduction: Issues in Affect Development

MICHAEL LEWIS AND LEONARD A. ROSENBLUM

Douglas, a 13-month-old sits quietly playing with blocks. Carefully, with a rapt expression, he places one block on top of another until a tower of four blocks is made. As the last block reaches the top, he laughs out loud and claps his hands. His mother calls out, "Good, Doug. It is a ta-l-l-l tower. Don't you feel good!" Returning to the tower, Doug tries one more block, and as he places it on top, the tower falls. Doug bursts into tears and vigorously scatters the blocks before him. His crying brings his mother, who, while holding him on her lap and wiping his tears, says softly, "Don't feel bad. I know you're angry. It's frustrating trying to build such a tall tower. There, there, try again."

How are we to describe or understand this series of events? We could talk about the child's growing knowledge about spatial representations, that is, his ability to place blocks in some spatial arrangement. In such a discussion, we could focus our attention on cognitive development. Likewise, we could discuss the development of motor dexterity and physical skills, looking at hand movements: the reaching, placing, building, and scattering of the blocks. Our attention then would be upon physical development. Another perspective is the social exchange and interaction between child and caregiver. Much study has recently been given to both the empirical and the theoretical analysis of dyadic interactions, social exchange, and communication, and we could characterize this set of events in terms of these dimensions. Sociolinguistic development would be still another view, the caregiver giving verbal comment and supplying a lexicon for the motor activity of her child. A final perspective, the one that we wish to pursue, is the affective dimension. In this framework, our interest is drawn to the behaviors of "rapt attention"; laughter at success and sadness and anger at failure;

1

verbal comments such as feeling good, bad, or frustrated; and the interface between action, such as in building a tower, and the internal states underlying or as a consequence of that action.

We view behavior, its ontogeny, and its developmental course as being a mixture, an interface of all these perspectives. Cognitive, motor, social, and affective growth all interact, as they are aspects of the same unified development of the individual. The taxonomies, developed by the Western mind in an attempt to delineate these separate categories of behavior, have had the effect of separating these elements. We prefer a model, an analogue of which is a house with many windows. Each of the windows we recognize as a different perspective, a different category of behavior. While the model does not allow for the exploration of the manner in which these categories interact, such a model does allow us both to differentiate and to conceptualize different categories of behavior, and at the same time it prevents us from holding to the existence of a single, noninteractive set.

The window we wish to open we will call *affective development.* Like other categories of behavior, possibly more familiar to the reader, it subsumes a set of behaviors and a set of conditions or situations in which these behaviors occur as well as assuming some internal state most commonly referred to as *feeling.*

GENERAL THEORETICAL ISSUES

For the construction of any kind of model of affective development, it is necessary to clarify some of the confusion in conceptualization and terminology that has emerged in the past. We suggest that what we term *affect* involves four essential elements: (1) the production of some alteration of an internal physiological state; (2) a correlated change in surface expressive behavior; (3) the individual's perception of these changes in himself; and (4) the individual's interpretation of these changes.

Let us attempt to examine and define some of the features of each. The internal changes that delineate affective state may be somatic or neural in character or some combination of the two. The exact nature of this constellation may be either learned or unlearned but must perforce be shaped by the genetic heritage of the organism. The stimuli that elicit these changes in state may similarly be largely encoded genetically, triggering specific receptor sites in the central nervous system or may develop similar stimulus–response regularity through experience. Indeed, it may be speculated that the confluence of a series of experiences, particularly in early childhood, may create linkages between stimuli and expressions that become deeply embedded in the child's developing personality. With sufficient repetition, enduring, fundamental structures similar to those that may emerge on a genetic basis can be found; in computer parlance, there can be a virtual conversion of "software" into "hardware."

With the elicitation of a change in the internal state, concomitant changes in affective expression generally ensue. The precision and fixity of the linkage of the two is an area of some dispute; nonetheless, at least at the extremes of some rough continuum of genetic and experiential contributions to such expression, we suggest that either force may be paramount in determining the production of a given expression. Even in animals, a painful stimulus does not uniformly produce a crouch or vocalization but rather may do either under some conditions and not under others. These variations in response emerge at least in part as a result of prior experience.

The surface expression of affect, once elicited, brings the organism's responses, potentially, into two significant perceptual spheres: its own and that of others in its social network. Clearly, overt expressive responses to affective elicitors can and do form a part of the individual's own percept of itself. It is the fact that affective expression joins the individual's perception of self with the perception of others that makes the individual's interpretation or experience of the affect a social-cognitive process.

Thus, as reflected in our opening example, others around us interpret, label, and differentiate our emotional expressions and their responses to them and help articulate the stimuli that appropriately elicit them. This social filter provides one way in which the child comes to develop its own sense of the nature of its affective response. This social-cognitive basis for interpreting one's own internal and expressive affective responses, although most dramatic during infancy, can occur throughout life. Indeed, some aspects of adult psychotherapy, for example, represent the socially mediated reinterpretation of emotional responses, which, in turn, effects a change in the person's own experience of them. Similarly, one cannot help but wonder at the possible effects of the incessant presentation of emotion-arousing, and hence emotion-defining, situations in the popular media. For both adults and children, the media explicitly define the stimulus events that should provoke affective response and verbally describe "the feelings one has" under such circumstances and the appropriate way to express those feelings. It is necessary that we consider just how well and how often life imitates art.

BASIC DEFINITIONS

1. *Affect*: Affect is defined as a consistent, temporarily delimited, multiphasic response pattern that involves four essential elements: (a) the production of a specific constellation of internal physiological and/or cognitive changes in the organism; (b) some concomitant of these changes in overt, surface expression in the individual; (c) the individual's perception of this pattern of changes; and (d) the individual's personal experience or interpretation of the perceived changes. It is assumed that the internal changes and expression and the individual's affective experience may vary in intensity over time but will be temporarily circumscribed, persevering for relatively short periods after the eliciting events.

2. *Affective elicitors*: These stimuli may be either internal or external in origin. Internal stimuli may range from specific physiological stimuli (e.g., low blood sugar) to complex cognitive activity (e.g., solving a problem). External affective elicitors may similarly range from concrete stimuli in our environment (e.g., a sudden noise) to social stimuli of a particular nature (e.g., the appearance of a loved one). The capacity of these elicitors to evoke responses may be either learned or unlearned.

3. *Affective receptors*: These are defined as relatively specific loci or pathways in the central nervous system (CNS) that mediate the production of changes in physiological and/or cognitive state of the organism. The process through which these receptors attain their affective function and the type of stimuli that trigger their activity may be genetically encoded or acquired through experience. Receptors may lie within more primitive midbrain areas or may be neocortical in locus. Although substantive data are generally lacking, it is assumed that the stimuli to which these receptors respond may be quite specific, unisensory inputs in some instances but may also be activated by more complex multisensory patterns in other cases. In our view, the essential element of the defined affective receptor is the relative specificity of the CNS structures that are involved in producing changes in affective state.

4. *Affective state*: The particular constellations of changes in somatic and/or neuronal activity that accompany the activation of affective receptors. Critical to this definition is its focus on *changes* from previous levels or modes of activity in given physiological domains, rather than the absolute dimensions of the physiological activity. Obviously, not all types of physiological change form a part of the organism's affective state; similarly, sustained alterations in functions may no longer bear upon the immediate affective state of the individual but come instead to provide the new background against which subsequent changes may be

viewed. Affective states, then, are largely specific, transient, patterned alterations in ongoing levels of physiological activity.

5. *Affective expression*: Those potentially observable, surface features of change in face, body, voice, and *activity* that accompany affective states. The constitutent elements and the patterning of particular expressions as well as the regularity with which they are associated with particular affective states may be either learned or unlearned. It is assumed that many aspects of affective expression may be perceived by the individual and may serve communicative functions to other members of the species. Similarly, since many aspects of expression are under potential conscious control, affective expressions may be produced intentionally.

6. *Affective experience*: The individual's conscious or unconscious interpretation and evaluation of its perceived affective state and expression. This cognitive process is influenced by a range of prior social experiences, in which the nature of the eliciting stimuli and the appropriateness of particular expressions have in part been articulated and defined for the individual by others. Central to this definition of affective experience is the individual's concept of self, for it is the perception of its own state and expression, as distinct from others, and its appreciation of itself in relation to a particular current context and past experiences that form the basis of the evaluative–interpretive processes involved.

MODELS OF AFFECTIVE DEVELOPMENT

The articulation of the possible models of affective development has hardly been undertaken. We shall present what we view as the two opposing views of affective development—the biological and the socialization—choosing the strong form of each model so as to delineate clearly the known conceptual space now available. We recognize that variations of these models are possible, indeed probable, and some of these will also be suggested.

Biological Model of Affective Development

The historical model is derived from the Darwinian view of the adaptive function of emotional behavior. Its focus is on unlearned complex behavior. Stated briefly, this model contains three features: elicitors, receptors, and responses. The elicitors are a class of events that have a one-to-one correspondence to a set of responses since they act on specific CNS receptors. An analogue can be drawn to other theories, particularly perceptual theories, having CNS specificity as their central feature; these are often called *grandmother cell theories*, implying that percepts are not created but that there exist specific cells, each created to respond to a different perceptual event. As there are specific cells in the retina that are stimulus- or elicitor-specific, such as specific to color curvature and contrast, there are specific cells in the CNS that respond to a specific set of affective elicitors. Thus, there are cells that respond with happiness to happy elicitors, anger to angry elicitors, etc. Lest this theory appear too farfetched, consider the discovery of pain and pleasure centers in the CNS.

Thus, the strong point of the biological model argues for (1) CNS specificity or a CNS affective template; (2) an unlearned relationship between elicitors and the activity of these receptors; and (3) an unlearned relationship between receptor activity and responses that include the surface features, that is, emotional expression. Usually, such models imply no distinction between the emotional state so produced and the subsequent emotional experience. Again, the strong form of the biological position would have state and experience associated with a minimum of learning.

The Socialization Model of Affective Development

This socialization or learning model contrasts with the biological model in that it does not hold either to CNS specificity (i. e., an affective template) or to any extensive elicitor–response correspondence. Responses, both surface features and internal states, are associated, though experienced with specific sets of elicitors. Consider the caregiver in our example, who defined both the elicitor for the specific set of affective behaviors and the "appropriate" response to them. Her definition included both a lexical component—that is, giving labels to behaviors—and giving the appropriate social responses to a specific emotional expression. Thus, the emotional state or experience is a consequence of the social environment's responses to the child's behavior in a specific context. More central to a theory of socialization is the belief that emotional states and experiences are a consequence of how the child's social environment reacts to the child's behavior as a function of the situation. Socialization, then, is, in part, communication through selective responsivity. The degree to which the social environment holds to the same shared meaning across individuals is the degree to which the socialization process creates similar affective experiences in these same individuals.

Both the biological and the socialization models contain the common features of elicitors, bodily change (in the CNS and/or elsewhere), and perception, which we have called *affective state* and *affective experience*. Given these sequentially related events, a wide variety of biological and social causes are possible in the chain of events that culminate in an affective experience. For example, there are sets of elicitors that appear to have a high correspondence to a set of responses (affective states). Consider, for example, the startle response to a loud and sudden noise. Thus, at least for some affective states, it appears reasonable to have unlearned and complex responses to sets of elicitors. Of course, not all elicitors, indeed very few, appear to have any simple one-to-one correspondence with responses, for either animals or humans.

Even given a high correspondence between elicitor and response (affective state), there may be little relationship between this affective state and affective experience. Two people each riding a roller coaster might have similar elicitors (the rapid drops) and responses (increased heart rate, kinesthetic changes, and more) but might have totally different affective experiences, one happy and excited, the other frightened. Given the set of events, including elicitors, affective states, and affective experiences, a wide range of models, combining to differential degrees a mixture of unlearned pattern and the products of socialization, are probable.

In this regard, two points are necessary to consider. It may well be the case that one simple model is insufficient to cover the array of differential affective experiences that occur among humans. That is, different affective experiences may have different determinants. Affective experiences, called by some *primary affects*, are those for which a more biological model is the best descriptor, whereas those called *learned affects* can best be accounted for by more of a socialization model. Even within a particular affective experience, such as fear, different models may be necessary. Thus, as Lewis and Rosenblum (1974), in a volume on fear, have already pointed out, the sequence responsible for the same affective experience may be quite different.

The need for multiple models may not only be a function of the particular affective experience but may be related to the developmental status of the child. It is not unlikely that biological models may have more heuristic value in a very young organism, while learning models may be more appropriate at later points in development. Even given these possibilities, we should not lose sight of the major events necessary for affective experience and, in this regard, of the importance of an evaluative function.

COGNITION AND AFFECT

The relationship between cognition and affect as processes in an experience is complex and poorly understood. Almost all theories of affective experience require cognitive aspects since the organism needs both to perceive the change in previous levels and to evaluate the changes in terms of both past experience and the present context. While the role of cognition in an affective experience has received some attention, almost no thought has been given to the role of affect in a cognitive experience. Cognitive experiences involve state factors, such as attention, and perhaps motivational factors, such as interest, and it may be possible to conceptualize a cognitive experience using affect in such a fashion. Clearly, more thought needs to be given to this type of problem.

What has received more effort in terms of conceptual issues is the relationship between cognitive and affective experiences. That is, does a cognitive experience lead to an affective experience, or is the reverse true? This type of argument can be conceptualized around two positions. For some theorists, affect is the consequence of cognition. Thus, for example, failure in assimilating discrepant information results in an affective experience. For others, affect can be viewed in motivational terms and is defined in the same manner that drive theorists thought of drives. That is, affects (either as states or experiences) are motivations and as such may be the instigators of cognitions.

Such linear models appear to be too simple to account for the continuity between these two categories of behavior. Neither:

$$\text{Cognition} \rightarrow \text{affect, nor}$$
$$\text{Affect} \rightarrow \text{cognition}$$

appears to be an adequate conceptualization. Rather, in their place, we would chose to offer a model that may be poorly articulated but nevertheless allows for more interaction and interdependence between these two behavioral categories.

In this model, we see that the relationship between cognition and affect is dependent on the point of entry into the observation. If, for example, one's observation starts with the cognition, then an affect will be seen as a consequence of this cognition. If, on the other hand, one starts with the detection of an affective response, a cognition will appear to be a consequence of that affect. For us, neither is right; rather, there is a flow between both factors: affects giving rise to cognitions that give rise to new affects and in turn to new cognitions. This flow—or circular rather than linear model—incorporates our belief in interaction both within and between individuals as well as the holistic approach to behavior; that is, all these behaviors occur within a single organism as a consequence of that organism's adaptation to a continuously changing environment.

AFFECT AND PATHOLOGY

Given the multiphasic model of affect that we propose, pathological affective patterns may be viewed as emerging at any of the phases of response or a combination of them. A child's sensitivity to a particular stimulus that is not usually an affective elicitor may be altered by physiological as well as experiential factors. Thus, for example, a simple auditory deficit may result in a sound that is normally ignored but that triggers affective receptors as it exceeds the child's threshold of tolerance. The result may be a seemingly pathological distress or fear in the infant. Similarly, an infant's (or indeed an adult's) responsivity to a generally neutral stimulus may be dramatically altered by its past experience with it.

It should be pointed out that although relatively simple notions of conditioning can be evoked in explaining many of experientially based pathological responses, this needn't always be the case. As suggested above, we must consider the role of cognitive processes in influencing the individual's interpretation of the stimuli with which he is confronted. Thus, a stimulus that the child interprets as involved in a task in which he cannot succeed may, if failure is equated with maternal rejection, respond violently to the simple neutral stimulus. For Douglas in our example, the building blocks could on the basis of cognitive processing of such past experience act as the elicitor of overtly pathological affective responses. As indicated above, the feedback of affect and cognitions in this sphere may further escalate the aberrant behavior as the infant's affective response further disorders his cognitive activity in the situation and absolutely ensures failure at figuring out the task if it is forced upon him.

The infant's perception and interpretation of his affective response—his affective experience—is particularly vulnerable to dysfunction. Since we suggest that this experience is largely mediated through social experience, all manner of disordered or inconsistent input can play havoc with the child's affective experience and indeed his basic conception of self. Thus, the child may be told that the arousal he feels when confronted with a model stimulus, either social or inanimate, is in fact fear and that the expressions and behaviors of fear are "expected" under such conditions. What might the sequelae of such mislabeling be in the emerging social and environmental interactions of such a child? Would it be surprising if this child, when forced to deal with new stimuli, and new situations, responded with disproportionate anxiety? We suggest that the reverberations of these early aberrant misinterpretations of one's own affective response are likely to emerge into potentially pathological affective states and experiences throughout life.

It is clear, then, that affect and its development may best be viewed as embedded in the child's total social, psychological, and physical maturation. In our view, study of neither the child's biology nor his experiences, neither his social network nor his intraindividual dynamics can afford us the body of information we seek for an understanding of affect, its expression, its development, and its meaning. It is only through diverse methodological and conceptual perspectives of the range embodied in the present volume that we can hope to achieve this significant goal.

REFERENCE

Lewis, M., & Rosenblum. L. A. (Eds.) *The origins of fear: The origins of behavior* (Vol. 2). New York: Wiley, 1974.

On Emotion and Its Development: A Working Paper

Jerome Kagan

Words . . . are the wildest, freest, most irresponsible, most unteachable of all things. Of course, you can catch them and sort them and place them in alphabetical order in dictionaires. But words do not live in dictionaries; they live in the mind. . . . Thus to lay down any laws for such irreclaimable vagabonds is worse than useless. A few trifling rules of grammar and spelling are all the constraint we can put on them. All we cay say about them, as we peer at them over the edge of that deep, dark and only fitfully illuminated cavern in which they live – the mind – all we can say about them is that they seem to like people to think and to feel before they use them, but to think and to feel not about them, but about something different. They are highly sensitive, easily made self-conscious. They do not like to have their purity or their impurity discussed. . . . Nor do they like being lifted out on the point of a pen and examined separately. They hang together, in sentences, in paragraphs, sometimes for whole pages at a time. They hate being useful; they hate making money; they hate being lectured about in public. In short, they hate anything that stamps them with one meaning or confines them to one attitude, for it is their nature to change.

Virginia Woolf, The Death of the Moth, *p. 131*

Introduction

This philosophical essay is a critique of some popular views of the concept of affect. It is neither a theory of emotion nor a synthetic review of the extensive literature on this topic — excellent reviews can be found in Mandler (1975), Izard (1971), Plutchik (1962), and Reymert (1950). Its

---

Jerome Kagan · Harvard University, Cambridge, Massachusetts. Preparation of this paper was supported, in part, by grants from the Carnegie Corporation of New York, and the Foundation for Child Development.

aims are far less ambitious: to suggest a new way to conceptualize the phenomena that have traditionally been called affective. Although I am critical of some current work in this area of inquiry, I do not wish to imply that the phenomena that have been called emotional are unimportant. Quite the opposite; these events must be represented in the written propositions that eventually will describe and explain human behavior. Hence, the critical tone is meant to be constructive and not derogatory.

There are two obvious issues that surround this domain of investigation. One controversy concerns the relation between the changes in somatic and visceral discharge to an incentive event, which are the essential features of most theories of emotion, and the central representation of those patterns of afferent impulses. Some believe that the relation is reliable, even fixed; others contend that it is always changing relative to cognitive evaluations of the situation and the incoming afferent sensations. At one extreme are those who assume that even when cognitive evaluations are absent—as is true of early infancy and special states of consciousness or when the changes are not perceived—it is still appropriate to talk of the existence of affect.

The second issue is semantic: What is the relation of the words we use to name our feelings and objective assessments of the material bases of those experiences? Stated baldly, is there a common envelope of phenomena that occurs every time a person says he is afraid, and is that envelope different from the one that accompanies a declaration of anger? Since both issues engage the classification of psychological phenomena, it seems useful to begin this essay with a discussion of the problems that surround classification. This section is followed by a brief history of the concept of affect and finally by some modest suggestions as to how future investigations might be structured.

THE PROBLEM OF CLASSIFICATION

The parsing of human experience has been the subject of philosophical essays for centuries, and the variety of classification systems reflects the profound presuppositions of the classifier. Nature presents us with an infinite number of discrete events, each of which shares some qualities with another. That experience seems sufficient to lead humans to group the envelopes of events that appear to share common dimensions and to classify them.

A central legend of the Mayan Indians who live in the villages that border Lake Atitlán in northwest Guatemala concerns the final battle between the great Indian warrior Tecun Uman, who was on foot, and the Spaniard Pedro Alvorado, who was on horseback. After hours of battle, Tecun Uman inflicted what he thought was a fatal wound on the horse. Since he had never seen a man on horseback, he thought the horse and rider were an organic entity and so turned away, believing that he was victorious. Alvorado dismounted and killed Tecun Uman, winning the Guatemalan territory for the Spaniards.

Although the risks we run in misclassifying phenomena are not as serious as those taken by Tecun Uman, scientists are always vulnerable to misdirection if they do not categorize phenomena in a way that is faithful to nature. A potentially serious error in the study of emotional (and motivational) phenomena is the acceptance of the validity of old categories and the attempt to define them in the best way, rather than first detecting the covariances that exist in nature and composing class names after the coherences have been discovered.

The mind seeks to understand events through the generation of propositions filled with categorical terms. The categories chosen to represent the phenomena of interest differ in their utility, validity, and mode of generation. In the mature sciences, categories are typically invented *a posteriori* to name a new phenomenon (new particle names are invented each time a physicist discovers a unique and reliable energy function in an accelerator) or, in the case of the quark, to point to a potential, as yet undiscovered phenomenon that might mediate events that are believed to be meaningfully related. In both cases, reliable phenomena led; the categories followed.

Unfortunately, that script is followed less frequently in the social sciences, where reliable relations are less common and the categories that are treated as theoretical terms are too often everyday words borrowed from the language of the larger society. This criticism is especially relevant to the category *emotion* and the terms that comprise the members of that superordinate class, for psychologists often assume that categories like fear and anger exist and try to locate their essence.

Hence, before we turn to the central mission of this paper, which is a psychological discussion of affect, it may be informative at the outset to ask a purely philosophical question, namely, What do we do when we classify events? What factors determine our classifications? Reflection on this issue may clarify the reasons for controversies and misunderstanding.

1. We begin with the assumption that each real event can participate in more than one category (by *category* we mean a set of shared dimensions) because each event possesses more than one dimension. Theoretically, an event can participate in as many categories as it has dimensions. Consider, as a simple example, the natural event we call "a cow." The dimensions of that event include, on the one hand, leather and meat but, on the other, the fact that a cow carries its young

internally and nurses its infant. The first set of attributes leads one to classify cows with alligators, peacocks, and chickens because they produce marketable commodities. The second set of dimensions leads one to classify cows with weasels, wolves, and gazelles under the superordinate category *mammals*. The category selected depends on the purpose of the classifier.

Consider an event more closely related to the topic of this paper; the 1-year-old child runs crying to his mother upon seeing a stranger. Presented with that event, we can focus on the "crying" and classify it as an instance of an emotion or focus on the "running to the mother" and classify it as motivational. We believe that it may not be useful to decide whether the child runs to the mother because he is "afraid" or because "he wants his mother's solace." Each classification is correct; the one we select depends on our purpose. We shall return to this issue in a moment.

2. Psychological events have as their major dimensions:

a. An overt action.

b. A change in feeling state.

c. Cognitive representations of past, present, or future events.

d. An incentive event.

e. A historical or genetic component.

f. A physiological component.

g. A context (social as well as nonsocial).

h. Ease of alteration . . . and perhaps many more.

An observer can selectively emphasize any one or more of the above dimensions in his classification, depending upon the use he wishes to make of the classification.

3. Some of the uses (or purposes) of a classification of an event include:

a. To describe (the child cried).

b. To explain by relating the event to inferred states in the present (the child is anxious; the child wants his mother).

c. To explain by relating the event to the product of past experience (the child is attached).

d. To include the classification as part of a larger logical or theoretical system (the child is in Stage IV object permanence).

e. To maximize communication with the largest number of people (the child is scared).

f. To generate an aesthetic feeling in another (the child is psychically vulnerable).

g. To relate an event normally classified in the language of one discipline to the language of another discipline (the child's reticular formation is physiologically aroused).

Each of these classifications would be potentially legitimate if one saw a 12-month-old child cry following departure of the mother. The one chosen would depend on the purposes of the observer.

4. There is disagreement among psychologists and philosophers with respect to the events that are classified as affective because scholars have different purposes. As a result, the observers selectively focus on different dimensions of the same event. Those who emphasize a change in feeling state as the central dimension of an affect may treat hunger and thirst as emotions. This position was popular during several historical eras when emotions were regarded as epiphenomenal to more fundamental physiological events.

Another group, which emphasizes the afferent feedback from the muscle movements that accompany facial expressions, does not regard hunger and thirst as affects. Since hunger has deprivation of food as a dimension, while sadness does not, it is reasonable at least to suggest that hunger and sadness be placed in different categories. But the reasons for insisting on that distinction are largely intuitive. A 5-year-old does not regard a mosquito as a member of the class *animal*, while a 15-year-old does, because the younger child focuses on the differences and is not yet aware of the similarities between insects and mammals.

Too much psychological classification rests on an intuitive base in which investigators selectively focus on certain qualities following hunch rather than theory.

The naturalist's classification of animals was originally guided by an atheoretical, descriptive morphology but gradually changed following Darwin's writings because evolutionary theory led biologists to focus on reproductive complementarity, common enzyme and blood groups, and even behavior. The theory of evolution replaced concrete morphological attributes as the basis for classification with more dynamic and less public dimensions that included potential behaviors and physiological characteristics.

Since the domain of phenomena we call psychological lacks strong theory, classifications have not been based on sophisticated foundations. Since action, feeling, and thought are so different in their objective and phenomenological qualities, it has been almost impossible for philosophers or psychologists to conceive of any other way to parse human psychological functioning. Although most contemporary investigators regard action and cognition as merely arbitrary envelope categories, that is not the case with emotion. That is, psychologists are not likely to define action in a formal way; attempt to discover, through rational analysis, the primary actions; or posit a group of secondary actions that are blends or derivatives of the primary ones. Similarly, few psychologists argue that there is a heirarchy of significance among the cognitive processes. Yet some scholars continue to approach the domain of emotion with the twin ancient prejudices of defining essences and hierarchically ordering them into pure and less pure categories.

The distinction between overt behavior, on the one hand, and cognition and affect, on the other, is the most obvious. The former is public and "point-at-able"; the latter two are private. The more subtle distinction between cognition and affect seems due to the fact that the latter experience has greater phenomenological salience than the former. The change in feeling that accompanies an insult to our dignity is far more distinctive than the change that occurs when we are planning the day's work. That simple fact of experience has led most to declare that emotions must be a special category different from action, on the one hand, and thought, on the other.

The contemporary separation of affect and cognition resembles, and is likely to be a derivative of, the older division between body and mind or the ancient distinction between spiritus and animus. Although such remarkable historical consensus might normally be taken to reflect the wisdom of that separation, it might also reflect an enduring historical error. It may be useful, therefore, to suspend prior prejudices, at least temporarily, and pretend that the terms we have used with such confidence for so long do not exist.

Emotional terms have been used in three quite different ways. They have been used most frequently to label conscious experience, less often to name physiological states (either objectively quantified or inferred), or to serve as hypothetical constructs to explain covariation between incentive events and behavioral consequences. To illustrate, there is typically a brief period of temporary inhibition of action accompanied by detectable changes in patterns of muscle and autonomic nervous discharge when a person encounters an unexpected external event. Scientists want to carve out the reliable coherences among incentive events, physiology, and subsequent behavior and assign them to some superordinate category. Hence, they have applied the name *surprise* to that coherence. However, *surprise* is not always the term used to describe the coherent set of events that follows the reading of an unexpected piece of new information on the world's fossil fuel reserves, nor is it the concept a physiologist chooses when his polygraph records reveal discharge in the reticular activating system.

5. At present, many psychologists, but certainly not all, regard the category *affective* as being characterized by the following dimensions:

   a. A change in feeling state that is derivative of internal physiological events
   b. produced by an immediate incentive event
   c. that is short-lived in duration,

d. linked to cognitive structures, and

e. not related to physiological deprivation.

There is a general, but implicit, agreement that those five dimensions are central to the category *affective*.

6. The dimensions of events that are classified as motives (in contrast to affects) are less clear but often include (a) anticipation of a future goal that (b) was acquired as a result of past experience.

7. The dimensions of those events that are classified as cognitive (in contrast to affective or motivational) are even less clear but appear to include (a) mental manipulation of schemata, symbols, concepts, and rules in the present with (b) no necessary change in feeling state or outward behavioral manifestation.

8. The above discussion implies that the popular use of the classifications *affective, cognitive,* and *motivational* tends to be correlated with the past, present, and future components of a continuous and dynamic unitary event.

Consider the event: the child who has just insulted a friend apologizes. If we focus on the child's evaluation of his act of insulting, we classify the event as cognitive. If we focus on the change in feeling, we call it affective. If we focus on the child's wish to make amends and apologize, we call the event motivational. The event (the child apologizes after insulting a friend) has thought, feeling, and wish as components. The classification imposed on that event announces the dimensions we wish to emphasize; in the same way, the classification of a woman as beautiful, arrogant, intelligent, or educated (as the first adjective used) reflects the dimensions we wish to award primacy.

9. The main purpose of a classification is to package a great deal of information efficiently. When we call an event a star rather than a planet, we communicate a great deal about the event. The classification *star* summarizes a great many qualities, including distance from the earth, light source, and probable size, age, and temperature. If we call the same event as astronomical object, we communicate only the fact that it is not located on the earth. Similarly, if an observer calls an event emotional, he implicitly announces that he wants to emphasize an incentive that produced a change in feeling state. If he calls the same event cognitive, he wishes to emphasize the evaluation and manipulation of information. If he calls the event motivational, he wishes to emphasize anticipation of a future state.

Many, but not all, psychological events are whole units with an incentive, a feeling state, a mediating cognitive process, and a consequent intention. When we wish to draw attention to the incentive and feeling state, we use classification words like *fear, guilt,* and *sadness.* When we wish to draw attention to the child's organization and processing of information, we use cognitive categories like *reflect, compare, infer* and *evaluate,* which share the manipulation of schemata, images, symbols, concepts, and rules. If we wish to draw attention to future aims and potential actions, we use motivational terms like *affiliation, achievement,* and *hostility.*

If an observer says, "The man is sad," he tells me of a likely incentive and a present feeling state. If the same observer says. "The man is thinking about his wife at home," he informs me of the content of his present thought. If the observer says, "The man wants to be with his wife," he informs me of his anticipations and likely future behavior. Each classification communicates something different about the same event.

10. There is potential utility in using separate affective, cognitive, and motivational categories, even though these categories are not normally explanatory. The classifications inform us of the qualities of an event that the classifier wishes to emphasize.

11. This discussion implies that states like hunger or thirst can be included or excluded from the category *affect.* If one could demonstrate that these drives shared a quality that the other affects did not, it might be potentially useful to separate them. Similarly, the affects accompanied by special facial feedback patterns might be separated from the others. But those who promote that view would have to show first that the classification of the states accompanied by facial feedback is theoretically useful, that is, that it leads to predictions and/or principles that are more powerful than those generated when the states with and without facial feedback are pooled. But this is not yet proved. Birds have many qualities that mammals do not, although both share some dimensions. Biologists find it useful at times to distinguish between these classes. But no biologist would argue that birds are a primary class of vertebrates, while mammals are secondary. That is why it is not clear why Tomkins and Izard want to claim that the affects associated with feedback from facial muscles are primary and all others are secondary. There is reason to believe that the affect states accompanied by facial feedback may be a special category, but it is less obvious that these events should be declared, *a priori,* the primary emotions.

12. There is a potential relation between affects and motives. The category *motive* refers to complementary representations of future and current states—a comparison of present and future. For example, the category *motivation for friends* implies the generation of a future experience with others that is different from one's current state. The specific motive category named often depends on the affect experienced, the one to be experienced, and the substantive goal sought. Hostility is placed in a category different from sexuality because of the differences in feeling

and content of the anticipated goals and state. Hence affect and motive are related since affect states contribute to the classification of motives. Assuming the validity of the categories (a) incentive events, (b) change in feeling state, and (c) anticipated goals, a combination of (a) and (b) makes up the superordinate category *affect*, while the combination of (b) and (c) makes up the superordinate category *motive.*

Since motive categories are influenced, in part, by the discrepancy between present state and an ideal state in the future, the motive categories that predominate in a society are influenced by local conditions, for societies differ in the magnitude of discrepancy between present and desired future for the varied goals humans seek. Wealth is a dominant motive in the West—while food is not—because many individuals experience a large discrepancy between the ideal and the present. The opposite profile exists in a Chilean concentration camp. This is another way of saying that nodes of uncertainty within a culture influence the hierarchy of motives.

The discussion thus far has been analytic and critical rather than constructive. We believe that the category *affective* has been used in a loose way to denote the universal but complex experience of detecting a sudden change in one's feelings or, by extension, inferring a similar change in another as a result of the recognition of certain unusual action patterns.

Since the occurrence of that class of event is relatively infrequent (i.e., the proportion of our waking hours that we are alerted by a serious discrepancy from our normal feeling tone is probably less than 10%), we naturally try to classify that experience. It is generally the case that the observer is initially tempted to base his classification on the dimension that is most discrepant from his corpus of knowledge. Hence, most classifications of affect award primacy to the changed feeling state. This cognitive disposition can also be noted when the Western anthropologist categorizes an African society as polygynous, even though less than a third of the families in that society practice polygyny. But since a household with several wives is so discrepant from the observer's norms, he is drawn to a classification based on that unusual quality and led away from other attributes that might be more critical to the functioning of the social group. We believe that this egocentric perspective has guided much theorizing on affect. But, as indicated earlier, there is a second strategy. One can first search for covarying phenomena and, if successful, invent categories to provide coherence. There is an important difference in the use of the term *fear* to explain the regular empirical relation in the 1-year-old between departure of the caretaker and subsequent crying and its contrasting use to name my sudden tachycardia following a near accident on a highway or to suggest the reason a 3-year-old child suddenly put his thumb in his mouth and lowered his head. Scientific progress in the study of emotion will be stalled as long as we fail to stipulate how we want to use affective terms.

WHAT HAVE WE WANTED TO UNDERSTAND? A HISTORICAL SURVEY

What phenomena do we wish to understand and/or predict that require the postulation of a concept like emotion? One popular answer is that we wish to explain the sudden changes in ongoing action and/or subjective experience that are lawfully yoked to certain contexts. A person is talking quietly with a friend when the former suddenly begins to wave his arms and raise his voice. Fom these data, we infer a change in internal state and perceived feeling. How shall we classify those phenomena? Whenever one's progress in solving a problem is stalled it is occasionally useful to inquire how scholars in the past approached the same problem. I believe that it will be useful, therefore, to present a brief historical survey of the concept of emotion. I have borrowed a great deal in the pages that follow from an infrequently cited book: Gardiner, Metcalf, and Beebe-Center (1970) entitled *Feeling and Emotion: A History of Theories*.

Plato's interest in emotion was guided by a transcendental concern with what was good. Affects either hindered or helped attainment of that precious state and were never ends in themselves. (As we shall see, Kant viewed affects hindering rationality—the modern West's symbolic substitute for virtue.) The feeling of pleasure, which is regarded as a final goal in modern writing, was only a "way station" in one's progress toward the more transcendental state.

Aristotle, like Plato before him and writers prior to the European Renaissance, also viewed emotions the way chemists regard catalysts. The focus of concern was man's movement toward the good. Emotions helped or hindered that process. Thus, emotions were typically evaluated as good or bad depending on their ability to move a human toward or away from morally proper action.

Aristotle divided man into three parts—faculties (potentialities to be actualized), formed habits, and passions—but he avoided defining the passions and merely gave examples. Like the writers of the Middle Ages, Aristotle believed that the passions did not belong to the soul but influenced the soul. Aristotle's classification of the passions, found in the 10th book of *Nicomachean Ethics* and the 2nd book of the *Rhetoric*, was composed of paired opposites that described an evaluative dimension: anger and the ease of being placated; love and hate; fear and confidence; shame and shamelessness; benevolence and churlishness; pity and resentment; emulation and contempt. He did not imply that the list was complete. Like Plato, Aristotle was concerned primarily with pleasure and pain, but he conceptualized pleasure as the concomitant of the normal exercise of human abilities. The actualization of any natural attribute was a source of pleasure, the degree of pleasure being proportional to the degree to which that talent was realized. It should come as no surprise that frustration of that human effectance, as Robert White might put it, was felt as pain. Unlike later writers, Aristotle made no analysis of affects. The affects were epiphenomena—something added to the normal functions of life, like the smile that follows a joke. Like most writers, Aristotle classified the affects by external incentives and associated cognitions. Anger was "an impulse attended with pain to avenge openly an undeserved slight openly manifested to ourselves or our friends." Love consisted in "wishing a person all the things you consider good, not for your sake, but for his and readiness, so far as in you lies, to bring them about." For Aristotle, as for most who followed him, drives, needs, feelings, and passions were all viewed as having something in common, namely, a distinct and salient subjective experience. Although there was some speculation on the role of bodily heat and blood in emotion, the key to Aristotle's classification was the contest and associated cognition; in that sense, it resembled the approach of the modern social psychologist.

The Stoics postulated four basic passions—desire, fear, pleasure, and pain—which were the result of a belief regarding the degree of good or evil inherent in the objects. The Stoics also defined emotion in terms of situation and target and acknowledged the contribution of cognitive factors. Although modern social scientists would reject those classifications in detail, they would at least be able to understand them.

The Middle Ages

By contrast, the scholars of the Middle Ages generated a classification of emotions that contained presuppositions that are more difficult for the modern mind to comprehend. Thomas Aquinas wrote one of the most systematic expositions in the 13th century. Aquinas believed that soul and body were connected and that passions could run in either direction. The consequences of a painful wound ran from body to soul, the results of anger from soul to body. Aquinas differentiated the purely intellective from the sensory and affective, the latter being divided into concupiscible and the irascible. The former concerned appetites, needs, and drives in the present with strong sensory components that could be gratified; the latter referred to future goals that were more difficult to gratify (see Table I).

TABLE I. AQUINAS'S TABLE OF PASSIONS

Concupiscible		Irascible	
Good	Evil	Good	Evil
Pleasure	Pain	Hope	Fear
Love	Hate	Despair	Courage
Desire	Aversion		Anger

It is doubtful that any modern scholar would ever classify the affects in this manner. Like the Greeks, Aquinas made an ambiguous differentiation between what we call *affect* and *drive* or *motive*. The primary passion, and the source of all the rest, was love, which was viewed as an aptitude to move toward the good. If one loves an object, one will move toward it. If one attains it, one will experience joy or pleasure. Although this medieval classification is based on presuppositions about good and evil that are alien to most modern psychologists, it served Aquinas and those of his century, who held a different set of *a priori* assumptions and had different purposes than Cannon, James, Schachter, or Tomkins. It is in this sense that we say that the Schachter and Tomkins positions are complementary and not inconsistent. If the purpose of the classification is to predict behavior, then Schachter's theory is more useful. If, on the other hand, the purpose is to understand the biological contributions to affective experience, the Tomkins and Izard propositions seem more useful.

Aquinas named 11 passions but argued that there are only four major affects, namely, pleasure and pain, on the one hand, and hope and fear, on the other. Pleasure and pain were states in the present, hope and fear anticipations of the future. Aquinas believed that the bodily changes were due to the appetite's being excited by the expectation of good or evil. But mind was the origin of a passion—a movement of soul in the body. "The affections of the soul are not caused by changes in the heart," Aquinas wrote, "but rather cause them." Thus, both the Greeks and the medieval scholars placed psychological factors, be they in the form of soul or in the form of thought, as the origin rather than as the consequence of biological changes.

The Renaissance

Renaissance writers introduced an important change in the classification of emotions. The rise of science and the hints of the Church's eventual decline led scholars away from inquiry into the purpose of affect and toward an attitude of analysis, even though the purpose of the analysis was left ambiguous. Gradually, the term *affectus* replaced *passiones*. Philipp Melanchthon, for example, defined pleasure not as the seeking or the attaining of good but in physiological terms: "The perception in the nerves or nerve coating or a congruent object, a perception not injuring or lacerating the nerves but totally adapted to their conservation." This defintion would have been foreign to Plato, Aristotle, and Aquinas and not unlike defining libido as a recursive polypeptide chain with four methylated hydroxyl groups. Morally neutral description and analysis were becoming the criteria for classification of affects and have remained so for over 500 years. Soul and body were now seen as less isolated, and a synergism between mind and biology was assumed. The actions of the heart were less epiphenomenal and played a more causal role. In a remarkably prophetic essay, Scipio Claramontius (1565–1653) argued that the most reliable signs of affect were to be found in the pulse and respiration because these two systems reflected the "heat of the heart." Modern writers have moved the site from the heart to the face and the brain.

A subtle but important change in the Renaissance attitude toward affective phenomena is captured by the contrast between the medieval concern with pleasure and grief and the Renaissance concern with laughter and weeping. The latter are objective behaviors, not inferred states. Antonius Laurentius wrote two books on laughter in the first decade of the 17th century, and even though the explanations are absurd ("tears flow when the brain is filled with moisture"), the form of the questions is modern, and the dependent variable is a public event, not a hypothetical, evaluative universal. Francis Bacon brought these threads together in *Advancement of Learning*, emphasizing the need for accurate description and analysis. By the middle of the 17th century, the empirical spirit was accelerating, and Descartes treated emotions in *Les Passions de l'Âme* in psychophysiological perspective. The original element in Descartes's discussion was to award biological forces a status independent of the soul but in a relation of influence to the soul, as one might conceive of a mother and child as separate and distinct entities, influencing each other. But Descartes was still close to the Greek view, for he regarded passion as an experience in which the soul was the subject, even though the source of the experience was the movement of forces in the body, in the spirit of James and Lange. Descartes speculated on the physiology of the passions. The body was the source of changes that, via the medium of animal spirits, influenced the soul, not unlike the statement that the discharge of cones in the retina via the ganglia in the thalamus eventually leads to the perception of color. Note that Descartes's concern was primarily with explanation, not with evaluation or purpose. Whatever teleology was present was distinctly modern in tone. The purpose of passions was survival, to dispose the soul to will the things that nature declared to be useful—an early version of the modern evolutionary biologist's view that the purpose of behavior is to ensure survival and reproduction of the next generation. The change from a "good" emotion to a "useful" one is profound! Unlike those of his predecessors, all the affects proposed by Descartes are in the immediate present, not in the future. They are not potential states or wishes but the consequence of bodily changes in the here-and-now. Descartes listed six primary emotions: admiratio (alertness, attentiveness, and surprise), love, hate, desire, joy, and grief. All others were derivative (one notes the absence of fear and guilt and the rejection of Aquinas's structure of the concupiscible and irascible passions).

Descartes's more empirical, pragmatic and materialistic view of affect was accompanied by a concern for the first time with the development of emotions. Descartes believed that the first passions were joy and sorrow (apparently Descartes called the crying of infants to the presence of strangers and on caretaker departure sorrow rather than fear, as we do). Sorrow subsequently was transformed into hate later in development. Thus, Descartes shares with modern theorists the assumption of an epigenetic relation between the affects of infancy and those of later childhood, as some modern writers posit a relation between infant attachment and later dependency. Descartes was also the first major associationist, for he believed that a person could learn a contiguous association between an idea and some bodily change—a conditioned link between visceral reaction and thought. He speculated that individual differences in the emotional reaction to roses, for example, were probably due to differences in prior experience.

The 17th and 18th Centuries: Hobbes, Spinoza, and Kant

Descartes's view of affects as natural phenomena to be explained was amplified by Hobbes, who carried Descartes's fragile materialism much further. For Hobbes, psychological life consisted of mechanically propelled motions of particles within the organism, and body and soul became one unity. Hobbes made the passions more important than any earlier writer. Passions were necessary for life: "to have no desires is to be dead, so to have weak passions is dullness." Affects sustained thought, determined intellectual and moral character, and were the sole incentives for action. Since Hobbes believed that passions guided thought, individual differences in behavior could be traced to emotions, especially the emotions related to the desires for power, wealth, honor, and knowledge, which Hobbes believed were environmentally determined rather than innate.

Hobbes completed the change in philosophical attitude that gradually replaced Plato's transcendental good as the criterion for evaluating an affect with individual survival by anticipating Darwin's assertion that the greatest good was the conservation of the individual. Self had replaced virtue as the entity to be preserved. Appetite and aversion were the primary affects, but Hobbes also posited desire, love, joy, and grief as simple passions. Contempt was a derivative emotion produced by an immobility of the heart in resisting the action of certain things, where the heart was already otherwise moved. Hobbes was concerned primarily with explaining man's behavior in society, not with analyzing physiological correlates.

Although Spinoza agreed that emotions were natural phenomena whose aim was self-conservation, he tried to reduce the enormous variety of experience to the smallest number of elementary units, and pleasure, pain, and desire became Spinoza's elemental trio.

Kant provided the next important set of changes in conception, for affect was again separated from cognition (Kant rejected Hobbes's attempt at unification) and motives were differentiated from emotions. The three faculties were knowing, feeling, and appetite; hence, Kant distinguished affects from what we call motives and drives. Kant believed that both feeling and appetite hindered rationality and, therefore, were potentially bad. Affect was evaluated once again, as it was much earlier, but this time the evaluation depended not on the relation of emotion to the seeking of an ethical or transcendental good but rather on the degree to which an emotion hindered or facilitated attempts at rationality, the West's version of virtue. Kant postulated a new set of primary emotions. For the first time, the innate passions were declared to be an inclination for liberty, love of life, and sexuality—all of which placed the self in the center as both subject and object of action. Once again, we note that nodes of uncertainty become the basis for classification. As it would have been impossible for Plato to have made "an inclination for liberty" a primary passion, so too it would have been impossible for Silvan Tomkins or Stanley Schachter to declare "love of God" as a primary emotion.

The Modern Era

During the late 19th century, we see for the first time an interest in emotional states that might not reach conscious experience. That novel idea was a result of the increased reliance on physiological factors as the criteria for emotion (Reymert, 1950). Scientists turned from phenomenology and observation of overt behavior to the quantification of physiological states. It was reasonable now, but not earlier, for James and Lange to assert that emotions were merely the perception of changes in bodily states, and for Spencer to argue that consciousness was due to physiological discharge. The enslavement of psychological products by physiological forces was carried to an extreme when Gall and Spurzheim postulated 35 faculties, each yoked to a specific cerebral organ, with over half of these faculties being affective in nature. Thus, by the late 19th century, conscious experience of a feeling became subordinate to biological events, a complete reversal of the views of Plato, Aristotle, and Aquinas, who saw the affective experience as origin rather than consequence.

That reversal has profound implications for our contemporary view of the orgins of man's actions, especially those related to morality. When consciousness is the source of passion and motivation, it is reasonable to argue that man is responsible for the actions that spring from strong feeling. When consciousness is merely the end of a series of physiological events, it is easier to defend the premise that man does not have total responsibility for all of the actions that are derived from passion. And during the last hundred years, we have seen an increasing friendliness toward the view that entities beyond the person's control—be they genes, neurotransmitters, madness, or poverty—can be the "causes" of behaviors that harm self or other.

The Present

We have several choices open to us if we still wish to classify affective phenomena. But we must first ask, What are our purposes? What uses do we want to make of emotional phenomena? We suggest that an important use of an affect category is to serve as a hypothetical construct to unite contemporaneous relations between incentives and resulting reactions or to serve as a conceptual entity to unite past with present—to explain how present behavior might be derived from the distant past. We suspect that most modern psychologists—or philosophers, for the matter—want to use emotional categories in this manner and not as terminal states to seek or avoid or as labels for phenomenological states. Unlike the Greeks, we do not want to posit an ideal telos for all actions and, therefore, are not burdened with a commitment to an evaluative veneer for emotions. Nor do we see emotions, as Kant did, as inimical to reason. But there is still detectable disagreement among those scholars who believe that emotion is an essence that will yield to definition.

Sartre (1962) regards emotions as a manner of apprehending the world. This cognitive view of affect is dictated, in part, by Sartre's philosophical agenda. Since consciousness is central to Sartre's philosophy and emotion is a form of consciousness, it was necessary that he define affect as a form of understanding.

But a psychologist like Plutchik (1962) cannot help but be influenced by the modern commitment to physiological reductionism and evolutionary theory, and so he makes physiological arousal and adaptive value fundamental qualities in his list of primary emotions. Nonetheless, his final definition of emotion is so inclusive that it admits almost any behavioral reaction to an incentive event: "Emotion is a patterned bodily reaction of either destruction, reproduction, incorporation, orientation, protection, deprivation, rejection, or some combination of these which is brought about by a stimulus" (Plutchik, 1962, p. 151).

In addition to the complementary views of Tomkins (1962, 1963) and Izard (1971), to which we have referred several times, Mandler's (1975) recent attempt to tame the many-headed entity of emotion also reflects the belief that although emotion is the result of an interaction of physiological changes and cognitive interpretations, the physiological arousal, which is not viewed as cognitive, is the quintessential first event: "The particular human behaviors and experiences of interest to us occur subsequent to the activities of the autonomic nervous system, particularly its sympathetic division. I shall refer to this activity as arousal" (p. 60), and "Arousal, as used here, refers to specific measurable events that occur external to the mental system; in a more ancient language, arousal is stimulation" (p. 111).

Mandler seems to side with Descartes in hinting at the independence of mind and body, but with James and Lange in making the former reactive to the vissicitudes of the latter—as most scholars have done since the early 19th century. The primacy of physiological arousal is seen most clearly in his discussion of the ontogeny of anxiety, where Mandler asserts that it is not necessary to specify the incentive for the fundamental distress state of the newborn, which he views as a combination of arousal and helplessness: "The schematic model suggested here for the occurrence of anxiety . . . is the cyclical distress of the human newborn. There may be antecedent events that could account for the crying and increased activity we recognize as distressful in the young infant . . . but it is not necessary to specify or even to assume such a specific antecedent event" (Mandler, 1975, p. 194).

This statement by a leading contemporary theorist reflects the popular presupposition that emotions are theoretically useful entities whose essences are to be found in autochthonous, physiological processes.

Since most theorists—including Mandler, Ekman, Izard, Plutchik, and Tomkins—view emotional terms as hypothetical constructs, they approach the classification of affect, as they do other concepts with this epistemological status, by asking what are the links to empirical reality.

The Central Characteristics of Affective Phenomena

The phenomena that have been called emotional by contemporary scientists generally share one quality. They always involve a change—usually perceived but for some theorists inferred—in internal milieu. We believe that there is a profound difference between the state of consciously perceived feeling changes and the state produced by bodily changes that are not detected. We shall consider only the first and postpone discussion of the psychoanalytic notion of "unconscious affective states" for another time.

Changes in Feeling Tone. Every person is aware of a typical feeling tone (or normal feeling state) to which he has become accustomed. The perception of a change in that tone has several consequences. The perceived change (1) alerts the person (the "admiratio" of Descartes); (2) may be accompanied by changes in bodily posture, facial expression, visceral reactions, or an alteration of the hierarchy of probable responses that might be issued; or (3) may be an incentive event for a cognitive interpretation. These are three quite different phenomena.

The phenomena that are associated with a change in facial expression more often have as their incentive a real external event in the present rather than a thought or an image. The primary emotions of Tomkins and Izard are typically triggered by the seeing, hearing, smelling, or experiencing of an external event. In a sense, they are special classes of orientation reactions. Since facial expressions produce afferent feedback to the central nervous system that might subsequently influence the feeling state, it is not unreasonable to regard those states produced by such real events and accompanied by changes in facial expression as a special category. But the decision to call those states the basic emotions and to imply that a feeling of emptiness in a hotel bedroom 1,000 miles from home on Christmas Eve is not a primary emotion because there is no necessary facial change has the flavor of theoretical imperialism. Nonetheless, the "face as seat of emotion" hypothesis is helpful, for it names two correlated events that can accompany a change in feeling tone, namely, an external incentive and a facial expression.

Quality of Feeling. Let us now examine more closely the quality of the change in feeling state. The change in state can vary in intensity, salience, perceived locus in or on the body, duration, and rise time. The change following an hour of exercise or a near accident on the highway is more intense than the change that follows violation of a standard on politeness. The locus of the change in feeling state can be the heart, chest, trunk, face, legs, stomach, or genitals. The change in feeling tone also has a salience, duration, and rise time that may provide important information. If a change in feeling tone is the essential event in emotion, it may be useful to specify, in a way that has not been done, how the combination of these five qualities might influence thought and action.

As we have indicated several times, we should differentiate between the use of emotional words to label conscious experience, to name physiological states, and to "explain" the relation between a set of incentive events and subsequent outcomes.

Since all changes in behavior are likely to be accompanied by changes in the central and autonomic nervous systems, theoretically all behavior change is accompanied by an affect. As we understand each new functional relation, we assign it a name, be it *hunger* or *pain*, and remove it from the larger unknown category called *affect*. One might conceptualize the task of scientific work as that of trying to empty the term *affect* of any content because we will have eventually grasped the more specific meaning of each of its exemplars. This view implies the wisdom of separating those changes in state we know something about—like hunger thirst, pain, warmth, or cold—from those we know little about. We might also eliminate the state of continued attention, for we are gaining understanding of those events that control attention, and they differ from those related to hunger and thirst.

But we are still left with a large set of psychological events that are (1) characterized by an incentive in thought or external information: (2) accompanied by a perceived change in feeling state; and (3) associated with a special set of reactions.

If one announces explicitly that one function of a classification of affective phenomena is to relate classes of incentive events to internal changes (acknowledging the legitimacy of other purposes), then the following discussion might be regarded as an initial attempt at categorization.

EXTERNAL EVENTS AS INCENTIVES

There is one class of external events that typically produces alerting, attention, and occasionally inhibition. These events are often called *discrepant*. This class of incentives includes all external events that require acquired knowledge for the change in state. These events are to be distinguished from those that innately produce a change in state, like a flash of bright light or a very loud sound. We are concerned here with those events that produce a changed state because they engage knowledge. This category would be closely related to the affects of surprise, fear, and interest postulated by Tompkins and Izard. We believe these to be among the first incentives for state change in the infant and have suggested that they are the origins of the phenomena that in modern terms are called *stranger* and *separation anxiety*.

A second class of external events that is linked to changes in state is caused by loss or absence of a target object toward which the child has established behavioral dispositions. These target objects can include caretakers as well as inanimate objects. When loss of a target object is recognized, a special state is created, different from the one created by discrepant events. If the target object remains absent and there is no coping response available, a different state is generated. A third class of external incentives with a special state involves some agent's interrupting a person's ongoing response routine—an incentive Mandler has awarded great power.

THOUGHT AS THE INCENTIVE

When reflections on the past or anticipations of the future are the primary incentives, there are important differences in the physical qualities of the change in state. The change is apt to be less intense and to have a slower rise time but a longer duration. We suspect that these factors may be critical. For example, Kearsley (1973) has shown that a slow rise time for an auditory event leads to interest in the newborn, while the same signal with a fast rise time leads to a defensive response.

One important class of mental incentives occurs when the child recognizes that his behavior or the behavior of others deviates from a standard. When the child recognizes that deviation, there is often inhibition. When the child is mature enough to anticipate or infer the psychological reactions of another to that deviation, another state is created. This state typically does not occur before 3 years of age because it requires the ability to infer the psychological state of another. Typical deviations are a failure to meet standards for a task and violation of parental prohibitions. When a standard becomes generalized across many contexts, the reaction to the violation may have a special quality.

There is a complementary state created when the child meets a standard following behavioral effort. In this sequence, the child generates a representation of a performance to be attained and invests effort in order to match his behavior to that ideal. If he is able to meet the standard, there is an internal state that some label *joy, pride,* or *happiness.*

Thus far, it has not been necessary to postulate a construct of self separate from the reactions of the child. By *self,* we mean the psychological function that evaluates alternatives and integrates the child's qualities into a coherent category. But by age 3 and maybe earlier, this new function has emerged. Now the child is aware that he has alternative actions or choices. The 2-year-old dirties himself, recognizes that a standard has been violated, and anticipates a reaction from others.

Although the 2-year-old does not appreciate that it could have been otherwise, the 4-year-old considers the possibility that perhaps he could have avoided that misdemeanor. Hence, the reaction has a different quality.

The emergence of a construct of self also permits the child to detect similarities and differences between himself and others. Since the self is old enough to evaluate those qualities, the child can categorize himself in desirable or undesirable terms, depending on the pattern of similarities. This process has been called *identification*. Additionally, if the child perceives that he is valued by another who possesses desired qualities, the child feels enhanced.

When either of these external events or thoughts are the primary incentives, we must posit a previously established structure. The incentive event is related to the knowledge in some way. The event can be discrepant from possessed knowledge, absence of a target one has oriented toward, violation of a standard, or meeting a standard. This approach to classification of affects makes cognition and cognitive structure necessary components of emotion. The perceived change in internal state—the phenomenon of interest—is due to the interaction of the incentive event and the cognitive structure, as radiation is the result of the interaction of an accelerating electric charge in an electromagnetic field. This position is incompatible with a division of affect and cognition, for affect is the phenomenon that emerges from the operation of cognition on information (see Sroufe, 1977, for a similar conclusion).

I have tried to avoid, as much as possible, using the common emotional terms found in textbooks because I am not sure how useful they are. But we might see how this discussion is related to two of those ancient categories. When an unassimilated discrepant event leads to a salient change in state that is intense, has a fast rise time, and is associated with special facial and postural reactions, many might use the word *fear*. The term *anxiety*, on the other hand, is often applied when an anticipation of the future leads to a change in feeling that has a slower rise time but no necessary sequelae in face or posture.

I suggest that affect states be characterized as classes of coherence among (1) the nature of the interpreted incentive; (2) the quality of the resulting feeling state; and (3) cognitive and behavioral sequelae. Trios of phenomena with a high degree of covariance might be grouped together. Consider the classification of the drive state hunger. Physiological psychologists have demonstrated the utility of taking into account the incentive, the state change, and the subsequent reaction. For example, the incentive for hunger is deprivation of food, the state change involves alterations in the lipid and glucose levels in blood and liver, and the reaction is a signal to the brain that prompts the organism to seek food. All three comprise a definition of hunger. The hunger state is not to be found in any one of these phenomena, and reliance on any one of these events may provide a misleading definition of hunger. One could be deprived of food for 10 hours but not be hungry because of high fat and sugar reserves. Or one might have a lower level of blood glucose because of "shock" rather than food deprivation. Or one might seek food and eat in order to be friendly. The coherence of a set of events seems to be a useful way to classify this concept and may be useful for affects as well. Note that this conceptualization implies a continuously dynamic state, not a static one. A person is not either hungry or not hungry but is characterized by a position on a set of potentially quantifiable dimensions. We experience hunger in degrees. It is unfortunate that our affect words—*fear, sadness, anger*—have such a static, dichotomous connotation. Perhaps research on their referents would have been more profitable had the terms implied a continuum, like *fearing, saddening,* or *angering.*

It is likely that there is a small set of incentive conditions, as interpreted by cognitive processes, that guarantees that certain states are likely to occur (perhaps must occur) in all settings in which children are raised by and live with human beings. The universally appearing incentives that contribute to these states include (1) encounter with unassimilable discrepant events; (2) encounter with assimilable discrepant events; (3) detection of inconsistency or deviation between acquired standards or between the standard and behavior; (4) loss of a target object to which the person has established a response routine; (5) anticipation of danger, harm, or an event with which the subject cannot cope; (6) an agent's blocking a goal or threatening ego's values and standards; (7) the meeting of a standard following effort or the realization of an anticipated state; (8) genital stimulation or the anticipation of genital stimulation; (9) the experience of a person requiring nurture; (10) the experience of a person violating a fundamental standard; and (11) release from a distress state.

Some of these incentive events fall into an approximate developmental sequence. For example, discrepant events are an incentive very early in development. Since the 12-month-old child can anticipate the future, he is vulnerable to a new feeling state. He can also hold a future goal in short-term memory for a longer time. Since that goal can be thwarted, a capacity for another state can occur. By 2 years of age, a child can reflect on the past, take the role of another, and make inferences. As a result, he can reflect on his own past behavior and the violation of standards and experience a special state. By 4 or 5 years of age, he is able to realize that he had a choice with respect to a prior action and is therefore vulnerable to still another state. By 7 years of age, he has acquired some absolute standards that generalize across many contexts, and events that violate those standards elicit additional feeling states.

The above list of incentives—and there are likely to be more— probably occurs in all humans who live with others. We believe that each of these is linked to changes in states (we acknowledge that there may not be distinctive changes in feelings linked to each incentive) and to sets of cognitions. These coherences might be called *affect states*. However, the name to be applied to each coherence is the least important consideration. We could number them from 1 to *n*.

Since some cultures present unique incentives not present in all locales, some affective states are unique to a community. The state that results from living alone in a foreign city for a year or the recognition that one shares few beliefs with others in the community in which one lives does not happen to millions of people who spend their lives in isolated, endogamous villages of less than 1,000 people. The affects we call *isolation, alienation,* or *depersonalization* are probably not actualized in these closed settings. However, the villager in these settings has a capacity for those affect states; many genetic predispositions are not actualized if the proper environmental conditions do not occur.

Some Final Suggestions

Since the category *affect* is so broad, it may have outlived its usefulness. Changes in feeling state are such a basic quality of human existence, as are interpretation, storage, and manipulation of information, that it is likely that the use of one term to cover the entire domain distorts nature's plan. Perhaps we should proceed on the assumption, as Guilford does for intelligence, that there are many theoretically independent classes of phenomena with different developmental functions, monitoring factors, and physiological correlates. Our task is to discern the most useful way to crack the domain so that the pieces that fall away are most faithful to the lines of coherence nature drew in initially, and then trace their structures ontogenetically.

If emotions have an internal state change as their essential attribute, it may be logically impossible to be in other than an emotional state, since each living creature is continually changing its state. Plutchik's definition of emotion has this inclusive quality. Perhaps this is one reason why, in practice, psychologists have been concerned with a very limited class of incentive–state change combinations. By popular consensus, these incentives have involved the relations between cognitive structure and experience in the form of recognizing either novelty, deviation from a standard, the meeting of a standard, anticipation of the future, or reflection on the past. These cognitive structures in conjunction with state changes—I avoid implying that the cognition occurs before or after the state change—comprise the coherence we wish to understand. The indifference to the temporal order of cognition and state change may strike some as cowardly and others as simply wrong, but it has a precedent in other natural phenomena. The introduction of an accelerating electrical charge into a field produces an effect similiar to the one produced by the creation of a field around an accelerating charge: radiation develops in both cases. A sudden ridge of cold air moving into a humid atmosphere produces snow, as does the sudden introduction of moist air into a frigid high-pressure system. A fertilized zygote can result from the introduction of an ovum into a sea of sperm or from the introduction of the sperm into a location where the ovum is present. Either sequence is effective and we do not ask about the temporal order. Our ancient commitment to a temporally linear causality may have prevented us from recognizing that in some cases (obviously, not in all) it is not very important to ask, "Which event occurred first?" and assign that incentive priority. In this sense, Aristotle, Descartes, and James were all guilty of seeking to assign primacy on the basis of temporal priority rather than looking for coherences. Changes that result from discharge in heart, muscle, or thalamus are necessary but insufficient for the state with which we are concerned. Each is a participant in an event that must involve cognition, and it may be that the temporal order of contribution is less relevant—though I hesitate to say it is irrelevant—than the elements that are combined.

What practical suggestions for the empiricist flow from this essay? We should begin to invent categories that summarize replicable functional relations or to generate the constructs that are necessary to render a set of empirically based propositions logically coherent. Rather than begin with the assumption that affects like joy or sadness exist and we must find their best definition, it may be more useful to search first for coherences among incentives, changes in state, and cognitive and behavioral reactions. We should also expect that some of those coherences will change over time. It is likely that loss of a parent in adolescence is associated with a reliable feeling state and a certain class of cognitions. It is just as certain that loss of a parent at 1 year of age does not produce the same state.

Let us consider two illustrations of the potential utility of this suggestion. As a result of a half dozen separate investigations of children living in the United States as well as in other cultural settings, it appears that the occurrence of serious inhibition of play and crying in response to the incentive of a primary caretaker's leaving a child alone in an unfamiliar setting or with an unfamiliar person follows an inverted U-shaped growth function over the period 7–36 months of age (Kagan, 1976). Here is one of the replicable functional relations we have been urging. Before suggesting a hypothetical state that might be applied to the child during this era, let us examine how some investigators have used this phenomenon.

Some had postulated an emotional state called *attachment* and subsequently tried to find some reactions that would define that construct. An early decision, now rejected, was to treat the protest following caretaker departure as indicative of the state of attachment. We can now see the problems with that assertion. Although protest begins to vanish after 2 years of age, no psychologist believes that the intensity of the attachment state is decreasing.

An older alternative was to declare that the emotional state "anxiety to anticipated loss of the mother" was indexed by the protest at separation. Again, no one wished to claim that the 3-year-old, who does not typically protest parental departure, does not experience a change in state following anticipation of the loss of a parent.

But suppose John Bowlby (1969) had first charted the developmental function for inhibition of play and fretting to maternal departure to see what course it took before inventing a name. He would have discovered the inverted U-shaped growth function and we suspect would have concluded something like, "During the period 7–30 months of age, the infant is made uncertain/anxious/fearful by the incentive event of parental departure in an unfamiliar context." Such a statement acknowledges the emotional quality of the young child's reaction but specifies both the incentive and the era when it is potent.

Consider a second, perhaps less persuasive, example. Nightmares are more frequent between the ages of 4 and 8 years than during the preceding or succeeding four-year period. It is less clear, in this case, what class of incentive is producing the sleep disturbances, and much more inference is required than in the case of separation protest. (I choose this example because I do not want the reader to be misled into thinking that I oppose theory; quite the contrary.)

One might infer that a major incentive for the nightmares is violation of standards on hostility to parents, obedience, sex play, masturbation, honesty, and stealing, since this is the time when these standards are being socialized in a serious way by the American family. As in the case of separation protest, even though the nightmares decrease after age 9, one would not conclude that the child does not experience a changed feeling state following anticipation of or committing a violation of those same standards. Nor would it be correct to assert that there is no change in state following violation of a standard on hostility prior to age 4, even though nightmares are less common during the first four years of life. As in the case of separation protest, a particular dependent variable (fretting, inhibition of play, or nightmares) bears a very specific developmental relation to a class of incentives. This situation, which is common, suggests at least three possible conclusions.

The internal state produced by the incentive is the same throughout development, even though the manifest behavioral reactions differ. This conclusion places a heavy burden on reasonableness, since it is hard to believe that a 10-year-old who wishes her parents a happy holiday on Barbados as they enter a taxicab is as distressed at their departure as she was at 15 months, when her mother walked out of the front door for a minute to allow a visitor to enter. Second, it is counterintuitive to assume that a 15-year-old who swears at his father following paternal insistence that the son stay home that evening is as distressed over his aggression as he was when he issued the same act at age 5. The fact that the dependent variable changes probably tells us something important about the emotional state of the child.

A second possibility is that both the incentive and the state have been altered because the child's interpretation of the event has changed with development. By interpretation, I mean the cognitive classification of the event. This is a tempting possibility, for psychologists acknowledge that from a psychological point of view, the incentive is not the objective stimulus but the person's interpretation. However, this posture also elicits some disquiet since it requires us to assume that the 15-year-old who swore at his father did not regard that act as violating a standard. This is questionable, for if we should ask, "Is it proper to swear at your father?" he would probably reply negatively. Thus, it is not clear that we can resolve our problem easily by simply declaring that the incentive event had changed.

A third possibility, and one I feel friendly toward, is that incentive events are accompanied by an evaluation of the individual's ability to understand, assimilate, or instrumentally deal with the incentive situation and the resulting state change. When there is uncertainty over assimiliation or action, a change in emotional state is most likely. Thus the 1-year-old cries to parental departure because of both uncertainty over parental return and the absence of coping behaviors that might be issued to deal with the uncertainty that follows departure. Similarly, the 5-year-old is probably more uncertain than the 15-year-old about the possible sequelae of hostile action or thoughts toward parents. Hence, the change in emotional state may be less intense in the older child.

These suggestions imply that study of the development of emotion must take into account both the altered interpretation of incentive events and changes in the ability to cope with the total event (i.e. to control the affect and respond to new information). These two may not develop in parallel fashion. I acknowledge that there are some changes in emotional state whose developmental course will not be handled easily by this last assumption. For example, children show an increased ability to experience a state change following an encounter with another person who is in distress. We cannot easily explain this phenomenon by referring to uncertainty over coping or understanding the event. Thus, the developmental course of this state is being monitored by other factors. Similarly, the likelihood of a state change following an insult is not easily understood by the above assumption. We take this to mean that state changes are influenced by a variety of qualitatively different factors and that the developmental course for each class follows different principles.

The importance of the child's ability to deal with the change in emotional state brings us to a final characteristic of affects that is often overlooked, namely, the ease with which an affect state can be altered by new information. Some affects are easily destroyed or altered by the introduction of a single fact. A person's anger at someone who failed to return a greeting can dissolve completely or be transformed to sympathy if he learns that the other is ill or blind. But affect states seems to differ in the ease with which they can be changed by new information. Guilt over causing the depression, distress, or death of another usually resists dissolution because the fact of the victim's state cannot be changed easily. The fact that an affect state—even an intensely felt one—can be dissipated by information is perhaps the best support for the statement that affects are dependent upon cognitive beliefs and processes.

It seems easier to alter the affects of young children than of adults because the former's beliefs, not his physiology, are more labile. As beliefs become resistant to change, acute, punctate affect states turn into chronic moods. The adjectives *angry, fearful,* and *joyful* typically refer to acute states; *mean, anxious,* and *happy* are more frequently used to describe the more permanent qualities of a person. As beliefs about self and the world become fixed in adulthood, the occurrence of acute changes in affect state are likely to decrease, while moods become more apparent. There are few dour children or silly adults.

There is a similarity in the theoretical status of the concepts of affect and intelligence. In the same spirit in which some psychologists reject the usefulness of a concept of intelligence because it is not representative of any unitary process, we suggest that the concept of emotion may be without much utility. For the domain of intelligence, Guilford has suggested that we must take into account the original materials, the cognitive processes, and the subsequent products, and he posits 120 different categories of cognitive ability. I do not know if there are 120 different emotional states but agree, in principle with Guilford that there are different classes of incentive events, state changes, evaluation of those state changes, and coping reactions.

In his 1940 William James lectures, *An Inquiry into Meaning and Truth*, Bertrand Russell wrote, "all the paradoxes arise from the attribution of significance to sentences that are in fact nonsensical." I have hinted that statements of the kind, "Emotions are————" fit Russell's definition of nonsense—one reason why many of us have the feeling we are caught in a sticky web. The term *emotion*, like the concept *weather*, must be analyzed if it is to have any meaning.

Summary

Since this essay may read more like a collection of dissatisfactions than a constructive critique, it may be helpful to summarize the points I have tried to make in the preceding pages.

1. Unlike physicists, chemists, and biologists, who frequently begin their theoretical work with a set of known functional relations they wish to explain, psychologists often begin with categories. They assume that certain words stand for something real and try to find their essence. Most of the affect words we currently use in our theories or everyday speech are labels for complex conscious experiences and, in a sense, are analogous to phrases like "tastes like lobster" or "smells like roses." Sensory physiologists would not have made much progress if they had tried to find where on the tongue the taste of lobster lay. For this reason, I suggest that it is probably not profitable to try to locate the essence of affects like fear or surprise in the face, the heart, or the hypothalamus, even though the reactivity of these material entities may participate in the state of interest.

2. Many of the events we call *affective* are dynamic, continuously changing coherences characterized by a change in feeling state, a class of incentives, and cognitive evaluations and intentions as major dimensions. We tend to classify an event as *emotional, cognitive,* or *motivational* depending upon which of those dimensions we wish to emphasize.

3. A change in internal feelings is the one dimension that all psychologists agree is central to affective phenomena. But since we are always undergoing changes in feeling state, that criterion is of minimal value. Psychologists have had a tacit understanding that the interest lay in a smaller set of changes in feeling state that were short-lived, provoked by an incentive, linked to a cognitive evaluation, and not the result of physiological deprivation. I have suggested that it might be useful to carve out trios of coherences that consisted of a class of

incentive (either external or mental), a quality of feeling, and cognitive structures and to treat these as the primary construct. For example, violation of a standard on aggression by a child who was able to evaluate his ability to instigate or inhibit the prohibition would be associated with a particular quality of feeling.

4. Since changes in feeling state are primary, it was suggested that we analyze the sensory qualities of these feelings, as we do any stimulus event, and take into account intensity, salience, locus, rise time, and duration.

5. Over the last century, we have awarded the physiological events associated with affect states primacy over the psychological ones, partly because of the rise of the biological sciences. I suggested that for some psychological phenomena, it may not be important to decide whether the physiological or the psychological event occurs first. Temporal priority does not always imply explanatory primacy.

6. I suggested that some incentives were likely to be universal and that a few might participate in an invariant developmental sequence. Some of the incentives included: reaction to discrepancy, inconsistency between standards or between standards and behavior, loss of a target object, anticipation of an event for which there was no coping response, blocking of a goal or a threat to one's values, the meeting of a standard following effort, genital stimulation, the experience of a person requiring nurture, the experience of a person violating a fundamental standard, and release from a distress state.

This discussion has been critical because it is easier to fault existing conceptualizations than to generate a better paradigm. Hopefully, this essay will provide a stage for discussion that will lead to more constructive ideas, for I agree with Sroufe (1977) that the child's growth will not be fully understood until we gain greater insight into those aspects of development that we call *emotional*.

ACKNOWLEDGEMENT

This paper was presented at a conference, The Origins of Behavior: Affect Development, February 11, 12, and 13, 1977, at the Educational Testing Service, Princeton, New Jersey.

GLOSSARY

affect: the emergent process resulting from the cognitive evaluation of
    information from visceral, somatic, mental, and external sources.
assimilable: able to be understood

classification: the grouping of events that share dimensions into a
category
epigenetic: having to do with necessary sequences in development
motive: the cognitive representation of a goal associated with a feeling
state
phenomenological: introspective description of one's internal states
separation anxiety: the occurrence of distress or inhibition of play shown
by a child during the period 6–30 months when his caretaker
departs in an unfamiliar setting
standard: the representation of an event, idea, belief, or feeling that is
linked to a good–bad evaluation.

REFERENCES

Aquinas, T. *Summa theologica*, opera editor vives. Paris: 1895.
Aristotle. *Nicomachean ethics* (F. H. Peters, trans.). London: 1881.
Bacon, F. *Advancement of learning*. (A. Spedding, Ed.). Boston: 1872.
Bowlby, J. *Attachment and loss* (Vol. 1), *Attachment*. New York: Basic Books, 1969.
Cannon, W. B. *Bodily changes in pain, hunger, fear and rage* (2nd ed.). New York:
Appleton-Century-Crofts, 1929.
Darwin, C. *The expression of the emotions in man and animals*. London: John Murray, 1872.
Descartes, R. *Les passions de l'Âme*. Paris: Oeuvre et Cousin, 1825.
Ekman, P., Friesen, W. V., & Ellsworth, P. *Emotion in the human face*. New York:
Pergamon, 1972.
Ekman, P. Crosscultural studies of facial expression. In P. Ekman (Ed.), *Darwin and facial
expression*. New York: Academic Press, 1973, pp. 169–222.
Gall, F. J. *On the functions of the brain and of each of its parts*. (W. Lewis, trans.). Boston: 1835.
Gardiner, H. M., Metcalf, R. C. & Beebe-Center, J. C. *Feeling and emotion: A history of
theories*. Westport, Conn.: Greenwood Press, 1970. (Originally published by the
American Book Company, New York, 1937).
Hobbes, T. *Leviathan* (T. Molesworth, Ed.) London: 1839.
Izard, C. E. *The face of emotion*. New York: Appleton-Century-Crofts, 1971.
James, W. What is an emotion? *Mind*, 1884, *9*, 188–205.
Kagan, J. Emergent themes in human development. *American Scientist*, 1976, *64*, 186–196.
Kearsley, R. B. The newborn's response to auditory stimulation. *Child Development*, 1973,
44, 582–590.
Lange, C. *Über gemuthsbewegungen*. Leipzig: Theodore Thomas, 1887.
Mandler, G. *Mind and emotion*. New York: Wiley, 1975.
Plutchik, R. *The emotions: Facts, theories and a new model*. New York: Random House, 1962.
Reymert, M. L. (Ed.). *Feelings and emotions*. New York: McGraw-Hill, 1950.
Russell, B. *An inquiry into meaning and truth*. Baltimore: Penguin Books, 1962.
Sartre, J. P. *Sketch for a theory of emotions*. London: Methuen, 1962.
Schachter, S. The interaction of cognitive and physiological determinants of emotional
state. In C. D. Spielberger (Ed.), *Anxiety and behavior*. New York: Academic Press,
1966.

Schachter, S., & Singer, J. E. Cognitive, social and physiological determinants of emotional state. *Psychological Review,* 1962, *69,* 379–399.

Sroufe, L. A. Emotional development in infancy. Unpublished manuscript, University of Minnesota, 1977.

Tomkins, S. S. *Affect imagery and consciousness* (Vol. 1 & 2). New York: Springer, 1962, 1963.

2

Facial Expression and Affect Development

Harriet Oster

The study of the causes of things must be preceded by the study of things caused.
Attributed to Hughlings Jackson (Beveridge, 1957)

One of my principal aims in this chapter is to introduce a new way of looking at infants' faces. The key to this approach is close observation and analysis of moment-to-moment changes in naturally occurring facial behavior, with an eye to discovering organized patterning both in the configuration of the facial features and in the timing and sequencing of facial movements. Beginning with a rich and fine-grained analysis of the infant's facial behavior, we can distinguish potentially meaningful expressive movements from random facial actions; we can refine grossly defined descriptive categories; and we can be more precise in relating facial movements to the infant's other behavioral responses and to particular stimulus situations. As a result, we can begin to specify more precisely the affective and communicative "meanings" of the infant's facial movements, as well as changes in function and meaning with age.

This approach depends on having an objective measurement system, one that allows us to describe all of the distinctions and changes the eye is capable of perceiving, while at the same time keeping track of what remains the same—for example, the common elements in two globally different facial expressions or constancies in facial expression

Harriet Oster · Human Interaction Laboratory, University of California, San Francisco, California. This work was supported by an Interdisciplinary Training Program postdoctoral fellowship (#5-T01-MH07082) and an NIMH postdoctoral research fellowship (#5-F-32-MH05012).

from infancy through adulthood. In the first part of this paper, I describe a newly developed system for coding facial movement that is uniquely suited to these purposes. In the second part of the paper, I illustrate several different strategies for analyzing the structure and meaning of infant facial movements, taking as examples smiling and brow knitting ("frowning") within the first three months of life. An unexpected temporal relationship between these two seemingly opposed actions is documented, raising questions about the usual interpretation of both behaviors. The findings presented here have implications for two larger issues: the nature and degree of organization of facial behavior in early infancy and the nature and origin of the relationships among facial behavior, emotion, and cognition.

The Facial Measurement System

The Facial Action Coding System (FACS) is a fine-grained, anatomically based measurement system recently developed by Ekman and Friesen (1976, 1978) and adapted to the infant's face by Oster (Oster & Ekman, 1977; Oster, in press). The basic units in FACS are discrete, minimally distinguishable actions of the facial muscles. Each of these *action units* is designated by a completely neutral number code and specified by an exhaustive set of dynamic cues, including the direction of movement and changes in the appearance of facial features and contours, wrinkles, pouches, dimples, etc. Though described in terms of visible appearance changes, the action units are defined in terms of facial muscle structure and function, that is, the "mechanics" of facial muscle action. By contrast, the basic descriptive categories of existing ethological measurement systems (cf. Blurton-Jones, 1971; Brannigan & Humphries, 1972; Grant, 1969; Young & Décarie, 1977) are defined largely in terms of phenomenological criteria, "a unit being all items of behavior which take the same form" (Brannigan & Humphries, 1972, p. 41). Although the basic units are similar in both types of system, an anatomically based system has several unique advantages, which are briefly highlighted here.

Unlike the ethological catalogs, FACS is a potentially comprehensive system: the anatomically defined elementary units of FACS can be combined to represent a virtually unlimited number of distinguishable facial movements. By contrast, the ethological catalogs cannot be comprehensive, since some of their categories are combinations of two or more distinctive actions that can occur independently or in combination with actions from different categories. This point is nicely illustrated by the treatment of brow movements and eye openness in the two types of system.

All possible movements in the brow–forehead region can be specified in FACS by three discrete action units (AUs) and their combinations: AU 1 and AU 2 correspond to two independent actions of the frontalis muscle, which can separately raise the inner and outer corners of the brows, respectively. AU 4, on the other hand, represents the combined actions of three closely associated muscles: procerus and depressor supercilii, which lower the brows, and corrugator, which draws the brows together and downward toward the root of the nose. Four distinctive configurations result from combinations of these actions: AU 1 + 2 (brows raised at both ends and slightly arched); AU 1 + 4 (oblique brows raised and drawn together in the middle); AU 2 + 4 (brows raised at their outer ends but lowered and drawn together in the middle); and AU 1 + 2 + 4 (brows evenly raised, flattened, and knit).[1] None of the ethological catalogs lists all of these actions, and some designate as separate categories what are merely intensity differences. (For example, Brannigan and Humphries's "sad frown" and "sad raise" seem to differ only in the extent to which the inner ends of the brows are raised.) In FACS three levels of intensity can be separately indicated for a number of action units, so that appearance differences due to the relative strengths of the constituent actions can be distinguished from differences in the actions themselves.

All of the ethological systems have units designating degrees of eye openness, but a single dimension fails to capture some important appearance changes that depend on the specific muscles acting. The eyes (i.e., the palpebral fissures) can be widened in only one way, by the raising of the upper lids (AU 5). However, they can be narrowed either by a drooping of the upper lids (AU 41) or by contraction of the muscles around the eyes (AU 6 and/or AU 7), actions that raise and straighten the lower lids and produce bagging or pouching below the eyes. (AU 6, corresponding to the outer pars orbitalis of the orbicularis oculi muscle, raises the cheeks as well as the lower eyelids; AU 7 corresponds to the inner pars palpebralis of this muscle. But the distinction between AUs 6 and 7 can be disregarded for the moment.) To appreciate the contrast between these two different forms of eye narrowing, compare Figure 7b, which shows drooping upper eyelids and relaxed lower lids, with

---

[1] The schematic descriptions in parentheses merely summarize the complex pattern of changes produced by each of the above actions and combinations—changes visible not only in the brows and the forehead but also in the upper eyelids and the eye cover fold (the skin below the brows).

Figures 7d, 7f, and 7g, in which the lower lids are raised and straightened, pouching the skin below the eyes.

FACS also takes into account interactions between movements of the brows and lids. For example, a strong brow-lowering action (AU 4) can narrow the eyes by pushing down the skin below the brows. As shown in Figure 2a, a distinctive, intensely alert appearance results when this lowering action is countered by a strong raising of the upper lids.

Practical Advantages

Without knowledge of the muscular basis of facial movement, static surface cues can be ambiguous or downright misleading. With FACS, behavior is scored on the basis of movement and change, which helps to make the observed surface appearance intelligible.[2] In addition, the detailed, dynamic cues specified by FACS make it possible to recognize a given action despite wide individual, group, or age differences in facial structure and appearance. To enhance interobserver reliability, the coding manual for FACS (Ekman & Friesen, 1978) further specifies minimum threshold requirements for scoring very slight facial actions. Finally, as illustrated in the second part of this paper, FACS is uniquely suited for analyzing the sequential, temporally patterned aspects of facial expression.

Limitations

In all, FACS specifies 24 discrete action units, 20 miscellaneous actions more grossly defined in terms of their anatomical basis (e.g., "cheek puff"), and 14 action units designating head and eye position. Although potentially capable of distinguishing among all visibly different facial movements, in practice FACS is limited by the ability of human observers to distinguish reliably among subtly different actions

[2] Example: Oblique eyebrows, raised at their inner ends, can be produced either by AU 1 or by AU 1 + 4. The brows cannot be "drawn down at their outer ends," as Brannigan and Humphries (1972) wrote in describing their category "sad frown." Technical points such as these can make an important difference in actual coding, determining where we would look for signs of movement (e.g., the inner, not the outer ends of the brows) and the precise appearance changes we would expect. Unfortunately, confusing errors tend to be perpetuated once they are in the literature.

or combinations of actions. (See Ekman & Friesen, 1976, 1978.) FACS specifies only visible movement and does not have categories corresponding to changes in complexion or muscle tone or to qualitative changes—often used to describe infants—such as "brightening" of the eyes. FACS was designed primarily for use with film or video, though still photos can also be scored with FACS. This system is not limited, therefore, by the constraints of real-time behavioral coding. Although the behavior being coded is almost always perceptible—and often identifiable—in real time, the precise scoring of facial actions requires repeated viewing, often in slow motion or frame-by-frame.

Facial Movements in Infants

Since FACS is an anatomically based measurement system, it can be applied to facial movements observed in infants only if these can be related to the same discrete muscle actions as in adults. This application would be possible only if the facial muscles—and the nerves innervating them—were sufficiently developed and differentiated at birth, and if the muscles had reached their definitive points of insertion in the tissues of the skin. As reported by Oster and Ekman (1977), the available data on the prenatal development of facial muscle structure and function indicate that these prerequisites are met by 18–29 weeks of gestation (cf. Gasser, 1967a, b).

Our own behavioral analysis confirmed that virtually all of the discrete elementary action units specified in FACS can be identified in the facial movements of both premature and full-term newborns. Moreover, despite the presence of some diffuse, low-level activity difficult to score with FACS, the facial muscle actions of young infants are often well defined and highly discriminable, even when occurring in complex configurations.

At the same time, the pattern of surface cues produced by a given action often differs in infants and adults, because of the considerable differences in their facial morphology. In particular, the extensive layers of subcutaneous fat in the full-term infant's forehead, across the bridge of the nose, and extending into the cheeks reduce the wrinkling and creasing associated with certain muscle actions, such as brow raising. As a result, slight upward movements of the brows may be difficult to detect in infants, particularly if the movement's onset is gradual. When the brows are drawn together (the corrugator component of AU 4), many infants do not show vertical furrows between the brows, as in adults. Instead, this action produces characteristic muscle bulges curling upward from the inner corners of the brow, as in Figure 2a.

Because of such differences, some modifications of specific coding criteria were required for scoring infants' facial movements. The process of adapting FACS to the infant's face is described in Oster and Ekman (1977). A detailed discussion of infant–adult differences and of the special problems involved in scoring infants' faces is presented in Oster (in press) along with systematic interobserver reliability data.

Level of Analysis

It is important to emphasize that FACS is a purely descriptive tool, an aid to analysis. It makes no prior assumptions about the "natural" or meaningful units of facial behavior or about the emotional correlates of facial muscle actions. At the same time, it is not assumed that facial expressions can be *reduced* to the level of individual action units or single "muscle twitches."

Like all complex behavioral systems, facial behavior is hierarchically organized. Thus, we cannot infer which discrete, elementary actions will co-occur (or be mutually exclusive) solely from a knowledge of which actions can *physically* co-occur. While facial movement can be characterized to a large extent in terms of sets of opposing muscle actions (up versus down, medial versus centrifugal, closing and narrowing versus opening and stretching, etc.), there are surprisingly few actions that are physically antagonistic in the sense that their simultaneous action is impossible. For example, as mentioned above, the action of lowering and knitting the eyebrows (AU 4) can combine with the action of raising the brows (AUs 1 and 2). Similarly, zygomaticus major (AU 12), which draws the mouth upward into a smile, and triangularis (AU 15), which lowers the mouth corners, can contract simultaneously. While the discrete facial actions specified by FACS can combine in a virtually unlimited number of different combinations, the configurations actually observed in distinctive human facial expressions represent a restricted range of these total possibilities. (This is a general property of hierarchically organized systems, as recently discussed by Jacob, 1977.) Therefore, only direct analysis of facial movements—and of the contexts in which they occur—can lead to a knowledge of the "co-occurrence rules" and hierarchical structure of facial behavior.

Moreover, the meanings of complex configurations can rarely—if ever—be inferred solely from a knowledge of their constituent actions, since single muscle actions are most often ambiguous: we cannot assume that a particular facial action has a single, fixed meaning, independent of the accompanying facial movements or the larger behavioral context and stimulus situation.[3]

We should not conclude from the above discussion that it is useless to describe facial behavior, or any complex behavior, in terms of its elementary constituent actions. On the contrary, the value of a system like FACS is that it permits an objective, comprehensive description of the behavior observed. The investigator can then determine empirically which actions are functional equivalents, which configurations are meaningful, and which differences in appearance are significant.

FACS does not offer any general solutions to the often-mentioned "problem" of how to go from the level of elementary units to more meaningful categories of behavior (cf. Lewis, Brooks, & Haviland, this volume). But with FACS, the task is at least well defined. Each distinguishable facial configuration can be represented, in FACS, by a unique string of action units. (Strings of more than 20 action units are theoretically possible. In adults, as many as 10 have actually been observed.) Alternatively, each configuration can be conceptualized as a unique point in a multidimensional "face space." The higher-level, meaningful categories can then be viewed as groupings of these unique strings or clusters of points in face space. The criteria for determining these higher-level categories and for deciding how finely or grossly they should be divided can probably not be fixed as general rules but must be determined by the investigator's specific aims. The problem of where to lump and where to split thus remains. The major difference is that with FACS, we are always aware of how much is being lumped. In addition, since this lumping occurs at a higher level of analysis—and not at the

---

[3] This is not to say that single muscle actions are necessarily without any "natural" or intrinsic meaning. As Darwin (1872/1965) first saw, many expressive movements (including single muscle actions and more complex combinations) can probably be traced to responses that once served a vital adaptive function (e.g., sensory or protective functions). Such natural associations, whether they originated in the evolutionary history of the species or during individual ontogenetic development, would be likely to restrict the potential meanings of an action. For example, we would not expect to find droopy, half-closed eyelids as an expression of surprise. At the same time, as Altmann (1967) and Ploog (1969) noted, there is no reason to expect a simple, one-to-one relationship between expressive movements and emotional states or signal functions. Because evolution is opportunistic, we would expect to find functional equivalents or "synonyms" in facial movements, as well as ambiguous movements that serve more than one biological or communicative function. The potential sources of expressive movements and the relative importance of phylogenetic, ontogenetic, and cultural influences have been the focus of much interest and controversy (cf. Allport, 1924; Ekman, 1977; Hinde, 1972; Oster & Ekman, 1977; Peiper, 1961/1963).

initial level of description—we can redefine our provisional categories as new empirical data are obtained and as new questions are raised.

In practice, the analysis of facial behavior can proceed from either of two starting points. On the one hand, we can begin by sampling facial behavior on the basis of provisional categories defined on some *a priori* grounds. These might include impressionistically defined descriptive categories (e.g., all configurations labeled *smiles*) or more precisely specified *a priori* categories for facial affect expressions (e.g., Ekman, Friesen, & Tomkins, 1971). Or they might include categories corresponding to particular situations or classes of stimuli that we think may be related to particular affects (e.g., all behavior observed in response to the approach of a stranger). Or the behavioral context might serve as the basis for sampling (e.g., all facial behaviors preceding some other act, like crying). On the other hand, we may sample facial behaviors more inductively, to see where regularities, nonrandom co-occurrences, and sequences of behavior might be found. This type of approach might begin, for example, with the sampling and analyzing of all facial movements involving upturned mouth corners or lowered brows. To specify and refine previously gross or subjective categories of facial expression, we might ask, for example, whether there are elements— either discrete action units or more complex combinations of action units—common to all facial behaviors labeled as *smiles* or to all behaviors occurring in situations that we would consider "fear"-inducing as opposed to painful or "frustrating."

The unique features of FACS are revealed most sharply in analyses that are not limited to refining or validating previously defined categories of facial expression but that focus instead on the organization or "structure" of facial behavior. Beginning with a knowledge of elementary facial muscle actions and the purely physical constraints on their co-occurrence, we can begin to discover more interesting and potentially meaningful regularities in the patterning of facial movements. Such discovery is particularly crucial for developmental research (cf. Oster, 1977; Oster & Ekman, 1977). Using FACS, we can investigate the quality and degree of organization (versus randomness) of facial movements in young infants, and we can compare the "combination rules" found in adult facial expressions with those seen within the first days or weeks of life. A system such as FACS is also indispensable for investigating the possible early precursors of distinctive adult facial expressions. To distinguish among alternative hypotheses about the origins of particular facial expressions, we must be able to specify the elementary actions making up complex behaviors such as crying, grimacing, startles, rooting, and responses to unpleasant taste substances, and we must also be able to analyze the timing and sequencing of such actions.

The Smiles of Two Infants

Data Collection

The material for this chapter is part of an ongoing longitudinal study of facial behavior and emotional development during the first year of life. Each infant participating in this study is videotaped during play sessions with its mother or its father at the ages of 3 and 4 weeks, then biweekly from 4 to 12 weeks, and monthly thereafter. I shall focus here on a small subset of these records: episodes of smiling in two healthy, full-term infants within the first three months of life. The two infants selected for study were the first two female infants in the sample. Both are Caucasian and the children of graduate students at the University of California at Berkeley.

The Setting

The usual setting for the recording sessions was the infant's home. However, the sessions with one infant were recorded at my home during the first three months. If the mother and the father were both home, part of the session was recorded with each parent.

The parents were asked simply to play with their infant in whatever way seemed most natural and enjoyable. They were free to use a variety of objects (rattles, rag dolls, brightly colored pieces of cloth), in addition to their own social behaviors, to engage their infant's attention. During the first three months, play consisted primarily of face-to-face interactions involving a rich array of animated facial, vocal, and gestural behaviors on the parents' part and including smiling and vocalizing on the infant's part (cf. Brazelton, Tronick, Adamson, Als, & Wise, 1975; Stern, 1974a, b). When the infant was 3–4 weeks old, the parent generally held the infant in a semiupright position on the lap, supporting the baby's back and head against his or her arms or raised knee. This position, which provided a rich and highly responsive pattern of stimulation, seemed optimally effective in eliciting smiling and alert attention at this age. With slightly older infants, an infant seat or floor cushion was often used to support the infant in the *en face* position.

Although the natural "goal" of such interactions is mutual delight, as Stern (1974b) has pointed out, my own principal aim during these sessions was to record a wide range of expressive behaviors and emotional responses in the infants, including periods of seeming unresponsiveness and inexpressiveness, as well as smiling, and including the transitions between these various states. For that reason, I chose to record the infants' behavior continuously during sessions lasting between 15 and 20 minutes. These sessions were scheduled at times when the infants were most likely to be alert and socially responsive. But the videotaping began whether or not the infants seemed "interested" and continued with only brief interruptions unless they fell asleep, cried persistently, or needed to have their diapers changed. Since the infants were not always optimally responsive and alert during these sessions, it was important to explain the broad aims of the study to the parents, so they did not feel under pressure to make their baby "perform" for the camera and to avoid disappointment when the infant did not smile. This procedure seemed to foster a general interest in the infants' expressive behaviors; indeed, some of the parents provided a running commentary on the baby's facial and vocal behaviors, spontaneously labeling them as "excitement," "anger," "concentration," and the like.

Videotape Recording

The investigator, using a portable, handheld Sony video camera with a zoom lens, stood behind the mother or the father and focused close up on the infant's face and upper body. (This close focus was essential for the fine-grained facial analysis used in this study.) Although the parent's face was not simultaneously recorded, adequate contextual cues for the purposes of this study were provided by the parent's voice and by other movements, such as postural adjustments and hands touching the infant's face. Gaze direction served as a fairly accurate indication of when an infant was looking at the parent's face. (To "calibrate" my judgments, at the beginning of each session I usually asked the parents to tell me when their child seemed to be making eye contact with them.) One possible advantage of focusing only on the infants was that the parents, knowing that their own behavior was not the object of the study, may have been more relaxed and spontaneous in their play.

Analysis

The video records of the first four sessions for each infant (at 3, 4, 8, and 10–11 weeks) were the subject of three quite different kinds of analysis with FACS. The aim of the first analysis was to specify the phenomenologically defined category of smiling and to explore, in a preliminary fashion, the distinctiveness and potential signal value of smiling in very young infants. The second type of analysis focused on the temporal relationship between smiling and various brow movements. Its aim was to investigate the extent to which smiling is a coordinated facial movement in early infancy. The aim of the third approach was to differentiate between two types of facial behavior involving brow knitting—behaviors that differ, I shall argue, in their affective significance. My purpose here is to illustrate the logic of each approach through analysis of a small sample of data. Data from a more extensive sample of subjects will be presented in a subsequent report.

WHAT IS A SMILE?

As a behavioral description, the term *smile* applies to a wide variety of facial configurations, which differ in their appearance and—according to some investigators—in their signal value in adults and children (cf. Brannigan & Humphries, 1972; Cheyne, 1976; Grant, 1969; Hooff, 1972). These different smiles share in common the action of zygomaticus major (AU 12 in FACS). Apart from producing the obliquely upturned mouth corners typifying—but not necessarily present in —smiling, AU 12 results in a variety of other cues, most of which are present in infants as well as in adults. As can be seen from a comparison of the nonsmiling faces in Figure 7 (a, c, and e) with the smiling faces (Figures 7b, d, f, g, and i), the smiles are associated with an elevation and "expansion" of the infraorbital triangle (the cheeks), a pronounced deepening and straightening of the infraorbital furrow below the lower eyelids, and a raising and pouching of the lower lids. These cues can be produced by a strong action of AU 12 alone but usually involve the synergistic action of AU 6 (orbicularis oculi). Other cues, such as deepening of the nasolabial furrow, may be less reliable in infants because of their full and firm cheeks.

If smiling is provisionally defined as a facial behavior involving AU 12 as a salient component, we can ask how well this definition corresponds to what an ordinary observer would call smiling in young infants. When AU 12 is pronounced, the appearance is distinctly one of smiling. But would less pronounced actions of AU 12 also be recognizable as smiles? Is AU 12 invariably present in facial behaviors that would be called smiles? Are there other un-smile-like actions that an observer—and the caregiver—might confuse with AU 12?

We approached these questions by looking at the discrepancy between objective and impressionistic codings of the same two video records: infant E. at 3 and 4 weeks. For the impressionistic coding, an assistant untrained in FACS went through each video record, first coding brow actions (discussed below) and then locating various movements of the lower face, including smiling. The assistant was not taught the specific cues to AU 12 but based her judgments purely on her own impression of which actions "looked like smiles." For the objective coding, I went through the same video records, noting the location of all facial movements with any cues to AU 12, whether or not they looked like smiles.

Findings

The 3-week session contained a total of 24 events that were scored as smiles or as AU 12 or both. There was agreement on only 14 (58%) of these: I saw no evidence of AU 12 in 1 item scored as a smile by the untrained coder, and she did not score as smiles 9 items that I thought involved AU 12. The record for the 4-week session contained a total of 15 events scored by either coder or both. This time, there was agreement on 13 (86%) of the events. This increased agreement at 4 weeks suggested that the high discrepancy between subjective and objective coding methods at 3 weeks may have been due to ambiguity in the infant's facial movements, rather than to a faulty definition of smiling or error on the part of the coders.[4]

To investigate this possibility more directly, I rated each of the 24 events observed at 3 weeks on a three-point scale: (1) AU 12 definitely present; (2) AU 12 possibly or probably present; and (3) AU 12 probably or definitely not present. A second coder trained in FACS independently rated the same segments of videotape. We agreed on 22 (92%) of the items: 6 items rated 1, 15 items rated 2, and 1 rated 3. The two disagreements were over items rated 2 by one coder and 3 by the other. In most of the items rated as ambiguous (a rating of 2), the cues to AU 12 were either slight or fleeting, or they were partly masked by other actions such as lip raising or lateral retraction of the lips. Comparing these ratings with the coding by the untrained observer, we found that all six items rated 1 had been identified as smiles, while all 9 of the items that she had "missed" were in fact ambiguous (rated 2). My own rating of infant E.'s facial movements at 4 weeks showed a decrease in ambiguous, fleeting instances of AU 12. A similar decrease was noted in infant L. between 3 and 8 weeks.

[4] The two coders scored both sessions before the results were compared. While I scored the 4-week session first, the other coder began with the 3-week session. I do not believe that the increased agreement on the 4-week tape was due to a practice effect, but this possibility cannot be ruled out until a larger sample of data is analyzed by this procedure.

Discussion

Though provisional, these findings seem to confirm my impression that the discrepancy between objective and impressionistic judgments at 3 weeks resulted from ambiguities in the infant's facial behavior. If we omit the ambiguous instances of AU 12, the results of the comparative coding show that facial actions involving AU 12 were indeed recognized as smiles and that nearly all facial behaviors described as smiles involved AU 12.

The above findings can be discussed from several different perspectives. First, if the findings are representative—as I expect they will prove to be—they support our provisional definition of smiling. AU 12 (when unambiguous) can thus be used as an objective criterion for categorizing infants' facial movements as smiles.[5] We can then specify other actions typically present (or absent) during smiling; we can try to find out whether morphologically different types of smiles (e.g., broad versus open-mouth) differ in their determinants or signal value in early infancy; and we can study developmental changes in infants' smiles. The example of smiling suggests that the "comparative coding" procedure illustrated above may be useful (with or without *a priori* definitions) in specifying the facial actions present in other grossly defined categories of facial expression in infants, such as "grimacing," "cry face," "sobering," "wariness," and "brightening."

Second, these findings suggest that the distinctiveness of smiling increased within the first weeks of life. This was indicated by the decreased discrepancy between impressionistic and objective codings and by a decrease in ambiguous instances of AU 12.

The procedures illustrated above may prove useful in developing objective measures of individual or group differences in the relative ambiguity or distinctiveness of an infant's facial movements. More elusive qualities of facial movement, such as "expressiveness" or "subtlety," may also be amenable in part to objective examination with methods such as these. Equally important, it should be possible to assess the relative sensitivity and accuracy of parents' responses to their infants' facial behaviors. This assessment could be done by a comparison of the parents' spontaneous reactions to these behaviors (or sys-

---

[5] Subjective ratings of when an infant appeared to be "happy" would not necessarily correspond to behavioral judgments of when smiling occurred. E.'s father, for example, commented on several occasions that the baby had "a happy look but not quite a smile." The cues that he was picking up were subtle: slight, uncodable increases of muscle tone in the cheek region and "brightening" of the eyes. On the other hand, a facial configuration that definitely involved AU 12 might not be judged as a "happy" expression if it involved other muscle actions that made it look "peculiar" or affectively ambiguous.

tematic impressionistic ratings of videotapes) with objective codings of
the infants' actual facial movements and ratings of the intensity and
distinctiveness of these movements. For example, the parents in my
sample often caught even subtle and fleeting smiles (such as the one in
Figure 5b, lasting barely 0.8 second), which they spontaneously
"acknowledged" either verbally ("*Thaaat's* a nice smile!") or by responses such as laughing or exclaiming, "Ooooh!" with rising voice
pitch. On the other hand, I have observed instances in which a parent
repeatedly interpreted as smiles facial movements not involving AU 12
and more closely resembling "grimaces" or "winces" of discomfort.

A number of investigators (e.g., Bell & Ainsworth, 1972; Brazelton
et al., 1975; Stern, 1974b) have hypothesized that there is a complex,
reciprocal relationship between the caregiver's "expressiveness" and
"sensitivity," on the one hand, and the infant's expressiveness and
competence in visual–facial signaling, on the other hand. In order to
clarify the nature of these relationships, it will be necessary to go beyond
qualitative ratings to identify the specific characteristics of distinctive
versus ambiguous facial movements in infants, and to specify the kinds
of cues that caregivers are able to pick up or are likely to ignore or
misread.

SMILING AS A COORDINATED FACIAL MOVEMENT

A smiling appearance can be produced by an action as simple as the
slight, isolated contraction of zygomaticus major, AU 12. Neonatal REM
(rapid eye movement) smiles, as described by Wolff (1963) and others,
often involve no more than a slight upward motion of the lip corners,
with the rest of the face relaxed. Most investigators, beginning with the
great anatomist Duchenne (1867/1959), have observed that something is
missing from such smiles and that to appear truly "natural" or
"genuine," a smile must be accompanied by the synergistic action of
orbicularis oculi, AU 6, which raises the cheeks and crinkles the skin
below the eyes. As shown in Figure la, this action may be present even
in neonatal smiles (See also Emde & Koenig, 1969.)

In REM smiles, the lips are usually completely relaxed—as in early
social smiles and the simplest of adult smiles. Indeed, Sir Charles Bell
(1883) believed that a complete relaxation of the lips (i.e., of orbicularis
oris) was as essential to the expression of smiling or laughter as the
zygomatic action itself. Complete relaxation of the lips is not always
found, however, in the more complex social smiles that begin to appear
in the second month of life. As previously reported by Oster and Ekman
(1977), these smiles may involve a wide range of facial actions, including

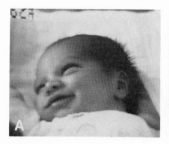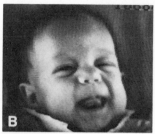

FIG. 1. (a) Smile elicited by the sound of a bell in a drowsy 5-day-old, (b) "Complex" smile in a 10-week-old participating in a visual preference experiment. (See text for descriptions of the facial actions illustrated in these and subsequent photographs. All photographs were taken from stopped frames of the videotapes.)

mouth opening, protrusion of the tongue, nose wrinkling, and lip actions such as tightening, pursing, protrusion, or—as in Fig. 1b—drawing down of the upper lip.

We cannot yet say whether the subjective qualities conveyed by these various actions correspond to specifiable differences in the affective meaning or signal value of the infant's smiles. What can be said on the basis of our previous study is that these actions do not represent a random selection of the facial actions that can (physically) co-occur with AU 12. Certain actions rarely occur with smiling in infants. One of these, AU 4 ("frowning" or knitting the brow), is the focus of the analyses reported below.

Smiling and Relaxation of the Brows

The fact that smiling nearly always goes with a smooth brow is not by itself remarkable. What I have discovered, however, is that the infants' smiles are not merely superimposed on a previously relaxed face; instead, early social smiling is frequently preceded by a 3–20 sec period of intensely knit brows, accompanied by visual fixation of the parent's face, as illustrated in Figure 2. Thus, the onset of smiling is accompanied by a *relaxation* of the brows.

This phenomenon was investigated by means of a fine-grained analysis of the video records for the two infants. In addition to identifying the action units occurring in the brow and mouth regions, it was necessary to determine the precise onset and offset of brow actions and smiles. Moreover, brow and mouth actions had to be coded independently, since distinctive actions such as AU 4 and AU 12 can have a powerful "halo" effect, influencing our perception of the entire face—an effect first noticed by Duchenne (1867/1959). The upper cheek and eyelid region contains important clues to smiling. Thus, when we

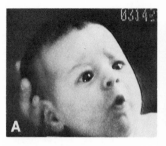

FIG. 2. (a) Brow knitting followed by (b) smiling in infant E. at 3 weeks, looking at her mother.

were coding brow movements, the face below the middle of the eyes was covered. When we were coding smiles, the face above the middle of the eyes was covered.

Coding Procedures

Precise timing of facial movements was made possible by electronic recording of a visible number on each 60th-of-a-second field of the videotapes. In a preliminary screening of the video records, the approximate beginning and ending frames of each smile were recorded. A larger "smiling episode" — covering a period beginning approximately 10 sec before the smile's onset to 10 sec after its offset — was then designated for finer analysis. If several smiles occurred within a short period of time, the entire sequence was designated. The fine-grained analysis of these segments was made in two passes: the first to identify each codable brow action and to locate its beginning and end, and the second to locate more precisely the beginning and end of each smile.

Categorization Criteria

For the analyses reported here, only unambiguous smiles were counted. Three criteria were used: (1) the action had to appear subjectively smilelike when viewed at normal speed; (2) there had to be more than a trace of AU 12; and (3) the AU 12 component of the smile had to be visible for at least 1 sec. Thus, the slight smile in Figure 5b, which lasted .8 sec, did not qualify, although it was recognized as a smile by the mother. If a smile faded and then increased in intensity again, it was considered as a single, continuous smile unless no trace of AU 12 was visible for at least .75 sec. Brow movements were scored in terms of the three discrete AUs and four combinations described above. All of these movements can be observed in infants within the first weeks of life. For the statistical analyses, these configurations were collapsed into the following mutually exclusive categories: raised, knit, any combination of raised and knit, and neutral—that is, relaxed—brows.

Interobserver Reliability

As noted above, a "naive" coder untrained in FACS made two passes through the entire 3-week and 4-week video records of infant E., locating and coding first brow movements and then a variety of mouth actions, including smiling. She was unaware of any hypothesized relationship between brow movements and smiling. For the coding of brow movements, she was shown the specific cues to each of the 3 brow–forehead action units and their four combinations. Her coding of brow movements—with approximate on- and offset times indicated—was condensed into the four categories listed above and then was compared with my own coding of brow movements within the time periods preceding and accompanying each of 19 previously designated smiles. We scored precisely the same brow movement category in 74% of the presmile periods and in 95% (all but 1) of the smiling periods. The principal source of disagreement during the presmile periods was brow raising: the untrained observer "missed" the 2 instances of raised brows that I had coded, and she scored as knit (AU 4) 2 of the 4 brow actions that I had designated as both raised and knit (AU 1 + 4 in both cases). There was high interobserver agreement (90%) on the presence of knit brows (AU 4), either alone or in combination with brow raising. The two coders concurred 7 of 9 times in scoring the brows as neutral before smiling, the 2 disagreements occurring where I had observed raised brows.

Brow Movements before and during Smiling

The frequency of each of the four mutually exclusive brow movement categories was determined for the periods immediately preceding and during smiling, for each infant during each of the four recording sessions. A brow movement was considered as "immediately preceding" a smile if it *ended* less than 1 sec before the smile's onset. Regardless of its total duration, if a brow movement ended more than 1 sec before a smile began, the brows were considered as neutral before the smile. In our classifying of brow movements "during" smiling, the brows were not counted as neutral unless they were relaxed during 81% or more of of the smile's total duration. (Thus, the brows could be classified as raised or knit both before and during a smile even if they relaxed a fifth of the way through the smile.) These conventions, though arbitrary, are conservatively biased away from the hypothesis that smiling is accompanied by a relaxation of the brows.

Findings

The results of this analysis confirmed my original impression. Figure 3 presents the data for E. during each of the four sessions analyzed. In nearly all cases, smiling was accompanied by a neutral brow. By contrast, 30–60% of her smiles at each age were preceded by knit brows, either alone or in combination with raised brows. The data for L. followed the same pattern at 8 and 10 weeks. At 3 weeks, however, no examples of brow knitting before smiling were observed; the nine smiles recorded during this session were all preceded and accompanied by neutral brows. At 4 weeks, L. was fussy and did not smile during the session. The data for the two infants, pooled across all four sessions, are summarized in Table I.

The transition diagrams in Figure 4 summarize the sequencing of brow movements associated with the onset of smiling in the two infants, with data pooled across all four sessions. For this analysis, the two

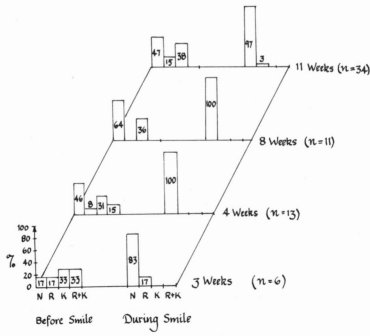

FIG. 3. Histograms showing the proportion of infant E.'s smiles preceded and accompanied by each of four brow movement categories at each of four ages: n = number of smiles recorded; brow positions: N = neutral, R = raised, K = knit, R + K = raised and knit.

TABLE I. DISTRIBUTION OF BROW MOVEMENTS BEFORE AND DURING SMILING[a]

	Infant	n^b	Brow movement categories		
			Neutral	Raised	Knit[c]
Brows before smile	E.	64	.47	.11	.42
	L.	66	.52	.08	.41
Brows during smile	E.	64	.97	.03	0
	L.	66	.86	.09	.05

[a] Entries correspond to the percent of smiles immediately preceded by and accompanied by each of the three mutually exclusive brow movement categories.
[b] n = total number of smiles recorded in all sessions
[c] The "knit" category includes brows that were coded as knit and brows that were coded as both raised and knit.

categories involving knit brows ("knit" and "raised + knit") were combined. As shown above, a substantial proportion of both infants' smiles were preceded by knit brows. Figure 4 shows that when the brows were knit before a smile (27 smiles in both E. and L.), they nearly always relaxed when the smile began and remained neutral throughout the smile (26 times in E., 21 in L.). The opposite sequence (neutral → knit) was never observed. In fact, in all but one instance (neutral → raised in L.), when the brows were relaxed before a smile they remained that way during the smile. The contrast between these transition probabilities was highly significant for both infants ($\chi^2 = 24$, $p < .001$ for E., $\chi^2 = 19$, $p < .001$ for L., using McNemar's test for correlated proportions [Hays, 1963]). Raised brows (with no knitting), representing a small proportion of brow movements before smiling, also tended to relax during the smile, though this tendency was stronger in E. than in L.

Cycles of Brow Knitting and Smiling

A striking feature of brow knitting and smiling in young infants is their occasionally cyclic appearance. In E. at 4 and 11 weeks and in L. at 8 and 10 weeks, there were extended episodes of social interaction characterized by repeated cycles of brow knitting and smiling succeeding each other with seemingly remarkable precision—the two actions separated by fractions of a second or overlapping by only a few frames of videotape.

Reliability of Timing Judgments

To determine how finely the onset and offset of these movements could reliably be coded, two episodes containing a high density of

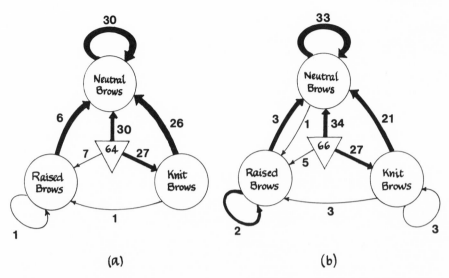

FIG. 4. Frequency of transitions between brow movement categories accompanying the onset of smiling in infants E. (a) and L. (b). The central triangle represents the total number of smiles recorded in all four sessions. Arrows leading from the central triangle indicate the number of smiles *preceded by* each of the three mutually exclusive brow movement categories. Arrows between circles indicate the frequency of transitions from one brow position to another when the smile began. Arrows leading back to the same circle indicate how often the brows remained the same before and during a smile.

smiling and brow knitting were selected. The two episodes, lasting 1.25 and 1.5 min, were independently scored by me and by another coder trained in FACS. As before, the coders made two passes through each segment, identifying first brow movements and then smiles. In each case, we tried to specify as precisely as possible the onset and offset of the action. (The first and last visible traces of the movement were taken as the beginning and end points.) This kind of analysis requires repeated back and forth viewing, alternating between real-time and slow-motion or frame-by-frame play. It proceeds at the rate of roughly 1 h of coding per minute of videotape. The results showed that, while laborious, the precise timing of facial actions can be done with a high degree of reliability: the two episodes contained a total of 18 instances of brow knitting (AU 4) and 12 smiles (AU 12). On the average, we were within .1 sec (or six video fields) of each other for the onset and offset of AU 4; in the case of AU 12, we were within .14 sec of each other for the onset, .3 sec for the offset. (Determining the offset of a gradually fading action such as smiling is subjectively very difficult, since a trace of high muscle tonus may remain in the cheeks, and the eyes may continue to appear "bright," as in Figure 7h.)

Findings

Figures 5 and 7 illustrate the two episodes (from the records of E. at 4 and 11 weeks, respectively) analyzed by the two independent coders. Both episodes began with E. looking past her mother's left shoulder. Her brows knit when her mother called to her, then relaxed as she smiled, still looking ahead. After turning to look at her mother, she continued to gaze at her mother's face throughout the remaining cycles of smiling and brow knitting. In both E. and L., the episodes of smiling and brow knitting typically ended when the infant turned away (with a neutral or knit brow) for a protracted "break" in the interaction.

Figure 6, which is keyed to the faces shown in Figure 5, graphically represents the temporal patterning of brow knitting and smiling in E. at 4 weeks. The average duration of the brow-knitting periods was 7 sec, of the smiles 5.5 sec. The interval between knit brows and smiles averaged .3 sec. On two occasions, the brows began to knit before a smile had completely faded, the two actions overlapping for .2 sec each time. In addition to indicating the precise timing of AU 4 and AU 12, Figure 6 schematically represents the relative intensities of the two actions and the rapidity of their on- and offsets. In general, AU 12 was more gradual in both its onset and offset and more variable in its intensity. As indicated in Figure 6, the smiles shown in Figures 5f and 5g, though different in appearance, represent two peaks of a continuous action that faded midway between the peaks but never disappeared completely. The onset of the second peak (5g) was accompanied by a brief but pronounced raise of the brows that was perceived by three independent coders. (Note the changed shape of the outer end of the right brow.)

In the 11-week episode, illustrated in Figure 7, there were a greater number of alternations within approximately the same time period (1.5 min): The brows knit 13 times, for an average of 4.5 sec, and there were 9 smiles, lasting an average of 2.9 sec. The average interval between smiling and brow knitting was 0.3 sec, and the two actions overlapped twice for 0.1 sec each time. In this episode, AU 4 was much attenuated, with corrugator action visible primarily in the left brow and with little or no lowering action.

Despite the similarity in temporal patterning in the episodes at 4 and 11 weeks, there were perceptible changes in E.'s appearance: her smiles at 11 weeks were more active, accompanied by tongue protrusions, vocalizing, arm waving, and lunging movements toward her mother. More difficult to define in objective terms, the smiles themselves appear less "vacuous" and the eyes more "focused" at 11 than at 3 or 4 weeks. These changes and the subjective impressions they convey are consistent with evidence of a change in the determinants (and hence psychological "meaning") of smiling around 3 months of age. As

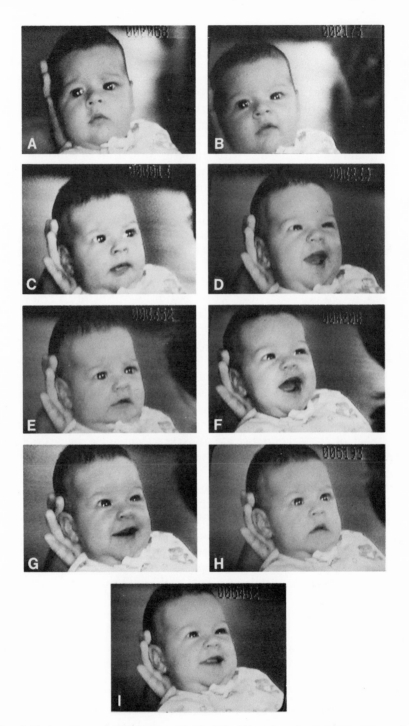

FIG. 5. Cycles of brow knitting and smiling in infant E. at 4 weeks. (a & b) Looking to her mother's left (c–i) Looking at her mother.

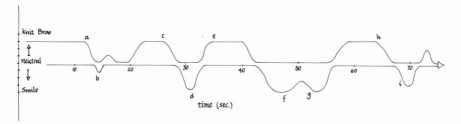

FIG. 6. Time course of brow-knitting and smiling cycles shown in Figure 5. The letters correspond to the facial expressions in Figure 5 (a–i).

interpreted by Emde, Gaensbauer, and Harmon (1976), Sroufe (in press), and others, this evidence suggests an increasing involvement of cognitive activity and an increasingly active and discriminating appraisal of the stimuli eliciting smiling. Some of these inferred psychological changes may be reflected in objectively definable changes in the appearance of smiling: changes, for example, in the specific actions accompanying AU 12; in the number and variety of distinguishable smile configurations; or in the timing and coordination of facial movements. Defining such age changes is one goal of my continuing analyses.

Discussion

The findings presented in this section can be discussed on two levels, the neuromuscular and the psychological. At the level of neuromuscular coordination, the relaxation of the brows immediately preceding a smile clearly demonstrates that smiling in infants as young as 1 month of age is a patterned, coordinated facial behavior simultaneously involving changes in the brows and in the lower face. Smiling in young infants is not just an isolated and local contraction of zygomaticus major and the synergistic orbicularis oculi, independent of whatever happens to be going on in the brows. Reciprocally, brow knitting does not occur randomly with respect to zygomatic activity.

In speaking of the relaxation of the brows before smiling, I have not speculated about the possible direction of influence, that is, whether the activation of zygomaticus major (AU 12) "causes" corrugator (AU 4) to relax; or whether AU 4 inhibits AU 12, so that a smile can appear only when AU 4 relaxes; or whether the relaxation of corrugator is in fact the "cause" of the smile. I suspect that the question of why knit brows relax before a smile—or why they are knit in the first place—cannot be resolved solely at an anatomical or neuromuscular level.

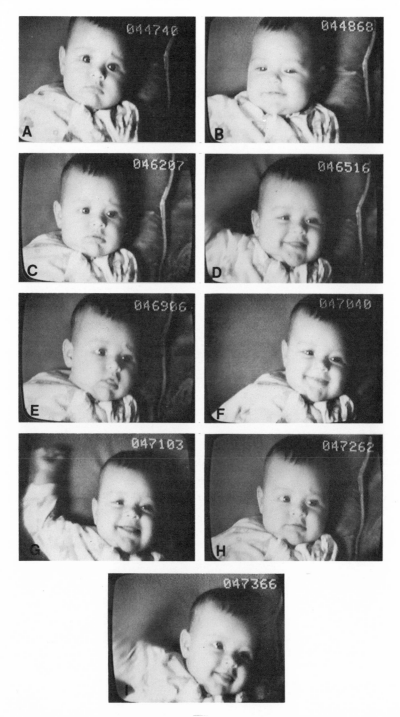

FIG. 7. Brow-knitting and smiling cycles in infant E. at 11 weeks. (a & b) Looking to her mother's left, (c–i) Looking at her mother. Several cycles from the 11-week episode are not illustrated here.

With respect to the relaxation of AU 4 before a smile, there is no purely anatomical reason why AU 4 and AU 12 should not be able to act simultaneously. Adults can voluntarily contract corrugator while smiling, although it may feel "unnatural." And as shown in Figure 4b, the two actions do co-occur in infants on rare occasions, generally during times of heightened attention to novel and arousing stimuli. Nevertheless, such examples are clearly exceptions to the general "rule" that smiling does not go with knit brows in infants.[6] The fact that reflexlike neonatal sleep smiles in both preterm and full-term infants are almost always accompanied by a smooth brow suggests that this "rule" is not dependent on learning or on a capacity for voluntary, conscious action; rather, it is part of the innate, subcortical "programming" for smiling.

The presence of knit brows before some 40% of the infants' smiles is more difficult to explain on purely physiological grounds. Several "simple" (i.e., nonpsychological) explanations can probably be ruled out. First, AU 4 and AU 12 are clearly not sequentially linked in an obligatory fashion: smiling is not invariably preceded by AU 4, nor does relaxation of AU 4 automatically activate AU 12. Second, there is no evidence that sequences or repeated cycles of AU 4 followed by AU 12 represent stereotyped, "preprogrammed," "fixed action patterns." To my knowledge, sequences of these two actions have not been observed as spontaneous, endogenous "discharges" (for example, during REM sleep), as one might expect if they were "preorganized" action patterns. Nor have I observed such sequences in response to relatively static, nonsocial objects.

While still incomplete, the evidence suggests that the observed sequences of facial activity are governed in large part by psychological processes, that is, that smiling and brow knitting reflect two distinct "states of mind" or psychological processes in the infant. If this view is correct, the finding of a temporal relationship between these two actions may be able to tell us something about the nature and organization of the underlying processes.

At the psychological level, however, interpretation of the data becomes more speculative, particularly with respect to the "meaning," if any, of brow knitting as a frequent precursor of smiling in young infants. In the final section of this paper, I illustrate the kind of analytic approach that will be necessary if we are to distinguish among alternative interpretations of "knit brow faces."

---

[6] Ekman (personal communication) believes that the mutual exclusivity of knit brows and smiling is also the general rule for adult smiles in most cultures. However, he has observed one interesting exception: the Kukukuku, a Southeast Highlands New Guinea group, frequently smile with knit brows when greeting strangers.

WHY DO INFANTS KNIT THEIR BROWS?

A number of other investigators have noted in passing that "frowning" or "sobering" is often seen alternating with smiling in response to social stimuli during the first three months of life (e.g., Emde, *et al.*, 1976; Stern, 1974a). These investigators have interpreted the infant's furrowed brow as a sign of negative affect, that is, as a state of tension or arousal sufficiently above the "optimal" level that it is experienced as unpleasant or aversive.

Implicit in this interpretation of brow knitting is the classical (and still prevalent) view that emotion in early infancy can be represented by a single dimension ranging from quiescence to distress (cf. Bridges, 1932) and that negative affect in young infants is wholly undifferentiated and diffuse (cf. Mandler, 1975; Sroufe, in press). The occurrence of smiling and "frowning" within a few seconds of each other has thus been seen as paradoxical—as an indication of the lability and disorganization of the young infant's emotional responses or as an indication that the smile is not yet a "true" expression of positive affect or a truly social response (cf. Emde *et al.*, 1976, p. 77).

I propose instead that the observed sequences of brow knitting and smiling are not paradoxical at all but that the apparent paradox arises in large part from the use of the term *frown* and from the prevalent assumption that this action reflects negative affect in infants. In fact, I believe that it can be shown that there is more than one kind of knit brow face and that the configurations that precede smiling reflect a heightened level of attention and arousal that is not experienced as distressing but is comprehensible as an antecedent of smiling.

One problem with the automatic assumption that brow knitting in young infants is invariably a sign of distress is that most investigators have disregarded the other facial actions that accompany AU 4 in various contexts. If brow knitting is indeed a sign of undifferentiated negative affect, varying only in intensity, we would expect to find some of the same actions and qualities of movement in the knit brow faces that precede smiling as in those preceding crying and defensive avoidance. We would not expect to find actions and qualities of movement characteristic of positive affect or alert attending.

Presmile versus Precry Faces

A differential analysis of the facial actions accompanying knit brows before smiling and before crying is currently under way. Thus far, I can report only qualitative observations, suggesting a different pattern of facial movements in these two contexts, at least within the first three months of life. To illustrate the logic of this approach, I briefly mention three differences that seem to be important:

1. *Differences in the brows and the eyes.* As noted above, AU 4 is a composite of three distinct muscle actions that generally occur together in infants and in adults. But in infants there are sometimes marked differences in the degree of contraction of the separate components, and these differences seem to differentiate presmile and precry faces. In the presmile faces shown in Figures 2, 5, and 7, corrugator action, which draws the brows together, seems especially salient. In overtly distressed or precry faces, on the other hand, the lowering actions of AU 4 predominate, producing a crease across the bridge of the nose and a muscle bulge above the nose bridge. Just before crying, the infant's gaze is likely to be averted, and the eyes are usually narrowed by strong contraction of orbicularis oculi (AU 6 or AU 7). In contrast, brow knitting before smiling is often accompanied by widened eyes and sustained fixation of the caregiver's face.

2. *Differences in the lower face.* The lower-face configurations that accompany AU 4 before a smile fall into two broad groups. In the first, we see pronounced and sustained pursing or protrusion of the lips, as in Figure 2a. In the second, the lower face is predominantly neutral, with a variety of relatively low-level and nonspecific actions around the mouth and lips: the relaxed cheeks may passively sag (as in Figures 5a and 7a), or there may be a slight downward tugging of the lower lip (5c) or mouth corners (5h). In precry faces, by contrast, there is usually a pronounced lateral or downward pulling of the mouth corners, along with a raising and lateral pulling of the upper lip.

3. *Differences in timing.* The onset of crying or of a precry face is usually very rapid in young infants, with brow lowering and knitting and the various "distress" components of the lower face occurring virtually simultaneously. By contrast, the knit brow configurations that precede smiling are sometimes held for several seconds before the smile begins. Low-level muscle actions such as those shown in Figures 5c and 5h are generally either transient or sustained at a tonic low level. This relative stillness of the face and the motor quieting that accompanies it contrast with the kind of restless, diffuse activity that often precedes fussiness (cf. Oster & Ekman, 1977).

To summarize, the knit brow faces observed immediately before smiling in young infants are not characterized by any signs of overt distress and do not resemble the immediate precursors of crying or fussiness. The specific facial actions involved, the timing and distinctiveness of the movements, and the infant's other behavior are different before smiling and before crying.[7]

Brow Knitting and Difficulty in Cognitive Activity

Certain aspects of the presmile knit brow faces—the occasional pursed or protruded lips, the widening of the eyes and sustained visual fixation, and the motor quieting—are characteristic of alert attending in young infants. However, brow knitting is not typically associated with attention in infants. Indeed, in many situations in which young infants engage in prolonged visual inspection of an object (for example, when 3-month-olds gaze at their own hands), the brow remains perfectly smooth. Therefore, brow knitting may reflect a special form of attention.

In adults, the action of lowering and drawing together the eyebrows is often associated with concentration or puzzlement. As Darwin (1872/1965) observed, "A man may be absorbed in the deepest thought, and his brow will remain smooth until he encounters some obstacle in his train of reasoning" (p. 221). Thus, according to Darwin, frowning occurs "whenever the mind is intent on any subject and encounters some difficulty" (p. 224).

Darwin's observation offers intriguing clues to the meaning of the behavior observed in young infants. Of course, we cannot attribute conscious reasoning to infants as young as those discussed in this paper. I suggest, however, that the knit brow faces that precede smiling may reflect the operation of perceptual, attentional, and cognitive processes that are early precursors of what we later interpret as "puzzlement" or difficulty in cognitive activity. In other words, I believe that the infant's knit brows may reflect an effort (not necessarily fully conscious) to "make sense of" or assimilate the complex, dynamic pattern of stimulation produced by the caregiver. When this effort is successful, the "tension" reflected in the knit brows is "released" and a smile follows.[8]

The specific nature or content of these psychological processes undoubtedly changes with age. Thus, we can speculate that at 3–4

---

[7] Thus far, I have not found any evidence indicating that the knit brow faces that precede smiling might correspond to specific negative affect expressions such as anger, sadness, or fear, as these appear in adults (cf. Ekman, Friesen, & Tomkins, 1971).

[8] In a natural social setting, in which the caregiver's behavior is constantly changing yet constantly repeating itself (cf. Stern, Beebe, Jaffe, & Bennett, 1977), "resolution" of the tension and hence smiling would be likely. In controlled experimental situations, such as those used by Stechler & Carpenter (1967), the infant might not be able to assimilate the "unnatural" stimuli received from the caregiver. In such cases, a prolonged period of what these investigators have referred to as "obligatory attention" might be accompanied or followed by fussiness or crying.

weeks, brow knitting may be related to the very early stages of forming a schema of the caregiver's face. By 3 months, it may be related to more specific aspects of the caregiver's behavior, such as unpredictable changes in facial expression and tone of voice. Or it may be related to the infant's efforts to detect contingencies between his or her own behavior and that of the caregiver (cf. Watson, 1977).

The above interpretation is clearly speculative at this point. Before accepting it, we would have to rule out a variety of simpler, more parsimonious explanations of brow knitting in young infants: for example, the possibility that brow knitting is narrowly associated with visual activity or that it is related in a purely "mechanical" way to babies' efforts to limit their field of view or to focus their eyes on a stimulus.[9] In the light of Meltzoff & Moore's (1977) recent findings, we cannot automatically discount the possibility that the infants are in some way imitating their partners' facial movements, though the timing and coordination of the observed sequences of smiling and brow knitting make this explanation seem implausible. A systematic test of these alternative interpretations will require additional data, including simultaneous recording of the infant and caregiver and systematic stimulus manipulations, as well as analysis of facial behavior in newborns and in blind infants.

EMOTION IN THE INFANT'S FACE?

The observations and analyses presented in the preceding sections have implications for the interpretation of both smiling and brow knitting in young infants. First, we cannot simply assume that the isolated action of knitting the brows is invariably a sign of negative affect without close analysis of the other facial actions present, the timing and coordination of the movements, and the larger behavioral context. If negative affect is at all reflected in the knit brow faces that precede smiling, it would have to be negative affect of a special kind, since it is accompanied by sustained attention and signs of positive "interest" and not by the signs of even mild distress. Thus, even in young infants, a single affect dimension may not adequately represent the behavior observed.

It is also difficult to conceive of the observed sequences or repeated cycles of brow knitting and smiling as fluctuations between negative and

---

[9] This possibility was proposed by Darwin (1872/1976) as one explanation of the evolution of "concentration frowns," but it has been questioned on purely physiological grounds by Ekman, in press.

positive affect, since as shown above smiling often follows brow knitting by only fractions of a second. It seems more plausible to view the infant's knit brows as a reflection of that "optimal range of attention and arousal" thought to be necessary for smiling and positive social responding (cf. Stern, 1974a).

The relaxation of the brows immediately before the onset of a smile fits well with a conceptualization of smiling as a "release of tension" (cf. Sroufe & Waters, 1976; and earlier, Tomkins, 1962). However, if the interpretation of brow knitting proposed above is correct, it would raise serious questions about the prevailing belief that early social smiling is a purely passive and reflexlike response (cf. Emde *et al.*, 1976; Sroufe, in press.).

According to Sroufe's (in press) recent account of the "tension release" hypothesis, the infant's early social smiles reflect fluctuations in the level of arousal produced by stimuli with certain prepotent characteristics, like highly contrasting contours. In Sroufe's view (shared by many cognitively oriented developmental psychologists), until the age of 2–3 months, there is no active "psychological engagement" or conscious cognitive processing of the stimulus and therefore no genuine experience of *emotion*. Lewis and Brooks (this volume), in a more extreme version of this view, propose that there is no "true" emotion until the infant develops the capacity for reflective, self-conscious awareness, toward the end of the first year of life.

At present, these hypotheses can be neither proved nor disproved. Though I would not deny the importance of the changes in cognitive capacities occurring around the third month and in the second half of the first year, it is not at all clear that these changes are prerequisites for the experiencing of emotion. The subjective experience of emotion is no doubt qualitatively different once the child acquires a capacity for reflective thought and for language; but this is not the same as saying that there can be no experience or awareness of emotion before that time. Moreover, it would be premature to conclude, on the basis of incomplete negative data, that infants are incapable of cognitive processing or active psychological engagement of stimuli (and therefore that they cannot experience emotion) before the age of 2 or 3 months. Such conclusions have the unfortunate effect of suggesting that there is nothing interesting to be discovered about emotional expression or affect development within the first three months of life. I believe that this is clearly not the case—as shown, for example, by the seminal work of Stechler and Carpenter (1967) and Wolff (1966).

At the very least, it could be easily demonstrated through the use of analytic techniques similar to those illustrated above that the infant's earliest social smiles, beginning around 3–4 weeks of age, bear little resemblance to reflexlike, sign-released responses—as was suggested by Alcock's (1975) contention that the month-old infant's smile is not fundamentally different from "the herring gull chick's pecking at a red dot on a yellow beak" (p. 152). Nor do these social smiles resemble reflexlike neonatal REM smiles: the brow knitting and prolonged periods of "fascinated" gazing at the caregiver's face that often precede smiling, the variability and complexity of the facial movements accompanying the infant's smiles, and their smooth onset and gradual fading are characteristic of genuine affect expressions, not reflexively elicited responses.

More generally, I believe that the findings presented in this paper, though preliminary, provide at least *prima facie* evidence that at as early as 3–4 weeks of life, there are organized, nonrandom patterns of facial behavior and that these reflect the operation of at least primitively psychological perceptual, attentional, and cognitive processes that are already intimately linked to affect.

ACKNOWLEDGMENTS

The research reported here and the preparation of this paper were carried out while the author was a postdoctoral fellow in the Human Interaction Laboratory, University of California, San Francisco.

I thank Paul Ekman and Wallace Friesen for making available an early prepublication copy of the Facial Action Coding System on which much of this research is based. I am especially grateful to Paul Ekman for his many valuable criticisms of and suggestions on this manuscript.

REFERENCES

Alcock, J. *Animal behavior: An evolutionary approach*. Sunderland, Mass: Sinauer Assoc., 1975.
Allport, F. H. *Social psychology*. Boston: Houghton Mifflin, 1924.
Altmann, S. A. The structure of primate social communication. In S. A. Altmann (Ed.), *Social communication among primates*. Chicago: University of Chicago Press, 1967.
Bell, C. *Expression: Its anatomy and philosophy* (2nd ed.). New York: Fowler & Wells, 1883.
Bell, S., & Ainsworth, M. Infant crying and maternal responsiveness. *Child Development*, 1972, 43, 1171–1190.
Beveridge, W. I. B. *The art of scientific investigation* (3rd ed.). New York: Random House, 1957.
Blurton-Jones, N. G. Criteria for use in describing facial expressions of children. *Human Biology*, 1971, 43, 365–413.
Brannigan, C. R., & Humphries, D. A. Human non-verbal behavior, a means of communication. In N. Blurton-Jones (Ed.), *Ethological studies of child behavior*. Cambridge, England: Cambridge University Press, 1972.

Brazelton, T. B., Tronick, E., Adamson, L., Als, H., & Wise, S. Early mother–infant reciprocity. In *Parent–infant interaction*. Amsterdam: Elsevier Excerpta Medica, 1975, pp. 137–154.

Bridges, K. Emotional development in early infancy. *Child Development*, 1932, *3*, 324–341.

Cheyne, J. A. Development of forms and functions of smiling in preschoolers. *Child Development*, 1976, *47*, 820–823.

Darwin, C. *The expression of the emotions in man and animals*. Chicago: Phoenix Books, University of Chicago Press, 1965. (Originally published, 1872.)

Duchenne, G. B. [*Physiology of Motion*] (E. B. Kaplan, Ed. & trans.). Philadelphia: Saunders, 1959. (Originally published, 1867.)

Ekman, P. Biological and cultural contributions to body and facial movement. In J. Blacking (Ed.), *Anthropology of the body*. New York: Academic Press, 1977.

Ekman, P. About brows: Emotional and conversational signals. In J. Aschoff, N. von Cranach, I. Eibl-Eibesfeldt, & W. Lepenez (Eds.), *Human ethology*. Cambridge, England: Cambridge University Press, in press.

Ekman, P., & Friesen, W. V. Measuring facial movement. *Environmental Psychology and Nonverbal Behavior*, 1976, *1*(1), 56–75.

Ekman, P., & Friesen, W. V. *Manual for the facial action coding system*. Palo Alto, Calif.: Consulting Psychologists Press, 1978.

Ekman, P., Friesen, W. V., & Tomkins, S. S. Facial affect scoring technique: A first validity study. *Semiotica*, 1971, *3*, 37–38.

Emde, R. N., Gaensbauer, T. J., & Harmon, R. J. Emotional expression in infancy: A biobehavioral study. *Psychological Issues Monograph Series*, 1976, *10*, Monograph 37.

Emde, R. N., & Koenig, K. L. Neonatal smiling and rapid eye movement states. *Journal of the American Academy of Child Psychiatry*, 1969, *8*, 57–67.

Gasser, R. F. The development of the facial muscles in man. *American Journal of Anatomy*, 1967, *120*, 357–375. (a)

Gasser, R. F. The development of the facial nerve in man. *The Annals of Otology, Rhinology, and Laryngology*, 1967, *76*, 37–56. (b)

Grant, E. C. Human facial expression. *Man*, 1969, *4*, 525–536.

Hays, W. L. *Statistics for psychologists*. New York: Holt, Rinehart, Winston, 1963.

Hinde, R. A. (Ed.). *Nonverbal communication*. Cambridge, England: Cambridge University Press, 1972.

Hooff, J. A. R. A. M. van. A comparative approach to the phylogeny of laughter and smiling. In R. A. Hinde (Ed.), *Non-verbal communication*. Cambridge, England: Cambridge University Press, 1972.

Jacob, F. Evolution and tinkering. *Science*, 1977, *196*, 1161–1166.

Mandler, G. *Mind and emotion*. New York: Wiley, 1975.

Meltzoff, A. N., & Moore, M. K. Imitation of facial and manual gestures by human neonates. *Science*, 1977, *198*, 75–78.

Oster, H. *The structure of infant facial behavior*. Paper presented at the meeting of the Society for Research in Child Development, New Orleans, March 1977.

Oster, H. Measuring facial movement in infants. In P. Ekman & W. V. Friesen (Eds.), *Analyzing facial action*. New York: Plenum, in press.

Oster, H., & Ekman, P. Facial behavior in child development. In A. Collins (Ed.), *Minnesota symposia on child psychology* (Vol. 11). Hillsdale, N.J.: Erlbaum Assoc., 1977.

Peiper, A. [Cerebral function in infancy and childhood] (B. & H. Nagler, trans.). New York: Consultants Bureau, 1963. (Originally published, 1961.)

Ploog, D. Prospects and problems of research in primate communication. In D. Ploog, & T. Melnechuk, Primate communication. *Neurosciences Research Program Bulletin*, 1969, *7*, 417–510.

Sroufe, L. A. The ontogenesis of emotion. In J. Osofosky (Ed.), *Handbook of infancy*. New York: Wiley, 1978.

Sroufe, L. & Waters, E. The ontogenesis of smiling and laughter: A perspective on the organization of development in infancy. *Psychological Review*, 1976, *83*, 173–189.

Stechler, G., & Carpenter, G. A viewpoint on early affect development. In J. Hellmuth (Ed.), *Exceptional infant* (Vol. 1) *The normal infant*. New York: Brunner/Mazel, 1967.

Stern, D. N. The goal and structure of mother–infant play. *Journal of the American Academy of Child Psychiatry*, 1974, *13*, 402–421. (a)

Stern, D. N. Mother and infant at play: The dyadic interaction involving facial, vocal, and gaze behaviors. In M. Lewis & L. A. Rosenblum (Eds.), *The effect of the infant on its caregiver*. New York: Wiley, 1974. (b)

Stern, D. N., Beebe, B., Jaffe, J., & Bennett, S. L. The infant's stimulus world during social interaction: A study of caregiver behaviours with particular reference to repetition and timing. In H. R. Schaffer (Ed.), *Studies on interactions in infancy*. New York: Academic Press, 1977.

Tomkins, S. S. *Affect, imagery, consciousness* (Vol. 1). *The positive affects*. New York: Springer, 1962.

Watson, J. S. Perception of contingency as a determinant of social responsiveness. In E. Thoman (Ed.), *The origins of the infant's responsiveness*. Hillsdale, N. J.: Erlbaum Assoc., 1977.

Wolff, P. H. Observations on the early development of smiling. In B. M. Foss (Ed.), *Determinants of infant behavior, II*. New York: Wiley, 1963.

Wolff, P. H. The causes, controls, and organization of behavior in the neonate. *Psychological Issues*, 1966, *5*, Monograph 17.

Young, G., & Décarie, T. G. An ethology-based catalogue of facial/vocal behaviour in infancy. *Animal Behavior*, 1977, *25*, 95–107.

3

Hearts and Faces:
A Study in the Measurement
of Emotion

MICHAEL LEWIS, JEANNE BROOKS, AND
JEANNETTE HAVILAND

Objects of rage, love, fear, etc., not only prompt a man to outward deeds, but provoke characteristic alterations in his attitude and visage, and affect his breathing, circulation, and other organic functions in specific ways. (James, 1890, p. 442)

. . . The bodily changes follow directly the perception of the exciting fact, and that our feeling of the same changes as they occur is the emotion. (James, 1890, p. 449)

Like many areas of psychological inquiry, the study of emotion and emotional development is cyclical. Relatively stagnant since the 1930s, there is currently a resurgence of interest and research in this area. As is often the case, this new research has rekindled old controversies and issues relevant to the study of emotion, in general, as well as raising many new issues pertinent to the study of emotional development. As one examines emotional responses from a developmental perspective, the traditional problems of definition and measurement take on new importance.

The thoughts of two men have largely determined the direction of the study of emotions, including both definitions and methodologies; they are William James (1890) and Charles Darwin (1872). If we focus

MICHAEL LEWIS, JEANNE BROOKS, and JEANNETTE HAVILAND · The Infant Laboratory, Institute for Research in Human Development, Educational Testing Service, Princeton, New Jersey. This research was in part supported by NIMH grant #MH 24849–04.

first on these two theorists and the work they generated, our interest in emotional development may be placed within a larger context: the measurement of emotion. Thus, we must examine the adult literature on the measurement of emotion first and then relate it to the study of infants and young children.

James's definition of emotion is in two parts stressing both the bodily changes—the soma—and the conscious feeling of these bodily changes. For James, emotion was not just the bodily change nor just the feeling of bodily change; it was both. While James attempted to measure the feelings of change introspectively, others, notably Lange, attempted to measure bodily change directly. Lange's approach was followed in the United States, and many subsequent definitions of emotions stressed the importance of physiological change, two classic examples being Wenger's definition of emotion as a visceral reaction (1950) and Cannon's as neural thalamic impulses generated by the release of cortical inhibition (1927). Thus, two traditions and methodologies arose from the James–Lange hypothesis: (1) introspection, as in the direct questioning of a person about his feelings, and (2) the response of the soma or physiological measures of emotion.

A third tradition and methodology emerged from the work of Darwin (1872). Darwin emphasized the surface aspects of emotion rather than feeling or soma. For Darwin, the "cause" of the surface change was found in the general theory of evolution: an adaptive response to environmental demands—the surface features being fixed by particular environmental patterns. Thus, the early work of James and Darwin gave rise to three different definitions and methodologies for studying emotion: emotion as introspective feeling, as physiological response, and as surface features.

Although a full review of the research literature pertinent to each tradition is beyond the task of this paper, we shall highlight the research to illustrate the three methodological approaches that have been generated. In addition, we present the interrelations among the three and their concomitant methodologies in order to provide a framework in which to consider the measurement of emotional development in infancy.

ADULT EMOTION

Introspection

Although James based many of his ideas about emotion on introspection—his own and others'—psychologists have been wary about accepting people's reports of their own emotions, recognizing that these subjective reports reflect the person's wishes and beliefs as much as any report of the "real" emotion. Also, as Skinner (1971) noted the language of emotion is perhaps less specific than the language of any other event, since the behaviors associated with the internal state may be less verifiable.

Most research that is related to introspection of emotion has been subsumed under indirect measures of personality. Psychoanalytic use of introspectionism has become very subtle, using the subject's actual words, his reactions to words, his lexical and linguistic expressions, his pauses, and so forth. The only tie to introspectionism that most of this approach retains is its use of language. Subjects are not trained to introspect using the methods that James (1890) or Wundt (1894) would have required.

In a peculiar sense, introspectionism has become the province of the experimenter. The experimenter designs situations that are intended to elicit particular emotional responses. In order to design such experimental situations, it is necessary that the scientist introspect as to which situations are likely to produce which emotions. Landis's (1924) unpleasant laboratory experiences, such as chopping off the head of a live rat to elicit strong emotional response, or even Ekman, Malmstron, and Friesen's (1971) showing of facial surgery so as to elicit fear and disgust are representative of this particular use of introspection, although many more could be mentioned. One might think that there would be some inquiry into the relationship among the experimenter's introspection, the experimental situation, and the emotions elicited; however, in that very intense laboratory situations have been used, where it is assumed that the experimenter's introspection is accurate, it is rare that inquiry has been made.

Facial Expression and Nonverbal Communication

The study of emotion as expression was pioneered by Darwin (1895/1965). His work on facial expressions and bodily posturing as signals of emotion in both humans and animals has for the most part been substantiated (Ekman, 1973). Most of Darwin's work has been pursued by animal ethologists, although there has been a small group of human researchers who have maintained an interest in facial expression and its measurement (Kanner, 1944; Schlosberg, 1952; Ekman, 1971).

From early studies using posed pictures of emotions as well as spontaneous photographs and even line drawings, it was found that most emotional expression could be described or classified at better than chance levels (Ekman, 1972; Kanner, 1944; Schlosberg, 1952; Tomkins &

McCarter, 1964). Some expressions seem to be more easily identified than others, the more easily identified ones being laughter or enjoyment and surprise and the less easily identified ones being pity, fear, and rage. Even children (Gates, 1923) can usually identify expressions fairly accurately, meeting adult standards somewhere around the age of 14. The measurement of facial expression does contain difficulties. Facial expressions are easily altered by suggestion (Fernberger, 1928). It is also the case that without knowing the context or the cause of the particular facial expression, the observer has difficulty interpreting what he sees. Facial expressions can be idiosyncratic: Ekman and Friesen (1975) referred to not just one but four different fear faces. Reliability has been obtained in studies of human expression and emotion, for example, the well-known scaling studies by Schlosberg (1952) and the studies of minute variations of expression portrayed in discrete muscular movements undertaken by Ekman *et al.* (1971).

There is now evidence that nonverbal facial signals have about the same meanings in most human societies (Eibl-Eibesfeldt, 1970; Ekman, 1972) and may be found in blind children and children both blind and unable to speak (Eibl-Eibesfeldt, 1973; Thompson, 1941). These studies suggest that there are certain invariances in nonverbal expression that occur across the species *Homo sapiens*. While most research has centered on the face, arguing for the evolutionary changes in facial muscles (Als, 1975) and the concomitant emotions, it is clear that other parts of the body need to be considered. While our discussion here centers on facial expression, it should be mentioned that other nonverbal expression involving other parts of the body than the face have been studied (see, for example, Argyle, 1972, on nonverbal communication in human social interaction). In dogs, tail wagging and tail-between-the-legs are certainly responded to as if they reflect different emotions. Body posturing has been (Schlosberg, 1952) and continues to be explored (Goffman, 1971). Another case not often used is vocal behavior (without the cues of formal language). Tomkins (1962) has argued that an important aspect of emotional expression is the concomitant use of vocal behavior: laughing when happy, crying when sad, growling when angry, and groaning when impassioned. The socialization process that results in the elimination of these vocal cues needs further study. The failure to relate bodily postures and facial expression constitute a sorry absence in the study of emotional expression.

Physiological Indices of Emotional Expression

The James–Lange hypothesis that somatic activity (muscular change) determines the conscious feeling of emotion gradually gave way to the Cannon–Bard (see Bard, 1934) hypothesis that activation through discharge from the hypothalamus to the cerebral cortex was involved in determining emotions. Both the James–Lange and the Cannon–Bard theories stressed the two aspects of emotions: the somatic changes (either muscular or neurophysiological) and the conscious feelings of these changes. Both these theories proposed that emotion is an activating or energizing system, a part of a drive system. Eventually, the focus of research changed from an interest in the felt change to a study of the physiological manifestations of the change. Research became oriented toward the activation of emotions and its concomitant physiological responses (Lindsley, 1951).

The focus on the autonomic nervous system (ANS) and sympathetic activity led to many studies using the galvanic skin response (GSR) as a physiological measure of emotion or, sometimes, merely of activation. Numerous studies were performed to determine whether subjects would be "activated" by different sorts of tasks, including electrical shock (Seward & Seward, 1934), free association (Jones & Wechsler, 1928), pleasant and unpleasant odors (Shock & Coombs, 1937), and various laboratory conditions, including loud noises, burning oneself with a lighted match, eating candy, and quizzes on laboratory apparatus (Bayley, 1928; Patterson, 1930). In general, the "stronger" the stimulus, the shorter the latency and the more extreme the GSR.

Other ANS responses could be used to study emotion and activation: blood pressure, heart rate (HR), and respiration. The history of the use of blood pressure and HR are as long as that for GSR (see for example, Shepherd, 1906). For the most part, the earlier findings seemed to show a consistent pattern of ANS activity, namely, that during arousal all ANS systems do, in fact, change. In the early 1950s, Lacey and his associates reported that "the autonomic nervous system does indeed respond to experimentally imposed stress 'as a whole' in the sense that all autonomically innervated structures seem to be activated . . . it does not respond 'as a whole' in the sense that all autonomically innervated structures exhibit equal increments or decrements of function" (Lacey, Batemen, & Van Lehn, 1953). Further investigation revealed differences in response specificity as a function of the organism's transaction with its environment. Thus, while GSR was shown to be relatively undifferentiated in terms of tasks requiring the organism to "take in" or exclude information, HR deceleration was more differentiated. Lacey, Kagan, Lacey, and Moss (1963) demonstrated that HR deceleration was a concomitant of the taking in of information (for example, attending), while HR acceleration was related to external stimulus rejection, such as the solution of mental arithmetic problems (Steele & Lewis, 1968). This differential HR response appeared to hold across a wide age range.

Continuing research with HR changes has raised important issues as to the role of the relationship between the central nervous system (CNS) and the ANS, with Lacey and his associates arguing for a more immediate relationship. Others, most notably Obrist, Webb, Stutter, and Howard (1970), have claimed that HR changes are to be considered more related to general bodily quiescence than to a CNS–ANS relationship.

Thus, the research literature indicates a movement away from the consideration of emotional responses to a more general issue of the ANS responses to stimulation in general and the organism's transactions with these stimuli (or contexts) in particular. In general, the studies have limited themselves to situations that appear to the experimenter (the neointrospectionist par excellence) to elicit stress or attention.

While it was originally thought that different affective states might be associated with different patterns of physiological response, the data provide little support for such a contention (for a review see Mandler, 1962). There has been little success in separating the various affective states through the use of physiological responses (or grouping of responses), although intensity of affect does show a relationship to intensity of physiological response. Whether this failure resides in the methodologies available or in the theories themselves will be determined by future research and technological advances. However, theories such as Schacter and Singer's (1962), which require only a general arousal state (in combination with the subject's cognitive evaluation of that state through the use of contextual cues), suggest in part that there may be no set of specific ANS or CNS responses corresponding to a set of felt emotions.

Relationship among Measurement Systems

Although the three traditions and methodologies exploring emotional expression have been available since the turn of the century, there is little research on the relationship between these methods. Studies of emotional response tend to use a single measure or at least to use a single measure to validate another measure within the same tradition, for example, the relationship between GSR and HR. In the following sections, the few studies that do examine emotional responses across traditional methodologies are examined.

Introspection and Facial Expression/Nonverbal Communication

It is difficult to find any studies in which facial expression and/or nonverbal communication and introspective accounts of affect were both examined. Introspection can be found, for example, when one considers the process of posing photographs as the poser is instructed to imagine (introspect) a situation in which he might feel the emotion that he is supposedly posing. However, the investigator does not question whether the subject actually uses the suggestion or whether this approach actually improves the poses; it is an instruction, not a condition of the study.

The other experimental condition in which one finds some form of introspection is one in which the experimenter creates a condition (for example, one thought to be fearful) and measures the subject's facial or other nonverbal responses. Although the condition is assumed to be fearful because of the introspection of the experimenter, it would be valuable to find out how the subject views the manipulation and to relate the subject's report to the measures being obtained.

Introspection and Physiological Indices

Although in recent years many advances have been made in the measurement of physiological parameters of emotion (see Levi, 1975), there has been little advance toward classifying responses that are particular to specific emotions. Most research has continued to concentrate on physiological parameters of stress and arousal without attempting to be more specific about emotions. Again, if the introspection of the experimenter is considered, there are a wide variety of studies looking at physiological indices of emotion-producing situations (for a review see Hamburg, Hamburg, & Bachas, 1975). As previously noted, the relationship between the situation and the organism's feelings about the situation are relatively unexplored.

Simonov (1969) has reported a study in which he asked actors to imagine being shocked with electrical stimulation and then measured their physiological responses. A high degree of similarity between the imagined shock and physiological response and the real shock and physiological response was found.

Physiological Indices and Facial Expression/Nonverbal Communication

The relationship between facial expression as well as other nonverbal behavior and physiological indices has also received scant attention. There are a few interesting exceptions. In one study, Ekman et al. (1971) reported some relationship between HR acceleration and the expressions of disgust and HR deceleration and the expression of surprise during the showing of a film of facial surgery. As Ekman et al. noted, there are unresolved difficulties with this study and the results are not conclusive, but it represents the integrated approach needed for the study of emotional expression. Such studies are rare.

Recent studies by Buck and his associates suggest that there may be an inverse relationship between naturally occurring facial expressions and either HR or GSR (Buck, Savin, Miller, & Caul, 1974) in the sense that either one system or the other is used to express emotion in relatively mild laboratory situations. These studies follow an earlier suggestion by Jones (1950) that different individuals tend to be "internal" or "external" expressors of emotion.

Although the postural and facial behavior was not analyzed, Simonov (1969) measured voice intonation by spectral analysis as well as changes in heart rate and found that change in both intonation and heart rate were related to stress. The subjects in this case were the Russian astronauts as they were circling the earth and the moon.

Summary

Although the study of emotions and emotional expression in adult humans has a long history in both European and American psychology, relatively little work has concerned itself with the integration of the various measurement systems derived from James and Darwin. The exclusion of introspection, at least from the subject, if not from the experimenter, has led to the study of the somatic correlates of emotion without consideration of the subject's feelings of these somatic changes. The notable exception is the Schacter and Singer theory, which allows introspection, although changed to evaluation of contextual cues, back into the study of emotion. Most of the work in emotional expression continues to be concerned with facial expression and its measurement (individual differences, cultural similarity, and observer bias) and physiological correlates of stress arousal and attention. Within the nonverbal expression literature there has been little attempt to integrate facial expression with body and postural effects, with some even arguing that the face is the center of emotional expression in humans. The physiological literature is also limited. For example, the conclusion that there does not exist a set or pattern of physiological responses that have a one-to-one correspondence with a particular affect was based on 30-year-old work, done prior to the use of computer technology through which patterning working such techniques as, for example, sequential lag could be detected. Clearly, research with adult humans can provide important methodologies and theories for our work with emotional development.

INFANT EMOTION

The interest in infant emotional expression is not new (Darwin, 1872; Bridges, 1930; Spitz & Wolf, 1946) and has a parallel history to that of the adult literature. Nevertheless, many of the same problems that surface in the measurement of emotion in adults are also problematic for infants and young children. The three traditions of introspection, facial and nonverbal expression, and physiological responses influence developmental research as well, although the introspective method is not available for the preschool child. Since the infant and the young child cannot verbalize their feelings, only their expression and our introspection are available, thus making it difficult to determine whether or not they feel. Moreover, given what we know about their limited cognitive abilities, the facial expression and any particular emotion may not be analogous; for example, a neonatal smile may or may not correspond to analogous emotional states, such as joy.

There are other difficulties with the study of the young; for example, the equivalence of behavior and the changing meaning of responses. Are crawling and walking always equivalent? Are the facial expressions and behaviors of smile, laughter, and giggling as expressions of joy equivalent for different ages? Consider a situation that may elicit joy, such as a mother and child at play. In this situation, the young infant may smile, the adult may laugh. Are these behaviors equivalent expressions of joy? Is laughter ontogenetically more advanced? Is laughter more intense than smiling? These are the types of questions and problems more apt to be confronted by those interested in emotional development.

One advantage often claimed for work with the young organisms is that the emotional expression available to them is not contaminated by socialization processes. There is no guile to their behavior; therefore, the correspondence between their emotional state and emotional expression is high. Moreover, one might suppose that the relationship between physiological responses and facial expression, as well as other nonverbal behaviors, would also be high. It is, of course, just as likely that these various response systems may not be related and become synchronized only as a function of development and socialization.

The careful study of emotional expression and its development in infants and young children is just beginning. In the following sections, some of the more relevant research is reviewed for facial expression and physiological indices of emotional expression.

Facial Expression and Nonverbal Communication

Studies of the facial expression of infants have a long history and include baby biographies with accounts of emotional behavior (Darwin, 1872), descriptions of gross behavior (Watson, 1921), and an examination of adults' impressions of infant expressions (Bridges, 1930, 1932). Studies examining a single response are relatively new, such as crying (Wolff, 1969), smiling (Ambrose, 1961; Sroufe & Waters, 1976; Emde & Harmon, 1972), and looking and attending (Lewis, Kagan, Kalafat, & Campbell, 1966). More recently, observers have started to examine large numbers of different responses and their relationship (Brooks & Lewis, 1976). Until recently, there have been no published lists or systematic analyses of ethograms of infants' facial expressions (see Oster, this volume), although such lists have been available for older children (Blurton-Jones, 1971), adults (Grant, 1969; Ekman, 1972) and for nonhuman primates (Chevalier-Skolnikoff, 1973).

Few emotional states have been studied with any intensity, although those that have been provide a rich behavioral base. The emotional states studied represent three general categories: positive, negative, and surprise or attention. Positive states, indicating such emotions as happiness, joy, and contentment, have been studied by use of the smiling response. The list of circumstances, social and nonsocial, that elicit smiles after the first few weeks of life has been extensively discussed (Ambrose, 1961; Sroufe & Waters, 1976; Kagan, 1971; Lewis, 1969; Watson, 1973). The responses of parents, other adults, or children to these smiles has not been carefully documented although infant's and mother's smiling are concomitant (Lewis & Freedle, 1973; Lewis, 1972). However, the difficulty is that the smile (or any facial response to be discussed) may reflect some internal state or may be the facial expression elicited by a class of endogenous events having little relationship to any internal state.

Negative states have received more attention, in particular fear and stress (Lewis & Rosenblum, 1974). Anger, rage, and frustration have received little study (Watson, 1919; Goldberg & Lewis, 1969; Brazelton, 1973), although rage was mentioned by Watson as one of the more primary affective states of the very young.

Crying and its various types have been carefully studied and various types of cries distinguished (Wolff, 1969). Fear and distress have been extensively studied in terms of situations, with two situations being prevalent: the approach of a stranger and the mother's separating herself from the child. How distressed the infant is, how many infants at what ages show stress, what the contextual features of the situation are, what the mother says on leaving, and how she detaches herself from her infant (Weinraub & Lewis, in press) are some of the issues under exploration (see for example Bronson, 1973; Lewis & Brooks, 1975). Recent research suggests that fear or distress in many situations may be overrated (Rheingold & Eckerman, 1973). Reasons that fear of strangers has been overemphasized include failure to observe carefully a variety of measures, to integrate these measures into patterns, and to study changes in them. In addition, very global behaviors sometimes used to indicate fear may be distorted by the adult's expectation (in this case a false introspection) of what ought to be seen; this may be labeled as a case of "selecting" the signal. Interestingly, the experimenters' expectations concerning fear seem to be changing, which can be inferred by the changing lexicon of the infants' responses. What was called *fear* is now called *wariness*, and *arousal* and *attending* are being considered instead of *distress*. Part of the problem stems from the use of a holistic versus a constructive approach. In the holistic approach, the experimenter rates the subject using broad categorizations. In the constructive approach, the experimenter rates each section of the face separately with facial patterns constructed from the individual parts. In both cases, facial patterns emerge, the latter method having the advantage of avoiding contamination of both general impressions as well as a reliance on one aspect of the face—the mouth for example—in the determination of the nature of the emotional expression. Besides fear, surprise and attention have received the most study (Charlesworth, 1964; Lewis & Goldberg, 1969; Vine, 1973). The issues raised in the study of fear are also relevant here.

One of the most critical aspects of the study of facial expression has been the lack of a systematic mapping of infant faces similar to what has been done for the adults. Oster (in this volume), Haviland and Lewis (1975), and Brooks and Lewis (1976) are all attempting to develop such ethograms. Another serious problem has been the utilization of single responses to infer an emotional state. Thus, crying or smiling alone without careful consideration of all aspects of the face has been used as an indication of particular emotions. Recently, Brooks and Lewis (1976) have looked at multiple measures and patterns of facial expression toward approaching strangers in an attempt to obtain patterning of facial expressions of fear and greeting.

Another difficulty involves the reliability of the measurement of infant emotions. Bridges (1930) and Sherman (1927) indicated that without situational information, perception of infant emotion was not reliable, although it was above chance for most emotions. Our own work with coding facial expression seems to bear this observation out. When adult observers were unaware of the situation in which the infant was being observed (the approach of a stranger), they often confused fear and interest. This effect suggests that the facial expressions of infants may be more ambiguous than those of adults. The impact of this fact, if verified by further study, on the development of emotions needs to be explored.

Physiological Indices of Emotional Expression

With few exceptions (Campos & Johnson, 1966), most of the research using physiological indices of emotional expression have centered on a single response, HR changes. Following upon Lacey's work on HR changes as a function of the organism's intended transaction with its world, Kagan and Lewis (1965) and Lewis et al. (1966) demonstrated the deceleration as an important concomitant to attending in infants. Subsequent research on the response has been summarized by Graham and Jackson (1970) and Lewis (1975) and indicates that across a very large age range, HR deceleration is related to the taking in and the attending to external stimulation when the organism is in an alert state. Moreover, the degree of HR deceleration was directly related to the degree of attention, and the acquiring of a subsequent task was dependent on that attention (Lewis, 1974). If we infer that attending is related to emotional states such as curiosity and exploration, the demonstration of a HR response concomitant with this internal state is some evidence of the relationship between emotion and physiological response; however, the claim of Obrist et al. (1970) that HR response represents no more than a concomitant response to motoric quiescence suggests nothing more than its relationship to a general arousal dimension as opposed to a specific emotion.

In infancy, HR changes and an emotional state have been studied in response to the visual cliff situation. Schwartz, Campos, and Baisel (1973) found that 9-month-old infants showed HR acceleration when placed over the high side of the cliff. They interpreted this response to indicate fear, although, as they reported, there were no behavioral manifestations of that fear. In an earlier paper, Campos, Langer, and Krowitz (1970) found, in 55-day-old infants, HR deceleration to the deep side, possibly an indication of attention and arousal at being off the ground.

The use of physiological indices of emotion has not received the attention it might. Elaborate equipment and data reduction contribute to its disuse, as well as problems having to do with measurement and data analysis. These issues become more apparent in the following sections.

Relationship among Measurement Systems

The relationship between physiological responses and introspection, facial expression, and nonverbal communication has received almost no attention with regard to emotional development in infancy. As stated earlier, introspection as a methodology is not relevant since the infant is not capable of self-report although the experimenter's introspection is widely used. Thus, placing the infant on a visual cliff should induce fear in an infant mature enough to "understand" that this is a fearful situation. Physiological and facial responses that occur in this situation are then assumed to be concomitants of fear. This procedure utilizing the introspection of the experimenter is reasonable; however, caution must be taken since the assumption that infants (and all infants, at that) will experience the same emotion as the experimenter may be faulty, especially for very young organisms, who certainly cannot order their experience as we do.

Moreover, there exists the possibility that even though the young infant exhibits a set of responses reminiscent of those of an adult feeling x emotion, there may be little relationship between expression and feeling. This relationship may be the consequence of socialization itself; the caregiver's responses, including verbalizations, may be the causal event relating expression to feeling.

Thus, the integration of methodologies and responses—in particular facial expression and physiological response—takes on a special significance for the study of emotional development. The very lack of any introspection or self-report suggests that careful attention should be given to those response systems available for study. Unfortunately, until recently, there was no research connecting facial expression and physiological responses.

Physiological Indices and Facial Expression

Two recent studies in infancy have measured HR responses and facial expression (Waters, Matas, & Sroufe, 1975; Campos, Emde, Gaensbauer, & Henderson, 1975). In both studies, HR responses and facial expressions were measured during a fear-inducing situation:the approach of a stranger.

In the Waters et al. (1975) study, wary infants, as measured by facial expression, were more likely to exhibit HR acceleration than less wary infants. However, there were serious methodological problems: there is little information about the time locking of the HR and facial expression data, about beat-by-beat changes in HR, and about when wary and nonwary faces were coded. The authors were sensitive to the problems of the contamination of motoric responses and the relationship between emotional expression and HR.[1] Even with its methodological problems, this

---

[1] The elimination of 10-month-old subjects showing motoric activity—avoiding infants—resulted in even stronger HR differences between wary and nonwary infants. This result is not well documented in the study, and because of its counterintuitive results—movement should increase HR level and therefore its elimination should decrease that level—further elaboration seems necessary.

study was the first to obtain data on the interrelationship of various response systems.

Campos *et al.* (1975) undertook a more extensive study of infants' cardiac and behavioral reactions to approaching strangers when the mother was present and absent. Unlike Waters *et al.* the authors time-locked filmed records of the infants' facial responses to a polygraph writeout. A base level HR was obtained 15 seconds prior to the entry of the stranger, and this mean value was subtracted from each "subsequent sampling point to give HR responses to each episode." Facial responses such as sobering and smiling were measured along with global judgments of distress. While Waters *et al.* eliminated active crying and presumably large motoric responses, the present investigation included these, which probably results in a spuriously high correlation between distress and HR acceleration due to the relationship between motor activity and HR. In the mother-present situation during the most intrusive point, only 25% of the 9-month-old infants show some indication of distress. These results do not support the contention that approach *per se* is fear-inducing, a finding reported by others (Brooks & Lewis, 1976). Although considerably more fearfulness was found in the mother-absent–stranger-approach condition, the mother's absence may be the more critical variable. Mean facial expression data by age and condition during the stranger's approach are presented, suggesting that the different facial expressions were summed. If this is the case, the procedure is somewhat questionable, since, for example, a frowning and fascinated face does not equal a sober face. Using mean data, Campos *et al.* found that only during the intrude phase in the first-approach, mother-present condition did the stranger elicit a mean face of "sober"; during the other phases, the face was more fascinated (or attentive in our nomenclature). The HR data are also averaged, and for the first stranger, mother-present condition there was, in general, HR deceleration.

The HR data of infants whose facial expression shifted from fascinated to whimpering or crying and infants whose expressions were rated as predominantly fascinated were selected. Progressive distress was related to HR acceleration. There was also acceleration in the fascinated group, although they showed less acceleration than the stressed group. That the mean facial expression and a mean HR response both showed covarying changes during distress is not proof of the relationship between HR acceleration and distress facial expression; mean data are insufficient for this purpose. Moreover, it may be the case that the motoric involvement of intense facial expression causes the reported relationship even though breath holding from crying does result in precipitous bradycardia. Bradycardia occurs rarely in just crying infants and usually only in very upset infants, few of which appeared in the present study. Finally, to prove their point more pervasively—that HR acceleration was always accompanied by facial distress—groups of infants showing or not showing acceleration could have been compared in terms of facial expression. Campos *et al.* may have overstated the relationship between HR acceleration and fear; however, their time-locking and measurement procedures provide an important addition to the Waters *et al.* results.

Summary

This review of the research on infancy reveals a paucity of data for either the study of facial expression, nonverbal cues, and physiological responses or their interrelationship. One of the most serious deficits rests in the failure to agree on a class of facial expressions and on the ability to classify types of faces. On the one hand, global facial categorization runs the risk of masking specific facial features and of biasing selection. On the other hand, specific facial feature measurement results in a fragmented face and with no underlying patterns. A measurement procedure that both measures facial expression in detail and at the same time allows for a system of classifying types of whole faces is sorely needed. Moreover, a system is needed for examining changes in facial expression. Most analyses (the Campos *et al.* study being a notable exception) would have us believe that the infant assumes a single-pattern facial expression, a static face, throughout a particular situation. The results from our own work as well as that of others indicates that faces are not static, especially during a complex approach sequence. How to characterize this change must be considered. Finally, the averaging of facial expression may be an unreasonable procedure, as it assumes some type of scaling of emotional expressions.

Physiological responses, too, are subject to similar errors. The averaging of HR may provide faulty results. The use of sampling techniques needs special attention; for example, results looking at peak acceleration can generate findings quite different from peak deceleration. HR response has many difficulties, for example, how to characterize the responses. Multiphasic responses cause particular difficulties since different phases can represent either responses to external events such as the approach of a stranger or an attempt of the system to regain homeostasis, a return to base levels.

Given the problems outlined above, the integration of facial expression and HR response is especially difficult. Beat-by-beat analyses are necessary as is time locking of the two response systems. When to time-lock presents particular problems since some response systems may be slower to respond than others. Peak HR responses, whether of an accelerative or a decelerative nature, are rather sluggish, having a latency of about 200–300 milliseconds. How fast do the muscles of the face move and how are we to time-lock them to HR change? It is clear that more research is needed to relate various response systems.

THE PRESENT STUDY

The present study was designed to examine the relationship between facial expression and HR responses in an emotion-inducing situation, in an attempt to answer some of the methodological considerations raised in the preceding section. We did not begin our study with the notion that HR and facial expression were necessarily coupled or that they covary in any simplistic fashion, as we believed that this relationship has not yet been conclusively demonstrated.

Experimental Methodology

The situation used to elicit emotional responses from the infant was one that has been commonly used to elicit fear: the approach of a stranger (Scarr & Salapatek, 1970; Morgan & Ricciuti, 1969). However, this situation has recently been shown to elicit a variety of responses other than fear, including wariness, attentiveness, and joy (cf. Rheingold & Eckerman, 1973; Brooks & Lewis, 1976). Findings suggest that the stranger-approach situation is ideal for eliciting a wide range of responses indicative of both positive and negative emotional states.

Infants accompanied by their mothers were brought into a room of 3 m × 4 m. The mothers sat to the left of their infants who were seated in high chairs. On signal, the stranger appeared at the doorway (E on our time-locked records and in the accompanying figures), smiled, but said nothing to the child. The stranger remained at the doorway until noticed by the child. She then walked, taking approximately 3 sec to reach Position 1 (1), which was approximately 1.5 m from the door. The stranger paused at Position 1 for approximately 1 sec. She then walked to Position 2 (2), which was 1.5 m from Position 1, and this took 3 sec. She then walked to Position 3 (3), which was 1.5 m from Position 2, paused, and finally walked to Position 4 (4), and touched the infant's hand. Then she turned, which was Position 5 (5), slowly walked to the door, and exited (E). The entire episode from entry to exit took approximately 25 sec. The mother remained next to the infant during the entire episode. The approach sequence was not begun until the infant was seated and relaxed and until its heart rate had stabilized at its baseline. Thus, the infants were made as comfortable as possible prior to the approach sequence.

The entire session was videotaped with a camera mounted on a wall opposite the infant, with the stranger's position marked by an audio signal and on the videotape and the polygraph recording. The auditory signal coordinated the two recording systems for each of the seven points of the approach.

For this study, 43 normal, full-term subjects were seen representing three age groups: 15 subjects (8 females, 7 males) were 6–8 months of age (mean 7-2); 15 subjects (7 females, 8 males) were 9–12 months of age (mean 11-4); and 13 subjects (7 females, 6 males) were 15–18 months of age (mean 17-2). All subjects (with one exception) were Caucasian. The subjects were all middle-to upper-middle-class infants, and one-half were firstborn, one-half later born. Subjects were recruited by telephone solicitation; 90% of those mothers contacted agreed to participate.

Facial Expressions, Definitions, and Measurement Procedures

Most observations of the infant's nonverbal affect system have relied on relatively holistic behavior categories (Bridges, 1930; Waters *et al.*, 1975; Campos *et al.*, 1975). The argument in favor of such categories is that a large number of discrete and subtle behavior patterns may be subsumed appropriately under a common rubric such as *excited* or *wary*, and the risk of overemphasizing a frequent but unimportant single variable is minimized. The holistic categories rest on the ability of the observer to make gestalt types of judgments, a task at which most observers are so good that attempts to replace such a functional system with a more discrete system ought to be carefully examined.

Interest in more discrete systems grew from several sources: the interest in the types of movement or signals that an infant uses relative to children and adults, the interpretation of these signals by adults, and the difficulties that began to arise when a holistic system of judging faces was related to other more discrete systems, such as physiological measures of ANS activity.

Blurton-Jones's (1972) and Grant's (1969) lists of facial and postural behaviors are two important discrete category systems that have been developed. Using both Blurton-Jones's and Grant's systems, we are in the process of developing rules for categorizing facial expression and establishing reliability (tasks with which Blurton-Jones and Grant are also currently involved). We establish high reliability by first having coders watch the moving sequence to establish a holistic sense of individual characteristics and range. After this, the actual coding is done by a study of the videotape at each approach position and an examination of each part of the face independently. The movement sequence tends to eliminate spurious differences due to structural differences, such as straight brows or curved brows, while the static coding eliminates the coders' natural tendency to see a "whole" expression when only part of it is there, such as "seeing" widely opened eyes or raised brows when the jaw drops.

The list of categories in Table I includes those categories that we could reliably code (at least 80% agreement between two coders in terms of absence or presence of categories). This system of coding is not exhaustive or simple. The four general categories coded included mouth position, eye direction, eye openness, and eyebrow position. *Mouth position* categories are highly reliable and are relatively clear-cut, with the exception of lips retracted. This category includes all signs of horizontal muscular tension with mouth open or shut. Lips retracted is often a transition category between corners up and down and has little stability. The *eye direction* categories are often inferred from head direction relative to body orientation or camera position because of the lack of clarity in the video production. Although reliabilities for eye direction are in the upper 80s, this reliability represents the use of consensus for resolving the problem. The *eye openness* categories are highly reliable (mid 90s). The *eyebrow* categories have been used in only one study so far and are highly reliable in the upper 90s, mainly because there is little perceivable change. More work needs to be done in other situations before these categories are finally accepted.

The central problem in discrete coding is how to collapse the discrete categories into types of faces. The holistic or gestalt interpretations resolve this problem by having the coder interpret the movements without discrete analysis. For the most part, we have relied on Grant's (1969) and Tomkins's (1962) descriptions of the expression of emotions, but blends—a combination of one feature from one emotion and another from a second emotion—are more frequent than not, giving rise to combination categories, for example, attention-negative tone facial expression. Without further exploration, some of these questions cannot be resolved. In the presentation of the data, we indicate the specific nature of the problems and the directions we have taken in interpretation.

The development of a discrete coding system raises some problems; however, such a system does allow for comparison with gestalt or holistic systems at the very least. At best, the discrete system may sensitize us to the tremendous variation in expression that exists, it trains us to be better observers of blends and contradictions, and it may allow us to find the part of the gestalt that is projected as opposed to the part that we project.

Heart Rate Responses, Definitions, and Measurement Procedures

Heart rate responses were obtained in the standard fashion. A Grass cardiotachometer printed out a continuous record of HR, and the stranger's position was recorded onto this record. Individual subjects' HR curves constitute the primary data for comparison with the facial

TABLE I. DESCRIPTION OF FACIAL FEATURES[a]

Mouth	
⬭	Squared upper lip
⬮	Squared lower lip: No muscular tension in cheek or jaw
◣	Relaxed
/‥\	Corners raised
(‥)	Corners lowered
¡‥¡	Lips retracted: open or closed mouth, lips narrow, tension visible in lower face
(O (	O-shape: vertical stretch, jaw drops
¡☉¡	Pursed

Eyebrows	
⌒ ⌒	Inside corners down
⌒ ⌒	Outside corners down (not raised)
⌒ ⌒	Relaxed: no tension
‾ ‾	Raised moderately and sustained
⌒⌒	Raised extreme: visible forehead wrinkles
⌒ ⌒	Flash brow, either or both: one second or less

Eye direction	Eye openness
Up	Wide: vertical stretch in corners, white visible
Down	Bit wide: pupil and iris visible
Mother side	Normal: no tension, pupil visible
Away side	Bit narrow: pupil partly hidden
Down side	Narrow: lid more than half down, horizontal tension
Ahead	Lid down: pupil not visible

[a] This coding system appeared in Haviland, J. Looking smart: The relationship between affect and intelligence. In M. Lewis (Ed.), *The origins of intelligence: infancy and early childhood.* New York: Plenum Press, 1975, pp. 353–377; also, Haviland, J., & Lewis, M. Infants' greeting patterns to strangers. Research Bulletin 76–2. Princeton, New Jersey: Educational Testing Service, 1976.

expressions at each of the seven positions. The use of the entire HR response curve, including the base period preceding the approach, eliminated many of the problems of curve averaging and allows for analyses based upon individual subjects' responses. Several aspects of each individual curve were examined: (1) the base period, the last four beats prior to the appearance of the stranger; (2) stimulus onset (E to 1), that period during which the stranger became visible but before she moved toward the subject; (3) the approach period (Positions 1–4), that period during which the stranger approached and touched the infant; and (5) stimulus offset (Positions 5–E), that period during which the stranger turned and left the room.

Several specific response parameters were obtained and examined: (1) base period—mean of last four beats prior to approach or the single beat prior to approach; (2) the approach period—(a) mean of four beats associated with each of the Positions 1–4; (b) the peak response or the high beat associated with one of the approach positions; (c) the trough response or the lowest beat associated with one of the approach positions. By use of these parameters, general response measures were obtained and included (1) peak response (base beat minus peak approach beat); (2) trough response (base beat minus trough beat); (3) mean change response ($\overline{X}$ four base beats minus $\overline{X}$ four approach beats); (4) change response (beat at Position 1 minus beat at Position 4).

Results

The results are divided into two sections. The first and most important is the presentation of individual subject data on the relationship between HR and facial expression. Given the problems as outlined above, the best way to examine the data is by individual cases. The complexity and variety of response patterns can be clearly demonstrated in this manner. The second section is a more traditional approach to the data, with group data presented. This approach is, of course, necessary to summarize the data and to examine the data for trends across subjects.

Individual Response Curves

The individual data are presented in terms of two criteria. First, subjects were selected on the basis of HR data. Subjects from each of the three age groups were chosen who showed the largest HR changes, either HR acceleration or HR deceleration. These infants' facial expressions were then examined. Second, infants exhibiting the most intense expressions were chosen and their HR responses were examined. Thus, the subjects chosen were representative of either large physiological or large facial expression responses. This procedure—using first HR and then facial expression as the criterion measure—was thought the most efficient for exploring, on an individual subject basis, the relationship between response systems.

Heart Rate as Criterion

The following figures illustrate the relationship between facial expression and HR response. On each figure the seven positions have been marked. For each position, a picture of the infant's face is also presented. The HR data represented in beats per minute (bpm), with the midpoint representing 120 bpm. Position E represents the appearance of the stranger, 1 represents the first movement toward the child, 2 and 3 are the continued approach, 4 is the actual physical contact, 5 is the turn of the stranger, and E is the departure of the stranger through the door.

Subject 64 was a 6-month-old female. Between E and 1 there was marked HR deceleration. The deceleration was maintained throughout the approach and gradually returned to the original base level as the stranger left the room. The predominant HR response to the approach was deceleration. The predominant facial expression was lips retracted and some tension in the lower face in addition to lip corners down at Position 3. This response suggests a wary infant. For this child, HR deceleration and a negative facial expression co-occurred.

The next figure is of Subject 71, a 7-month-old male. This child showed HR deceleration as a response to the approaching stranger; unlike the previous child, this subject exhibited a smiling face with no

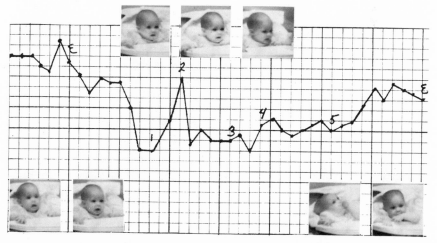

FIG. 1. Individual heart rate and facial expression data: Subject 64.

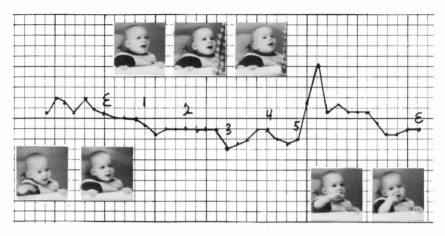

FIG. 2. Individual heart rate and facial expression data: Subject 71.

indication of any tension; indeed, this face appears to be happy, attentive, and receptive to the approaching stranger. Thus, for this child HR deceleration and a positive facial expression co-occurred.

The next subject, 83, was an 8-month-old male. Between Position E and 1, HR deceleration to the onset was accompanied by an attentive face. The HR response remained decelerative, and although there was some acceleration from 1 to 4, the response at 4 was still below the base. This HR response would therefore have to be characterized as decelerative, yet the face at Positions 2, 3, and 4 shows some mouth tension

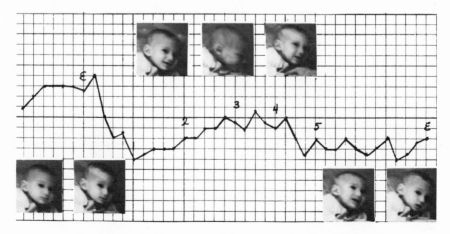

FIG. 3. Individual heart rate and facial expression data: Subject 83.

along with turning away and therefore suggests a somewhat negative facial expression.

The next figure is that of Subject 82, an 8-month-old female. She showed a large decelerative response to the onset of the stranger and returned to base level during the approach only to be followed by a marked decelerative response when the stranger turned and left the room. Here is an excellent example of HR deceleration to onset and offset of an event not unlike those reported by Lewis (1971) for onset and offset of auditory stimulation in the same-aged children. The facial expression of this child varied from a happy expression to one of slight tension reminiscent of an attending response.

Subject 60 was a 6-month-old female. The HR response of this child showed very little deceleration at the onset of the stranger and a slow cardiac acceleration accompanying the stranger's approach. There was some deceleration as the stranger turned and left the room. Unfortunately, the infant turned toward the mother, one of the few cases to do so, and it was not possible to code the child's facial expression at all positions. The child's face at Position 4, the point of contact, along with the gaze aversion, suggests a negative face accompanied by HR acceleration. Interestingly, at Position E, the exit, the child showed the same corners-down mouth, although the eyes, which were opened more widely, suggest more of an attentive face co-occurring with deceleration.

A characterization of these five subjects between 6 and 8 months of age reveals that the most prevalent response to the appearance and approach of the stranger was HR deceleration. There were cases of

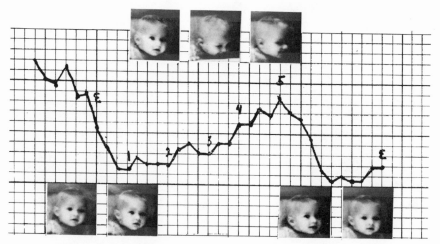

Fig. 4. Individual heart rate and facial expression data: Subject 82.

acceleration, but in general the deceleration was the prevalent response. Some infants showed HR increases as the stranger approached them. Whether these HR increases (which were still below the base level) were a function of the approaching stranger or were homeostatic responses—that is, the adjustment of the HR to its base level—needs to be determined. Finally, the turning of the stranger and her exit from the room often resulted in HR deceleration. Thus, both the entrance and the exit of the stranger had concomitant HR deceleration responses. A facial expression of attention often accompanied the onset and the termination of the approach experience. Individual subjects differed in whether or not they showed a facial expression of tension during the approach. In general, the observation of HR and facial expression in this age group showed little covariation. Facial expressions of distress had concomitant deceleratory as well as acceleratory responses. Likewise, faces showing positive affect also showed no covariation with HR responses.

Let us turn toward some records of infants 9–18 months of age, children who might be expected to show more negative affect at the approach of a stranger. Subject 18 was an 11-month-old female. Her HR response to the approaching stranger was a monophasic deceleration. The corners of her mouth were raised, the brows appeared relaxed, and the face could be characterized as smiling.

The next figure is of Subject 11, a 9-month-old male. The initial response was a deceleration accompanied by HR acceleration as the stranger approached. After the stranger touched the child and turned to leave, there was an immediate decelerative response. The facial expres-

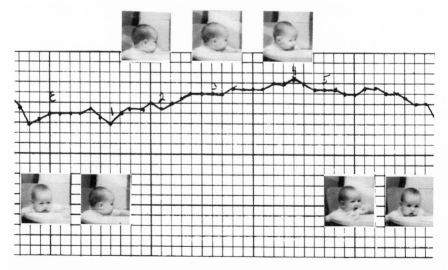

FIG. 5. Individual heart rate and facial expression data: Subject 60.

sion was one of a smiling face. Notice that at the onset and offset of the stranger, the child showed a sobering and what we call *attentive* expression, which accompanied HR deceleration.

The next is Subject 4, a 12-month-old female. The child showed little initial HR response to the approach of the stranger, possibly a slight acceleration, followed by a decelerative response at Position 3 when the stranger was close, and once again a decelerative response when the stranger left the child. The child's face can be characterized as lips retracted for most of the approach and lowered corners of the mouth at the touch. Thus, this child exhibited negative affect with some deceleration.

Subject 17 was a 9-month-old male. The child showed initial HR deceleration followed by acceleration. In general Subject 17 showed little HR change, although there was deceleration when the stranger left. At Position 1, the lips were retracted, the brows showed some tension, and he was averting his gaze, suggesting wariness; yet, at Position 5, he appeared to be smiling and showing positive affect.

Subject 36 was a 17-month-old female. She decelerated in response to the appearance, approach, and departure of the stranger. The concomitant facial expressions were pursed lips, mouth corners lowered, and gaze aversion. This child had a wary facial expression and HR deceleration in response to the approach of the stranger.

Subject 31 was an 18-month-old male. His HR response was triphasic: acceleration to the appearance, deceleration during the approach, and acceleration as the stranger departed. The facial expression

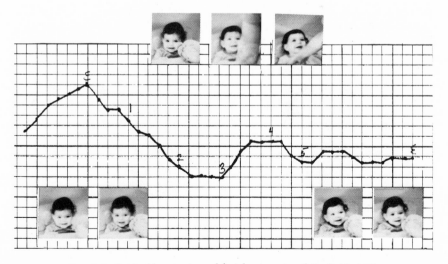

FIG. 6. Individual heart rate and facial expression data: Subject 18.

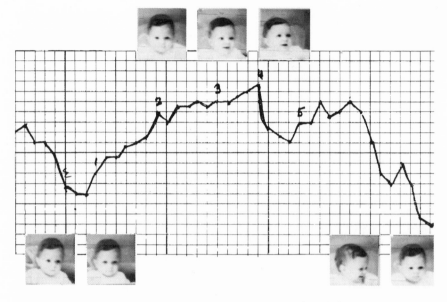

FIG. 7. Individual heart rate and facial expression data: Subject 11.

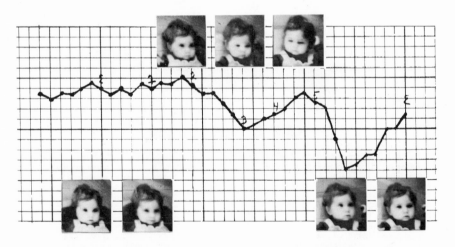

FIG. 8. Individual heart rate and facial expression data: Subject 4.

associated with this deceleration was, in general, one of tension with lips protracted and mouth corners lowered (especially at Position 3).

In summary, the observation of the facial expression of infants showing large HR changes reveals only a slight relationship between these two systems. In general, the predominant HR response was deceleration, although this was somewhat dependent on the measurement procedure employed. If the HR level during base minus HR level during approach is used, deceleration was the characteristic response. However, if the slope of the HR during the approach, excluding the base level (Positions 1–4 only) is examined, HR acceleration sometimes accompanied the approach of the stranger. Whether this HR acceleration was caused by the approach of the stranger or was part of the homeostatic response associated with the initial deceleration—the return of HR to a base level—is not clear. If the base level is taken into account, HR deceleration was again the predominant response.

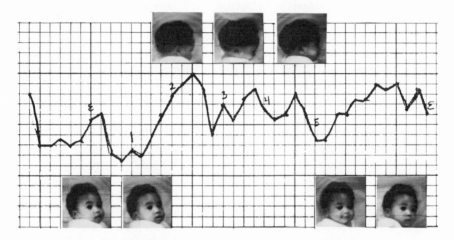

FIG. 9. Individual heart rate and facial expression data: Subject 17.

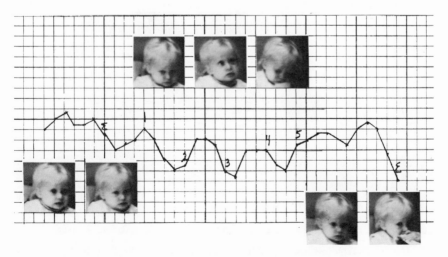

FIG. 10. Individual heart rate and facial expression data: Subject 36.

There is little relationship between HR and facial expression. Subjects who showed HR deceleration were as likely to exhibit positive or negative facial expression. In fact, HR deceleration to the appearance and disappearance of the stranger was most often accompanied by an attentive face; this appears to be part of an orienting response, which shows concurrence of looking and HR deceleration (Lewis *et al.*, 1966). Interestingly, HR acceleration, when it occurs, is more frequently but not exclusively related to negative facial expressions.

Although negative facial expressions were observed, what has been termed *fear* was not seen; the infants did not cry or attempt to escape, although some frowned or retracted their lips during the approach. When wariness was seen, it was not very intense. An attentive or even a positive facial expression was exhibited by many of the infants at the approach of the stranger. These findings, consistent with several other studies of approach (Lewis & Brooks, 1974; Brooks & Lewis, 1976; Rheingold & Eckerman, 1973), are in disagreement with other studies reporting considerably more negative tone associated with the approach of the stranger. This discrepancy is probably multiply determined. The presence of the mother may reduce stranger wariness, since infants show relatively little fear or wariness in her presence as compared to in her absence (Campos *et al.*, 1975). Our attempts at testing only when the infants were comfortable may also have reduced the incidence of wariness associated with the stranger situation rather than with the approaching strange adult. Facial expressions, often reported as negative in tone, may reflect an attentive rather than a wary face. Finally, when coders know that they are coding a fearful situation, they may

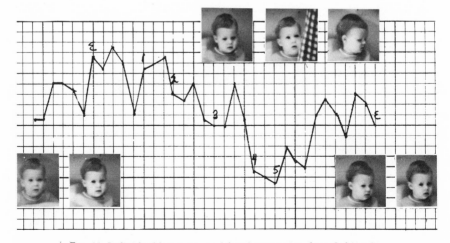

FIG. 11. Individual heart rate and facial expression data: Subject 31.

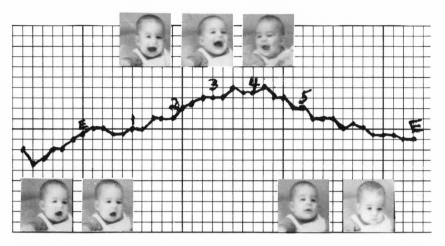

FIG. 12. Individual heart rate and facial expression data: Subject 61.

expect the infants to be frightened and may mistake attentiveness for wariness.

Facial Expression as the Criterion

While the first set of figures were chosen because the subjects exhibited the largest HR change, the next set were chosen because of the display of facial expressions, and their HR responses were examined.[2]

Subject 61 was a 6-month-old male child. The infant's face shows a smiling, open-mouthed grin; it is a happy face. The HR response was one of acceleration reaching a peak and then declining as the stranger turned and left the room. A positive facial expression was associated with HR acceleration and may be an example of high levels of affectual response resulting in acceleration—motoric activity being the causal factor.

Subject 75 was an 8-month-old male. This subject also showed a positive affect; yet the predominant HR response was deceleration.

The next subject (13) was an 11-month-old male. His expression is one of an attentive and positive facial expression accompanied by HR deceleration.

Subject 14 was a 10-month-old female who showed a negative-attentive face with lip corners down. Observation of her HR responses

[2] Those subjects who qualified under this criterion but who were presented before are not included.

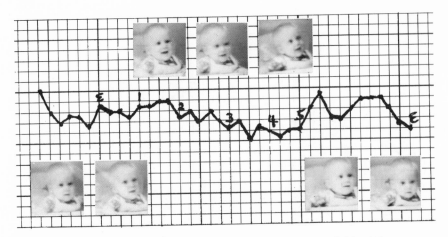

FIG. 13. Individual heart rate and facial expression data: Subject 75.

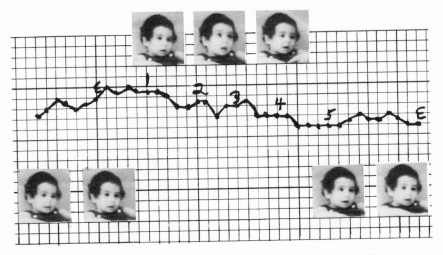

FIG. 14. Individual heart rate and facial expression data: Subject 13.

indicates a triphasic response, deceleration during the approach, acceleration at contact, and deceleration during the departure. The triphasic HR response was unrelated to the relatively static face.

Subject 8 was a 10-month-old female who appeared to be wary—evidenced by tension in her mouth and gaze aversion—although she was also attentive. The initial response (E–1) was HR deceleration followed by acceleration, which returned to the resting level. In general, there was relatively little change in the HR response of this child, although the facial expression does show some wariness.

Subject 1 was a 9-month-old male with a negative facial expression characterized by retracted and slightly open lips in addition to some gaze aversion as the stranger approached. The predominant HR response was deceleration.

Subject 20, a 17-month-old female, showed corners of her mouth lowered in addition to some tension in her face. This negative tone was present at the approach and during the touch; however, at the turn, the subject exhibited a more relaxed face. The subject showed a minimum HR response characterized by deceleration, the greatest between Positions 5 and E.

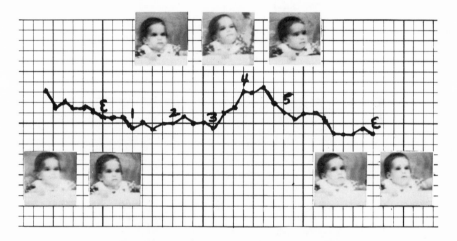

FIG. 15. Individual heart rate and facial expression data: Subject 14.

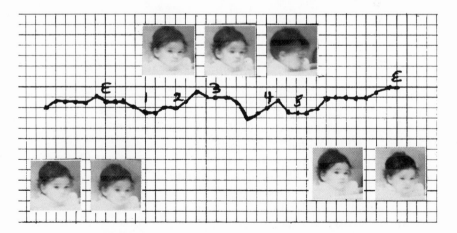

FIG. 16. Individual heart rate and facial expression data: Subject 8.

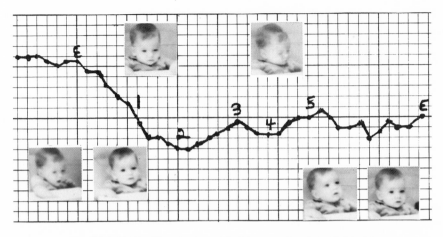

FIG. 17. Individual heart rate and facial expression data: Subject 1.

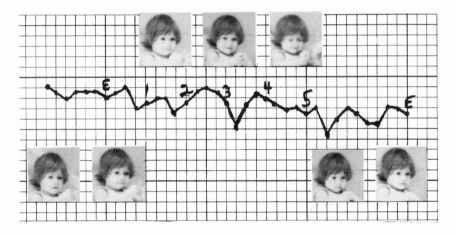

FIG. 18. Individual heart rate and facial expression data: Subject 20.

In summary, when facial expression was used as the criterion measure, the findings were the same as when HR was used as the criterion measure. Observation of the individual records of 26 subjects reveals very little covariation in facial expression and HR change. The most consistent finding for either criterion measure is that HR deceleration accompanied an attentive face. There is little support for a wariness–HR acceleration relationship.

The failure to find a concomitant relationship between facial expression and HR may be due to many causes. There may be no such relationship. The lack of response specificity that Lacey *et al.* (1963)

reported for the autonomic nervous system may also apply to the ANS and other systems such as facial expression. Alternatively, there is always the possibility that a more careful measurement procedure would reveal a relationship. In the following section, this possibility is further explored.

Group Data

Four major facial patterns occurred: a positive face (corners of the mouth raised, no corners lowered or lips retracted, and eyes directed up and/or ahead); a negative face (corners lowered or lips lowered and including gaze aversion—looking down or to the mother's side); an attentive face (a squared upper or lower lip or relaxed mouth with eyes mainly ahead and up); and an attentive-negative face (retracted lips with eyes and forehead relaxed). These four faces were scored with relatively high reliability and were used to look at group data. (See Table II for the specific criteria we used in determining these faces.)

Four HR change parameters were obtained and their relationship to the facial patterns were compared by the use of chi-square statistics. In the first analysis, the mean HR in base period was compared to the mean HR during the approach. Since the approach started at Position 1, the mean of the beats associated with Positions 1, 2, 3, and 4 were subtracted from the mean of the last four beats prior to E. As might be expected, 28 out of 43, or 65%, of the subjects showed HR decreases from base to approach. The two chi-squares shown in Table III were based on the "predominant" facial expression at the four approach points for HR accelerators or decelerators. (See Table II for facial expression criteria.) The predominant facial expression was obtained by a selection of the facial expression that occurred most frequently. The predominant face was used since it might reflect the facial expression tendency. There was no significant relationship between the four facial expressions and HR changes, although there was a trend for attentive faces to be related to HR deceleration ($p < .10$). No age differences were found. However, since a "predominant" face may mask certain individual facial expressions, we undertook other analyses to explore this relationship further.

In the next analysis, facial expression and HR change at a particular point in the approach was examined. (See Table II for facial expression criteria.) Independent of the base level, the position corresponding to the lowest heartbeat (trough point) and to the highest heartbeat (peak point) was examined in conjunction with the facial expression at these two points. For the trough point (see Table IVa), the χ^2 between HR and facial expression was significant, with the attentive face being associated

TABLE II. DETERMINANTS OF POSITIVE (+), NEGATIVE (−), ATTENTIVE (ATT.), AND
ATTENTIVE-NEGATIVE (ATT-NEG.) CATEGORIES

Pattern

I.   For a single point in time.
    + a. Any expression that includes mouth corners up (Figure 19, Faces 1 and 2).
    − a. Any expression that includes mouth corners down (Figure 19, Faces 5 and 6).
    OR
       b. An expression that includes mouth contracted *and* gazing away.
  Att. a. An expression that includes eyes ahead *or* up *and* eyes normal *or* a bit narrow or wide *and* excludes mouth corners down or mouth contracted (Figure 19, Faces 7 and 8).
Att-Neg. a. An expression that includes mouth contracted *and* eyes ahead *or* up *and* any eye openness (Figure 19, Faces 3 and 4).

II.   Predominant pattern during four points in the approach from enter to touch.
    + a. A "+" label at two points.
       b. A "+" label at one point and an "Att." label at three points.
    − a. A "−" label at two points.
       b. A "−" label at one point and "Att." label at three points or "Att-Neg."
  Att. a. "Att." label at all points. A single glance away with no other expressive change is permitted.
Att-Neg. a. A combination of "−" and "Att." within a single point. Usually means contracted mouth, eyes ahead and up with a single glance away during the approach.

III.   Change pattern from enter to touch.
    + a. "+" label at touch; any other label at enter.
    − a. "−" label at touch; any other label at enter.
  Att.
  OR
Att-Neg. a. "Att." or "Att-Neg." label at touch, any other label at enter.
No change a. "+" "+" at enter and touch.
       b. "−" "−" at enter and touch.
       c. "Att." or "Att-Neg." at enter and touch.

with deceleration ($p < .05$). At the peak point, there was no relationship (see Table IVb). Again, there were no age differences.

Since the trough or peak point for some subjects might not be lower or higher than the base level, a stronger relationship between facial expression and HR might be found if the base level were taken into account. The last base beat was compared to the trough point, with only those subjects whose lowest beat during the approach was lower than the base beat being included in the trough analysis. The same procedure

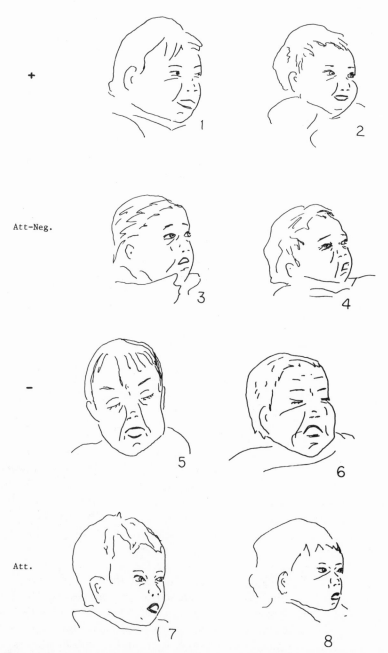

FIG. 19. Visual description of facial expressions presented in Table II. Reprinted from Haviland, J. Sex-related pragmatics in infants' nonverbal communication. *Journal of Communication*, 1977, **27** (2), 21–27.

TABLE III. THE RELATIONSHIP BETWEEN FACIAL PATTERN AND HR ACCELERATION AND DECELERATION DURING THE APPROACH

(a)

HR Deceleration during approach
(considering base)

Facial pattern			
	+	5	
	−	8	
	Att.	12	$\chi^2 = 6.57, p < .10, df = 3$
	Att-Neg.	3	
	Total	28	

(b)

HR acceleration during approach
(considering base)

Facial pattern			
	+	4	
	−	4	
	Att.	4	$\chi^2 = 1.13, df = 3$
	Att-Neg.	1	
	Total	13	

was used for the peak point, with the last base beat compared to the peak point. Likewise, χ^2 was recomputed and a subject was included in the peak point only if the highest beat during the approach was higher than the base beat. These results are presented in Tables Va and Vb. For the trough analysis, the relationship between attentive faces and deceleration became stronger ($p < .02$), while there was still no relationship between the peak point and facial expression.

One final analysis was of some interest. It was observed that during the approach, 25 subjects showed HR acceleration. This acceleration could have been caused by the approach of the stranger or could have been a reflection of the heart's homeostatic response as it returned to base level. If it were related to the approach of the stranger, there might be some relationship between changes in facial expression and acceleration. In order to examine this hypothesis, we obtained change scores for

TABLE IV. THE RELATIONSHIP BETWEEN FACIAL PATTERN AND THE TROUGH AND REAL HR
POINTS DURING THE APPROACH

(a)

Trough during approach
(independent of base)

Facial pattern	+	6	
	−	10	
	Att.	17	$\chi^2 = 8.28, p < .05, df = 3$
	Att-Neg.	6	
	Total	39[a]	[a] Four subjects' faces were not clear enough to score.

(b)

Peak during approach
(independent of base)

Facial pattern	+	7	
	−	12	
	Att.	13	$\chi^2 = 2.60, df = 3$
	Att-Neg.	8	
	Total	40[b]	[b] Three subjects' faces were not clear enough to score.

facial expression using the facial expression categories already discussed. (See Table II for facial expression criteria.) Four change scores
(based on the change from Position 1 to Position 4) were possible: a
change to a positive face, a change to a negative face, a change to an
attentive or attentive-negative face, and no change.[3] As can be seen in
Table VIa there was no significant relationship between the change in
facial expression and HR increases. In this analysis, the increase in HR
from Position 1 to Position 4 did not take the base level into account.
Thus, while 25 subjects showed an increase, only 11 subjects' increase
reached a level *greater* than their base level. There was no significant
relationship between facial expression and acceleration when the base

[3] Heart rate change was obtained by subtraction of the HR value at Position 4 from the HR
value at Position 1. Base level was not taken into account.

TABLE V. THE RELATIONSHIP BETWEEN FACIAL PATTERN AND THE TROUGH AND PEAK HR POINTS
DURING THE APPROACH

(a)

Trough during approach
(considering base)

Facial pattern		
	+	5
	−	10
	Att.	16
	Att-Neg.	4
	Total	35[a]

$\chi^2 = 10.39, p < .02, df = 3$

[a] Only 35 subjects' lowest HR beat during approach was lower than base.

(b)

Peak during approach
(considering base)

Facial pattern		
	+	3
	−	6
	Att.	4
	Att-Neg.	4
	Total	17[b]

$\chi^2 = 1.12, df = 3$

[b] Only 14 subjects' HR beat during approach was higher than base.

level was taken into account (Table VIb). These results support the notion that the HR acceleration between Position 1 and Position 4 was a homeostatic response rather than one tied to emotional expression.

These results are consistent with the idiographic analysis presented earlier. Both lend little support to any synchrony between facial expression and HR changes. The only consistent finding was that HR deceleration and attentive faces were related.

ISSUES OF SYNCHRONY

The search for a relationship between ANS functioning and behavior has been a long one. For the better part of a century, we have

TABLE VI. THE RELATIONSHIP BETWEEN CHANGES IN FACIAL PATTERNS AND ACCELERATION
DURING THE APPROACH (POSITIONS 1–4)

(a)

Acceleration during approach
(independent of base)

Change to +		2
Change to −		6
Changing facial pattern	Change to Att. or Att-Neg.	7
	No change	10
	Total	25[a]

$\chi^2 = 5.24, df = 3$

[a] Only 25 subjects showed HR increases from Positions 1 to 4.

(b)

Acceleration during approach
(considering base)

Change to +		1
Change to −		4
Changing facial pattern	Change to Att. or Att-Neg.	1
	No change	5
	Total	11[b]

$\chi^2 = 4.63, df = 3$

[b] Only 11 subjects showed HR increases from Positions 1 to 4 that were greater than base.

assumed with James that no feeling or true expression of feeling would occur without concomitant bodily change, since the former is considered, at some level, a reflection of the latter. The relationship has not been found. This should not be surprising in light of Lacey's findings that there is relatively little response specificity and covariation even within the ANS itself; for example, HR changes and GSR are not related (Lacey et al., 1963). Given that the responses within the ANS do not covary in some obvious sense, it would be unusual to expect a high correspondence between behavior and soma as part of ANS functioning. Even so, there has been some success in finding a relationship between cardiac deceleration and attending among infants and young children. Lewis and Goldberg (1969) found correlations of .60–.70 between visual fixation and cardiac deceleration, and correlations of

.30–.50 have often been reported. Likewise, in this study, an attentive face and HR response were related.

How then do we explain the lack of synchrony found in studies of this type? Two answers are possible: (1) as stated above, synchrony cannot be expected, and (2) there are measurement problems and issues still to be dealt with, and once one has considered them, covariation between some behavioral manifestation and ANS functioning might be found.

It may be the case that once the measurement of facial expression and cardiac response is refined, a stronger relationship will emerge. The measurement of facial expressions in infants and young children is not complete. The problems, as discussed earlier, need further attention and study. In the last two decades, the study of the cardiac response has received considerable attention; sampling procedures, base level effects, state changes, etc., have been explored. This information should be incorporated into the study of synchrony. Even with the existence of adequate measurement procedures for facial expression and HR changes, there are important issues on how to measure their covariation. Group averaging may mask the phenomenon, and issues of adequate time-locking still need consideration. From a purely measurement point of view, it is too early to conclude that there is no relationship between an ANS response such as HR and some behavioral manifestation such as facial expression, although the majority of the adult literature points in this direction.

The Concept of Synchrony

If there is little support for a notion of general synchrony among response systems, is this notion useful? Synchrony and asynchrony may be structural properties of the nervous system; both are essential for efficient functioning in that *organisms need both to act and to stop acting.* It is this principle and its accommodation that may influence synchrony. While synchrony might be efficient in any action—all response systems acting together in concern would provide a most powerful response set—it would not be efficient for stopping that response or action. If all response systems are equally activated and covary when activated, there are few ways that the organism can stop acting. There are no response systems left to stop the ongoing behavior, since they are all activated and responding together. It is hypothesized that a critical feature of the nervous system is its ability both to activate and to terminate ongoing behavior. Hull (1943) discussed the notion of retroactive inhibition, and more recently, Solomon and Corbitt (1974) have proposed a competitive process theory of appetitive behavior. Both these theories are constructions to explain how organisms stop behaving as well as behave. We would propose that the asynchrony within the ANS itself and between the ANS and behavioral systems functions in order to stop the organism's ongoing behavior. The lack of covariation, therefore, is the structural process that creates "drag" on the responses of the organism, thereby allowing for the cessation of ongoing behavior.[4] Thus, in any response-producing situation, there is a competitive system: response synchrony or covariation for more efficient behavior and response asynchrony for the termination of ongoing behavior. In situations where the need to act predominates—in case of extreme stress or where efficient processing is necessary—more responses may covary. These cases may be exemplified by situations of emergency where survival is in danger.[5] This suggests that in high arousal conditions, response sets both are activated faster and take longer to terminate, the termination being effected by the general inhibitory activity of responses, a kind of neuronal fatigue. For everyday situations, with lower or little arousal, response sets are more likely not to covary.

Attending behavior, which could be placed at a moderate level on an arousal continuum, would be expected to show some correlations between two response systems. Synchrony and covariation of response systems are a function of the competitive need for action and cessation of action and rest on the nervous system's resolution of this conflict, with high states of arousal leading to more covariation. Campos *et al.'s* (1975) results and the present findings make sense in light of these comments. Very frightened infants, left alone without their mothers and being approached by a stranger in a strange manner, are in a high state of arousal; facial expression, motoric activity, and heart rate are more likely to show a high correspondence. When the infant's mother is physically close, an approaching stranger is less arousing and therefore causes less covariation. This theory of synchrony, as outlined, fits these divergent results and suggests that studies of covariation, depending on the situations used, will result in varying degrees of synchrony.

Individual Differences in Synchrony

Although there are no data to support individual differences, it does not seem unreasonable to imagine individual differences in nervous system synchrony. Some organisms—as a function of some combination of temperament, nervous system efficiency, or socialization—may show more covariation of systems than others. Prideaux (1920) found

---

[4] The amount of drag or, conversely, efficiency of a response may be a function of the number of covarying responses: the more drag or efficiency needed, the more the covarying or noncovarying responses.

[5] States of high arousal may be examples. Under these conditions, covariation may be more likely.

individual differences in synchrony. Adults who showed large and/or frequent GSR also showed less overt emotional behavior than less GSR-responsive individuals. Similar findings have been reported by others (Buck, Savin, Miller, & Caul, 1972, 1974). This lack of synchrony has been used by Jones (1950, 1960) to categorize individuals into "internalizers" and "externalizers," those who express emotions internally, as in GSR, and those who express emotions externally, as in facial changes. Individual differences in arousal level may also affect synchrony, since arousal level may act as a mediating factor, organizing both the behavioral manifestations, such as facial expression, and ANS responding: the higher the arousal level, the more synchrony between systems. Thus, individual differences in arousal level, the ease of evocation, etc., may be related to synchrony.

Age differences are a special case. Recall that one view of emotional expression holds that prior to socialization (and the advent of guile), there should be more synchrony than after socialization; that is, socialization serves to unlink facial expression from somatic response. An alternative position argues that socialization itself integrates facial expression and soma.

There may be age differences in synchrony that are not a function of socialization but are instead a function of arousal level. As was stated earlier, there may be a relationship between synchrony and arousal level: greater synchrony with higher arousal levels. It may be the case that younger infants, with more immature nervous systems, show higher arousal levels under a given situation.[6] These higher arousal levels may facilitate the synchrony and result in greater covariation of behavioral responses with ANS functioning. Thus, under a situation designed to evoke fear (the approach situation), younger infants may be more aroused—although not necessarily more fearful. This heightened arousal should result in a higher covariation between facial expression and HR responses, a conclusion our data support in that the youngest groups showed the highest covariation between faces and HR responses.

Synchrony of Expression and Feeling

This discussion has, for the most part, concerned itself with the synchrony of such events as facial expression and ANS functioning. Finally, there is the issue of synchrony between facial expression/ANS functioning and feeling states, that is, the relationship or synchrony

---

[6] *Arousal level* and *emotional tone* are not considered synonymous and can vary independently (see, for example, Schacter & Singer, 1962).

between emotional expression and emotional states. The various models proposed earlier are relevant here. The strong form of the biological model would suggest that there is, especially in infancy and early childhood, a greater synchrony between emotional expression and emotional state since the socialization process has not yet been able to unlock these two aspects. For such a model, the two systems of emotional expression and internal state must be synchronous. A happy face reflects an internal state of happiness. In the alternative socialization model, it would be argued that emotional expressions are biological givens but that the emotional states are caused by the interaction of the social world and these expressions. Thus, for example, the caregiver, seeing the infant cry (an emotional expression), reacts with an interpretation of the emotional state of the infant ("Why are you unhappy?"). This interpretation is both verbal and behavioral, with a different set of responses elicited by a different set of expressions in specific contexts. These expressions and context are what the adult uses to interpret the internal state—giving them both a verbal label and a set of expected outcomes. As Mead (1934) and Lewis and Brooks (1975) have pointed out, the infant becomes, in part, what others think him to be. Thus, the very act of interpretation and response has a potential for the creation of internal states. Consider this example. The infant cries in two situations. In the first, he is building a tower of blocks; in the second, he runs into a table corner. In the first case, his mother says, "Don't be frustrated, try again." She may hold him but also encourages him to try to rebuild the tower. In the second case, she says, "Don't worry, it will feel better." In this situation, she holds him and physically comforts him. In both cases, she interprets the cry, using the context to define the internal emotional state. Whether the infant has such differentiated internal states is not clear. However, the differential labeling and response of the social world set the stage for the infant's acquisition of a differential expectation and the acquisition of a set of cognitive labels related to internal feeling states. Whether this is the material that creates these differential emotional states or, in fact, only the more limited case of supplying the cognitive evaluation ability is as yet unclear. Even so, the response of the social world must play a role in the cognitive assessment and evaluation of internal expressions of oneself and others.

ACKNOWLEDGMENTS

We would like to thank Christine Brim Hogan for her help in collecting and Steven Grossman for his help in analyzing the data.

REFERENCES

Als, H. The human newborn and his mother: An ethological study of their interaction. Unpublished doctoral dissertation, University of Pennsylvania, 1975.

Ambrose, J. A. The development of the smiling response in early infancy. In B. M. Foss (Ed.), *Determinants of infant behavior* (Vol. 1). London: Methuen, 1961, pp. 179–196.

Argyle, M. Non-verbal communication in human social interaction. In R. A. Hinde (Ed.), *Non-verbal communication.* Cambridge: University Press, 1972.

Bard, P. Emotion: I. The neuro-hormonal basis of emotional reactions. In C. Murchison (Ed), *Handbook of general experimental psychology.* Worcester, Mass.: Clark University Press, 1934, pp. 264–311.

Bayley, N. A study of fear by means of the psychogalvanic technique. *Psychological Monograph,* #176, 1928.

Blurton-Jones, N. G. Criteria for use in describing facial expressions of children. *Human Biology,* 1971, 43(3), 365–413.

Blurton-Jones, N. G. Categories of child–child interaction. In N. G. Blurton-Jones (Ed.), *Ethological studies of child behavior.* Cambridge, England: Cambridge University Press, 1972.

Brazelton, T. B. Neonatal behavioral assessment scale. In *Clinics in Developmental Medicine,* No. 50, Spastics International Medical Publications. Philadelphia: Lippincott, 1973.

Bridges, K. M. B. A genetic theory of the emotions. *Journal of Genetic Psychology,* 1930, 37 514–527.

Bronson, G. W. Infants' reactions to unfamiliar persons and novel objects. *Monographs of the Society for Research in Child Development,* 1973, 37(3).

Brooks, J., & Lewis, M. Infants' responses to strangers: Midget, adult and child. *Child Development,* 1976, 47, 323–332.

Buck, R., Savin, V. J., Miller, R. E., & Caul, W. F. Nonverbal communication of affect in humans. *Journal of Personality and Social Psychology,* 1972, 23, 362–371.

Buck, R., Savin, V. J., Miller, R. E., & Caul, W. F. Sex, personality, and physiological variables in the communication of emotion via facial expression. *Journal of Personality and Social Psychology,* 1974, 30, 587–596.

Campos, J. J., Emde, R. N., Gaensbauer, T., & Henderson, C. Cardiac and behavioral interrelationships in the reactions of infants to strangers. *Developmental Psychology,* 1975, 11, 589–601.

Campos, J. J., & Johnson, H. J. The effect of verbalization instructions and visual attention on heart rate and skin conductance. *Psychophysiology,* 1966, 2, 305–310.

Campos, J. J., Langer, A., & Krowitz, A. Cardiac responses on the visual cliff in prelocomotor human infants. *Science,* 1970, 170, 196–197.

Cannon, W. B. The James–Lange theory of emotions: A critical examination and an alternative theory. *American Journal of Psychology,* 1927, 39, 106–124.

Charlesworth, W. B. Instigation and maintenance of curiosity behavior as a function of surprise versus novel and familiar stimuli. *Child Development,* 1964, 35, 1169–1186.

Chevalier-Skolnikoff, S. Facial expression of emotion in nonhuman primates. In P. Ekman (Ed.), *Darwin and facial expression.* New York: Academic Press, 1973.

Darwin, C. *The expression of emotions in man and animals.* London: John Murray, 1872.

Darwin, C. A biographical sketch of an infant. *Mind,* 1877, 2, 285–295.

Darwin, C. *The expression of the emotions in man and animals.* Chicago: University of Chicago Press, 1965. (Originally published, 1895.)

Eibl-Eibesfeldt, I. *Ethology: The biology of behavior.* New York: Holt, Rinehart & Winston, 1970.

Eibl-Eibesfeldt, J. The expressive behavior of the deaf- and blind-born. In M. von Cranach & I. Vine (Eds.), *Social communication and movement.* New York: Academic Press, 1973.

Ekman, P. Universals and cultural differences in facial expressions of emotion. In J. K. Cole (Ed.), *Nebraska Symposium on Motivation* (Vol. 19). Lincoln: University of Nebraska Press, 1971.

Ekman, P. Crosscultural studies of facial expression. In P. Ekman (Ed.), *Darwin and facial expression.* New York: Academic Press, 1973, pp. 169–222.

Ekman, P., & Friesen, W. V. *Unmasking the face.* Englewood Cliffs, N. J.: Prentice-Hall, 1975.

Ekman, P., Malmstron, E. J., & Friesen, W. V. Heart rate changes with facial displays of surprise and disgust. Unpublished manuscript, 1971.

Emde, R. N., & Harmon, R. J. Endogenous and exogenous smiling system in early infancy. *Journal of the American Academy of Child Psychiatry,* 1972, *11*(2), 177–200.

Fernberger, S. W. False suggestion and the Piderit Model. *American Journal of Psychology,* 1928, *40,* 562–568.

Gates, G. S. An experimental study of the growth of social perception. *Journal of Educational Psychology,* 1923, *14,* 449–461.

Goffman, E. *Relations in public: Microstudies of the public order.* New York: Basic Books, 1971.

Goldberg, S., & Lewis, M. Play behavior in the year-old infant: Early sex differences. *Child Development,* 1969, *40,* 21–31.

Graham, F. K., & Jackson, J. Arousal systems and infant heart rate responses. In H. W. Reese & L. P. Lipsett (Ed.), *Advances in child development and behavior,* (Vol. 5). New York: Academic Press, 1970, pp. 59–117.

Grant, E. C. Human facial expression. *Man,* 1969, *4,* 525–536.

Hamburg, D. A., Hamburg, B. A., & Bachas, J. D. Anger and depression in perspective of behavioral biology. In L. Levi (Ed.), *Emotions: Their parameters and measurement.* New York: Raven Press, 1975.

Haviland, J., & Lewis, M. Infants' greeting patterns to strangers. Paper presented at the human ethology session of the Animal Behavior Society meetings, Wilmington, N.C. May 1975.

Hull, C. L. *Principles of behavior.* New York: Appleton-Century, 1943.

James, W. *Principles of Psychology.* New York: Henry Holt, 1890.

Jones, H. E. The study of patterns of emotional expression. In M. Reynart (Ed.), *Feelings and emotions.* New York: McGraw-Hill, 1950.

Jones, H. E. The longitudinal method in the study of personality. In I. S. Coe & H. W. Stevenson (Eds.), *Personality development in children.* Chicago: University of Chicago Press, 1960.

Jones, H. E., & Wechsler, D. Galvanometric technique in studies of association. *American Journal of Psychology,* 1928, *40,* 607–612.

Kagan, J. *Change and continuity in infancy.* New York: Wiley, 1971.

Kagan, J., & Lewis, M. Studies of attention in the human infant. *Merrill-Palmer Quarterly,* 1965, *11,* 95–127.

Kanner, L. Early infantile autism. *Journal of Pediatrics,* 1944, *25,* 211–217.

Lacey, J. L., Batemen, D. E., & Van Lehn, R. Autonomic response specificity. *Psychosomatic Medicine,* 1953, *15,* 8–21.

Lacey, J. I., Kagan, J., Lacey, B. C., & Moss, H. A. The visceral level: Situational determinants and behavioral correlates of autonomic response patterns. In P. H. Knapp (Ed.), *Expression of the emotions in man.* New York: International Universities Press, 1963.

Landis, C. Studies of emotional reactions: II. General behaviors and facial expression. *Journal of Comparative Psychology,* 1924, *4,* 447–509.

Levi, L. *Emotions: Their parameters and measurement.* New York: Raven Press, 1975.

Lewis, M. Infants' responses to facial stimuli during the first year of life. *Developmental Psychology,* 1969, *1,* 75–86.

Lewis, M. A developmental study of the cardiac response to stimulus onset and offset during the first year of life. *Psychophysiology*, 1971, *8,*(6), 689–698.

Lewis, M. State as an infant–environment interaction: An analysis of mother–infant interaction as a function of sex. *Merrill-Palmer Quarterly*, 1972, *18*, 95–121.

Lewis, M. The cardiac response during infancy. In R. F. Thompson & M. M. Patterson (Eds.), *Methods in physiological psychology: I. Bioelectric recording techniques, Part C, Receptor and effector processes.* New York: Academic Press, 1974, pp. 201–229.

Lewis, M. The development of attention and perception in the infant and young child. In W. M. Cruickshank & D. P. Hallahan (Eds.), *Perceptual and learning disabilities in children* (Vol. 2). Syracuse: Syracuse University Press, 1975, pp. 137–162.

Lewis, M., & Brooks, J. Self, other, and fear: Infants' reactions to people. In M. Lewis & L. Rosenblum (Eds.), *The origins of fear: The origins of behavior* (Vol. 2), New York: Wiley, 1974, pp. 195–227.

Lewis, M., & Brooks, J. Infants' social perception: A constructivist view. In L. Cohen & P. Salapatek (Eds.), *Infant perception: From sensation to cognition* (Vol. 2.) New York: Academic Press, 1975.

Lewis, M., & Freedle, R. Mother–infant dyad: The cradle of meaning. In P. Pliner, L. Krames, & T. Alloway (Eds.), *Communication and affect: Language and thought.* New York: Academic Press, 1973, pp. 127–155.

Lewis, M., & Goldberg, S. The acquisition and violation of expectancy: An experimental paradigm. *Journal of Experimental Child Psychology*, 1969, *7*, 70–80.

Lewis, M., Kagan, J., Kalafat, J., & Campbell, H. The cardiac response as a correlate of attention in infants. *Child Development*, 1966, *37*, 63–71.

Lewis, M., & Rosenblum, L. (Eds.). *The effect of the infant on its caregiver: The origins of behavior* (Vol. 1.) New York: Wiley, 1974, pp. 21–48.

Lindsley, D. B. Emotion. In S. S. Stevens (Ed.) *Handbook of experimental psychology.* New York: Wiley, 1951.

Mandler, G. Emotion. In R. W. Brown, E. Galanter, E. H. Hess, & G. Mandler (Eds.), *New directions in psychology.* New York: Holt, Rinehart & Winston, 1962.

Mead, G. H. *Mind, self, and society.* Chicago: University of Chicago Press, 1934.

Morgan, G. A., & Ricciuti, H. N. Infants' responses to strangers during the first year. In B. M. Foss (Ed.), *Determinants of infant behavior* (Vol. 4), London: Methuen, 1969.

Obrist, P. A., Webb, R. A., Stutter, J. R., & Howard, J. L. Cardiac deceleration and reaction time: An evaluation of two hypotheses. *Psychophysiology*, 1970, *6*, 695–706.

Patterson, E. A qualitative and quantitative study of the emotion of surprise. *Psychological Monographs*, #181, 1930.

Prideaux, E. The psychogalvanic reflex: A review. *Brain*, 1920, *43*, 50–73.

Rheingold, H. L., & Eckerman, C. O. Fear of the stranger: A critical examination. In H. W. Reese (Ed.), *Advances in child development and behavior* (Vol. 8), New York: Academic Press, 1973.

Scarr, S., & Salapatek, P. Patterns of fear development during infancy. *Merrill-Palmer Quarterly*, 1970, *16*, 53–90.

Schacter, S., & Singer, J. E. Cognitive, social and physiological determinants of emotional state. *Psychological Review*, 1962, *69*, 379–399.

Schlosberg, H. The description of facial expression in terms of two dimensions. *Journal of Experimental Psychology*, 1952, *44*, 229–237.

Schwartz, A., Campos, J., & Baisel, E. The visual cliff: Cardiac and behavioral correlates on the deep and shallow sides at five and nine months of age. *Journal of Experimental Child Psychology*, 1973, *15*, 86–99.

Seward, J. P., & Seward, G. H. The effect of repetition on reaction to electric shock. *New York Archives of Psychology*, 1934, *168*, 103.

Shepherd, J. F. Organic changes and feeling. *American Journal of Psychology,* 1906, *17,* 522–584.

Sherman, M. C. The differentiation of emotional response in infants: I. Judgment of emotional response from motion picture views and from actual observation. *Journal of Comparative Psychology,* 1927, *7,* 265–284.

Shock, N. W. & Coombs, C. H. Changes in skin resistance and affective tone. *American Journal of Psychology,* 1937, *49,* 611–620.

Simonov, P. V. Studies of emotional behavior of humans and animals by Soviet physiologists. *Annals of the New York Academy of Sciences,* 1969, *159,* 3.

Skinner, B. F. *Beyond freedom and dignity.* New York: Bantam/Vintage Books, 1971.

Solomon, R. L., & Corbitt, J. D. An opponent-process theory of motivation: I. Temporal dynamics of affect. *Psychological Review,* 1974, *81,* 119–146.

Spitz, R., & Wolf, K. The smiling response: A contribution to the ontogenesis of social relations. *Genetic Psychology Monographs,* 1946, *34,* 57–125.

Sroufe, L. A., & Waters, E. The ontogenesis of smiling and laughter: A perspective on the organization of development in infancy. *Psychological Review,* 1976, *83,* 173–189.

Steele, W., & Lewis, M. A longitudinal study of the cardiac response during a problem-solving task and its relationship to general cognitive function. *Psychonomic Science,* 1968, *11*(8), 275–276.

Thompson, J. Development of facial expression in blind and seeing children. *Archives of Psychology,* 1941, *264,* 1–47.

Tomkins, S. S. *Affect, imagery, consciousness,* (Vol. 1), *The positive affects.* New York: Springer, 1962.

Tomkins, S. S., & McCarter, R. What and where are the primary effects? Some evidence for a theory. *Perceptual and Motor Skills,* 1964, *18,* 119–158.

Vine, I. The role of facial-visual signaling in early social development. In M. von Cranach & I. Vine (Eds.), *Social communication and movement.* New York: Academic Press, 1973.

Waters, E., Matas, L., & Sroufe, L. A. Infants' reactions to an approaching stranger: Description validation and functional significance of wariness. *Child Development,* 1975, *46,* 348–356.

Watson, J. B. *Psychology from the standpoint of a behaviorist.* Philadelphia: Lippincott, 1919.

Watson, J. B., & Watson, R. Studies in infant psychology. *Science Monitor,* 1921, *13,* 493–515.

Watson, J. S. Smiling, cooing and "the game." *Merrill-Palmer Quarterly,* 1973, *18,* 323–339.

Weinraub, M., & Lewis, M. Departure and separation. *Monographs of the Society for Research in Child Development,* in press.

Wenger, M. A. Emotion as visceral action: An extension of Lange's theory. In M. L. Reymert (Ed.), *Feelings and emotions: The Mooseheart Symposium.* New York: McGraw-Hill, 1950.

Wolff, P. H. The natural history of crying and other vocalizations in early infancy. In B. M. Foss (Ed.), *Determinants of infant behavior* (Vol. 4). London: Methuen, 1969, pp. 81–109.

Wundt, W. *Grundriss der Psychologie* (C. H. Judd, trans.), Leipzig: Engleman, 1894.

4

Emotional Expression in Infancy: I. Initial Studies of Social Signaling and an Emergent Model

ROBERT N. EMDE, DAVID H. KLIGMAN, JAMES H. REICH, AND TED D. WADE

This story, one of description, began as a bothersome byroad in a research odyssey concerned with understanding emotional development, but it has now become an absorbing adventure in its own right. Our program started in what seemed like a direct and simple fashion, first with studies of babies who smiled and then with babies who cried. We studied these behaviors in multiple contexts, physiological, social, and developmental (Emde & Harmon, 1972; Emde, Gaensbauer, & Harmon, 1976), but then, as psychiatrists, we encountered a concern. In the course of our longitudinal studies, we became increasingly bothered by a nagging question: How did we know that what we were calling *emotional* in babies was related to the later emotional experience that older patients talk about and that we find so central in our clinical work? Obviously, the preverbal infant could not tell us how he felt. In using a variety of viewpoints to bear on this problem, we soon learned that

ROBERT N. EMDE, DAVID H. KLIGMAN, JAMES H. REICH, AND TED D. WADE · University of Colorado Medical School, Denver, Colorado. This work was supported by NIMH Project Grant MH 28803. Dr. Emde is supported by Research Scientist Award K02 MH 36808.

defining or "indexing" emotions by physiological or situational correlates alone was unreliable and made little sense. But as we continued
our longitudinal studies, both in the home and in the laboratory, we
reassured ourselves with one view, firmly rooted in the naturalistic
setting. When we concentrated on viewing emotions as expressions, as
nonverbal communications, we were reassured because we found that
facial expressions and other behaviors that we presumed to call *emotional*
regularly communicated (1) feelings *and* (2) messages for caretaking and
social interaction, and that both of these were meaningful for parents.
Nonetheless, our observations were at the anecdotal–descriptive level,
and we realized that more systematic efforts were needed.

A review of the literature about infant emotions was discouraging.
On the one hand, researchers seemed to imagine almost anything about
the subjective experience of infants based on what they wished for or,
more accurately based on what was consistent with their theories. Thus,
a research tradition seemed to include James, who spoke of the
newborn's "blooming, buzzing, confusion" (1890); Watson, who spoke
of the newborn's "love, rage and fear" (1930); and Freud, who spoke of
the young infant's hallucinatory wish fulfillment in the absence of the
breast (1930/1958). Spitz had spoken of the tendency of adults to view
infants in terms of adult experience as using "adultomorphism." This
literature seemed more infected by another ism ailment, namely, that of
"theoreticomorphism": Researchers tended to see the young infant in
terms of what was consistent with their theories. On the other hand,
this seemed to lead to a countertendency. More empirically oriented
researchers gathered evidence that seemed to refute the usefulness of
the abstract, theoretical views while at the same time adding little
systematic data to replace them. A well-known study of this type was
that of Mandel Sherman (1927a,b) who demonstrated that when they
viewed motion pictures of newborns, judges could accurately discern
neither the emotional categories of Watson nor the eliciting circumstances that Watson had linked to these categories. This study
effectively challenged Watson's position but did not go on to explore
what regularities existed in regard to judgments of infant emotions.
Subsequent thinkers tended to adopt particular viewpoints about infant
emotions largely in the absence of systematic data about what is
expressed, how accurately it can be judged, and what it means in terms
of communication (see, for example, Bridges, 1933; Werner, 1948/1957;
Erikson, 1950; Spitz, 1965).

While we appreciated the need for theories with their organizing
perspectives, we concluded that there was a need for a systematic
description of expressive behaviors, their developmental sequences,
and their context. We found encouragement in our ethnological observations in the home since we came to appreciate striking regularities in

certain affective messages communicated to mothers by infant facial expressions. As Stechler and Carpenter (1967) emphasized in their seminal paper, mothers rarely mistook the meaning of a newborn's crying, for example: a distress feeling would be communicated and the mother would go to the infant and change something. Smiling communicated a good and pleasant feeling, often leading to a continuation of the social encounter. In addition, when we took still photographs of other infant facial expressions and showed them to students and colleagues, similar regularities were apparent; people would more often than not use the identical labels that mothers had used who had also looked at these same pictures of their own infants.

Another source of encouragement for continuing this line of study came from recent adult work in the tradition of experimental psychology. Research concerning discrete *categories* of facial expression of emotion had its origin in Darwin's classic treatise (1872/1904) and was revived by Silvan Tomkins's later theoretical (1962, 1963) and empirical (Tomkins & McCarter, 1964) work. It also had strong roots in clinicians' experience with nonverbal communication. However, it remained for two different volumes, published in successive years, to bring contemporary excitement to this field. The books of Izard (1971) and of Ekman, Friesen, and Ellsworth (1972) critically and masterfully reviewed previous work on the accuracy of judgments of adult facial expressions of emotion and turned up striking consistencies in the experimental literature that previously had been unappreciated. Ekman and his group found that most investigators who used posed facial expressions collected evidence from them of the ability to judge at least seven categories of emotion. The list included *happiness, surprise, fear, anger, sadness, disgust/contempt,* and *interest.* Izard developed a similar list which, in effect, also included *distress* and *shame.* Each of these investigators and their colleagues also reported results of cross-cultural studies. Findings included dramatic evidence of regularities. Particularly impressive was Ekman's demonstration of universal agreement about posed still photos of peak emotional expressions in *preliterate* as well as in a number of literate cultures. Such agreement about verbal labeling, even in a forced-choice paradigm such as they used, seemed to imply a universal "basis" not only for the *expression* of particular emotions but also for their *recognition.* Izard, from his cross-cultural studies and other work, reached similar conclusions: there are discrete patterns of facial expression that represent universal systems of emotional expression. Izard's list of "fundamental emotions" is slightly longer than that of the Ekman group. Both lists are presented in Table I. It is also noteworthy that each of these investigators has spelled out specific facial movements involved in each of these patterns of emotion (see Izard, 1971, 1972; Ekman & Friesen, 1975).

Table I. Primary Categories of Emotional Expression

Ekman et al. (1972)	Izard (1971)
1. Happiness	1. Interest–excitement
2. Sadness	2. Enjoyment–joy
3. Fear	3. Surprise–startle
4. Surprise	4. Distress–anguish[a]
5. Disgust/contempt	5. Disgust–revulsion
6. Anger	6. Anger–rage
(7. Interest)	7. Shame–humiliation[a]
	8. Fear–terror
	9. Contempt–scorn[a]

[a] Additional Izard categories; in some studies disgust and contempt are combined into one category.

Limits of a Forced-Choice Categories Rating Technique for Infancy

From our longitudinal home observations of normal infants (Emde et al., 1976), we would not expect that most adult categories as enumerated by Ekman or by Izard would apply in any simple fashion. Categories involving labels such as *anger, contempt/disgust,* and even *fear* were unusual in mothers' spontaneous descriptions of early infancy. Nonetheless, it seemed worthwhile to do some simple classroom experiments to document the usefulness and/or limits of the Ekman and Izard forced-choice techniques for labeling infant emotional expressions.

Classroom Study Using an Adaptation of Ekman's Forced-Choice Paradigm

Twenty-five still photographs (35mm) were sampled from a "pool" of photos of 3½-month-old infants originally taken in standardized home sessions that included spontaneous infant expressions as well as responses to social and nonsocial stimuli. When these pictures were shown to a class of graduate psychology students ($N = 13$) who had to make a choice among the six categories, only *five* of the 25 pictures produced major agreement.[1] These were all in the *happiness* category and all, interestingly enough, agreed with the mother's original in-

[1] We chose a criterion of 70% agreement as representative of "major agreement"; the choice was made on an intuitive basis. Interestingly, we later realized that Izard had chosen the same criterion level in one of his studies (1971).

terpretations. Perhaps the most striking aspect of this experiment was the subjective discomfort expressed by classroom raters in the forced-choice paradigm. Only *happiness* was easy to judge, and other categories often seemed inappropriate or silly. When another sampling of 10 slides was presented and a free choice for labeling was allowed, judgments were easier. Furthermore, the vast majority of class responses included many primary labels that the mothers had originally used.

Classroom Study Using an Adaptation of Izard's Forced-Choice Paradigm

Similar results were obtained with the Izard forced-choice paradigm. The same 25 photographs were shown to a large class of graduate nursing students ($N = 49$), who were asked to place them in one of the nine Izard categories. Results were somewhat more positive in that 9 of the 25 pictures reached major agreement; 4 of these were in the *enjoyment–joy* category, 4 in the *interest–excitement* category, and 1 in the *distress–anguish* category. Again, classroom raters expressed that they could tell a lot more from the pictures than was allowed by the forced-choice categorizing task. Similarly, in a second part of this classroom study, when free choices were allowed in labeling, judgments were easier.

These results would probably surprise few researchers working in the field of infancy (e.g., see Charlesworth and Kreutzer's review of 1973): forced judgments using categories derived from adult peak emotional expression appear to be inappropriate for the 3-month-old, whereas encouraging consistencies in judgments emerge from free-choice responses. Our sampling of infant pictures was vastly different from Ekman's or Izard's sampling of actor-posed peak expressions; our study infants did not dramatize their facial expressions or "pose" for our pictures, and in real life, "blends" or more neutral expressions would probably be more common than expressions of peak states.

A Note About Sampling

As a result of the classroom studies, we wanted to continue our efforts in systematic description, using approaches more specifically adapted to developmental studies in infancy. We soon learned that the sampling problems in a beginning venture of this sort are enormous; still, we had the feeling that we could not afford to be fainthearted. We simply had to plunge in, start in a small way somewhere, hope for the best, and then if initial results were encouraging, expand sampling later in multiple directions (such as by increasing the number of infants, sampling throughout the infant's "behavioral day," increasing the number of ages studied, increasing the number of mothers, increasing the number and type of raters, etc.). The same initial photographic sampling was used as a basis for analysis in the two approaches to be reported.

Obviously, photographs were not actor-posed emotional expressions of infants: they consisted of 20 35mm color photographs of normal young infants taken during standardized home sessions. We began all sessions with infants in a wakeful state. Each mother was asked to talk and play with her baby, and the first five photos were taken at 30-second intervals during this interaction. The next two photos were taken with a stranger nodding his or her head and talking to the baby, and this was followed by two more photos taken during the presentation of a standard inanimate visual pattern. Then 10 photos were taken at 30-second intervals without any stimulus presentations. A final photo was taken during a loss of support stimulus (Moro response).[2] One week after the taking of these photographs, a visit was made to each mother and an interview was conducted that was tape-recorded for later transcription. During the interview, each mother viewed her baby's pictures, which were randomized (to eliminate sequence cues), and she was instructed to say what the photographically captured expressions told her, if anything. Mothers' verbatim responses to individual photos were later typed on 3-by-5 cards. Because of this procedure, we were able to base later ratings and analyses on either (1) photographs of infant facial expressions or (2) original mothers' interpretations of these photographs.

Our initial results are based on five normal infants, sampled longitudinally on a monthly basis from 2.5 to 4.5 months. Because these results seemed consistent and meaningful, we are now involved in a 24-hour study of expressions sampled throughout the day and an expanded age study. Until these and other studies of context (including an analysis of signal-operating and receiver-operating characteristics) are completed, the results reported below must be considered preliminary. Nonetheless, we believe that they are sufficiently compelling to suggest a model that can be tested for its usefulness.

---

[2] We have reason to believe that this sampling procedure underrepresents sleep, crying, and expressions occurring around feeding. A 24-hour sampling study will test this hypothesis, which is based on our naturalistic longitudinal home observations (Emde *et al.*, 1976).

TWO APPROACHES FOR DESCRIBING THE FACIAL EXPRESSION OF EMOTION IN INFANCY

Free Responses and Subsequent Categorizing

Since the forced-choice paradigm seemed inappropriate for our studies, another question arose. Could one develop a free-response labeling technique that could then yield categories appropriate to infancy? A requirement for any categorization would be that raters agree with themselves and also with mothers' original labels. Since we wanted to avoid the imposition of our own theoretical biases, we decided to begin with a modification of a free-response labeling technique that had been devised for use with judges of adult expressions. Such a technique had been designed by Izard in his study of four cultures (Izard, 1971). Using his array of photographs of peak emotional expressions, he found that the number of words used to label emotions were limited. When words used by only one subject were omitted, 268 subjects used less than that number of words (224) in responding to 32 photographs. Izard then obtained a pool of judges who were asked to categorize these words in accordance with his scheme of eight fundamental emotions. As a result, Izard was able to construct what one might call a lexicon or a list of words grouped according to each of the eight emotional categories.

We used 35 mm color photographs taken of normal 3.5-month-old infants during standardized home sessions as previously described and randomly sampled them for our judgment studies. In these studies, raters were adult women who had had experience with children. They were given a set of instructions modified from the Izard study, in which they were asked to record in one word or phrase "the strongest and clearest feeling" that the baby was expressing.[3]

Figure 1 summarizes our results of three different studies with infants of 3–4 months and illustrates the remarkably similar findings from each. The first study made use of a classroom exercise with 42 graduate nurses who gave free-response judgments of 11 pictures.

---

[3] The actual instructions for this task were as follows: "We are going to show you some photographs of babies who might be expressing feelings. The purpose of this experiment is to see how clearly these feelings are expressed. When we show you a picture, we want you to look at it carefully and then describe how the baby seems to be feeling. In some photos, you may judge that more than one emotion is apparent. However, please decide which one emotion is expressed most strongly and most clearly and write this in the first column. Use one word, if at all possible. You may then record the other feeling(s) in the second column and also say whatever else you may wish to make clear what the baby is expressing. Remember, the first column is for the strongest and clearest feeling that the baby is expressing; anything else can go in the second column."

	STUDY 1	STUDY 2	Sample 1	Sample 2	Sample 3
				STUDY 3	
No. Raters	N = 10	N = 42	N = 22	N = 22	N = 22
No. Slides	25	11	25	25	25
Enjoyment	36%	26%	39%	38%	37%
Interest	26%	32%	26%	25%	27%
Distress	12%	10%	15%	16%	10%
Sleepy	8%	6%	6%	5%	9%
Fear	6%	5%	3%	2%	3%
Anger	2%	6%	2%	5%	3%
Passive/ Bored	5%	3%	2%	1%	2%
Surprise	1%	3%	2%	2%	3%
Shame	.4%	.4%	.1%	1%	2%
Disgust	0	5%	.5%	.5%	.3%
Other	4%	4%	4%	5%	5%
					F.R-CRT

FIG. 1. Categories of emotion from free-response judgments.

Using the Izard word lists, we found that 86% of the responses could easily be classified within his scheme of eight categories. Adding two categories of *passive–bored* and *sleepy* (with clear-cut descriptive words, as determined by three judges) resulted in 96% classified, with only 4% in "other." Our *free-response categorizing* instrument, therefore, evolved to have 10 categories plus an 11th of "no emotion." All words that are not easily categorized from our "dictionary" listing are tallied separately. This instrument has now been applied with similar results in two other studies. In one study, 10 raters gave free-response judgments to 25 stimulus items (either photos alone or photos with 30-second movie segments) in three separate sessions, and in another, 25 raters gave free responses to three separate sets of 25 photos.

Sorting by Similarities and Multidimensional Scaling

Another approach in our descriptive efforts to understand the expression and recognition of emotions in infancy involved the application of a multidimensional scaling (MDS) technique as devised by Shepard (1962a,b; 1974). Our interest was directed toward it because of its advantage in not requiring researcher-imposed categories and even more because of its potential for model building.

In our application of the MDS, 25 judges are asked to sort stimulus cards (either infant pictures or verbal responses of mothers to their own infants' pictures) into one or more piles, putting those that seem to belong together in the same pile. After they have completed this task with 25 cards, they are asked to "label" each pile. Our computer analysis then takes the data from 25 raters and yields an output of (1) *a frequency count of labels* applied to each card; (2) *a similarity matrix* giving numerical expression to the number of times each pair was placed together; and (3) the MDS output itself (the program is one developed at Bell Labs by Kruskal, 1964a,b). In studies so far, all raters have also been adult women, experienced with children, and the original photographs of infant expressions were taken in standardized home sessions, as described above. The results we summarize here are based on a random selection from a "pool" of such pictures, with multiple samples taken longitudinally from five normal infants.

The MDS program gives us a spatial model of the data points (e.g., pictures) so that pictures judged as relatively similar are relatively close together in the model and pictures judged as relatively dissimilar are relatively far apart. We seek the minimum number of spatial dimensions necessary to adequately "fit" the similarities. We then examine the labels of the pictures to try and interpret these dimensions.

At this juncture, we have completed 18 MDS analyses, involving sortings of the pictures themselves and involving sortings of stimulus cards that list mothers' verbal interpretations of their own infants' pictures. Sortings have been done for infants' expressions at 2½ months, 3½ months, and 4½ months of age. The following pattern of results emerges, as Table II documents. At 2½ months, solutions have been two-dimensional. The first dimension is easily characterized as "hedonic tone" and the second is more difficult to interpret, sometimes best characterized as "activation" and sometimes as "state." At 3½ months, there is a mixture of two-dimensional and three-dimensional solutions from sortings of mothers' verbal responses, and three-dimensional solutions appear in the three sets of picture sortings. At 4½ months, three-dimensional solutions appear in all of the six MDS sortings we have done.

TABLE II. MDS WITH NORMALS

Group	Best solution (Number of dimensions)	Stress value[a]	Dimension labels	
Mothers' responses to pictures of their infants:				
2.5-month infants (Denver raters)				
Set 1	2	.24	1. Hedonic	2. Activation
Set 2	2	.25	1. Hedonic	2. State
Set 3	2	.23	1. Hedonic	2. State
3.5-month infants (Toronto raters)				
Set 1	2	.22	1. Hedonic	2. Activation
Set 2	2	.20	1. Hedonic	2. State
Set 3	3	.15	1. Hedonic 3. Internal/External	2. Activation
3.5-month infants (Denver raters)				
Set 1	2	.14	1. Hedonic	2. Activation
Set 2	2	.23	1. Hedonic	2. Activation
Set 3	3	.10	1. Hedonic 3. Internal/External	2. Activation
4.5-month infants (Toronto raters)				
Set 1	3	.19	1. Hedonic 3. Internal/External	2. Activation
Set 2	3	.14	1. Hedonic 3. Internal/External	2. Activation
Set 3	3	.09	1. Hedonic 3. Internal/External	2. Activation
4.5-month infants (Denver raters)				
Set 1	3	.18	1. Hedonic 3. Internal/External	2. Activation
Set 2	3	.16	1. Hedonic 3. Internal/External	2. Activation
Set 3	3	.12	1. Hedonic 3. Internal/External	2. Activation
Direct sorting of pictures:				
3.5-month infants (Denver raters)				
Set 1	3	.18	1. Hedonic 3. Internal/External	2. Activation
Set 2	3	.22	1. Hedonic 3. Internal/External	2. Activation
Set 3	3	.14	1. Hedonic 3. Internal/External	2. Activation

[a] The stress value can be thought of as referring to the "goodness of fit" between the similarities in the data and the distances between stimulus items in the MDS model. Although stress values decline as the number of dimensions increases, low stress values are only one basis for deciding which dimensional solution is acceptable. Interpretability of dimensions after appropriate rotation of axes is crucial. The "best solution," therefore, is the one with lowest stress value that contains substantively interpretable dimensions. A discussion of factors involved in choosing the "best solution" can be found in Shepard (1974).

Not only is there an apparent developmental pattern in these results, but interpretability and labeling of dimensions are consistent throughout. *Hedonic tone* is always present and readily interpretable in all solutions, accounting for about three quarters of the variance in two-dimensional solutions and half of the variance in three-dimensional solutions. *Activation* appears as an interpretable dimension with some two-dimensional solutions and with all three-dimensional solutions, and an *internally oriented/externally oriented* dimension appears in three-dimensional solutions. Table III illustrates labels that define the extremes of the various dimensions. (In some two-dimensional solutions, the two-dimensional solution is less easy to interpret and *state* seems a better descriptor than *activation*.) Figure 2 illustrates a plot from a three-dimensional solution.

We find it encouraging that not only are our results internally consistent, but *soon after three months*, the suggested pattern of results shows consistency with studies of adult emotional expression. In fact, there is a history containing striking regularities consistent with these results. In discussing adult feelings, Spencer (1890) and Wundt (1896) suggested dimensions of pleasantness–unpleasantness and something similar to relaxation–tension. Freud (1915/1957) discussed vicissitudes of instincts in terms of polarities of pleasure–unpleasure, active–passive and ego–external world.

The well-known set of chapters in Woodworth and Schlosberg's textbook of experimental psychology of 1954 summarized the dimensional way of thinking and the empirical research it spawned in the days prior to factor analysis. Schlosberg noticed that Woodworth's linear

TABLE III. LABELS DEFINING POLES OF MDS DIMENSIONS

Positive pole	Negative pole
Two-dimensional solution	
happy ⟵⟶ 1. HEDONIC ⟵⟶	unhappy, upset, frustration, dislike
bored, sleep, tired, content, happy, unhappy ⟵ 2. STATE ⟶	concentrate, curious, excited, attention
Three-dimensional solution	
happy ⟵ 1. HEDONIC ⟶	unhappy, upset, frustration, dislike
startled, excited, concentrate ⟵ 2. ACTIVATION ⟶	relaxed, asleep
curious, interest ⟵ 3. EXTERNAL–INTERNAL ⟶	happy, sleepy, bored

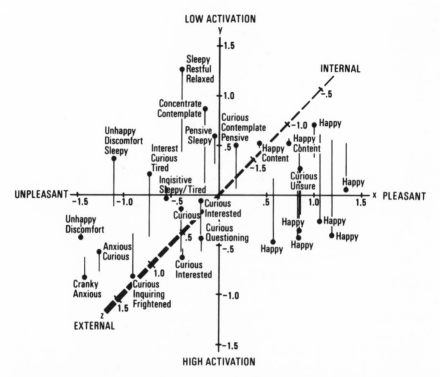

FIG. 2. Three-dimensional solution from MDS resulting from judgments of infant pictures taken at 3.5 months.

scale of categories of facial expression could be converted to a model in which categories were displayed on a circular surface with two axes: pleasantness–unpleasantness and attention–rejection. This model was then demonstrated to be useful for experimental data, especially when a third dimension, that of "sleep–tension" (activation) was added (Engen, Levy, & Schlosberg, 1958). Subsequent studies employed factor-analytic techniques (for example, Osgood, 1966; Frijda & Philips-zoon, 1963; Frijda, 1970) and multidimensional scaling techniques (Gladstone, 1962; Abelson & Sermat, 1962) to quantify adult facial expressions, with similar results.

It is easy to be critical of these studies on the basis of the selection of stimuli used (usually posed still photographs), the limited selection of dimensions to be rated, and the instructions to the raters (see, for example, discussions in Izard, 1971, and in Ekman et al., 1972). Nonetheless, we are impressed with the pattern of findings. As in our results, pleasantness–unpleasantness emerges as a major dimension, taking up more variance than other dimensions. A second dimension is present in most but not all analyses; namely, an activation or intensity dimension. A third dimension is often suggested but is frequently difficult to interpret and has variously been called *acceptance–rejection, control,* or something like *expressed feeling versus inner feeling.*

A CROSS-VALIDATION STUDY USING OUR FREE-RESPONSE CATEGORIZING TECHNIQUE AND MDS

We established that the MDS procedure had the appearance of reliability; that is, the results of multiple samplings from a pool of photographs seemed to be consistent. In addition, the scale seemed to have some face validity in the developmental sense, since there was a pattern of increasing differentiation in the narrow age range we studied. Would the scale also be of value in refining our free-response categorizing technique? (The free-response technique is one that we hope to simplify, collect data on, and ultimately make available for clinical application.) In order to approach this question, we did a study in which we took the same group of 75 pictures (i.e., three sets of 25) and obtained raters who either sorted them by similarities (for MDS analysis) or gave free-response labels (for categorizing). A total of 50 raters were randomly assigned to either one or the other of these tasks over a two-day period. We examined the data to see if pictures similarly categorized on the free-response paradigm would also "clump" together in the MDS spacial model. Table IV summarizes these results.

Using a criterion of at least one-third agreement among judges for assignment of a given picture to a category resulted in 69 of the pictures being categorized from the free-response technique. Of these 6 were "blends"; that is, they were judged so as to meet the one-third agreement criterion for two categories. To test for "clumping," we selected from a set of pictures those that belonged to any category where at least one other picture also met criteria for that category. Turning to the MDS models on the same pictures, we could then compare the average (straight-line) distance of a picture from others of its category with its distance from all other pictures in the entire set not of its category. The t values for this comparison were highly significant ($p <$ .0001, $p <$ .001, and $p <$ .0001 for three different sets of pictures) reflecting a strong tendency for pictures similarly labeled to be close together in the MDS model. Significance values were necessarily inflated because only those pictures that had within-category distances could have values entering into the t test.

TABLE IV. Free-Response Categorizing of 3.5-Month Denver Picture Sample

	Categories						Other categories: Surprise–startle Shame–humiliation Passive–bored Disgust–contempt No emotion	Blends				Sum of classified pictures	Significance level: Free-response categorizing–MDS concordance
	Interest–excitement	Enjoyment–Joy	Distress–anguish	Sleepy	Anger–rage	Fear–terror		Interest & enjoyment	Interest & distress	Interest & surprise	Enjoyment & sleepy		
Set 1 (N = 25)	7	11	2			1	0	1	1		1	24	$p < .0001$
Set 2 (N = 25)	6	10	2	1			0	2				21	$p < .001$
Set 3 (N = 25)	7	13	1	1	1		0			1		24	$p < .0001$
Sum of pictures:	20	34	5	2	1	1	0	3	1	1	1	69	
Sum of pictures (N = 75):	.27	.45	.07	.03	.01	.01	0	.04	.01	.01	.01	.92	

STILL PHOTOGRAPHS AND MOVIES

It is a matter of some surprise that so much information can be transmitted from still photographs. In real life, contingencies in early infant–caretaker interactions are embedded in temporal patterns of activity. Movement—whether in facial expressions (Brazelton, Koslowski, & Main, 1974) or in gaze behaviors (Stern, 1974)—provides much of the substrate for the meaning of a message. Because of this, we became interested in comparing movies with still photographs. We asked the question: Would viewing a movie segment substantially change judgments of infant facial expressions made from the viewing of still photographs?

In three of the photographic sampling sessions, we took simultaneous 16mm movies involving close-ups of the infant's face and upper body. After film processing, we sampled 25 still photographs from these sessions and then found the corresponding 30-second movie segments that led up to each picture. Thus, either slides alone or movie segments and slides were available for judgment studies.

In our studies, order of presentation of all film material was randomized to eliminate sequence effects. Our procedure was as follows. Ten raters, all adult women experienced with children, came to the laboratory for three experimental sessions, approximately one week apart. The instrument for judging facial expressions of emotion during all sessions was the free-response categorizing technique. One half of the group ($N = 5$) rated the 25 slides alone during the first session, and the remaining half rated film units that included a 30-second segment of a movie, followed immediately by its appropriate 35mm still photograph containing the facial expression found at the end of the 30 seconds. During the second session, each group was assigned the task it had not had during the first session. The third session (for all raters) again involved judgments of the slides alone; this procedure enabled us to assess stability of judgments over time for the slide-alone task.

Table V presents the results of this study for the 18 still photographs that met criteria for stability (i.e., more than one-third of the raters agreed on the same category on the two different slide-alone presentations). Categories are listed for each photograph, along with the proportion of raters who agreed on that category. One can see that of the 18, 14 (78%) were judged to be in the same category during the movie and slide presentation, using the one-third agreement criterion. The disagreements were instructive, since they were explained readily by the addition of new information during the 30-second movie preceding the slide. In those instances, events such as a yawn, eyelid closure, a fleeting smile, or the appearance of glassy eyes contributed to a facial

TABLE V. FREE RESPONSE CATEGORIZING FROM STILL PHOTOGRAPHS AND MOVIES

Slide No.	Experiment 1: still photographs — Categories	Experiment 3: Repeat still photographs — Categories	Experiment 2: Movies and still photographs — Categories	Agreement	Additional event in movie
1	Interest .6[a], Enjoyment .4	Interest .7	Enjoyment .4, Interest .5	Yes	
2	Enjoyment 1.0	Enjoyment 1.0	Enjoyment .7	Yes	
3	Distress .7	Distress .9	Distress .8	Yes	
4	Enjoyment .4	Enjoyment .4	Enjoyment .4	Yes	
5	Interest .8	Interest .8	Enjoyment .3, Interest .3, Sleepy .3	No	Yawn
6	Interest .4	Interest .6	Interest .8	Yes	
7	Enjoyment .6	Enjoyment .7	Enjoyment .4, Interest .5	Yes	
8	Enjoyment .9	Enjoyment 1.0	Enjoyment .9	Yes	
9	Enjoyment .8	Enjoyment .9	Enjoyment .9	Yes	
10	Enjoyment .6	Enjoyment 1.0	Enjoyment .9	Yes	
11	Enjoyment .6	Enjoyment .5	Enjoyment .3, Sleepy .3	No	Glassy-eyed, eyelids droop
12	Enjoyment .5	Enjoyment .6	Enjoyment .6	Yes	
13	Enjoyment .9	Enjoyment .9	Enjoyment .7	Yes	
14	Interest .4	Enjoyment .4, Interest .5	Enjoyment .4, Interest .3	No	Smile
15	Interest .7	Interest .7	Interest .4	Yes	
16	Enjoyment .4	Enjoyment .4	Sleepy .7	No	Eyelids closed
17	Enjoyment .4	Enjoyment .7	Enjoyment .7	Yes	
18	Interest .6	Interest .7	Interest .9	Yes	

[a] Numbers beside categories refer to proportion of raters agreeing on that category.

expression composite that resulted in a different judgment (*sleepy* and *enjoyment–joy*).

Thus, it would seem that within 30 seconds and under the conditions of our sampling, discrete events of emotional expression are reasonably well captured by our still photographic techniques. Putting it another way, emotional expressions seem to be communicated in small time units that may or may not depend upon sequential coding for interpretation.

SPECULATION: AN EMERGING MODEL OF EARLY HUMAN AFFECT EXPRESSIONS

Our view of emotions as social signals is obviously incomplete. Emotional expressions not only communicate messages to others, they reflect complex and changing organismic states. Biological adaptation has led not only to systems of *external regulation* but to systems of *internal regulation* (both physiological and psychological), and there must be crucial interrelationships between domains. Still, in spite of these complexities, we are persuaded that it is quite useful to study emotional expressions as response systems in their own right. Such a strategy has the promise of avoiding definitional problems that have surrounded constructs of emotion in the past, and thus far, developmental results seem consistent and meaningful. Furthermore, we are prompted to offer the following preliminary biological speculations, even though, at this moment in our research program, we must skip the intermediate level of analysis, according to which internal states underlying emotional response systems might be understood.

When we consider the preliminary result of our descriptive efforts and add them to our previous research experience in social affective development (see summaries in Emde & Harmon, 1972, and Emde *et al.*, 1976), the following picture emerges. We consider it likely that a fundamental characteristic of human affective expressions is that they communicate in such a way that one can discern two or three dimensions. These dimensions, especially ones of hedonic tone and activation, are not only consistently found in studies involving judgments of adult facial expression but are also found in studies involving judgments of verbal expression of emotion (see reviews of the verbal expression data in Osgood, 1966, and Arnold, 1970). Furthermore, they are in striking agreement with the three essential response characteristics of emotional behavior that emerged from the infancy studies of Ricciuti (1968; Ricciuti & Poresky, 1972). Based on our preliminary MDS data and on our experience in infant longitudinal studies, we propose that these dimensional properties are manifest beginning after the neonatal period and remain throughout the life span. Further, we propose that they must represent dimensions of biologically meaningful messages, vital for adaptation and survival, with varying degrees of peremptoriness attached to them. A neurophysiological substrate for the first two dimensions could involve diencephalic–reticular core brain structures. These include reward and aversion systems, mediating "hedonic tone" (Olds & Olds, 1963), and the reticular activating system, mediating "activation" (Lindsley, 1951). (The reader might also see Riss and Scalia, 1967, for a motivational–affective model that juxtaposes the neurophysiology of both of these systems.) As Bergstrom (1969) has documented, core brain structures involve a variety of homeostatic survival systems, and these tend to mature early in ontogenesis. The third dimension, which seems less homogeneous and somewhat more difficult to interpret, is perhaps expressive of a motivational aspect of affect, perhaps having to do with the regulation of incoming stimulation. (See discussion of emotions as regulators of input in Pribram, 1967, and Pribram and Melges, 1969). Its neurophysiology would, therefore, be less certain, although we feel it is not too farfetched to think of it as involving primitive brain structures that mature early.

We also consider it a basic characteristic of human affect expressions that they communicate in such a way that one can discern a number of categories. Each of these categories carries rather discrete information, although we believe that such information quite often occurs in combinations or "blends" and usually at much less than peak intensity.

From an evolutionary standpoint, these categories, since they appear to be universal, must also represent biologically meaningful messages. Based on our own longitudinal and cross-sectional studies (Emde & Harmon, 1972; Campos, Emde, Gaensbauer, & Henderson, 1975; Emde et al., 1976) and on extensive literature of similar observations by others (for example, Bridges, 1933; Hetzer & Wolf, 1928; Gesell & Amatruda, 1945; Spitz & Wolf, 1946; Spitz, 1965; Bayley, 1969), we conclude that categories of affect expressions are not present at birth but appear according to an epigenetic sequence. Ethologists have pointed to the existence and the functional significance of such sequences in mammals. Hinde (1974), for example, stated that various social releasers in a species' repertoire tend to appear in a fixed developmental sequence; perhaps this is in part a consequence of the biological importance of expressive movements of communication with mother and sibs preceding those with sex partners. Fox (1970) and Chevalier-Skolnikoff (1971) have also discussed such sequences, along with the possible phylogenetic mechanisms that may have been involved in producing them. Most recently, Redican (1975), in his review of facial expressions in nonhuman primates, has pointed to a particular ontogenetic sequence of affect expressions—one that is analogous to the sequence we have postulated in the human infant and one that is completely compatible with Bronson's (1968) early human infant model. The developmental sequence that Redican found is one beginning with social cohesive expressions (lip smacking and play face), followed by fearful expressions (grimace), and then by aggressive (threat and yawn) expressions.

In terms of neurophysiology, we postulate that structures involved in regulating categorical aspects of affect expression require more complex organization than those involved in regulating dimensional aspects; they may require considerable feedback relationships between hypothalamic, thalamic, and autonomic nervous system regulatory centers, as well as forebrain areas, for cognition. Therefore, the underlying structures mediating categories of affect expressions are presumed to be of later development.

Our experience (Emde et al., 1976) corresponds with that of Sroufe (1976) that the affect expressions of fear, surprise, and anger become prominent in development only during the latter half of the first year. Furthermore, in terms of what we know about cognitive development, it is only in Piaget's Stage 4 of sensorimotor development (Piaget, 1936/ 1952), usually around 7–9 months, that an infant's cognition reaches the point that it is in some ways independent of his activities and that there is evidence for intentionality in the sense of a capacity for delay between an initial perception of a goal and a final action and in the sense of detours being circumvented from which we can infer the existence of means–ends relationships. At this age, there is an evidence of anticipation beyond the motor act, and this extends to the affective realm: by 9 months, the infant laughs in anticipation of the mother's return in a peek-a-boo game rather than in response to a completed sequence. The child expresses fearfulness at low levels of stimulation and in advance of noxious stimulation, thus implying that it is the meaning of the stimulation and not just the stimulation itself that is reacted to (Emde et al., 1976; Sroufe, 1976). It is only at this stage that we can see that affective expression leads to behavior and is, in fact, probably motivating subsequent behavior on the part of the infant instead of merely signaling change to the caretaker. We would say that at 9 months, affect provides a signal to the inside (used cognitively), not just to the outside (as an appeal to others); in other words, social signals become psychological signals as well.[4] Elsewhere, we have discussed the evidence supporting

---

[4] We do not mean to imply that there is no internal feedback before this age or that such a process appears without precursors. It goes without saying that there is inner regulation of behavior from birth. At first, such regulation is largely physiological, and then with the impact of maturation and experience, it comes more under psychological control. At 9 months, the qualitative change in emotional signaling to which we refer corresponds to the momentous change in means–end relationships that Piaget has described for cognition.

the notion that one could consider that there is the onset of a capacity for fearfulness at this age (Emde *et al.*, 1976) and that it could be viewed in terms of a two-phased affective response sequence and, for the first time, could bear analogy to adult emotional responses as conceptualized by Magda Arnold (1970): the entire affective sequence seems to involve an initial phase of evaluation or appraisal and a subsequent motoric phase of obvious distress with attempts at avoidance.

Finally, since experiential factors have increasing importance as the child gets older, we would not expect categories of affect expressions to emerge suddenly, as "fully developed" during the first two years, at least in the sense in which they are measured by Ekman and Friesen (1975). A recent study of facial patterns in 10 to 12-month-old infants (Hiatt, Campos, & Emde, 1977) suggests that fearfulness and surprise may emerge in undifferentiated form. These categories of emotion were judged reliably from facial expressions alone, despite the absence of the patterns of components as enumerated for adult facial expressions. We also assume that the epigenetic process is such that before their complete patterned emergence, *components* of emotional expressions may appear as *developmental antecedents* that are not yet thoroughly organized or integrated. Theoretically, it should be possible to predict the multidimensional space where a category of expression will appear, ahead of its actual developmental appearance; this should assist us in our future searching for antecedents. Our work (Emde *et al.*, 1976) has already shown developmental antecedents for social smiling and for stranger distress. When an affect expression appears fullblown, there is a new organization to it that combines already existing components and enables expressive meaning to be integrated within a cognitive and social context.

Summary

The need for an unbiased description of the social signaling system that derives from infant facial expressions of emotion was highlighted by the recent adult work of Izard and Ekman and led to our initial studies. Since the forced-choice paradigm used in adult work was found to be unsatisfactory for infant facial expressions, two other approaches were developed. One involves free responses to pictures, with subsequent categorizing according to a technique modified from Izard. The other involves sorting by similarities and multidimensional scaling.

Multidimensional scaling results are presented for two types of data: (1) the sorting of infant pictures and (2) the sorting of the mothers verbal responses to viewing pictures of their own infants. By 3½ months of age, a three-dimensional solution in the multidimensional scaling is predominant: a *hedonic tone* dimension is always present and readily interpretable, an *activation* dimension is the next most prominent and an *internally oriented—externally oriented* dimension appears as a third dimension.

A cross-validation study using our free-response categorizing technique and the technique of multidimensional scaling yielded highly significant results, increasing our confidence in the potential usefulness of the multidimensional scaling technique for model building and for further refining aspects of our free-response technique. A study comparing still photographs alone with still photographs supplemented by movies gave results that increase our confidence in the usefulness of the still-photograph sampling procedure. Still photographs apparently capture discrete and useful message units in the emotional signaling system.

Finally, we have presented a developmental model for the early human affect expression system that takes account of both its dimensional and its categorical properties. We have suggested that the organization of the central nervous system is such that soon after 3 months of age, the three dimensions of emotional expression are apparent. In contrast, categories of emotional expression, characterized by discrete messages, undergo an epigenesis continuing through the first postnatal year and beyond. Cognitive development plays an increasingly important role in this epigenesis, and the study of its integration with ongoing motoric components of expression offers an exciting challenge.

References

Abelson, R. P., & Sermat, V. Multidimensional scaling of facial expressions. *Journal of Experimental Psychology*, 1962, *63*, 546–554.

Arnold, M. B. (Ed.). *Feelings and emotions.* New York: Academic Press, 1970.

Bayley, N. *Bayley Scales of Infant Development.* New York: Psychological Corporation, 1969.

Bergstrom, R. M. Electrical parameters of the brain during ontogeny. In R. J. Robinson (Ed.), *Brain and early behavior.* London: Academic Press, 1969, pp. 15–41.

Brazelton, T. B., Koslowski, B., & Main, M. The origins of reciprocity: Early mother–Infant interaction. In M. Lewis & L. Rosenblum (Eds.), *The effect of the infant on its caregiver* (Vol. 1). New York: Wiley, 1974, pp. 49–76.

Bridges, K. M. B. Emotional development in early infancy. *Child Development*, 1933, *3*, 324–341.

Bronson, G. W. The fear of novelty. *Psychological Bulletin*, 1968, *69*, 350–358.

Campos, J., Emde, R., Gaensbauer, T., & Henderson, C. Cardiac and behavioral interrelationships in the reactions of infants to strangers. *Developmental Psychology*, 1975, *11*(5), 589–601.

Charlesworth, W., & Kreutzer, M. Facial expressions of infants and children. In P. Ekman (Ed.), *Darwin and facial expression: A century of research in review*. New York: Academic Press, 1973.

Chevalier-Skolnikoff, S. The ontogeny of communication in Macaca speciosa. Ph. D. thesis, University of California, Berkeley, 1971.

Darwin, C. *The expression of emotions in man and animals*. London: John Murray, 1904, (Originally published, 1872.)

Ekman, P., & Friesen, W. *Unmasking the face*. Englewood Cliffs, N.J.: Prentice-Hall, 1975.

Ekman, P., Friesen, W. V., & Ellsworth, P. *Emotion in the human face: Guidelines for research and an integration of findings*. Elmsford, N.Y.: Pergamon Press, 1972.

Emde, R. N., Gaensbauer, T., & Harmon, R. J. Emotional expression in infancy: A biobehavioral study. Psychological Issues, Monograph Series, Inc. 1976, *10*, Monograph #37. New York: International Universities Press.

Emde, R. N., & Harmon, R. J. Endogenous and exogenous smiling system in early infancy. *Journal of the American Academy of Child Psychiatry*, 1972, *11*(2), 177–200.

Engen, R., Levy, N., & Schlosberg, H. The dimensional analysis of a new series of facial expressions. *Journal of Experimental Child Psychology*, 1958, *55*, 454–458.

Erikson, E. *Childhood and society*. New York: Norton, 1950.

Fox, M. W. A comparative study of the development of facial expressions in canids: Wolf, coyote and foxes. *Behavior*, 1970, *36*, 49–73.

Freud, S. *Instincts and their vicissitudes*. Standard Edition: 1915 (Vol. 14). London: Hogarth Press, 1957, pp. 117–140.

Freud, S. *Formulations on the two principles of mental functioning*. Standard Edition: 1930 (Vol. 12). London: Hogarth Press, 1958, pp. 218–336.

Frijda, N. Emotion and recognition of emotion. In M. B. Arnold (Ed.), *Feelings and emotions*. New York: Academic Press, 1970.

Frijda, N., & Philipszoon, E. Dimensions of recognition of expression. *Journal of Abnormal and Social Psychology*, 1963, *66*, 45–51.

Gasell, A. L., & Amatruda, C. *The embryology of behavior: The beginnings of the human mind*. New York: Harper, 1945.

Gladstone, W. H. A multidimensional study of facial expression of emotion. *Australian Journal of Psychology*, 1962, *14*, 19–100.

Hetzer, H., & Wolf, K. Babytests. *Zeitschrift für Psychologie*, 1928, *107*, 62–104.

Hiatt, M., Campos, J., & Emde, R. N. Fear, surprise and happiness: The patterning of facial expressions in infants. Presentation to the Society for Research in Child Development, New Orleans, March 20, 1977.

Hinde, R. A. *Biological bases of human social behavior*. New York: McGraw-Hill, 1974.

Izard, C. *The face of emotion*. New York: Appleton-Century Crofts, 1971.

Izard, C. *Patterns of emotion: A new analysis of anxiety and depression*. New York: Academic Press, 1972.

James, W. *Principles of psychology*. New York: Henry Holt, 1890.

Kruskal, J. B. Multidimensional scaling by optimizing goodness of fit to a non-metric hypothesis. *Psychometrika*, 1964, *29*, 1–27. (a)

Kruskal, J. B. Non-metric multidimensional scaling: A numerical method. *Psychometrika*, 1964, *29*, 28–42. (b)

Lindsley, D. Emotion. In S. S. Stevens (Ed.), *Handbook of experimental psychology*. New York: Wiley, 1951.

Olds, M. E., & Olds, J. Approach–avoidance analysis of rat diencephalon. *Journal of Comparative Neurology*, 1963, *120*, 259–295.

Osgood, C. Dimensionality of the semantic space for communication via facial expression. *Scandinavian Journal of Psychology*, 1966, *7*, 1–30.

Piaget, J. *The origins of intelligence in children* (2nd ed.). New York: International Universities Press, 1952. (Originally published, 1936.)

Pribram, K. H. Emotion: Steps toward a neuropsycholgical theory. In D. C. Glass (Ed.), *Neurophysiology and emotion*. New York: Rockefeller University Press and Russell Sage Foundation, 1967.

Pribram, K. H., & Melges, F. T. Emotion: The search for control. Reprinted from the *Handbook of clinical neurology*. In P. J. Vinken & G. W. Bruyn (Eds.), *Disorders of higher activity*. Amsterdam: Elsevier, 1969.

Redican, W. K. Facial expressions in non-human primates. In L. Rosenblum (Ed.), *Primate behavior* (Vol. 4). New York: Academic Press, 1975, pp. 103–194.

Ricciuti, H. N. Social and emotional behavior in infancy: Some developmental issues and problems. *Merrill-Palmer Quarterly*, 1968, *14*, 82–100.

Ricciuti, H. N., & Poresky, R. H. Emotional behavior and development in the first year of life: An analysis of arousal, approach–withdrawal, and affective responses. In A. D. Pick (Ed.), *Minnesota Symposium on Child Psychology* (Vol. 6). Minneapolis: University of Minnesota Press, 1972.

Riss, W., & Scalia, F. *Functional pathways of the central nervous system*. Amsterdam: Elsevier, 1967.

Shepard, R. The analysis of proximities: Multidimensional scaling with an unknown distance function: I. *Psychometrika*, 1962, *27*, 125–140. (a)

Shepard, R. The analysis of proximities: Multidimensional scaling with an unknown distance function: II. *Psychometrika*, 1962, *27*, 219–246. (b)

Shepard, R. Representation of structure in similarity data: Problems and prospects. *Psychometrika*, 1974, *39*(4). 373–421.

Sherman, M. The differentiation of emotional responses in infants: I. Judgments of emotional responses from motion pictures views and from actual observation. *Journal of Comparative Psychology*, 1927, *7*, 265–284. (a)

Sherman, M. The differentiation of emotional responses in infants: II. The ability of observers to judge the emotional characteristics of the crying of infants and of the voice of an adult. *Journal of Comparative Psychology*, 1927, *7*, 335–351. (b)

Spencer, H. *The principles of psychology* (Vol. 1). New York: Appleton, 1890.

Spitz, R. *The first year of life: Normal and deviant object relations*. New York: International Universities Press, 1965.

Spitz, R., & Wolf, K. M. Anaclitic depression, an inquiry into the genesis of psychiatric conditions in early childhood: II. *Psychoanalytic Study of the Child*, 1946, *2*, 313–342.

Sroufe, A. Emotional expression in infancy. Unpublished manuscript, 1976.

Stechler, C., & Carpenter, G. Theoretical considerations. *Exceptional Infant Normal Infant*, 1967, *1*, 165–189.

Stern, D. N. Mother and infant at play: The dyadic interaction involving facial, vocal, and gaze behaviors. In M. Lewis & L. Rosenblum (Eds.), *The effect of the infant on its caregiver* (Vol. 1). New York: Wiley, 1974, pp. 187–213.

Tomkins, S. S. *Affect, imagery, consciousness: The negative affects* (Vol. 1). New York: Springer, 1962.

Tomkins, S. S. *Affect, imagery, consciousness: The negative affects* (Vol. 1). New York: Springer, 1963.

Tomkins, S. S., & McCarter, R. What and where are the primary affects? Some evidence for a theory. *Perceptual and Motor Skills*, 1964, *18*, 119–158.

Watson, J. B. *Behaviorism* (1st ed.). Chicago: University of Chicago Press. 1930.

Werner, H. *Comparative psychology of mental development* (rev. ed.). New York: International Universities Press, 1957. (Originally published, 1948.)

Woodworth, R. S., & Schlosberg, H. S. *Experimental psychology*. New York: Holt, 1954.

Wundt, W. *Grundriss der Psychologie* (C. H. Judd, trans.). (1896) Cited in C. Izard, *The face of emotion*. New York: Appleton-Century Crofts, 1971.

The Emergence of Fear on the Visual Cliff

JOSEPH J. CAMPOS, SUSAN HIATT, DOUGLAS RAMSAY, CHARLOTTE HENDERSON, AND MARILYN SVEJDA

We have two major objectives in this chapter. One is to present empirical evidence confirming the existence of an unexpected developmental shift in emotional expression in the human infant, and the second is to discuss the role of a number of possible determinants of this shift.

There has been considerable interest in recent years in verifying and explaining the onset of negative emotional reactions in infancy. Much of this interest has centered on the developmental shifts taking place in two social situations. One, the separation of the infant from the mother, begins to elicit distress between 5 and 8 months of age (Schaffer & Emerson, 1964; Stayton, Ainsworth, & Main, 1973). The second is the close approach of an unfamiliar person (or, perhaps, a person acting strangely), which elicits distress at roughly the same period in life (Campos, Emde, Gaensbauer, & Henderson, 1975; Emde, Gaensbauer, & Harmon, 1976; Schaffer, 1966; Waters, Matas, & Sroufe, 1975).

The present chapter describes the study of a similar developmental shift in a very different situation. There is now abundant evidence, from both our laboratory and others, pointing to a change in how infants react

JOSEPH J. CAMPOS, SUSAN HIATT, DOUGLAS RAMSAY, CHARLOTTE HENDERSON, and MARILYN SVEJDA · University of Denver, Denver, Colorado. This research has been supported by NIMH grant #MH 23556 to J. J. Campos and a grant from the Grant Foundation to the developmental psychology division of the Psychology Department of the University of Denver. Dr. Ramsay was supported by NIMH fellowship MH 57090.

to heights—a change from initial absence of wariness and distress to subsequent avoidance and fear of heights.[1] We present here evidence linking this developmental shift to events occurring *after* the onset of locomotion. Of the possible factors that may prove to be playing a critical role in accounting for this shift, we discuss the role of five: (1) perceptual and cognitive development, such as an increasing ability to calibrate distances, especially relatively great distances; (2) discrepancies from past experience, and in particular discrepancy from the experience of locomoting on opaque surfaces; (3) specific experiences, such as falls of a certain type; (4) the role of self-produced locomotion and reafference and their subsequent effects on the guidance of visually controlled behavior; and (5) the development of an aversive ("fear?") system, allowing reactions to the *threat* of danger, rather than to the danger itself.

One point of view that we feel is clearly *not* supported by the data we present is a strict nativistic and ethological orientation toward fear of heights. According to Bowlby (1973), height is a "natural clue" to danger. According to this view, innate sensitivity to height is biologically adaptive for the organism, since avoidance of heights from the first opportunity has obvious competitive evolutionary advantage. No evaluation of the significance of height needs to be postulated; the organism's reaction is both aversive and automatic. Similar thoughts have been recently expressed by Freedman (1974). The well-known reports by Walk and Gibson (1961; Gibson & Walk, 1960) of chicks avoiding the deep side of a visual cliff shortly after hatching, of baby goats doing the same shortly after the acquisition of locomotion, and of the performance of dark-reared animals when tested on the visual cliff have created a set of data in apparent support of the notion that fear of heights is inborn or, at the very least, awaits only the development of response capacities for its manifestation. So widespread is the acceptance of this position that few in developmental psychology challenge the widely cited conclusion that the young of the species, including human infants, "perceive depth" (i. e., show aversion to the deep side of the visual cliff) as soon as they can locomote.

However, the results of our research program have pointed to a very different picture of the development of fear of heights. On the basis of our data and those of others, we conclude that the *human infant*

---

[1] Throughout this chapter, the term *fear* is used with the understanding that it is being treated as a hypothetical construct and that its manifestation can take many forms (e. g., cardiac acceleration, aversive responding, distress vocalizations, response suppression in an operant conditioning paradigm, etc.). It is also recognized that the construct requires converging operations for its validation. Many of the studies described in the chapter are aimed at providing at least partial convergence on the construct.

perceives depth (at least crudely) *before he can locomote but does not manifest fear of heights until some time after he can locomote.* The time lag between the onset of depth perception and locomotion, on the one hand, and the apparent onset of fear of heights, on the other, appears to us to create problems for strict ethological theories, at least as they are currently formulated. There clearly is a time in the infant's life when depth perception is not sufficient to mediate avoidance of potentially dangerous precipices.

REVIEW OF PREVIOUS EVIDENCE FOR A DEVELOPMENTAL SHIFT ON THE VISUAL CLIFF

The visual cliff is one of the most widely used apparatus for the study of depth perception in infants of many species. It is a large, glass-covered table divided into two equal halves. One half of the table has a textured surface immediately underneath the glass and is called the *shallow side.* The other half has a similar surface, but it is placed on the floor, nearly 4 ft (1.21 m) below the glass. Gibson and Walk (1960) described two paradigms for testing subjects on the visual cliff. One paradigm involves a comparison of locomotion across the two sides of the cliff; if the infant refuses to cross the deep side to get to a lure (such as a toy or the mother or both), fear of heights, and hence depth perception, is inferred. A second, much less widely used paradigm is called by us the *direct placement* technique and has the distinct advantage of being useful with infants of any age—locomotor or otherwise. With this technique, fear of heights and depth perception are inferred from the presence of wariness or distress when the subject is perched directly over the glass covering the deep side and from the absence of such when the subject is perched on the shallow side.

One of the first indications that fear of heights undergoes a developmental shift in human infants came from studies with the visual cliff that used the direct placement technique in order to remove the task requirement of locomotion on visual cliff performance. That task requirement had effectively prevented the testing of human infants younger than crawling age on the visual cliff. In two studies reported by Campos, Langer, and Krowitz (1970), heart rate and recordings of visual attention and distress vocalization were taken with the direct placement procedure. The assumption of those studies was that very young infants would manifest heart rate acceleration and distress vocalizations on the deep but not on the shallow side of the cliff. (The expectation of heart rate acceleration on the deep side was consistent with both Graham and Clifton's [1966] theory predicting accelerations in defensive or distressed states, and Obrist's [Obrist, Webb, Sutterer, & Howard, 1970] theory of cardiac–somatic coupling, since tension or vocalizations would be expected to be correlated with accelerations.) Since cardiac accelerations can be readily elicited even in the newborn (cf. the review by Graham & Jackson, 1970), the method seemed potentially applicable with extremely young subjects.

The results of the two studies presented in the Campos *et al.* (1970) report were counter to expectations. In groups of both 2- and 3½-month-olds, the deep side of the cliff was discriminated from the shallow side, but apparently not on the basis of fearfulness. Heart rate *decelerated* on the deep side of the cliff in both studies, crying was significantly less frequent on the deep side in one of the studies, and attentiveness to the deep side was greater than to the shallow side, again in both studies.

Although the results of Campos *et al.* (1970) were interpreted to indicate that young, prelocomotor infants were not afraid of the deep side of the cliff, considerable experimental work remained before the tentative conclusion could be confirmed. For example, one obvious alternative interpretation of these results stemmed from the work, current at the time, on pattern complexity as a determinant of visual attentiveness and cardiac deceleration (Bond, 1972). That is, when the textured elements composing the surface of the deep and shallow sides of the cliff are the same in physical size, their retinal projections are of a different retinal angle and hence differ in density and complexity. Since the projections of the deep side were those that were retinally more complex in the initial study, they could well have elicited more frequent and longer fixations. This hypothesis could account for the early visual cliff data from prelocomotor infants without invoking any explanation involving detection by the infant of depth-specifying stimulation.

Therefore, a subsequent study (Campos & Langer, 1971) equated for retinal projections of the two sides of the visual cliff to test this hypothesis. The results of this study replicated the earlier report of heart rate deceleration on the deep side, no cardiac change on the shallow side, and significant discrimination of the two sides of the cliff. This finding suggested that infants, even at 2 months of age, are capable of discriminating the two sides of the visual cliff on the basis of their detection of stimuli that specify depth.

Further evidence that prelocomotor infants have the capacity to detect stimuli that specify depth came from a study (Appel & Campos, 1977) demonstrating that 2-month-olds are sensitive to binocular disparity. Such disparity is considered to be one of the most critical sources of information about depth in the visual world (Gibson, 1950), and the discrimination was demonstrated through the use of a dishabituation paradigm. Infants were given repeated trials with a stereoscopically presented display containing no binocular disparity (each eye was presented a slide of an object photographed from the same vantage point), then dishabituated to an otherwise identical display, save for the presence of disparity (accomplished by the presentation to each eye of a slide of the same object photographed from two different vantage points). Infants in this study discriminated such a change, evident in recovery of both heart rate and sucking responses. However, they did not discriminate the reverse sequence of presentations—initial trials with displays producing disparity and dishabituation trials with no disparity.

These early studies from our lab, taken in conjunction with a number of reports from Bower and his collaborators (Bower, 1964, 1965, 1966; Bower, Broughton, & Moore, 1970a, b), suggested, but did not prove, that infants perceive depth by 2 months of age. The visual cliff studies, furthermore, suggested that discrimination of the two sides of the cliff was accomplished without the expression of fear at these early ages. This conclusion was consistent with incidental observations made by Scarr and Salapatek (1970). In a study of fear reactions of infants in a wide variety of situations, Scarr and Salapatek noted that prelocomotor infants pulled across the deep side of the visual cliff on a small, wheeled platform (a "crawligator") showed no evidence of fear of the deep side.

Since Walk and Gibson (1961) and others (e.g., Scarr & Salapatek, 1970; Walk, 1966) had shown evidence of wariness by older infants of crossing the deep side, the implication of the Campos *et al.* studies was that a developmental shift must be taking place on the visual cliff. To test this implication, a study was conducted of 5- and 9-month-old infants, again with the use of the direct placement procedure, with heart rate and behavioral observations as dependent variables (Schwartz, Campos, & Baisel, 1973). In this study, a clear developmental shift was obtained in heart rate on the deep side, with 9-month-olds producing approximately a 6-bpm (beat per minute) accelerations and 5-month-olds producing approximately a 4-bpm deceleration. Behavioral observations, except for ratings of visual attentiveness downward to the surface of the visual cliff, were generally insensitive to the developmental shift. However, an examination of the correlations between heart rate responses and behavioral indices suggested that attention was associated with cardiac deceleration and defensiveness with acceleration. That is, heart rate showed a median correlation of $p = +.38$ with distress vocalization, indicating that as distress vocalization time increased on a given trial, the heart rate response tended to be more acceleratory. On the other hand, heart rate correlated negatively with ratings of duration of visual attention ($p = -.29$).

Nevertheless, because of the absence in these studies of clear evidence of behavioral changes on the visual cliff, the interpretation of a developmental shift on the visual cliff rested primarily on the cardiac response. This created grounds for interpretational caution. In the first place, as is well known, the quest for physiological differentiation of emotions (such as is implied, by extrapolation, from the various studies cited above) had led to weak, equivocal results (cf. Ax, 1953; Lacey, 1959). Furthermore, there was evidence in both the human (e.g., Obrist, Wood, & Perez-Reyes, 1965; Wilson, 1969) and animal (e.g., Anderson & Brady, 1973) literature that conditioned "fear" reactions frequently were associated with cardiac *decelerations*, although more recent evidence has found cardiac accelerations when UCS parameters are sufficiently intense (Obrist, Howard, Lawler, Galosy, Meyers, & Gaebelein, 1974). Thus, the possibility existed that the finding of cardiac deceleration on the deep side of the visual cliff in prelocomotor infants had been erroneously interpreted: the decelerations may have been indicating fearfulness, not merely attentiveness. This possibility did not seem likely to us, however. First, we were persuaded by the arguments put forth by Graham and her colleagues (Graham & Clifton, 1966; Graham & Jackson, 1970) to the effect that heart rate acceleration is a component of the defensive response described by Sokolov (see Lynn, 1966). Furthermore, the findings of the Schwartz *et al.* (1973) study would have to be interpreted as indicating that the same psychological state is associated with cardiac decelerations in infants less than 5 months old and with cardiac acceleration in older ones. Nevertheless, the interpretation of the heart rate developmental shift required further support.

This support was provided in a study of cardiac reactions to the approach of a stranger in infants 5 and 9 months of age (Campos *et al.*, 1975). It is well known that, at least in some situations, the typical reaction to strangers shows a marked shift from attentiveness to wariness or distress.[2] Consequently, heart rate would be expected to decelerate, on the average, at the age when attentiveness is predominant and to accelerate when wariness is predominant. Furthermore, the

---

[2] There is controversy at present sparked by Rheingold and Eckerman's (1973) critique of the stranger distress research. Some of this controversy concerns whether the evidence shows that infants are afraid of strange persons or of a person *acting strangely*. Much of the rest of the controversy concerns the adequacy of rating scale data in preference to objective quantifications of variables and the lack of a contrast condition to allow the inference that the developmental change is due to strangers. None of these concerns applies to the Campos *et al.* (1975) study, which was less concerned with whether there is fear of *strangers* than with whether a developmental shift in affective expression can be elicited and recorded reliably, with the approach of a stranger used as the eliciting circumstance.

behavioral changes infants show in reactions to strangers can be readily quantified and thus related to concomitantly measured cardiac responses, which allows for more suitable "anchoring" of the interpretation of heart rate to behavior. Third, some 5-month-olds can be expected to show stranger distress and some 9-month-olds not. Therefore, heart rate reactions of 5-month-olds who were behaviorally rated as distressed could be compared with heart rate reactions of 5-month-olds who were not, and the same could be done with parallel data from 9-month-olds. This procedure allowed us to test the interpretation of the direction of heart rate change with age held constant.

The results of this study were generally positive and were simultaneously buttressed by findings from other laboratories bearing on the same issue. We found (1) that heart rate responses elicited by the approach of a stranger tended to be predominantly deceleratory in 5-month-olds, and predominantly acceleratory in 9-month-olds (*although generally only when the mother was not in the room with the infant*); (2) that behaviorally distressed infants at either 5 or 9 months of age gave progressively acceleratory responses, while behaviorally undistressed infants did not; and (3) that the accelerations of heart rate were maximal when the stranger was closest to the infant. Meanwhile, Provost and Décarie (1974) reported finding that 9- and 12-month-old infants who were behaviorally rated as distressed showed cardiac accelerations, while those who were not so rated showed decelerations. Sroufe, Waters, and Matas (1974; Waters, Matas, & Sroufe, 1975) also reported finding large-magnitude heart rate accelerations in wary infants and also reported that the presumably more stressful conditions of laboratory testing produced greater heart rate accelerations than did home testing.

Thus, although we know that heart rate accelerations can occur in nonstressful conditions such as smiling (Emde, Campos, Gaensbauer, & Reich, 1975), the weight of the evidence in our laboratory as well as in those of others (e. g., Sroufe & Waters, 1977) supported the interpretation of a close linkage between heart rate deceleration and attention, and heart rate acceleration and distress, at least in situations in which the mother is not present in the room with the infant, which was the case in all our visual cliff studies. Thus, the interpretation of the findings of Schwartz *et al.* (1973) on the visual cliff seemed appropriate.

Further Evidence of a Developmental Shift on the Visual Cliff

Although the stranger distress study successfully confirmed our predictions regarding the interpretation of directional changes in heart rate, the developing controversy over methodological and inferential problems in research on fear of strangers (Harmon & Morgan, 1975; Rheingold & Eckerman, 1973) focused interest on alternative means of documenting the presence of a developmental shift on the visual cliff. Walk and Gibson (1961) had, of course, presented data that suggested little tendency for an age effect on the visual cliff, but we were struck by the possibility that the locomotor crossing method (that is, the method in which a locomotor infant is placed on the center of the cliff and induced to crawl to the mother over one side or the other) might *also* be tapping a developmental shift.

One source of evidence suggesting that possibility was the study by Scarr and Salapatek (1970). They reported a developmental trend indicating that infants seemed to be more afraid of crossing over the deep side of the cliff with increasing age. They also reported that three infants who had not been locomoting for very long "were uniform in their lack of fearfulness and rapid crossing of the gradient" (p. 70). Their evidence, however, was in many respects marred by problems of interpretation, resulting from their use of a three-point scale of fearfulness, and lack of clarity as to how a single index of fearfulness was computed.

A second major source of evidence alluding to the same possibility came from a review by Walk (1966) of his research with the visual cliff. Walk clearly showed that young infants do not necessarily avoid crossing to the mother over the deep side as soon as they can locomote. (Locomotion such as crawling has an expected onset age of 7.1 months [Bayley, 1969]). Infants between 200 and 300 days of age demonstrated a surprisingly large incidence (between 43% and 48% of those tested) of crossing to the mother over the deep side. After 300 days of age, there was a sharp increase in the proportion of infants avoiding the deep side. Walk's data are reproduced in Figure 1.

Other data alluded to by Walk in that report heightened the possibility that the locomotor crossing method was tapping the same developmental shift that was discovered by the direct placement procedure; these data also suggested that locomotor *experience*, and not age *per se*, might account for the increase in avoidance of the deep side. Walk reported that of the 24 late crawling infants he tested (i. e., infants who started to crawl between 9 and 11 months of age), 46% crossed to the mother over the deep side, in contrast to 20% of infants the same age who had longer locomotor experience. He also reported great difficulty in matching for age infants who crossed to the mother over the deep side with those who did not, finding that those who did *not* cross over the deep side tended to be a month and a half older than those who did. Walk interpreted these data as reflecting the development of perceptual

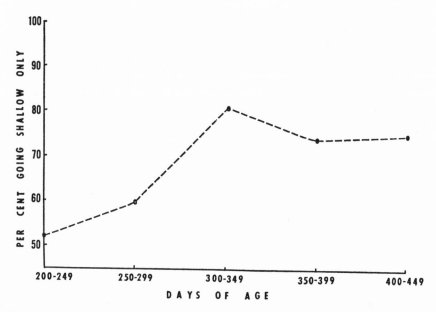

FIG. 1. The percentage of infants reported by Walk (1966) as going only to the shallow side of the visual cliff, as a function of chronological age. (The figure is taken from Walk, 1966.)

capacities in locomotor infants, an interpretation that is discussed below but that thoroughly ignored the possibility that the infants' depth perception was adequate all along, while the *index* of depth perception, the fear of heights, was the factor showing the developmental trend. In view of findings by Fields (1976), Day and McKenzie (1973), and others demonstrating depth perception in prelocomotor infants, the latter interpretation needed to be addressed.

Furthermore, although Rosenblum and Cross (1963) had earlier shown fear of heights to be present in 3-day-old rhesus monkeys, tested with both the locomotor crossing and the direct placement methods, Walk demonstrated in his monograph that a developmental shift on the visual cliff is not limited to human infants. Figure 2 is a reproduction of Walk's data with kittens, showing the percentage of descents to the shallow side as a function of age. (Kittens were tested from the day their eyes first opened.) Between 9 and 23 days of age, kittens descended equally to the shallow and deep sides of the cliff, according to Walk's narrative. After 23 days of age, the kittens showed a marked increase in avoidance of the deep side of the cliff.

Figure 3 reproduces analogous data for albino rabbits. For both these species, then, Walk found that young animals went equally to the two sides of the cliff at the beginning of visually controlled locomotion,

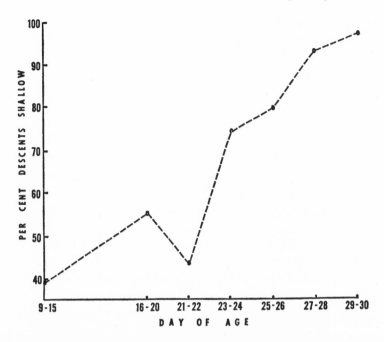

Fig. 2. The percentage of descents to the shallow side of the visual cliff of kittens tested from soon after eyes were open until 30 days of age. (Figure is from Walk, 1966.)

after which there was a sharp increment in avoidance of the deep side with increasing age.

Still one more suggestion that human infants show a developmental shift in reactions to heights comes from a telephone interview we conducted, for heuristic purposes, with mothers who had previously volunteered their infants' services in our laboratory. Of more than 60 mothers contacted, not a single one has failed to report that there was a stage during which their infants would readily crawl over the edge of a bed, or off a sofa, in apparent nonchalance over the consequences, but that subsequently, often after a fall, their infants showed clear wariness of edges and staircases. These data, although suffering the weaknesses of maternal reports, have been noted before (e.g., Freedman, 1974) and explained away. But they encouraged us to believe that the phenomenon we were hypothesizing to take place on the visual cliff is "ecologically valid" and worthy of more detailed, and better controlled, investigation.

The human infant data we have described from Walk's studies were reported in a discussion section, and many important details about the study and the sample were not given, such as how long the infants had been locomoting, or whether they had been tested repeatedly with the visual cliff. Most importantly for our purposes, no information was given about the possibility that even though the infants crossed readily to their mother over the deep side, they may have been frightened while doing so. Nor was there any attempt to unconfound the interpretation of the infants' behaviors. That is, did the infants cross the deep side because of an inability to perceive depth adequately or because of an inability to show *fear* of depth, even when the depth was perceived, at least to some extent, on the cliff? As a result, we embarked upon a pilot investigation in our laboratory to test longitudinally infants' reactions on the visual cliff when required to cross to the mother.

Experimental Procedure: Locomotor Crossing Study

The primary purpose of this study was to determine whether infants undergo a developmental shift from initially crossing to the mother with equal facility on either side of the visual cliff to differential crossing indicative of aversion of the deep side and no aversion to the shallow. This study involved testing three groups of subjects. One was a longitudinal group ($n = 15$; 4 male, 11 female, ranging in age from 6.2 months to 8.3 months, mean age 7.3 months) tested from shortly after the onset of locomotion until they met a terminal criterion of two

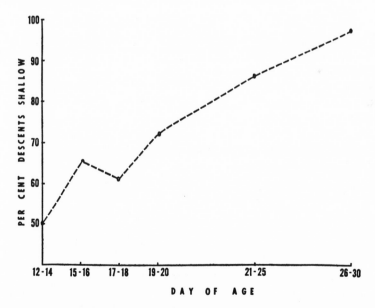

FIG. 3. The percentage of descents to the shallow side of the albino rabbits tested from soon after eyes were open until 30 days of age. (Figure is from Walk, 1966.)

consecutive sessions of differential crossing to the mother over the deep side. The second was a group of 15 subjects (8 male, 7 female) tested at 9 months of age, the approximate age of termination of testing for the longitudinal subjects. The third was a group of 15 subjects (8 male, 7 female), matched in age with the longitudinal subjects at the beginning of testing and tested for the presence of depth perception on the visual cliff with the *placing response,* as previously studied by Walters and Walk (1974) in young infants. The placing response is a preparatory adjustment of the infant's arms and hands made just before contact with a solid surface. It consists of a rapid extension of the arms, and usually a fanning of the fingers, when a threshold distance from an approaching surface has been reached. An additional 8 infants assigned to the longitudinal group, 2 infants assigned to the 9-month-old group, and 2 infants assigned to the placing response group could not be tested because of fear of the strange experimenter or the strange situation or the inability of the parents to continue participation in the longitudinal testing of the subjects.

So that we could ensure the initiation of testing of the infant shortly after the onset of locomotion, the mothers were contacted when their infants were approximately 6 months of age and asked to contact us as soon as their infants were locomoting a distance of 4 ft (1.21 m). (That was the distance that infants needed to negotiate to cross either side of the visual cliff.) When the mothers notified us of their infants' locomotion, an appointment was immediately set up for testing the infant at our laboratory. There, we verified the infant's locomotor activity by placing the infant on a 4-ft (1.21-m) Plexiglas panel on the floor. (This Plexiglas mimics the surface of the visual cliff that the infant had to locomote.) If the infant negotiated the panel, testing was started on the visual cliff. If the infant did not negotiate the panel, a new appointment was set up for a few days later.

Each testing session involved the administration of two deep and two shallow crossing trials. All possible orders of testing were used, and the infants were randomly assigned to an order on each day of testing. Trials involved the female experimenter's placing the infant on the center board of the visual cliff, at the farthest distance from the mother, and having the child's mother call the infant to her from the corner of the cliff opposite to the child, on either the deep or the shallow side. In addition to calling the child, the mother used an attractive gear toy to lure the child to her. Each trial lasted a maximum of 120 sec, and timing was initiated by the experimenter via a foot switch the moment the infant was placed on the center board of the cliff. The trial was terminated when the infant entered a 15 in × 15 in (38 cm × 38 cm) square zone in front of the corner from which the mother called to the infant.

Testing was repeated at 10-day to 2-week intervals until the infant showed, during two consecutive sessions, either of two criterion reactions that we had noted in pilot-testing the procedure. One criterion was failure to cross to the mother over the deep side and no such failure over the shallow side. The second criterion was what we called *detour crossing* to the mother over the deep side (i.e., crossing to the mother not on a beeline but rather by using the center board to get near the mother, and then traversing the now much shorter "chasm" to get to the mother along the long wall of the visual cliff).

Only one test session was administered to the 9-month-olds, who were otherwise treated in the same manner as were the longitudinal infants.

The placing response group was tested in only one session on the visual cliff. These subjects were held horizontally 3 ft (.91 m) above one or the other side of the visual cliff and then slowly lowered to the glass surface of the cliff. A descent rate of approximately 1 sec per vertical foot was used. Visual placing was scored if the infant demonstrated (1) extension of the limbs toward the surface to which he was being lowered and (2) fanning outward of the fingertips *prior to* contact with the glass surface. Those reactions were scored from videotapes recorded from a camera placed in the adjacent control room. Failure of depth perception was taken to be evident by the *absence* of placing response on either side of the visual cliff. Depth perception was indicated by the infant's demonstration of visual placing on the shallow surface approach but not on the deep surface approach. Two trials were given on each side.

The apparatus used in testing these subjects was the Visual Cliff Model III (Walk & Gibson, 1961), an 8 ft × 6 ft (2.43 m × 1.82 m) Herculite-glass-covered table, with 3-in (7.62 cm) red and white squares covering the shallow side and 6-in (15.24 cm) red and white squares covering the deep side. Heart rate was not recorded in any phase of this study. All sessions were videotaped from an adjacent control room through a large clear glass window, otherwise curtained to minimize visibility of the control room by the infant.

Videotapes were subsequently scored by two raters for a number of variables of interest in the study. These response variables included: (1) visual fixation (the duration in seconds of direction of gaze downward to the side the infant was required to cross); (2) surface testing (the number of trials in which the infant patted, licked, struck, or otherwise appeared to verify the solidity of the surface he was required to cross); (3) latency to locomote (the number of seconds from the moment that both hands and knees were on the center board to the time that the infant had moved all four hands and knees); (4) avoidance (moving of the entire body, including all hands and knees, off the center board in the direction opposite to that from which the mother called to the infant); and (5) the presence of detour behavior (crawling along the center board of the cliff toward the opposite wall of the cliff table, then crossing to the mother via the minimum distance on the deep or shallow sides). Interrater reliabilities ranged from 85% to 95% for perfect agreement and were above .90 for correlations of measurements involving time units.

RESULTS

In order to place the longitudinal data from the present study in better perspective, we will first discuss the data from the two cross-sectional groups.

As expected from previous studies (Schwartz et al., 1973; Walk, 1966; Walk & Gibson, 1961), the cross-sectional 9-month-old group (who had been locomoting, on the average, for over two months) showed clear aversion to the deep side of the visual cliff. Of 15 infants tested, none ventured across the deep side of the cliff on the first deep trial, and only 2 did on the second deep trial. By contrast, all crossed the shallow side of the cliff on both trials. The mean latency to reach the mother over the shallow side was 24.3 sec, while over the deep side, it was 115.0 sec, a highly significant difference ($p < .0001$). The infants in this group did not merely fail to cross. Of the 15 infants in this group, 11 showed active avoidance of the deep side of the cliff when called by their mothers, literally retreating, in many cases, to the extreme opposite end of the cliff table from the mothers. No such avoidance was ever shown on the shallow trials.

Furthermore, infants at 7.3 months of age were shown to possess depth perception adequate to guide their visual placing responses appropriately. Every single infant tested placed differentially over the two sides of the visual cliff, with (1) all infants demonstrating the placing response on both shallow trials; (2) all *failing* to place on the first of two deep trials; and (3) all but two infants continuing *not* to place on the second deep trial. These data are highly significant by even the insensitive sign test ($p < .001$).

Finally, the longitudinal subjects provided evidence for a developmental shift in locomotor crossing to the mother. On the first testing session, 10 of the 15 infants crossed to the mother over the deep side of the cliff. The other 5 infants crossed to the mother over the shallow but not over the deep side. At the final test session, *all* subjects crossed to the mother very differentially on the two sides or else failed to cross the deep side altogether. The failure of the infants to avoid descending onto the deep side was not a function of inattention: a mean of 18.07 sec was spent in visual fixation to the deep side on Test Session 1, compared to a mean of 16.09 sec on the shallow side.

The data on latency to initiate locomotion and to reach the mother gave entirely congruent results. Figure 4 presents the data obtained with the more stringent of the two indices, latency to reach the mother across the deep and the shallow sides. Three sessions are presented because all subjects had at least that many sessions, although most had more than three before reaching criterion for termination of the study. (The mean number of sessions to criterion was four, with a range of three to eight sessions.) The data graphed in Figure 4 were submitted to analysis of variance, the factor of central interest being the interaction between the test session and the side of the cliff. This interaction proved to be highly significant ($F = 14.55, p < .005$). Follow-up Scheffé tests were employed to clarify the nature of the interaction. Although there was a trend toward a latency difference in crossing the two sides in the first test session, the Scheffé test showed the difference not to be significant ($p < .15$). However, latency differences in both subsequent test sessions proved highly significant. The analysis of variance also revealed highly significant main effects of test session ($F = 11.65, p < .01$), of side of the cliff ($F = 46.61, p < .001$), and of trials ($F = 6.62, p < .02$).

Although the latency to cross the deep side does not appear in Figure 4 to demonstrate any developmental change, the obtained developmental function masked two qualitatively different manners of crossing the deep side. That is, six of the subjects refused to cross to the mother on the deep side in the later test sessions, even though all of them had freely crossed to the mother in previous sessions, including

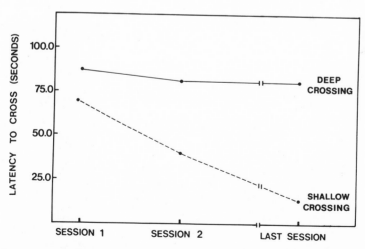

FIG. 4. Latency to cross to the mother over the deep and the shallow side of the visual cliff as a function of longitudinal test session number.

the initial one. These subjects showed a marked increase in latency to reach the mother over test sessions. The remaining nine subjects continued to cross to the mother over the deep side with continued testing and, in fact, crossed more quickly to the mother in the criterion sessions than in the initial one (the latency being 55.6 sec at end of testing compared to 72.2 sec at the beginning). However, *how* they crossed the deep side was dramatically different in the last sessions when compared to the first. Whereas before they crossed to the mother on the deep side in a diagonal beeline, they now crossed to her on the deep side by taking a detour, consisting of the use of either the shallow side or the center board to get as close to the mother as possible, and then crossing to the mother over a much shorter distance on the deep side. By contrast, shallow crossings continued on the beeline in all subjects (latency to cross, 11.8 sec).

An increase in *avoidance* was also evident in the longitudinal subjects. Eight infants retreated from the center board in the final test session, compared to only three who did so in the first. (These three subjects were also noncrossers in Test Session 1.)

Furthermore, the *duration of time locomoting* prior to initial testing on the cliff proved to be an important factor in determining latency differences in crossing to the mother over the two sides. In the present study, a time lag existed between the age of onset of any locomotion, as observed by the mothers, and the criterion of the infant's being able to crawl 4 ft (1.21 m), the minimum distance necessary for testing the infant on the cliff. Consequently, our sample of longitudinal infants had some degree of variation in locomotor history. Dividing the subjects in this study into four groups on the basis of time between maternal report of day of onset of locomotion and the day of initial testing resulted in the data presented in Figure 5 on the mean difference in crossing to the mother over the two sides of the cliff on the first testing day.

As can be seen, there is a nearly monotonic relationship between degree of locomotor history and deep–shallow crossing differences. Although we caution that the sample size was small, infants with the briefest crawling history in this study showed *no difference in latency to cross to the mother over the two sides* in the initial test session. Infants crawling for two or three weeks before testing was initiated showed some difference in crossing time over the two sides, although in neither group was the difference statistically significant. Interestingly, four of the five babies who initially did not cross the deep side to the mother were in the three-week testing lag group, and all of the infants with brief (seven days, on the average) locomotor history crossed to the mother over the two sides on all trials. The mean ages of these three subgroups proved to be identical.

In addition to demonstrating a developmental shift in the manner in

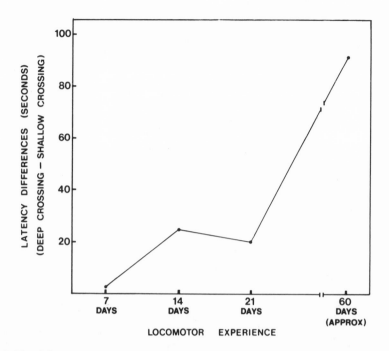

FIG. 5. The difference in the latency to cross the deep and the shallow sides of the cliff as a function of reported duration of any locomotion. Data from the 7-day, 14-day, and 21-day groups were taken in Session 1 of the longitudinal testing. Data from the 60-day locomotion group were from the 9-month cross-sectional subjects.

which the infants cross to the mother over the two sides of the cliff, the present study provided evidence that repeated longitudinal testing of infants *attenuated* the expression of fear in the infants. A comparison of the performance of the 9-month-old longitudinal subjects with the cross-sectional controls matched for age demonstrated more of a tendency for longitudinals to cross to the mother and for fewer of the longitudinals to show active avoidance.

In summary, then, the results of this study demonstrated the following points:

1. A developmental shift interpretable as a marked *increment* in fear of heights was evident in both longitudinal and cross-sectional comparison. Subsidiary analysis suggests that fear of heights may not even be present when locomotion is first acquired.

2. The evidence is now clear that by 7 months, infants possess depth perception sufficient to guide visual placing responses, and therefore any absence of fear of heights is *not* due to an absence of depth perception.

3. The importance of locomotor history in accounting for the onset and increment in fear of heights on the visual cliff was underscored.

4. The interesting detour behavior with which 9 of the 15 longitudinal infants continued to cross to the mother over the deep side suggests the onset of problem-solving behavior by infants tested on the cliff, as well as the possible use by the infants of strategies for *coping with stress*.

5. These findings are analogous to results previously reported by others.

Further Evidence of a Developmental Shift as a Function of Locomotion

We conducted a second study to serve as a converging operation with the locomotor crossing study, bearing on the role of locomotor experience on the developmental shift. Such a converging operation is particularly necessary because the locomotor crossing paradigm may underestimate the child's true aversive reactions to height as a result of the need to use the mother to call the infant to cross to her. The child's eventual crossing to the mother may therefore reflect the outcome of two separate valences: the fear of heights and the infant's trust in the mother. Although the eventual cessation of crossing to the mother would be no less remarkable when viewed in this light, any observed developmental shift in crossing to the mother may not reflect the onset of fear of heights so much as its intensification above levels of trust in the mother.

This particular problem does not affect research with the direct placement method because the mother need not be in the visual cliff testing room with the child. Furthermore, the direct placement method is the paradigm of choice when nonlocomotor infants are to be tested. Consequently, we tested prelocomotor and locomotor infants, matched for age and cognitive level, using a variant of the direct placement technique.

Previous unpublished work in our laboratory had repeatedly shown that direct placement at 6½–8 months of age did not elicit any significant cardiac changes during the period when the infant was actually perched atop the glass surface. However, the experimenters working with the 7-month-old placing response subjects in the previous study had noted a marked tensing of some of the infants as they were brought down to the deep side of the cliff (that is, before contact with the glass surface). The experimenters did not observe such tension on the shallow placements. Consequently, we focused our attention on the differences in heart rate between the 3-sec period just prior to initiating the descent onto one side or the other and the 3-sec period of the actual descent onto the table surface.

The study was planned as a 2 × 2 design, in which locomotor status (pre- versus postlocomotion onset) was crossed with object permanence level (Stage 3 versus beyond Stage 3). As will be discussed shortly, Piagetian theory gives object permanence a critical role in the construction of spatial relationships by the infant, and we had hoped to test for such an effect in a study in which age was held constant across the four cells. However, we succeeded only partially in our attempt to hold age constant, and in addition, we have found it very difficult to obtain nonlocomoting Stage 4 infants. Thus, one cell of the design remains incomplete. However, for the present purposes, a comparison of the performance of the Stage 3 infants as a function of their locomotor status is the central point of interest. In addition, we make reference to the data of the Stage 4 locomotor subjects.

Subjects were assigned to groups as follows. In the prelocomotor Stage 3 group, there were 20 infants (8 male, 12 female), with a mean age of 6.83 months. In the locomotor Stage 3 group, there were 19 infants (12 male, 7 female), with a mean age of 6.90 months and 4.1 weeks of locomotor experience. In the locomotor Stage 4 and 5 group, there were 15 infants (8 male, 7 female), with a mean age of 7.8 months and 5.3 weeks of locomotor experience. We succeeded in obtaining only 5 prelocomotor Stage 4 or 5 infants, and their data are not discussed here. An additional 15 infants were not tested because of sustained crying, which prevented initiation of testing, or because of equipment difficulties. The mother observed testing from an adjacent control room.

Procedure

The Object Permanence Testing

Infants received at least three object permanence items to test for Stage 3 and post-Stage 3 object permanence functioning: a partial hiding, a hiding-in-the-act-of-reaching, and a complete hiding. If the subject succeeded in solving the complete hiding with one screen, he was then tested with two screens and finally with multiple visible displacement using two screens. The items were administered in order of increasing difficulty. Infants were considered to be in Stage 3 if they passed the partial hiding or the hiding-in-the-act-of-reaching but failed the complete hiding. Infants were considered to have entered into Stage 4 if they passed the complete hiding and to be beyond Stage 4 if they passed any items using multiple visible displacements (Uzgiris & Hunt, 1975).

The Visual Cliff Direct Placement Procedure

There were two orders of testing: deep–shallow–deep–shallow, and the reverse. The orders were randomized across subjects. Each infant received at least two trials, one on each side. Most subjects received all four trials. Prior to each placement, the infant received a baseline period during which he sat on top of the shallow side of the cliff for 15 sec. After the baseline period, the experimenter moved to the appropriate side of the cliff, held the infant for 3 sec, raised the infant horizontally to a position 3 ft (.91 m) above one or the other surface of the visual cliff, and then slowly lowered the baby to the surface at the rate of approximately 1 vertical foot/sec (.30 m/sec). The baby then was left for 15 sec on the surface before being picked up, and the next baseline trial started.

Heart rate was recorded via a Biocom Telelink telemetry system and a Grass Model 5D polygraph with a specially designed cardiotachometer. Behavioral reactions were recorded via the system described for the first study.

From the videotapes, we scored the presence of the placing response, as described for the previous study, in order to determine whether the infants could show appropriate placing even prior to the onset of locomotion.

Results

The results analyzed so far demonstrate that every single infant tested, whether locomotor or not, and whether in Stage 3 or beyond, placed differentially on the two sides of the cliff. We take this to mean that infants possess depth perception on the visual cliff even *prior to* locomotion.

Furthermore, the heart rate response during the descent trials showed a developmental shift as a function of locomotor experience. These data are presented in Figure 6. The shallow descent trials showed no developmental trend, being a consistently nonsignificant acceleration (probably associated with the motoric activity of the placing response) of some 2 bpm. The heart rate response on the deep descent trials was a slight (nonsignificant) deceleration in the prelocomotor Stage 3 infants. For the two locomotor groups, on the other hand, the response was both markedly acceleratory and significantly different from predescent heart rate levels and from the shallow descent heart rate response ($p < .01$ by t test).

Although we want to underscore the tentative nature of the latter findings, we feel that two experimental paradigms with the visual cliff—the locomotor crossing method and the descent portion of the

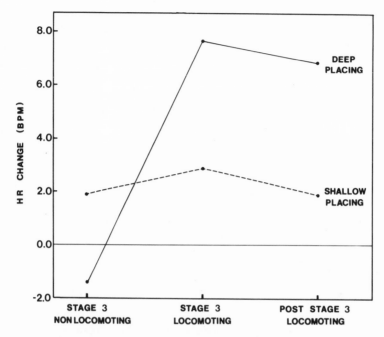

FIG. 6. Changes in heart rate during descent toward the deep or the shallow side of the visual cliff as a function of object permanence stage and of locomotor experience.

direct placement method—are pointing to a developmental shift that is in part a function of locomotor experience. Furthermore, although the results of the second study do not rule out the possible role of cognitive level independent of locomotor experience, the results so far clearly point to locomotor experience as being sufficient, and for cognitive level (i.e., Stage 4 of object permanence) not to be necessary, in producing this shift.

Possible Determinants of the Developmental Shift on the Visual Cliff

What factors could be determinants of an obtained developmental shift on the visual cliff? Among many alternatives, the following generic categories of determinants immediately come to mind: (1) specific experiences; (2) discrepancy explanations, such as have been invoked to account for the onset of fear of strangers; (3) the development of fearfulness *per se* as an *output* system; (4) cognitive-perceptual (i.e., information-processing) developments allowing improved estimation of distances; and, a related explanation, (5) the role of self-produced movement and reafference in the visual guidance of behavior.

Specific Experiences

One possible interpretation of the data amassed so far on visual cliff performance is that infants have keen distance perception from an early age but no appreciation that depth-at-an-edge is dangerous, in the absence of experience with falls. Locomotion serves as an opportunity to increase the possibility of such falls. In short, the infant may need classical conditioning with height as the conditioned stimulus and a painful experience as the unconditioned stimulus.

There is evidence that falling accidents may be playing a role in the infants' behavior on the visual cliff. Walk (1966) reported that the "tendency in the sample of 71 [infants] was for the infants with two or more accidents to be more cautious [than were those with one or no falling accidents]" (p. 103). However, in a different study, Scarr and Salapatek (1970) reported no relationship between falling accidents and fear of heights on the visual cliff. In our study, at least five mothers had reported a fall to have taken place during the interval just prior to the manifestation of the developmental shift in crossing behavior, but unfortunately, the absence of a systematic collection of data on falling accidents makes the above data from our study merely suggestive. A similar comment applies to our telephone interview results.

We think that there is a second type of experience that could be playing a role in the onset of fear of heights, and that is the mother's reaction to a "near fall" by her infant. Infants at the ages tested on the visual cliff can detect and react appropriately to negative emotional expressions on the part of adults (Charlesworth & Kreutzer, 1973; Haith & Campos, 1977). The infant can thus associate heights with potential danger not through actual experience with falls but through the mediation of the mother's social communicative systems. The role of both types of experiences are probably playing an important role in the developmental shift on fear of heights.[3]

Discrepancy Explanations

In the past few years, considerable interest has been generated in

---

[3] There are at least two other ways in which experience plays a role in visual cliff performance, although these are not determinants of the developmental shift. We have already alluded to one in a previous section: infants repeatedly tested on the cliff showed a greater readiness to be coaxed across the cliff than subjects matched for age without prior experience on the cliff. We interpret this readiness to mean that infants remember the solidity of the surface of the deep side of the cliff from previous sessions. A second way in which experience plays a role has been demonstrated by Warnberg and Somervill (1973), who first conditioned a pattern preference in infants and then obtained a greater tendency for infants to cross the deep side when the preferred pattern constituted the floor of the deep side.

explanations of emotional development using the so-called discrepancy hypothesis or fear of novelty (e.g., Bronson, 1968; Hebb, 1946; Schaffer, 1966). This hypothesis has been widely used to explain phenomena such as fear of the strange, which is interpreted to be the result of a present perceptual input's (a stranger) being sufficiently discrepant from a central representation (a storehouse of past experiences, e.g., familiar persons) so that disruption of phase sequences (Hebb, 1946) or fear (Bronson, 1968) results. A number of corollaries have been added to this assumption in recent years. For example, Kagan (1974) described fear as due in particular to unassimilable discrepancies, to events that the infant tries to but cannot understand.

This hypothesis has never been extended to findings obtained with the visual cliff, but it can readily be extrapolated to account for the onset of a developmental shift. The extrapolation, furthermore, implies that any obtained fear on the cliff is not due to heights but to visual–tactual incongruity. In other words, early in development, the infant perceives no incongruity on the surface of the deep side and hence manifests no fear. As locomotor and other perceptual experiences are acquired by the infant, the infant gains the knowledge that horizontal crawling surfaces are both solid to the touch and opaque to the eye. If, at this point, the infant is required on the visual cliff to cross a surface that is *solid* to the touch and *transparent*, incongruity is detected, and fear results. Such a discrepancy between touch and vision would be otherwise experienced in the ordinary world of the child only when infants look *horizontally* out of windows.

All discrepancy explanations have been seriously criticized recently (Haith & Campos, 1977; Sroufe, in press; Sroufe, Waters, & Matas, 1974). Basically, it is argued that discrepancy can account for the arousal component of affect but not for the quality of the affect itself, since discrepancy seems to play such an important role in laughter, anger, and surprise, as well as fear. In the present context, although we believe that this theory can account for some of the data we have presented so far on the locomotor crossing paradigm, it does not seem to us to account for two very significant observations made in the course of our studies. First, it cannot explain the cardiac accelerations observed in the descent toward the deep side of the visual cliff in postlocomotor infants. In that paradigm, the indications of fear are recorded *before* there is any contact with the glass, and hence before any visual–tactual incongruity. Second, we do not see how such a discrepancy can fully account for the mother's reports in our telephone interview that after a period of no fear of going over the edges of beds, tables, stairs, etc., the infant suddenly balks when encountering any of these situations. Such reactions seem to imply more the role of specific experiences, more complex cognitive factors than discrepancy, or maturational factors.

The Development of Fearfulness as an Output System

There has been considerable interest in the possibility of the development of a reaction system (sometimes called a *fear system*) that begins to operate at the third quarter-year of life (Bridges, 1932; Emde *et al.*, 1976; Scarr & Salapatek, 1970). This response system shares features with response systems present in very early infancy (e.g., distress) but differs from earlier systems in a number of ways. First of all, the later system is triggered by the *threat* of danger or hurt rather than by the danger or the hurt itself. Thus, while Watson (1924) may have been right in speaking of loud sounds and sudden loss of support as eliciting "fear" (i.e., distress) in neonates, the later system would involve reactions to the threat of loss of support. A second difference is that the response organization of the two systems is not the same. For example, facial expressions communicative of fear (Ekman, Friesen, & Ellsworth, 1972; Izard, 1971) should be present in the later system but not in the earlier. Although it has proved difficult to find such response specificity up to now, a recent study in our laboratory with 10- to 12-month-old infants placed directly atop the visual cliff uncovered evidence of some of the classic facial features linked theoretically to fear, such as the opening of the mouth and the tensing and drawing back of the lips (Hiatt, Campos, & Emde, 1977). Unpublished observations suggest no such facial features to be evident in 6- and 7-month infants.

In apparent further support of the emergence of this reaction system is the finding of a rough simultaneity in the age of onset of negative reactions to strangers, separation protest, the visual cliff, and most recently, looming stimuli (Cicchetti & Sroufe, 1977; Yonas, Becktold, Gordon, Frankel, McRoberts, Norcia, & Sternfels, 1977). The rough similarity of age of onset of these phenomena has been taken as evidence by Emde, Gaensbauer, and Harmon (1976) for the existence of an "organizer"—that is, a central neurophysiological nodal development that becomes manifest in many ways in organism–environment transactions. There is evidence from both our laboratory and others that the simultaneity in age of onset is not precise. For example, Schaffer and Emerson (1964) reported that separation distress generally, but not invariably, preceded stranger distress. In our lab, we have found evidence for stranger distress (Campos *et al.*, 1975) at 5 months, and in unpublished work at 6½ months—that is, generally before we see a developmental shift on the visual cliff. (However, it should be kept in mind that we have not yet explicitly compared reactions to the two situations.) However, the viewpoint of Emde and his colleagues does not require precise timing of onset of these developments any more than the Piagetian theory requires precise simultaneity of time of onset of indices of representation or of any criterion for stage attainment.

A related point of view has been adopted by Kagan (1976a, b). Kagan believes that the changes evident in affect in the second half-year of life are probably a reflection of fundamental changes in the cognitive abilities of the infant—either the "origin of hypotheses" (Kagan, 1971) or the maturation of memory capabilities (Kagan, 1976a, b). Although Kagan believes that experience enters into play in these developments, the universality of many of the developmental changes in the second half-year of life argues for a maturational basis.

Because of the absence of any method of untangling the effects of experience and biological maturation in the intact human infant, it is very difficult to evaluate these positions. One observation from our longitudinal study, however, is consistent with a maturational viewpoint—although we hasten to emphasize that it also may result from the specific experiences alluded to above. The observations we refer to come from the five infants who initially failed to cross to the mother in the first longitudinal test session. Despite this initial wariness of crossing the infants were coaxed across the deep side by the mothers on subsequent test sessions, only to manifest a new upwelling of fearfulness that led them to become hesitant to cross to the mothers once again. Others, such as Scarr and Salapatek (1970), as noted before, have also reported a marked increase in fearfulness on the visual cliff with increasing age, and in their study, no experiential or cognitive factor proved predictive of the increment in fearfulness they observed, leading them to postulate a biological maturational variable as one possible determinant.

Cognitive-Perceptual Development

There is currently considerable interest in the relationship between cognitive and emotional development in the human infant (Décarie, 1974 and in this book; Kagan, 1974; Sroufe, in press). Typically, investigators have focused on the development of Stage 4 (or more rarely, Stage 5) of Piagetian sensorimotor development and have attempted to find in these stages a logical prerequisite for separation protest (Ainsworth, 1973; Bowlby, 1960) or for stranger distress (Décarie, 1974; Emde et al., 1976; Paradise & Curcio, 1974; Scarr & Salapatek, 1970; Schaffer, 1966). The linkage between cognitive and emotional development has often been proposed in vague, unpersuasive fashion (see Fraiberg, 1969; Jackson, Campos, & Fischer, 1977). With the visual cliff, however, the linkage between perceptual-cognitive and emotional developments seems more direct and testable and need not involve postulating (as was mentioned above) the total absence of depth perception in the infant prior to showing aversion of heights.

Piagetian theory, for example, states that infants go through stages in which the perception of near space is slowly constructed, only to be followed by the construction of far space (see Piaget, 1954, Chap. 2). That is, infants can initially perceive depth only to the extent that vision and prehension are intercoordinated (in Stage 3 of sensorimotor development). During this stage, infants can perceive planes of depth to the extent that they can reach and perhaps a little beyond (since they can lean forward and stretch somewhat). This zone of near space, as Piaget calls it, does not possess well-developed size and shape constancy, especially since the visual world just beyond the zone of near space is perceived by the infant as a flat plane (much in the way we perceive the sky at night, in which moon and stars occupy the same plane despite light-years distance between them). Piaget holds that this flat plane of far space becomes progressively stretched out as a result of a number of developments, the one most clearly described by Piaget being the construction of the relationships "in front of" and "behind," which the infant manifests for the first time in his search for hidden objects. (Hence our initial attempt to assess the role of object permanence independent of that of locomotion on the visual cliff.) Only alluded to by Piaget, but perfectly consistent with his theoretical position, is the possibility of the intercoordination of *locomotion with vision,* an intercoordination that would duplicate in the perceptual world of far space the construction of planes of depth previously accomplished for near space by the intercoordination of prehension and vision. In other words, the infant learns to calibrate visual distances in one of two ways: through accomplishments related to object permanence (the construction of the relationships "in front of" and "behind") or through locomotor experience.

Note the implications of this theoretical approach for affective developments on the visual cliff. Since Stage 3 infants (who, by Piaget's and our own data, can be 7 or even 8 months of age) possess depth perception in near space, they should be expected to demonstrate the placing response appropriately at this age; the placing response is only a special case of visually elicited reaching. Placing occurs because a surface is beginning to approach the child in the zone of near space, and consistent with the theory, our observations suggest that the placing response begins when the surface is some 10 in (25.4 cm) from the infant's eyes. On the other hand, since far space has yet to be constructed, its distance, being indeterminate or else localized just beyond the zone of near space, is not as yet sufficiently calibrated or adequate to trigger reactions to great distances, to distances far enough to produce reactions to a danger. As soon as far space becomes calibrated, however, such a perceptual mechanism, assumed necessary to trigger fear of heights, now becomes functional.

Two very testable predictions are postulated by the theory. One is that infants with no active locomotor history but with other active schemes for the construction of the visual world will be able to show avoidance of heights. An infant who, by reason of cerebral palsy, meningomyelocele, or orthopedic handicap preventing locomotion, may be *retarded* in the onset of far space perception but should be able eventually to construct mentally what he may not otherwise be able to construct via his own locomotor experiences. The second testable prediction is that a Stage 3 infant with no locomotor history should show no far space perception and hence no fear of heights.

Two issues can be raised at this point: (1) Is the distinction between near space and far space viable in the light of recent experimental evidence presented on perception of constancies and of looming stimuli in very young infants? (2) If the distinction is viable, how can it be tested readily for coordination with findings with the visual cliff?

It will be recalled that between the mid-1960s and the early 1970s, there was a plethora of reports, mostly from the same laboratory, suggesting very early visual competence in infant depth perception (Ball & Tronick, 1971; Bower, 1964, 1965, 1966, 1974; Bower, Broughton, & Moore, 1970a, b). These studies are now extremely controversial, apparently defying attempts at replication. For example, Yonas (Yonas, *et al.*, 1977) has reported failure to replicate avoidance of looming stimuli in infants 2 months of age and younger. Cicchetti and Sroufe (this volume) also report a marked increase in fear of looming stimuli in the second half-year of life in normal subjects. McKenzie and Day (1972) failed to extend Bower's (1964) findings on size constancy using a dishabituation paradigm, while others have reported informally great difficulty in replicating Bower's operant conditioning paradigm. The report that neonates reach to visually presented objects (Bower, Broughton, & Moore, 1970a) has also not replicated (Dodwell, Muir, & DiFranco, 1976). Finally, although shape constancy has been demonstrated in 2- to 4-month-old infants in one study (Day & McKenzie, 1973), a recent thorough study on shape constancy in 3-month-olds (Caron, Caron, & Carlson, 1977) concluded, "Clearly, [infants] don't see retinal images, but that they see objects in a functionally significant way is also doubtful"

In brief, the answer to the question whether very young infants perceive depth sufficiently to mediate size and shape constancy is still very much in doubt.

The answer to the second question is much more problematic. There are numerous methodological problems in testing for infants' reactions to distal stimuli (see Bower, 1974; Yonas & Pick, 1975). To add the further requirement of testing for the effects of successful processing of depth in near space versus in far space would seem to tax the creative capacities of the most thorough researcher. Nevertheless, the results on the visual cliff appear to us thoroughly congruent with Piaget's thinking: there is a stage in which stimuli specifying depth are registered by the sense organs but not given meaning by the infant (the 2-month-old's cardiac deceleration on the visual cliff), and then there is the stage of near space perception (producing accurate placing responses in the infant but no fear of great distances as yet). Finally, there is the stage of far space perception and the concomitant fear of heights.

One other observation from our longitudinal study is relevant to Piagetian theory. We observed a developmental shift in the manner of crossing to the mother over the deep side in some of our infants. As we noted above, nine of the infants in that study crossed to the mother at the end of testing by use of detour behavior. These nine subjects initially crossed over both sides on a beeline. Yet, at the end of testing, they crossed on the deep side through the use of clear detour behaviors, while they continued to cross on the beeline on the opposite side. We interpreted this behavior as evidence of the development of fearfulness because the barrier the infants were detouring around was psychological and not physical. But we also interpret this behavior as indicative of the difference between a Stage 4 infant's direct, nondetour approach to problem solving and that of a Stage 5 infant, who possesses, for the first time, the cognitive prerequisites for use of multiple means to the same end (the tertiary circular reaction, or the intellectual criterion called "associativity" by Piaget, 1950).

The Role of Self-Produced Movement

Perhaps the most parsimonious interpretation of our results is based upon the previous work by Held, Hein, and their collaborators (e.g., Held & Hein, 1963: Hein, 1972; Hein & Diamond, 1972). They have produced a wealth of evidence that feedback correlated with self-produced movement (which feedback they call *reafference*) is necessary for adaptation to prismatic rearrangement, for visually guided reaching, and for avoidance by kittens of the deep side of the visual cliff. Passive transport of the subject in space is not only ineffectual in producing appropriate visually directed behavior but can actually impede the eventual acquisition of such behavior.

The most relevant of their studies for our purposes is the study of the kitten carousel (e.g., Held & Hein, 1963). This study used an ingenious apparatus that allowed dark-reared yoked kitten littermates to obtain comparable levels of visual stimulation as a function of active or passive movement in space. One kitten was given visual experience in patterned light while moved about passively. (The kitten was placed in a gondola that prevented any movements from being translated into locomotion.) The other kitten moved actively in the apparatus and, via a mechanical linkage, caused equivalent movement of the gondola containing the yoked littermate. Held and Hein's results were striking: every kitten who moved actively about in the apparatus showed avoidance of the deep side of the cliff, while every passively transported kitten failed to avoid the deep side. Future work not only replicated the importance of self-produced locomotion but also uncovered negative transfer effects from the passive movement condition (Hein, 1972). The passively transported kittens actually required extra experience compared to a group not placed in a gondola before they showed normal visually guided behavior. Hein (1972) interpreted this effect to mean that the passively transported kittens' normal reafference from head movements was disrupted by the addition of visual movement created by the passive transport in space.

We feel that in many respects the human infant prior to the onset of locomotion is in a state analogous to that of the passively transported kittens of the kitten carousel study. It is a state in which reafference from self-produced locomotion is absent and in which passive transport by the caregiver ensures that reafference from head movements during such transport is confounded with afference produced by the passive movement itself. Consequently, visually directed behavior such as avoidance of the deep side of the visual cliff would not be expected to be present in prelocomotor infants, unless some other factor intervened. Unfortunately, the analogy is not precise: in contrast to the dark-reared kittens of the carousel study, the human infant obtains reafference from hands and legs prior to locomotion. Held and Hein have not described studies of kittens' behavior on the visual cliff under circumstances of forelimb reafference in the absence of locomotor reafference. However, it does not strain Held and Hein's theory to suggest that under such circumstances, one might obtain visual placing responses of one sort or another prior to avoidance of the deep side of the cliff—which is precisely the pattern of findings we have obtained.

A number of tests of this theory are immediately suggested. One prediction concerns the presence of significant individual differences in visual cliff performance after locomotion onset as a function of prior transport history. The more passive transport a child has had in the presence of head movements on his part, the longer it will take him to establish correct correspondence between reafference and "correlated storage"—the residue of prior afferent and efferent signals associated with movement—and hence the longer it will take the infant to establish correct visually guided behavior. A second prediction concerns artificial means of creating self-produced locomotion: an infant given extensive experience with a "walker" prior to true self-produced locomotion may well establish reafference sufficiently to generate avoidance of heights even prior to normal crawling age.

Although similar in many ways to Piaget's theory, Held and Hein's approach differs in a number of critical respects. First of all, Held and Hein refer to their work as elucidating visuomotor coordinations. They are ambiguous as to whether self-produced locomotion affects visual perception or the guidance of behavior, or both. However, some of their work suggests that it is the guidance of behavior, and not perception, that is affected. For instance, Hein (1972) described a study in which a kitten showed correct placement of a previously seen forelimb but not of one that was previously unseen. Since vision was the same in both conditions, it seems more likely that it was the response process that was affected. In Piaget's theory, by contrast, the distinction between near and far space is a perceptual one, even though space is constructed through motoric activity. Thus, there may be two points of view with fundamentally different implications for the understanding of human infant visual cliff behavior. One implies that depth perception possibly has been there all along but that only behavior in space (e.g., avoidance of heights) is affected, while the other implies that there are changes in depth perception as a function of self-produced locomotion. The former position requires a mechanism to couple avoidance of heights with a preexisting perceptual capacity. The latter (among a number of alternatives) can accommodate a revised ethological view on fear of heights; that is, avoidance may be innately triggered by a percept, but experience is necessary to construct the percept.

There is a second way in which the theories differ. Piaget posits multiple routes to correct localization of the body in space and to perception of great distances. Held and Hein, by contrast, stress only self-produced movement. Because an infant can construct a relationship intellectually, even when lacking certain critical schemes like locomotion, a paralyzed infant would be predicted to show a developmental shift on the visual cliff, albeit delayed in origin, according to Piaget's view. This shift should not be possible, according to our understanding of Held and Hein's theory: in the absence of self-produced locomotion, avoidance of the deep side of the cliff would be impeded.

Summary

The study of the development of negative emotions in infancy has until recently centered exclusively on social situations, but now it has been broadened to include more purely perceptual elicitors. The data we presented, together with results previously described in both the human and the animal literature, leave no doubt that a major developmental shift is taking place in reactions to heights. Furthermore, our results implicate the emotion of fear in that shift. The onset of refusal to cross the deep side of the visual cliff is one such indication. Retreat from the edge of the cliff is a second. Facial expression components of fearfulness in connection with direct placement atop the deep side is still a third.

The onset of fear of heights appears to come about very shortly after the onset of locomotion, but there appears to be a second surge of fearfulness occurring well after the onset of locomotion. Nevertheless, there remains the possibility that avoidance of heights can be shown prior to the age of onset of locomotion, perhaps through the mediation of falling experiences or artificially produced locomotion (e.g., walkers). Verification of that possibility remains for future research. Our data suggest that such early fearfulness may be rare.

There is also little doubt that infants can perceive depth to some extent prior to the onset of locomotion. Nevertheless, theoretically critical questions remain about certain aspects of the veridicality of the infant's depth perception at the time of the developmental shift. Piaget's distinction between near-space and far-space perception seems important to pursue. Far-space perception could prove a necessary cognitive accomplishment underlying the onset of fear of heights. The role of self-produced locomotion on visual perception as opposed to the guidance of behavior also needs clarification. In any event, visual cliff performance is not going to be determined by a single factor. The infant's temperament, its prior experiences, and a host of contextual variables, such as trust in the mother, are all likely to have measurable importance.

References

Ainsworth, M. The development of infant–mother attachement. In B. Caldwell & H. Ricciuti (Eds.), *Review of child development research* (Vol. 3). Chicago: University of Chicago Press, 1973.

Anderson, D., & Brady, J. V. Prolonged preavoidance effects upon blood pressure and heart rate in the dog. *Psychosomatic Medicine*, 1973, *35*, 4–12.

Appel, M., & Campos, J. Binocular disparity as a discriminable stimulus parameter in early infancy. *Journal of Experimental Child Psychology*, 1977, *23*, 47–56.

Ax, A. The physiological differentiation between fear and anger in humans. *Psychosomatic Medicine*, 1953, *15*, 433–442.

Ball, W., & Tronick, E. Infant responses to impending collision: Optical and real. *Science*, 1971, *171*, 818-820.

Bayley, N. *Manual for the Bayley scales of infant development*. New York: Psychological Corporation, 1969.

Bond, E. Perception of form by the human infant. *Psychological Bulletin*, 1972, *77*, 225–245.

Bower, T. Discrimination of depth in premotor infants. *Psychonomic Science*, 1964, *1*, 368.

Bower, T. Stimulus variables determining space perception in infants. *Science*, 1965, *149*, 88–89.

Bower, T. Slant perception and shape constancy in infants. *Science*, 1966, *151*, 832–834.

Bower, T. *Development in infancy*. San Francisco: Freeman, 1974.

Bower, T., Broughton, J., & Moore, M. The coordination of visual and tactual input in infants. *Perception and Psychophysics*, 1970, *8*, 51–53. (a)

Bower, T., Broughton, J., & Moore, M. Demonstration of intent in the reaching behavior of neonate humans. *Nature*, 1970, *228*, 679–680. (b)

Bowlby, J. Separation anxiety. *International Journal of Psychoanalysis*, 1960, *41*, 89–113.

Bowlby, J. *Attachment and loss separation* (Vol. 2). New York: Basic Books, 1973.

Bridges, K. M. Emotional development in early infancy. *Child Development*, 1932, *3*, 324–341.

Bronson, G. The fear of novelty. *Psychological Bulletin*, 1968, *69*, 350–358.

Campos, J., Emde, R., Gaensbauer, T., & Henderson, C. Cardiac and behavioral interrelationships in the reactions of infants to strangers. *Developmental Psychology*, 1975, *11*, 589–601.

Campos, J., & Langer, A. The visual cliff: Discriminative cardiac orienting responses with retinal size held constant. Paper read at the meetings of the Soceity for Psychophysiological Research, 1970. *Psychophysiology*, 1971, *8*, 264–265. (Abstract)

Campos, J., Langer, A., & Krowitz, A. Cardiac responses on the visual cliff in pre-motor human infants. *Science*, 1970, *170*, 195–196.

Caron, A., Caron, R., & Carlson, V. Do infants see objects or retinal images? Shape constancy revisited. Paper read at the meetings of the Society for Research in Child Development, New Orleans, March 1977.

Charlesworth, W., & Kreutzer, M. Facial expressions of infants and children. In P. Ekman (Ed.), *Darwin and facial expression*. New York: Academic Press, 1973.

Cicchetti, D., & Sroufe, L. An organizational view of affect: Illustration from the study of Down's Syndrome infants. In M. Lewis & L. Rosenblum (Eds.), *The origins of affect*. New York: Wiley, 1977.

Day R., & McKenzie, B. Perceptual shape constancy in early infancy. *Perception*, 1973, *2*, 315–320.

Décarie, T. *The infant's reaction to strangers*. New York: International Universites Press, 1974.

Décarie, T. Affect development and cognition in a Piagetian context. In M. Lewis & L. Rosenblum (Eds.), *The origins of affect*. New York: Wiley, 1977.

Dodwell, P., Muir, D., & DiFranco, D. Responses of infants to visually presented objects. *Science*, 1976, *194*, 209–211.

Ekman, P., Friesen, W., & Ellsworth, P. *Emotion in the human face: Guidelines for research and an integration of findings*. New York: Pergamon Press, 1972.

Emde, R., Campos, J., Gaensbauer, T., & Reich, J. Smiling to strangers at five and nine months: Analysis of movement and heart rate. Paper read at the meetings of the Society for Research in Child Development, Denver, April 1975.

Emde, R. N., Gaensbauer, T. J., & Harmon, R. J. Emotional expression in infancy: A biobehavioral study. *Psychological Issues*, 1976, *10*(1, Monograph 37).

Fields, J. The adjustment of reaching behavior to object distance in early infancy. *Child Development*, 1976, *47*, 304–308.

Fraiberg, S. Libidinal object constancy and mental representation. *Psychoanalytic Study of the Child*, 1969, *24*, 9–47.

Freedman, D. *Human infancy: An evolutionary perspective*. Hillsdale, N.J.: Erlbaum, 1974.

Gibson, E., & Walk, R. The "visual cliff." *Scientific American*, 1960, *202*, 64–71.

Gibson, J. *The perception of the visual world*. Boston: Houghton, Mifflin, 1950.

Graham, F., & Clifton, R. Heart-rate change as a component of the orienting response. *Psychological Bulletin*, 1966, *65*, 305–320.

Graham, F. K., & Jackson, J. C. Arousal systems and infant heart rate responses. In H. W. Reese & L. P. Lipsitt (Eds.), *Advances in child development and behavior* (Vol. 5). New York: Academic Press, 1970.

Haith, M., & Campos, J. Human infancy. *Annual Review of Psychology*, 1977, *28*, 251–293.

Harmon, R., & Morgan, G. *Infants' reactions to unfamiliar adults: A discussion of some important issues*. ERIC, 1975.

Hebb, D. On the nature of fear. *Psychological Review*, 1946, *53*, 259–276.

Hein, A. Acquiring components of visually guided behavior. In A. Pick (Ed.), *Minnesota symposia on child psychology* (Vol. 6). Minneapolis: University of Minnesota Press, 1972.

Hein, A., & Diamond, R. Locomotory space as a prerequisite for acquiring visually guided reaching in kittens. *Journal of Comparative and Physiological Psychology*, 1972, *81*, 394–398.

Held, R., & Hein, A. Movement-produced stimulation in the development of visually-guided behavior. *Journal of Comparative and Physiological Psychology*, 1963, *56*, 872–876.

Hiatt, S., Campos, J., & Emde, R. Fear, surprise, and happiness: The patterning of facial expressions in infancy. Paper read at the meetings of the Society for Research in Child Development, New Orleans, March 1977.

Izard, C. *The face of emotion*. New York: Appleton-Century-Crofts, 1971.

Jackson, E., Campos, J., & Fischer, K. The question of decalage between object permanence and person permanence. *Developmental Psychology*, 1978, in press.

Kagan, J. *Change and continuity in infancy*. New York: Wiley, 1971.

Kagan, J. Discrepancy, temperament and infant distress. In M. Lewis & L. Rosenblum (Eds.), *The origins of fear*. New York: Wiley, 1974.

Kagan, J. Emergent themes in human development. *American Scientist*, 1976, *64*, 186–196. (a)

Kagan, J. Three themes in developmental psychology. In L. Lipsitt (Ed.), *Developmental psychobiology: The significance of infancy*. Hillsdale, N.J.: Erlbaum, 1976. (b)

Lacey, J. Psychophysiological approaches to the evaluation of psychotherapeutic process and outcome. In E. A. Rubenstein & M. Parloff (Eds.), *Research in psychotherapy* (Vol. 1). Washington, D.C.: American Psychological Association, 1959.

Lynn, R. *Attention, arousal and the orientation reaction*. New York: Pergamon Press, 1966.

McKenzie, B., & Day, R. Object distance as a determinant of visual fixation in young infants. *Science*, 1972, *178*, 1108–1110.

Obrist, P., Howard, J., Lawler, J., Galosy, R., Meyers, K., & Gaebelein, C. The cardiac-somatic interaction. In P. Obrist, A. Black, J. Brener, & L. DiCara (Eds.), *Cardiovascular psychophysiology*. Chicago: Aldine, 1974.

Obrist, P. A., Webb, R. A., Sutterer, J. R., & Howard, J. L. The cardiac–somatic relationship: Some reformulations. *Psychophysiology*, 1970, *6*, 569–587.

Obrist, P. A., Wood, D. M., & Perez-Reyes, M. Heart rate during conditioning in humans: Effect of UCS intensity, vagal blockade, and adrenergic block of vasomotor activity. *Journal of Experimental Psychology*, 1965, *70*, 32–42.

Paradise, E., & Curcio, F. Relationship of cognitive and affective behaviors to fear of strangers in male infants. *Developmental Psychology*, 1974, *10*, 476–483.

Piaget, J. *The psychology of intelligence*. Paterson, N.J.: Littlefield, Adams, 1950.

Piaget, J. *The construction of reality in the child*. New York: Basic Books, 1954.

Provost, M., & Décarie, T. Modifications du rhythme cardiaque chez des enfants de 9–12 mois au cours de la rencontre avec la personne étrangère. *Canadian Journal of Behavioral Science*, 1974, *6*, 154–168.

Rheingold, H., & Eckerman, C. Fear of the stranger: A critical examination. In H. W. Reese

& L. P. Lipsitt (Eds.), *Advances in child development and behavior* (Vol. 8). New York: Academic Press, 1973.

Rosenblum, L., & Cross, H. Performance of neonatal monkeys in the visual cliff situation. *American Jouranl of Psychology*, 1963, *76*, 318–320.

Scarr, S., & Salapatek, P. Patterns of fear development during infancy. *Merrill-Palmer Quarterly*, 1970, *16*, 53–90.

Schaffer, H. The onset of fear of strangers and the incongruity hypothesis. *Journal of Child Psychology and Psychiatry*, 1966, *7*, 95–106.

Schaffer, H., & Emerson, P. The development of social attachments in infancy. *Monographs of the Society for Research in Child Development*, 1964, *29* (Serial No. 94).

Schwartz, A., Campos, J., & Baisel, E. The visual cliff: Cardiac and behavioral correlates on the deep and shallow sides at five and nine months of age. *Journal of Experimental Child Psychology*, 1973, *15*, 86–99.

Sroufe, L. A. Emotional development in infancy. In J. Osofsky (Ed.), *Handbook of infant development*. New York: Wiley, in press.

Sroufe, L. A., & Waters, E. Heart rate as a convergent measure in clinical and developmental research. *Merrill-Palmer Quarterly*, 1977, *23*, 3–27.

Sroufe, L. A., Waters, E., & Matas, L. Contextual determinants of infant affective response. In M. Lewis & L. Rosenblum (Eds.), *The origins of fear*. New York: Wiley, 1974.

Stayton, D., Ainsworth, M., & Main, M. Development of separation behavior in the first year of life: Protest, following, and greeting. *Developmental Psychology*, 1973, *9*, 213–225.

Uzgiris, I., & Hunt, J. *Assessment in infancy: Ordinal scales of psychological development*. Urbana: University of Illinois Press, 1975.

Walk, R. The development of depth perception in animals and human infants. *Monographs of the Society for Research in Child Development*, 1966, *31*(Whole No. 5).

Walk, R., & Gibson, E. A comparative and analytical study of visual depth perception. *Psychological Monographs*, 1961, *75*(15, Whole No. 519).

Walters, C., & Walk, R. Visual placing by human infants. *Journal of Experimental Child Psychology*, 1974, *18*, 34–40.

Warnberg, L., & Somervill, J. Effects of a shaped pattern preference on depth avoidance by human infants in the visual cliff situation. *Perceptual Motor Skills*, 1973, *36*, 919–925.

Waters, E., Matas, L., & Sroufe, L. Infants' reactions to an approaching stranger: Description, validation, and functional significance of wariness. *Child Development*, 1975, *46*, 348–356.

Watson, J. *Behaviorism*. Chicago: University of Chicago Press, 1924.

Wilson, R. Cardiac response: Determinants of conditioning. *Journal of Comparative and Physiological Psychology Monograph*, 1969, *68*, 1–23.

Yonas, A., Bechtold, A., Gordon, R., Frankel, D., McRoberts, G., Norcia, A., & Sternfels, S. Development of sensitivity to information for impending collison. *Perception and Psychophysics*, 1977, *21*, 97–104.

Yonas, A., & Pick, H. An approach to the study of infant space perception. In L. Cohen & P. Salapatek (Eds.), *Infant perception: From sensation to cognition* (Vol. 2), *Perception of space, speech and sound*. New York: Academic Press, 1975.

6

Affect Development and Cognition in a Piagetian Context

Thérèse Gouin Décarie

For more than half a century, Jean Piaget's unique concern has been epistemology. As a young student of zoology, back in 1916, he dreamt of "constructing a biological epistemology based exclusively on the concept of development" (1950, Vol. 1, p. 5). In order to attain such an ambitious goal, Piaget was led to analyze the growth of intelligence, and in so doing, he began systematically to observe the schoolchild, the infant, the toddler, and eventually the adolescent. However, Piaget has always maintained that he is not a child psychologist, that his monumental work in child psychology has been only a "detour," a "by-product" (Piaget, 1970a).

Since there exists an unavoidable link between cognition and perception, Piaget and his co-workers devoted a great deal of time and energy to the study of perceptual processes (e.g., Piaget, Albertini, & Rossi, 1944–1945; Piaget, 1955–1956, 1961; Piaget & Morf, 1958a,b); in comparison, affective development occupies a rather small place in Piaget's omnia opera, which covers nearly 70 years of publications.[1] Is this because of neglect, lack of interest or prejudice? Once asked why he so seldomly referred to affective processes, Piaget replied: "Freud focused on emotions, I chose intelligence."[2] Nevertheless, Piaget has explicitly and repeatedly expressed the point that for him affectivity remains an essential dimension of human development.

---

[1] Piaget's first publication was a 1907 article on an albino sparrow: he was 11 years old. His last book, *Le Comportement, Moteur de l'Evolution*, is dated 1976.
[2] "J'ai choisi l'intelligence." Personal communication.

Thérèse Gouin Décarie · Université de Montréal, Montreal, Quebec, Canada.

PIAGET'S POINT OF VIEW ON THE RELATIONSHIP BETWEEN INTELLIGENCE AND AFFECTIVITY

The clearest statement of Piaget's position on this subject is to be found in his 1954(b) lectures at the Sorbonne. Whenever he has touched upon this theoretical issue in his ensuing works (1960, 1962b, 1967, 1968, 1974, 1976; Piaget & Inhelder, 1966), he has merely reaffirmed his initial stand. In the mimeographed report of these lectures, we find a systematic analysis of the relationship that Piaget assumes to exist between mental and emotional developments. This relationship is threefold: indissociability, functional parallelism, and interaction.

For Piaget, cognition and affectivity are inseparable from one another and they are irreducible one to the other: "There are no affective behaviors and cognitive behaviors: they are always both at the same time. These two characteristics become distinct only through analysis since abstraction permits a study of their respective mechanisms whereas in reality both aspects are present *simultaneously*" (1954b, p. 67).

Piaget stresses that if we accept that affect and cognition are two indissoluble aspects of behavior, it is a pseudoproblem to ask which comes first or which causes which. One aspect does not produce the other, nor is one aspect anterior to the other; rather they are both complementary, since neither can functionally exist without the other.

Consequently, Piaget vigorously rejects the idea that affectivity can modify or create new mental operations or that intelligence can create emotions. He readily admits that the intervention of emotional processes can accelerate, delay, or disturb mental acquisitions, but this does not mean that affectivity, as such, plays a role in the structuration of intelligence.

Piaget conceives of affectivity as the energy source upon which the good functioning of intelligence depends, as in a car where gas is necessary to make the motor run but does not affect the design of the motor: "l'affectivité constitue l'énergétique des conduites dont l'aspect cognitif se réfère aux seules structures" (Piaget & Inhelder, 1966, p. 125).

This point is illustrated by reference to the problem of spatial localization. Piaget wrote (1954b) that in a normal family environment, the infant's love for his mother makes the mother an object of interest from both a cognitive and an emotional point of view, but that it is the cognitive factor that accounts for the detailed facts that determine at any particular moment in time her localization in space:

> If love for the mother obviously constitutes the motive for the need to localize her in space, the affective motive adds nothing to the explanation of the structuration of space. Spatial structuration with its organization of displacements and localizations implies something more than just affective

motivation: there is no measurement common to both love and space. The
disorders that have been described in this field, including the many cases
reported in differential psychology, involve both factors simultaneously, but
we cannot thus conclude that one factor is antecedent to the other nor that
one is the cause of the other, and specifically we cannot reduce the factors of
localization to mere emotional factors. (p. 68)

As one can well imagine, Piaget's point of view differs greatly from
the first psychoanalytic model of mental functioning where one finds,
even at birth, the following sequences:

$$\text{Drive} \rightarrow \begin{cases} \text{absence of drive object:} \\ \text{delay of discharge} \end{cases} \rightarrow \begin{cases} \text{hallucinatory image of} \\ \text{the memory of gratification} \end{cases}$$

According to Freud, the delay of gratification, with its accompanying frustration, is a prerequisite to the emergence of the ego, and the
concepts of objects spring from primitive hallucinatory images (see
Rapaport, 1951).

Piaget's conceptualization had led him, back in 1954, to interpret
Spitz's hospitalism syndrome as being due more to a lack of sensorimotor stimulation than to a lack of love, and since that time, a great
many data seem to bear him out (e.g., Casler, 1961, 1965a,b; Yarrow,
1961; White & and Held, 1966; White, 1967; Ambrose, 1969; Brossard
& Décarie, 1971; Rutter, 1972).

Thus, the first kind of relationship between affectivity and intelligence postulated by Piaget is one of inseparability. In the second part of
this paper, I try to illustrate this first aspect by presenting a few
experimental studies in which researchers have utilized primary emotions to infer cognitive evolution.

If Piaget vigorously rejects the hypothesis of a causal relationship
between affectivity and cognition, he stresses, on the other hand, the
existence of a functional parallelism between their two evolutions:

If our previous hypotheses are correct, we shall be able to parallel, stage by
stage, the intellectual structures and the levels of emotional development.
Since no structure exists without dynamic and since, respectively, a new
form of energizing regulation must correspond to any new structure, a
certain type of cognitive structure must correspond to each new level of
emotional behavior (1954b, p. 10).

It is certainly this parallelism that constitutes, for Piaget, the most
important aspect of the relationship between mental and emotional
phenomena, and he has summarized this parallelism covering the
whole of the life span in Table I, which is seldom referred to and is
extremely difficult to translate adequately.

Of greater interest to those of us who are infancy researchers is
Piaget's discussion of the first emotional decentrations and the problem
of the object choice (e.g., 1954b, p. 33). When read in the light of the

Table I. Parallel Tables of the Stages of Intellectual and Affective Developments[a]

A	
Sensorimotor intelligence (= nonsocialized)	Intraindividual feelings (accompanying every action of the subject)
I. *Hereditary baggage* Reflexes Instincts (collections of reflexes)	*Hereditary baggage* Instinctive tendencies Emotions
II. *First acquisitions* as a function of experience during first stages of sensorimotor intelligence First habits Differentiated perceptions	*Perceptual emotions* Pleasure and pain tied to perceptions Feelings of well-being and of uneasiness
III. *Sensorimotor intelligence* (From 6 to 8 months until language acquisition in the second year)	*Elementary regulations* (As defined by Janet): activation, braking, reactions of termination, with feelings of success or failure.

B	
Verbal intelligence (conceptual = social)	Interindividual feelings (affective exchanges among people)
IV. *Preoperational representations* (Interiorization of actions in the form of thoughts that are not yet reversible)	*Intuitive emotions* (Elementary social feelings, appearance of first moral feelings)
V. *Concrete operations* (7–8 years to 10–11 years) (Elementary operations of classification and relationships = nonformal thought)	*Interiorized social emotions* Appearance of autonomous moral feelings with the intervention of the will (the just and the injust no longer depend on obedience to a rule)
VI. *Formal operations* (Beginning at 11–12 years, to be fully attained at 14–15 years): logic of propositions freed from content	*"Ideological" feelings* Interindividual feelings combine with other feelings whose aims are collective ideals Parallel elaboration of the personality: the individual assigns himself a role and goals in society

[a] From Piaget, 1954b, p. 12–13.

evolution of psychoanalytic thinking during these last 20 years, Piaget's attempt to systematically compare the appearance of the infant's focused relationship and his construction of reality appears naive and outdated. It is no accident that Piaget never published the 1954 Sorbonne lectures. At L'Institut Universitaire des Sciences de l'Education in Geneva, he was among the first young psychologists to recognize Freud's genius and the importance of psychoanalysis, and he recalls with a certain degree of nostalgia and warm humor a conference that he gave in the 1930s during which he did his best to explain Freud's hypotheses to an audience of teachers. His "flirt with psychoanalysis," as James Anthony has put it, had been a real attempt to understand Freud's works and he read them thoroughly, but probably because he had "chosen intelligence," he didn't try to remain well informed of the evolution of the psychoanalytic school as he has constantly done in other fields, such as biology, philosophy, and the computer sciences. Piaget was thus aware that his lectures were limited to Freud's original hypotheses and that as such might not be fully satisfactory in 1954.[3]

In addition to theoretical studies (e.g., Cobliner, 1965; Fraiberg, 1969; Kaplan, 1972), the last decade has seen a few experimental studies that have attempted to test the existence of a functional parallelism between certain emotional phenomena (considered within the psychoanalytic framework or within the theory of attachment) and the six stages of sensorimotor intelligence. In order to illustrate Piaget's second basic assumption, I refer to a few of these studies later on in this paper.

The third and last kind of relationship that Piaget postulates between affectivity and intelligence is one of an intricate interaction. It is perhaps in *Études Sociologiques* (1967) that we find it most clearly described. Here Piaget readopted Durkheim's thesis, which states that the individual, if left to his own resources, would attain only practical intelligence and images, whereas the play of concepts, the categories of the mind, and the rules of thought consist of "collective representations" and as such are products of continual social interaction. Piaget believes that even the interaction between just two individuals can result in lasting modifications and can be considered as a social phenomenon. Society "would be the expression of the collection of these interactions among 'n' individuals ('n' beginning at two and extending indefinitely) and at its maximum would include all actions

---

[3] Others, such as Wolff (1960), have developed in a much more satisfying manner than Piaget himself this comparison between psychoanalytic theory and the six stages of sensorimotor intelligence. It is my belief that if one wishes to attempt a theoretical parallelism between Piaget's stages of development and the Freudian theory of affectivity, the correspondence could probably be best established by reference to a neo-Freudian, Erik H. Erikson. The definition of what constitutes a stage for Piaget and a critical stage for Erikson holds many similarities.

performed by the most distant ancestors on all their social inheritors" (1967, p. 146).

Piaget's own genetic studies reveal that logic is not innate, that it is constructed gradually in the course of development precisely as a result of social interactions, especially those of reciprocity.

The developmental experiments referred to by Piaget as the basis for the establishment of a connection between logic and social development are to be found primarily in his first works: *The Language and Thought of the Child* (1923/1926b), *Judgment and Reasoning in the Child* (1924/1926a), and *The Moral Judgment in the Child* (1932), the latter being elaborated by the work of Kohlberg and his collaborators (e.g., Kohlberg, 1971; Kohlberg & Ruriel, 1971). We also find a fascinating analysis in the last chapter of *The Growth of Logical Thinking from Childhood to Adolescence* (1955), written with Inhelder: in this chapter, the authors discussed the relationship between the operational acquisitions characteristic of formal thought and the psychosocial mechanisms typical of puberty.

Piaget believes that this interactionist hypothesis does not apply at the level of sensorimotor intelligence and he wrote:

> During the sensori-motor period preceding language acquisition, we cannot yet speak of the socialization of intelligence: it is only during this period that we can speak at all of a purely individual intelligence. It is true that the child learns to imitate before learning to talk, but he imitates only those gestures that he can already perform by himself or those gestures that he has learned to understand sufficiently on his own. Sensori-motor imitation does not influence intelligence, rather it is a manifestation of intelligence.[4] As for the emotional contacts of the baby with his surroundings (smiles, etc.), these are not interactions which affect the intellect as such. (1967, pp. 155–156)

This statement does not at all mean that empirically the interactionist hypothesis is not extremely fruitful even at the level of infancy: the last studies that I present are all implicitly or explicitly inspired by this very hypothesis.

Conclusion

Piaget's point of view on the relationship between affectivity and cognition was already clearly delineated in the early 1950s, and it has not really varied since. He has never been interested in affectivity *per se* because, in his eyes, the problem of affectivity is not an epistemological

---

[4] Because of the limited scope of this article, I have refrained from discussing the complex problem of language in the light of the interactionist hypothesis. Recent data on infantile imitation, which is for Piaget at the root of the first words, show his first stages of the evolution of imitation to be in need of revision.

problem. Recently, he expressed the opinion (in his own unambiguous way) that all the theories on affectivity seem "bougrement provisoires" (damned provisional) but that hopefully, one day, physiologists will succeed in giving us precise endocrinological explanations (Bringuier, 1977, p. 79).

SOME ILLUSTRATIVE DATA

As we have just seen, Piaget's conception of the relationship between affectivity and intelligence is characterized by three main modalities: inseparability, functional parallelism, and constant interaction. In the second part of this paper, I shall try to illustrate these three modalities by summarizing a few recent studies that in one way or another refer to Piaget's theoretical standpoint. This is not a review of the literature: I have deliberately limited myself to (1) the level of sensorimotor intelligence, for the simple reason that this is the level I know best, and (2) a small number of researches that differ widely in aim and context but that, in my opinion, illustrate rather well the difficulties inherent in "mixed" investigations. Consequently, I have omitted a large number of studies treating the relationship between affectivity and intelligence, even though many of these unmentioned studies are of great interest.

Inseparability of Emotion and Cognition

Until recently, there were no systematic studies of the expression of emotions in infants, despite Darwin's (1872–1890) auspicious beginning and 100 years of ensuing research. This dearth of data might explain why we still lack an ontogeny of emotions in man, while our understanding of the evolution of facial expressions and vocal sounds in primates is beginning to be rather well documented. In spite of our lack of knowledge, we seem to have reached a certain degree of agreement as to which emotions are considered primary (Bridges, 1932, 1933; Plutchik, 1970; Tomkins, 1970; Izard, 1971; Ekman, Friesen, & Ellsworth, 1972; Lewis & Rosenblum, 1974; Sroufe & Waters, 1976).

The emotions seen as primary are interest, surprise, joy, distress, anger, fear, and disgust. To my knowledge, all of these emotions—with the exception of disgust—have been used at one time or another as indices of infant's cognitive development. Haviland (1976) has shown how Piaget himself has used affect to infer cognition and how prevalent this procedure is even in standard baby tests such as the Bayley Scales of Mental and Motor Development. It is, of course, impossible to assess

mental development by observing emotions as such: certain researchers
evaluate interest by measuring the duration of visual attention; others
infer surprise by a change of cardiac or sucking rhythm; some use
vocalizations; a great number rely in the infant's facial expression.
Charlesworth's study (1966) is of the latter kind.

In his theoretical exposé, Charlesworth (1969) carefully distinguished between surprise, startle, and orienting reflexes. He analyzed
two complex and related phenomena: *surprise*, that "logical emotion"
(Baldwin, 1894) that occurs when events present themselves unexpectedly, and *the way* in which surprise is implicated in cognitive development. Charlesworth (1969) listed six generalizations pertinent to his
argumentation:

> (1) Surprise results when an expectation is not confirmed. [Not all writers
> agree with this generalization.]
>
> (2) Surprise is sometimes manifested in certain characteristic facial expres-
> sions, sometimes by vocalization, frequently by particular changes in gross
> motor behavior, and always by certain physiological events, such as
> peripheral vasoconstriction, cerebral vasodilation, changes in respiration,
> cardiac activity, and skin potential.
>
> (3) Surprise is associated with the cessation of ongoing motor activities and of
> certain cognitive activities, such as complex symbolic processes.
>
> (4) Surprise is followed by a sudden, frequently involuntary focusing of
> attention upon the surprise stimulus accompanied by heightened conscious-
> ness of the stimulus at the expense of other stimuli.
>
> (5) Surprise diminishes as a result of the attention it arouses, i.e., most of the
> surprise responses habituate relatively rapidly once the stimulus is attended
> to. The stimulus is usually not effective in eliciting surprise reactions on
> subsequent occasions.
>
> (6) Surprise has a mixed effect on the ability to retain in memory stimulus
> aspects associated with the surprise situation. (p. 266)

The rational of the use of surprise as a clue to early mental
development is clear. On the one hand, in some cases, surprise follows
unfulfilled expectancies. This presupposes a conflict, a disequilibrium
between cognitive structures (or schemes). On the other hand, surprise
is also one of the determinants of attentional processes upon which
cognitive development depends.

In an unpublished experimental study, Charlesworth (1966)
suggested that surprise responses obtained under what he labeled "trick
conditions" are better predictors of *object concept* level than instrumental
(motor) responses obtained under the real condition.

To my own surprise, I find that the words *object concept* appear for
the first time in this paper, when I am already half through its
presentation! Must I define, then, what is an *object* for the infant? Bower
(1975) has written, "I would hazard a guess that the object-concept is the

most studied problem in infancy, bar smiling, perhaps. Certainly, every one seems to have read Chapter I of Piaget's *Construction of Reality in the Child* (1954b) where the basic phenomena are described though few seem to have penetrated to the second and third chapter of this masterpiece" (p. 38). As we shall see, it is evident that when one refers to cognitive development in early infancy within a Piagetian framework, one thinks almost exclusively of the evolution of the object concept. Trusting that Bower is also right about the fact that everyone has read the first chapter of *The Construction of Reality*, I will not present the main steps of the evolution of the object concept here nor describe the scales usually used to assess them (an excellent comparison of the various scales can be found in Uzgiris, 1976).

In his 1966 study, Charlesworth did not use a standardized scale. Depending on the child's failures or successes in giving a series of responses, he classified his subjects (58 four-to-twelve month old infants) into three levels: (1) no object concept (NOC); (2) object concept (OC); and (3) transitional, that is, a level between NOC and OC.

In fact, the data that Charlesworth reported, based on 116 observations, apply mainly to the third and fourth stage of object permanency.

The procedure used (or trick condition) involved (a) covering a desired object within view of the infant; (b) removing the object surreptitiously while it is hidden from view; (c) lifting the cover and then noting the infant's reactions. In the conventional test situation (Real Condition) the object is covered, left in its original position, and revealed when the experimenter or subject lifts the cover.

The results of the study revealed significant changes in the infants' behavior toward objects hidden from view, and the changes occurred at approximately the same age as observed by Piaget. In the trick condition, when the cover was removed and the object was no longer in its original position, OC subjects reacted differently than NOC subjects: significantly more OC subjects than NOC subjects showed a change in affect and puzzlement (or bewilderment) when they discovered that the object was absent.

When one mentions authors whose data seem to contradict Piaget's work on sensorimotor intelligence, a name that immediately comes to mind is T. G. R. Bower. In the last decade, Bower appears to have been the infancy researcher who most systematically questioned Piaget's data and hypotheses. He has been especially interested in two points: (1) the evolution of the object concept and (2) a notion closely akin to the first, the gradual coordination of sensorimotor schemes.

Bower has published prolifically, and his numerous astute experiments (e.g., 1966, 1967, 1971, 1974a,b, 1975) have met with ever-increasing recognition—and, simultaneously, with some doubts and misgivings (Gratch, 1975). His publications started a kind of "chain reaction," long overdue, which provoked a series of systematic studies (e.g., Ball & Tronick, 1971; Charette & Delorme, 1976; Dodwell, Muir, & Difranco, 1976; Sobey, 1977) that challenge Bower's conclusions in his challenge of Piaget's conclusions.

Bower's work is of interest to us in this paper because of his frequent use of emotions, such as surprise and distress, as clues to mental processes. I mention here only one such experiment, in which crying as a sign of distress was the main criterion of cognitive development.

In the first part of this experiment, as described by Bower, Broughton, and Moore (1970b), an intangible object (a red transparent plastic tetrahedron, a red transparent plastic hexahedron, or a blue transparent plastic sphere) was produced by a shadow caster (two oppositely polarized beams of light casting a double shadow of an object on a rear projection screen). An infant viewed the double shadows through polarizing goggles that made a different shadow visible to each eye. According to the authors, the innate processes of stereopsis fused the two images to make the infant think that he was seeing a solid object in front of the screen.

The infants ($N = 11$) were between 8 and 31 days. According to Bower (1974a), all the infants reached out and all the infants cried (with a latency after the first reach of 15–75 seconds) when their hands failed to make contact with the object. A comparison group of 40 infants in the same age range but not wearing goggles was run in a simular setup with real objects. None of these infants cried.

The authors stressed, that the crying could not be attributed to the goggles because the infants were preselected for their ability to wear goggles without crying during 3 minutes—much longer than any of them managed in the virtual object experiment.

In a further study (Bower, Broughton, & Moore, 1970a), the same experiment was repeated with a larger sample of subjects ($N = 80$) and a larger range of ages (from 7 days to 6 months). The virtual object situation produced frustration and tears at every age up to 5 months. Bowers considered these emotional reactions as proof of intentionality in the reaching behavior of neonates and concluded that oculomanual coordination is innate.

A few questions could be asked here. Was a 3-minute tolerance of goggles sufficient to ensure that later crying could not be explained by discomfort associated with the apparatus? Reactions to real objects were always studied without goggles. The stereopsis situation was not really identical to the real object situation in terms of demands to the visual system. Images of the virtual object create a conflict between accommodation and convergence not normally produced by a real object. When the virtual object is seen as unique, it is a little out of focus; when the shadows on the screen are well focalized by the infant, there should be some diplopia. This could be a second source of discomfort that is likely to produce crying in infants or neonates.

A pilot study by Charette and Delorme (1976) gives some weight to these alternative explanations of Bower's results. They replicated the experiment but with goggles much more comfortable than those used by Bower. Bower's goggles were made of two polaroid filters fixed to a velcro band that circled the head; Charette and Delorme used a kind of light helmet with the polaroid filters that did not even touch the baby's face. The real object as well as the virtual object was seen through the goggles. A further experimental condition was added to verify the possibility of an effect of discomfort related to the stereopisis condition. The virtual object was produced by means of a half-silvered mirror tilted at a 45° vertical angle in front of the subject. Independent control of lighting in different parts of the device permitted simultaneous vision of the virtual object and of the hand without requiring goggles.

In this study, 14 subjects aged from 18 to 38 weeks were submitted to the virtual object situation. Motor reactions to the virtual object were comparable to those observed by Bower *et al*. (1970a,b), but even in the youngest subjects, no cries or tears were observed that could be associated with the intangibility of the object. However, while these results do not definitively rule out Bower's interpretations since only 5 subjects were under 6 months old, they do suggest that the distress associated with the intangibility of the object is not as general as Bower thought it was.

The Problem of a Functional Parallelism between Some Emotional Phenomena and Object Permanency

In the last decade, quite a few studies have attempted to establish a relationship between the evolution of some psychosocial phenomena (in which the affect component is obvious) and the different stages of sensorimotor intelligence. The phenomena under scrutiny have usually been "fear of strangers" and "separation anxiety" (or protest), and the category of intelligence analyzed has been object permanency.

In this paper, I have omitted the separation protest studies (Littenberg, Steven, Tulkin, & Kagan, 1971; Lester, Kotelchuch, Spelke, Sellers, & Klein, 1974) and retain only two experiments on fear of strangers and object permanency which were carried out simultaneously but independently. Their unexpected results are all the more interesting and must be "explained away."

Scarr and Salapatek (1970), in their study on *Patterns of Fear Development during Infancy*, used Schaffer's (1966) series of six steps to elicit fear of strangers and two of the seven cognitive scales developed by Uzgiris and Hunt (1975): permanency of object (P-O) and means–end (M-E). Each step in the stranger's approach was scored on a three-point scale of fear (1 = no evidence of fear; 2 = sober, cautious, quits ongoing activity; 3 = fretting, crying, fleeing to mother). There were 91 infants, 2–23 months old. The authors' conclusions were the following:

> In general, no relationship was found between object permanence skills and the fear of strangers during the first two years, once age variance had been removed. At any given age, infants with precocious object concepts were not more fearful than those with a less well developed concept of object permanence. If anything, the less precocious infants tended to be more fearful. . . . No threshold could be identified in the cognitive scale that would predict the presence or absence of fear of strangers. (pp. 81–82)

In Brossard's (1974), experiment, the stranger's mode of approach was inspired by Morgan and Ricciuti's (1969) five-phase procedure, and the Piagetian scale used was derived from the unpublished work of Saint-Pierre (1962). The latter researcher modified Décarie's (1962) object concept scale that was restricted to inanimate objects so that it could also be applied to the vanishing human person. The method used to evaluate the infant's reaction to the stranger was a complex technique—both quantitatively and qualitatively—based on fine and gross motor responses, facial expressions, and vocalizations. It is fully described in Goulet's (1974) study on fear of strangers and the infant's conception of causality.

The age levels were 32, 40, 48, and 56 weeks, with 8 subjects in each age group for a total of 32 subjects in the full sample. Brossard's main conclusion is the same as that of Scarr and Salapatek: "Our results indicate that at the age of 7½ to 13 months no clear correspondence exists between the infant's affective reactions to strangers and his cognitive development as evaluated in terms of his conceptualization of the human object" (Brossard, 1974, p. 116).

These results contradict Spitz (1950, 1955), Spitz and Cobliner (1965), Schaffer and Callender (1959), Schaffer and Emerson (1964), and Bowlby (1960, 1969), who assumed that a certain stage of object permanence must be reached before a negative reaction to strangers can appear.[5] Do they also contradict Piaget's assumption of a functional

---

[5] Though they found no correlation between object permanence and fear of strangers, Paradise and Curcio (1974), with a sample of thirty 9–10 months male infants, did find that 13 of the 15 subjects demonstrating fear had reached Stage VI in person permanence, while this was true of only five of the nonfearful subjects. Because the authors admitted that "Typically the intensity of fear was mild and might be more accurately described as wariness" (p. 481), I am inclined to interpret these results as indicating a

parallelism? Are these unexpected results due, as Gratch (1975) has stated, to the premature development of object concept scales based on Piaget's theory? When Gratch (1976) wrote that "The leap [between theory and the construction of the scale] would be warranted if object-concept scale performance were found to have important correlates, but at present, no compelling correlations have been found" (p. 69), he was quite right about the absence of clear-cut correlations, but he did not consider the possibility that this absence of correlations might be due to the fact that the dimension that one seeks correlation with might not have the developmental significance that the object-concept has.

In other words, fear of strangers might not after all be the developmental milestone that it has always been considered to be since Spitz (1950) unfortunately labeled it "the eight month anxiety."

The findings recently published by Solomon and Décarie (1976) strongly challenge the universality of the negative response. Their study shows that the positive response of infants between 8 and 12 months when confronted by three strangers (one male and two females) within a maximum of 10 days is a stable one. The negative response is not. [6] This finding seems to indicate that negative reactions to strangers might be just as, meaningful as, but not more meaningful than, negative reactions to father or to siblings, or (as Rheingold and Eckerman, (1973), have pointed out) to mothers. While many researchers would not agree with the foregoing, there is a growing consensus (see Ainsworth, 1973; Sroufe & Waters, 1976) that the response to strangers is highly subject to situational variables that make the appearance of a fearful or friendly response unpredictable. It may be possible eventually to correlate the Piagetian scales with the emergence of a fear system (Emde, Gaensbauer, & Harmon, 1976) in 8–12-month-old infants and thus illustrate the correlation between two profound developmental milestones. However, to reject the object concept scales as being unreliable because they do not correlate with a behavior as unreliable as stranger fear seems, at the least, premature.

---

relationship between person permanence and wariness, rather than between person permanence and fear of strangers. We agree with Sroufe (1977) when he distinguishes wariness from fear of strangers and defines wariness as an organizational construct, which has significance as "a balance for the infant's strong approach and exploration tendencies" (p. 732). Wariness does not necessarily imply fear and could well be conceived as a cognitive attitude: in French, wariness is *circonspection*.

[6] In a recent article, Sroufe (1977) criticized this study on a number of points. The criticisms seem to be based, however, on a profound misunderstanding of our methodology. For instance, Sroufe reports our study as involving one stranger whereas in fact there were three. He reports that following our scoring system "an infant that was positive throughout the first 2 min, then clearly distressed at pick up, still would be classed as positive" (737). On the contrary, our scoring system was designed specifically to prevent this kind of error.

When Piaget postulates a functional parallelism between affectivity and cognition, he obviously refers to developmental phenomena that are universal and constant and species-specific. He is not interested in individual differences, except maybe when it can be demonstrated that in spite of them, the developmental sequences he has described remain irreversible.

Interaction between Emotional and Mental Processes

In *Les mécanismes perceptifs* (1961), Piaget rejected the hypothesis of a direct filiation between perception and cognition and suggested instead a reciprocal interaction that is already active during the first weeks of life. Though he also assumes an interactionist relationship in the case of affectivity and cognition, he unexpectedly seems to believe, as I have previously mentioned in the first part of this paper, that this interaction does not take place during the two first years of life but intervenes only at the level of preoperational thought. Recent studies on infants have brought to light some fascinating data that might be explained through such an interaction, though the exact developmental processes that come into play are still far from being understood.

I will conclude the second and last part of this paper by mentioning briefly two such studies, but first, I must replace them in the Piagetian context. Piaget has repeatedly stressed the importance of the human being, not only as an essential element of the emotional universe of the infant but also as a privileged agent of cognitive acquisitions:

> The other person is of course an emotional object to the highest degree but at the same time it is the most interesting cognitive object, the most alive, the most unexpected, at this level the most instructive one, an object, I repeat, which is the source of perception, of actions of any kind, of imitation, of causality, of spatial structuring. Thus, the other person is an object which implies a multitude of exchanges in which cognitive as well as affective factors play a role, and if this object is of paramount importance in one of these respects, it is, I think, equally important in the other. (1954b, p. 66)

This unique kind of animate object (and especially the person-mother) happens to be on a number of occasions at the point of intersection of the basic sensorimotor schemes:

> The mother can be sucked (sucking scheme)[7] and heard (auditory scheme). She smells (olfactory scheme) and even tastes something (gustative scheme). She can be grasped (prehensive scheme) and she can take and rock (kinesthetic scheme) and caress (tactile scheme). Finally, she is one the things

---

[7] To follow Piaget's suggestion in a footnote (Piaget, 1970b, p. 705), we now use the term scheme (plural schemes) instead of the more usual term schema (plural schemata).

which enter the visual field of the baby most frequently (visual scheme) and in many contexts: sometimes she is far away and cannot be grasped, sometimes she can be seen but not heard, sometimes she can be heard without being seen, she changes in color, form (with or without hat) and even is size (near or far). (Décarie, 1965, pp. 25–26)

Thus, she activates simultaneously more than any other element of the infant's outer world (certainly more than the breast) the different schemes through which the infant apprehends reality and should therefore be among the first things to be conceived of as permanent, substantial, identical, and external to the self, that is, to become an object in the "Piagenetic" language.

The hypothesis by which the conceptualization of the human person—while developing in parallel with the inanimate object concept—begins and is completed first simply means that "usually a 8–9 month old baby might be capable of finding his mother in a simple hide and seek game, but not of retrieving an interesting toy comparably hidden" (Bell, 1970, p. 292). This hypothesis, first advanced by Piaget 40 years ago (Piaget, 1937/1954a, p. 50), has been confirmed by Saint-Pierre (1962) (see also Décarie, 1966; Bell, 1968, 1970; Lamb, 1973). [8]

This hypothesis implies a very particular kind of "décalage," which is in itself an intriguing epistemological problem, for I do not believe that it can simply be assimilated to a classical horizontal décalage. The basis of the décalage might prove of a tremendous importance in what has been called "the learning of the parent"—a process about which we still know very little and which, as Lewis's work suggests, seems closely related to the learning of the self (e.g., Lewis & Brooks, 1974, 1975).

The dimension of identity that is slowly emerging as an important aspect of the object concept (Gardner, 1971; Gratch & Evans, 1972; Lecompte & Gratch, 1972; Saal, 1974; Bower, Broughton, & Moore, 1971; Moore, Borton, & Darby, 1975; Moore & Meyers, 1975) might, in fact, be at the root of this permanency décalage. At our own lab, Ricard (1976) is working along these lines, prompted by the hypotheses that an animate

---

[8] In the first experiment of a recent study (Jackson, E., Campos, J. J. and Fischer, K. W. The question of décalage between object permanence and person permanence, *Developmental Psychology* [1977]) the authors conclude that there is no décalage when the task demands are equated. In this important experiment, the apparatus is such that the *whole* inanimate object is seen by the infant, but only *part* of person (the face) can be seen. Therefore, only for the very first item where both objects are partially hidden, are the task demands really equal. Moreover the possibility of a critical décalage (because it is akin to a vertical décalage) between stages V and VI is precluded by the experimental design: the last item tested being that of *one* hidden displacement which according to Piaget, characterizes not stage VI but the end of stage V (Piaget, 1937/1954a, p. 70). The results of the second experiment of this study are much more conclusive."

object is easier to identify than an inanimate one and that logically and developmentally, identity should precede permanence.

Bell's (1970) ingenious experiment on the relationship of infant—mother attachment to the development of the object concept appears as a good example of an interaction between affectivity and cognition. Her project was a short-term longitudinal study in which she devised two scales, the first to test for object permanency and the second to test for person permanency, that "social concept," as Lewis and Brooks (1975, p. 106) put it. In Bell's study, 33 babies were tested, at home, three times between the age of 8½ and 11 months. One week after the third testing session, the babies were introduced to the strange situation designed by Ainsworth and Wittig (1969) to evaluate attachment behavior. The results, as summarized by the author herself in her Ph. D. thesis (1968), were rather clear-cut:

> Two-thirds of the sample had a positive décalage[9], whereas the remainder had a negative or no décalage. A notable relationship between type of décalage and quality of attachment was observed: babies who had a positive décalage displayed active efforts to establish contact, proximity, or interaction with the mother, whereas babies with a negative or no décalage showed either little interest in proximity and contact-seeking or reacted with highly ambivalent behavior towards her. Finally, there is evidence that the type of décalage is related to the rate of development of object-permanence. Babies with a consistently positive décalage are not only accelerated in the development of person-permanence, but also complete the development of the concept of the permanence of inanimate objects sooner than do infants with a negative or no décalage. (p. iii)

and Bell (1970) concluded:

> There is an important dimension affecting the development of the object concept which transcends socioeconomic boundaries and often goes unexamined in studies aiming to isolate the essential features of "enrichment" or "deprivation." Specifically, the findings of the present study lead us to the hypothesis that the quality of a baby's interaction with his mother is one of the crucial dimensions of "environmental influence" to affect this type of sensori-motor development. (p. 310)

Additional support for the hypothesis that there exists an interrelationship between development of the object concept and development of the infant–mother relationship has been provided by Serafica and Uzgiris (1971) in their study of 38 infants between 4 and 12 months. They defined the tie of the infant to the mother not in terms of pat-

---

[9] A positive décalage is one in which person-permanency precedes object-permanency, a negative décalage is simply the reverse.

terns of attachment but within the broader context of the construct "interpersonal relationship." They hypothesized the development of this relationship as a progression from a state of relative undifferentiation to increasing differentiation and hierarchic integration among main components, namely: (1) discrimination, (2) affect, (3) approach, and (4) expectancy.

Each element was scored while the infant was placed in a series of natural situation, such as being given toys, asking for toys, feeding, and being left by the mother. For the entire sample, with age held constant, the results indicated a significant correlation between scores on the IPDS for object permanence and scores on the interpersonal relationship.

Correlations between object concept and each of the four posited components of the relationship were also analyzed during different periods of the infant's development and were found to vary during the third and fourth quarter. The authors concluded that a changing reciprocal interaction exists between the infant–mother relationship and object concept during the first year of life.

Notwithstanding their interest, what these studies do not yet do is tell us what are the basic affective processes and cognitive processes that interact with one another. By distinguishing components within the infant–mother relationship, Serafica and Uzgiris's study appears as a step in the right direction; nevertheless, it is not only the infant–mother relationship that needs unraveling but also the object concept, whose simplicity is deceitful, as researchers such as Lucas and Uzgiris (1976) and many others have found out.

BY WAY OF CONCLUSION

Up to now, infancy researchers interested in mental evolution within a Piagetian context have focused almost exclusively on the problem of object permanency, so much so that we are beginning to forget that object concept is much more than object *permanency*. It includes the development of exteriority, of identity, of substance—and cognitive development itself is much more than object concept; it is also the evolution of time, space, causality, the problem of imitation, play, and language.

We seem to have reached a crossroad. On the one hand, we are badly in need of systematic studies in one precise dimension of cognition that will tell us more about the basic processes intervening in the development of that well-delineated notion. On the other hand, if we ever hope to be able to describe the 3-month-old infant or the 1-year-old child as a whole, and not "en pièces détachées," we have to work toward an apparent contradictory goal by studying simultaneously the perceptual, mental, and affective components of true developmental phenomena. Maybe Kagan's suggested strategy (see this volume) is one way out of this dilemma, but whatever we choose to do in our own researches, I believe that Piaget's data and hypotheses will sometime, somewhere, somewhat influence us.

REFERENCES

Ainsworth, M. D. S. The development of mother–infant attachment. In B. M. Caldwell & H. N. Ricciuti (Eds.), *Review of Child Development Research* (Vol. 3). Chicago: University of Chicago Press, 1973.

Ainsworth, M., & Wittig, B. Attachment and exploratory behavior of one-year-olds in a strange situation. In B. M. Foss (Ed.), *Determinants of infant behavior* (Vol. 4). New York: Wiley, 1969, pp. 11–136.

Ambrose, A. *Stimulation in early infancy*. London and New York, Academic Press, 1969.

Baldwin, J. M. *Handbook of psychology: feeling and will*. New York, Henry Holt, 1894.

Ball, W., & Tronick, E. Infant response to impending collision: Optical and real. *Science*, 1971, *171*, 818–820.

Bell, S. The relationship of infant–mother attachment to the development of the concept of object permanence. Unpublished doctoral thesis, Johns Hopkins University, 1968.

Bell, S. The development of the concept of object as related to infant–mother attachment. *Child Development*, 1970, *41*, 291–311.

Bower, T. G. R. The visual world of infants. *Scientific American*, 1966, *215*(6), 90–92.

Bower, T. G. R. The development of object-permanence: Some studies of existence constancy. *Perception and Psychophysics*, 1967, *2*(9), 411–418.

Bower, T. G. R. The object in the world of the infant. *Scientific American*, 1971, *225*,(4), 30–38.

Bower, T. G. R. *Development in infancy*. San Francisco: Freeman, 1974. (a)

Bower, T. G. R. Repetition in development. *Merrill-Palmer Quarterly*, 1974, *20*, 303–318. (b)

Bower, T. G. R. Infant perception of the third dimension and object concept development. In L. Cohen, & P. Salapatek, (Eds.), *Infant perception: From sensation to cognition* (Vol. 2). New York: Academic Press, 1975, pp. 33–50.

Bower, T. G. R., Broughton, J. M., & Moore, M. K. The coordination of visual and tactual input in infants. *Perception and psychophysics*, 1970, *8*, 51–53. (a)

Bower, T. G. R., Broughton, J. M., & Moore, M. K. Demonstration of intention in the reaching behaviour of neonate humans. *Nature*, 1970, *228*(5272), 679–681. (b)

Bowlby, J. Separation anxiety. *International Journal of Psycho-Analysis, 1960, 41*, 89–113.

Bowlby, J. *Attachment*. New York: Basic Books, 1969.

Bridges, K. Emotional development in early infancy. *Child Development*, 1932, *3*, 324–341.

Bridges, K. Emotional development in the young child. Unpublished doctoral thesis, Université de Montréal, 1933.

Bringuier, J. P. *Conversations libres avec Jean Piaget*. Paris: Robert Laffont, 1977.

Brossard, M. The infant's conception of object permanence and his reactions to strangers. In T. G. Décarie (Ed.), *The infant's reaction to strangers*. New York: International Universities Press, 1974.

Brossard, M. & Décarie, T. The effects of three kinds of perceptual-social stimulation on the development of institutionalized infants. *Early Child Development and Care*, 1971, 111–130.

Casler, L. Maternal deprivation: A critical review of the literature. *Monographs of the Society for Research in Child Development*, 1961, *26*, 1–64.

Casler, L. The effects of extra tactile stimulation on a group of institutionalized infants. *Genetic Psychology Monograph*, 1965, *71*, 137–175. (a)

Casler, L. The effects of supplementary verbal stimulation on a group of institutionalized infants. *Journal of Child Psychology and Psychiatry*, 1965, *6*, 19–27. (b)

Charette, J. M. & Delorme, A. Réaction du jeune enfant de 4 à 6 mois à un object virtuel. Paper presented at: Congrès de l'Association canadienne française pour l'avancement des sciences. Sherbrooke. 1976.

Charlesworth, W. R. Development of the object concept: A methodological study. Paper presented at the meeting of the American Psychological Association, New York, 1966.

Charlesworth, W. R. The role of surprise in cognitive development. In D. Elkind & J. H. Flavell (Eds.), *Studies in cognitive development*. New York: Oxford University Press, 1969.

Cobliner, W. C. The Geneval School of genetic psychology and psychoanalysis: Parallels and counter parts. In R. A. Spitz and W. G. Cobliner (Eds.), *The first year of life*. New York: International Universities Press, 1965.

Darwin, C. *The expressions of the emotions in man and animals*. London: Murray, 1890. (Originally published, 1872.)

Décarie, T. *Intelligence and affectivity in early childhood*. New York: International Universities Press, 1965.

Décarie, T. Intelligence sensori-motrice et psychologie du premier áge. In F. Bresson & M. Montmollin (Eds.), *Psychologie et* épistémologie génétiques. Paris: Dunod, 1966.

Dodwell, P. C., Muir, D., & Difranco, D. Responses of infants to visually presented objects. *Science*, 1976, *194*, 209–211.

Ekman, P., Freisen, W. & Ellsworth, P. *Emotion in the human face*. New York: Pergamon, 1972.

Emde, R., Gaensbauer, T., & Harmon, R. Emotional expression in infancy. *Psychological Issues* (Vol. 10, No. 1, Mon. 37). New York: International Universities Press, 1976.

Fraiberg, S. Libidinal object constancy and mental representation. *Psychoanalytic study of the child*, 1969, *24*, 9–47.

Gardner, J. K. The development of object identity in the first six months of human infancy. Paper presented at the meeting of the Society for Research in Child Development, Minneapolis, 1971.

Goulet, J. The infant's conception of causality and his reactions to strangers. In T. G. Décarie (Ed.), *The infant's reaction to strangers*. New York: International Universities Press, 1974.

Gratch, G. Recent studies based on Piaget's view of object concept development. In L. Cohen & P. Salapatek (Eds.), *Infant Perception: From sensation to cognition* (Vol. 2). New York: Academic Press, 1975, pp. 51–99.

Gratch, G., & Evans, W. F. The stage IV error in Piaget's theory of object concept development: Difficulties in object conceptualization or spatial localization? *Child Development*, 1972, *43*, 682–688.

Haviland, J. Looking smart: The relationship between affect and intelligence in infancy. In M. Lewis, (Ed.), *Origins of intelligence*. New York and London: Plenum Press, 1976, pp. 353–377.

Jackson, E., Campos, J., & Fischer, K. The question of decalage between object permanence and person permanence. *Developmental Psychology*, in press.

Kaplan, L. Object constancy in the light of Piaget's vertical decalage. *Bulletin of the Menninger Clinic*, 1972, *36*, 322–334.

Kohlberg, L. From is to ought. In M. Lewis (Ed.), *Cognitive development and epistemology*. London and New York: Academic Press, 1971, pp. 151–235.

Kohlberg, L., & Ruriel, E. *Recent research in moral development*. New York: Holt, 1971.

Lamb, M. E. The effects of maternal deprivation on the development of the concepts of object and person. *Journal of Behavioural Science*, 1973, *1*(5), 355–364.

Lecompte, G. K., & Gratch, G. Violation of a rule as a method of diagnosing infants' level of object concept. *Child Development*, 1972, *43*, 385–396.

Lester, B., Kotelchuch, M., Spelke, E., Sellers, S., & Klein, R. Separation protest in Guatemalan infants: Cross-cultural and cognitive findings. *Developmental Psychology*, 1974, *10*, 79–85.

Lewis, M., & Brooks, J. Self, other and fear: Infants' reactions to people. In M. Lewis & L. Rosenblum (Eds.), *Fear: The origins of behavior* (Vol. 2). New York: Wiley, 1974.

Lewis, M., & Brooks, J. Infant social perception: A constructivist view. In L. Cohen, & P. Salapatek, (Eds.), *Infant perception: From sensation to cognition*. New York: Academic Press, 1975, pp. 101–148.

Lewis, M. & Rosenblum, L. A. *The origins of fear*. New York: Wiley, 1974.

Littenberg, R., Steven, R., Tulkin, A., & Kagan, J. Cognitive components of separation anxiety. *Developmental Psychology*, 1971, *4*(3), 387–388.

Lucas, T. C., & Uzgiris, I. Spatial factors in the development of object concept. *Developmental Psychology*, 1977, *13*(5).

Moore, M. K., Borton, R., & Darby, B. L. Visual tracking in young infants: Evidence for object identity or object permanence? Paper presented at the meeting of the Society for Research in Child Development, Denver, 1975.

Moore, M. K., & Myers, G. D. The development of object permanence from visual tracking to total hidings: two new stages. Paper presented at the meeting of the Society for Research in Child Development, Denver, 1975.

Morgan, G. A., & Ricciuti, H. N. Infant's response to strangers during the first year. In B. M. Foss (Ed.), *Determinants of infant behaviour* (Vol.4). New York: Wiley, 1969.

Paradise, E. B., & Curcio, F. Relationship of cognitive and affective behaviors to fear of strangers in male infants. *Developmental Psychology*, 1974, *10*(4), 476–483.

Piaget, J. *Judgment and reasoning in the child*. New York: Harcourt Brace, 1926. (Originally published, 1924.) (a)

Piaget, J. *The language and thought of the child*. London: Kegan Paul, 1926. (Originally published, 1923.) (a)

Piaget, J. *The moral judgment of the child*. New York: Harcourt Brace, 1932.

Piaget, J. La psychanalyse et le développement intellectuel. *Revue française de psychanalyse*, 1933, *6*, 404–408.

Piaget, J. *Introduction à l'épistémologie génétique* (Vol. 1), *La pensée mathématique*. Paris: Presses Universitaires de France, 1950.

Piaget, J. *The origins of intelligence in children*. New York: International Universites Press, 1952. (Originally published, 1936.)

Piaget, J. *The construction of reality in the child*. New York: Basic Books, 1954. (Originally published, 1937.) (a)

Piaget, J. *Les relations entre l'affectivité et l'intelligence dans le développement mental de l'enfant*. Paris, C.D.U., 1954.(b)

Piaget, J. Recherches sur le développement des perceptions. XXII. Essai d'une nouvelle interprétation probabiliste des effets de centration de la loi de Weber et de celle des centrations relatives. *Archives de Psychologie* (Genève), 1955–1956, *35*, 1–24.

Piaget, J. The general problems of the psychobiological development of the child. In J. M. Tanner & B. Inhelder (Eds.), *Discussions on child development* (Vol. 4). New York: International Universities Press, 1960, pp. 3–27.

Piaget, J. *Les mécanismes perceptifs: Modèles probabilistes, analyse génétique, relations avec l'intelligence*. Paris: Presses Universitaires de France, 1961.

Piaget, J. *Play, dreams and imitation in childhood*. New York: Norton, 1962. (Originally published, 1945.) (a)

Piaget, J. Will and action. *Bulletin of the Menninger Clinic*, 1962, 26(3), 138–145. (b)

Piaget, J. Le développement des perceptions en fonction de l'âge. In P. Fraisse & J. Piaget (Eds.), *Traité de psychologie expérimentale, : La perception*. Paris: Presses universitaires de France, 1963, pp. 1–57.

Piaget, J. *Études sociologiques*. Geneva: Droz, 1967.

Piaget, J. Le point de vue de Piaget. *International Journal of Psychology*, 1968, 3(4), 281–299.

Piaget, J. *L'épistémologie génétique*. Paris: Presses Universitaires de France, 1970. (a)

Piaget, J. Piaget's theory. In K. Mussen, (Ed.), *Carmichael's Child Psychology*. New York: Wiley, 1970, pp. 703–732. (b)

Piaget, J. "Piaget now," Times Ed. Suppl. Feb. 1972 cited by S. Modgil, *Piagetian Research: a handbook of recent studies*. New York: NFER, 1974.

Piaget, J. *Le comportement, moteur de l'évolution*. Paris: Gallimard, 1976.

Piaget, J., Albertini, B. von, & Rossi, M. Recherches sur le développement des perceptions: IV. Essai d'interprétation probabiliste de la loi de Weber et de celle des centrations relatives. *Archives de Psychologie* (Genève), 1944–1945, 30, 95–138.

Piaget, J., & Inhelder, B. *The growth of logical thinking from childhood to adolescence*. New York: Basic Books, 1958. (Originally published, 1955.)

Piaget, J., & Morf, A. Les isomorphismes partiels entre les structures logiques et les structures perceptives. In J. S. Bruner, F. Bresson, A. Morf, & J. Piaget (Eds.), *Logique et perception: Études d'épistémologie génétique* (Vol. 6). Paris: P.U.F., 1958, pp. 49–116. (a)

Piaget, J., & Morf, A. Les "préinférences" perceptives et leurs relations avec les schèmes sensori-moteurs et opératoires. In J. S. Bruner, F. Bresson, A. Morf, & J. Piaget (Eds.), *Logique et perception. Études d'épistémologie génétique* (Vol. 6). Paris: P.U.F., 1958, pp. 117–155. (b)

Piaget, J., & Inhelder, B. *La psychologie de l'enfant*. Paris: Presses Universitaires de France, 1966.

Plutchik, R. Emotions, evolution and adaptive processes. In M. Arnold (Ed.), *Feelings and emotions*. New York: Academic Press, 1970, pp. 3–24.

Rapaport, D. *Organization and pathology of thought*. New York: Columbia University Press, 1951.

Rheingold, H., & Eckerman, C. O. Fear of the stranger: A critical examination. In H. W. Reese (Ed.), *Advances in Child Development and Behavior*. New York: Academic Press, 1973.

Ricard, M. Le développement de l'identité et son rapport avec la permanence dans l'élaboration de la notion d'objet. Unpublished dissertation proposal, Université de Montréal, 1976.

Rutter, M. *Maternal deprivation reassessed*. New York: Penguin Science of Behavior, 1972.

Saal, D. A study of the development of object concept in infancy by varying the degree of discrepancy between the disappearing and reappearing object. Unpublished dissertation proposal, University of Houston, 1974.

Saint-Pierre, J. Étude des différences entre la recherche active de la personne humaine et celle de l'objet inanimé. Unpublished thesis, Université de Montréal, 1962.

Scarr, S., & Salapatek, P. Patterns of fear development during infancy. *Merrill-Palmer Quarterly of Behavior and Development*, 1970, 16, 53–90.

Schaffer, H. R. The onset of fear of strangers and the incongruity hypothesis. *Journal of Child Psychology Psychiatry and Allied Disciplines*, 1966, 7, 95–106.

Schaffer, H. R., & Callender, W. M. Psychological effects of hospitalization in infancy. *Pediatrics*, 1959, 24, 528–539.

Schaffer, H. R., & Emerson, P. E. The development of social attachment in infancy. *Monograph of the Society for Research in Child Development*, 1964, (Serial No. 94), *29*(3), 1–77.

Serafica, F., & Uzgiris, I. Infant–mother relationship and object concept. *Proceedings of the Annual Convention of the American Psychological Association*, 1971, *6*, 141–142.

Sobey, K. Perception and cognition in the construction of the object concept. Unpublished manuscript, 1977.

Solomon, R., & Décarie, T. Fear of strangers: A developmental milestone or an over-studied phenomenon? *Canadian Journal of Behavioral Science*, 1976, *8*(4), 351–362.

Spitz, R. A. Anxiety in infancy: A study of its manifestation in the first year of life. *International Journal of Pscyho-Analysis*, *1950*, *31*, 138–143.

Spitz, R. A. A note on the extrapolation of ethological findings. *International Journal of Psycho-Analysis*, 1955, *36*, 162–165.

Spitz, R. A., & Cobliner, W. G. *The first year of life*. New York: International Universities Press, 1965.

Sroufe, L. A. Wariness of strangers and the study of infant development. *Child Development*, 1977, *48*, 731–746.

Sroufe, L. A., & Waters, E. The ontogenesis of smiling and laughter: A perspective on the organization of development in infancy. *Psychological Review*, 1976, *83*(3), 173–189.

Sroufe, L. A., & Wunsch, J. P. The development of laughter in the first year of life. *Child Development*, 1972, *43*, 1326–1344.

Tomkins, S. Affect as the primary motivational system. In M. Arnold (Ed.), *Feelings and emotions*. New York: Academic Press, 1970, pp. 101–110.

Uzgiris, I. Organization of sensori-motor intelligence. In M. Lewis, (Ed.), *Origins of intelligence*. New York: Plenum Press, 1976, pp. 123–163.

Uzgiris, I., & Hunt, McV. *Assessment in infancy: Ordinal scales of psychological development*. Urbana: University of Illinois Press, 1975.

White, B. An experimental approach to the effects of experience on early human development. In J. P. Hill (Ed.), *Minnesota Symposia on Child Psychology*. Toronto: Clark, 1967, pp. 201–226.

White, B., & Held, R. Plasticity of sensorimotor development in the human infant. In J. F. Rosenblith & W. Allinsmith (Eds.), *Causes of behavior: Readings in child development and educational psychology*. Boston: Allyn and Bacon, 1966, pp. 60–71.

Wolff, P. H. The developmental psychologies of Jean Piaget and psychoanalysis. *Psychological Issues, Monograph 5*. New York: International Universities Press, 1960.

Yarrow, L. J. Maternal deprivation: Towards an empirical and conceptual re-evaluation. *Psychological Bulletin*, 1961, *58*, 459–490.

7

Self-Knowledge and Emotional Development

MICHAEL LEWIS AND JEANNE BROOKS

When Benjamin was 2 years and 9 months, his family moved from one house to another. Benjamin had spent all of his life in the first house. One week after moving to the new house, he was asked whether he liked the new house. "This house doesn't taste good," he said, as he stuck out his tongue.

This example of a child, not yet 3 years old, who is able to express his emotions quite eloquently, highlights several features related to the development of emotional states. First, children prior to 3 years of age are capable of understanding at least some questions pertaining to feelings (in this case, "How do you like . . . ?"). Second, young children are capable of making at least limited verbal replies related to feelings (in this case, ". . . doesn't taste good"). Third, children recognize that feelings have a location and that this location is inside the body (in this case, the sticking out of his tongue and the use of the word *taste* were an indication that the location of the feeling was inside his body, specifically in his mouth).

This child's verbal and expressive behavior represents an early example of the acquisition and understanding of emotional experience. Our use of the word *experience* rather than *expression* is deliberate; we wish to distinguish between the expression of an emotion and the emotional experience.

MICHAEL LEWIS and JEANNE BROOKS · The Infant Laboratory, Institute for Research in Human Development, Educational Testing Service, Princeton, New Jersey. This paper was supported in part by a NIMH grant #5 R01 MH 24849-03 and a grant from the Foundation for Child Development.

The example of Benjamin's response to his moving illustrates another phenomenon besides his realization of his emotional state. Specifically, Benjamin indicated an awareness of himself as a distinct entity. By sticking out his tongue when stating that the house did not taste good, he indicated that the house did not taste good *to him*, not that the house in general did not taste good. We believe that such self-knowledge is necessary for the experience of emotion. This hypothesis is developed in the following comments. In general, we believe that self-awareness is an organizing principle around which infants develop the ability to experience emotion rather than to express emotion.

A DEFINITION OF EMOTION

Our thoughts concerning emotion and emotional development are influenced primarily by two men: James (1890) and Darwin (1872). Darwin and the tradition that followed him emphasized the surface expression of emotion rather than feeling or emotional state. In Darwin's view, a particular event—some external situation—elicits both the surface expression and the emotional state. In this tradition, the elicitor produces both the emotional state and the surface expression. Thus, state and expression are intimately connected; for example, a happy face would be equivalent to a happy feeling. However, it is not clear that there is any one-to-one correspondence between emotional expression and emotional states. For example, the neonate has been shown to have penile erections and to smile during REM sleep, but we would be reluctant to say that the newborn is experiencing a happy state or having a happy dream. Likewise, we might laugh at the boss's joke, which we may not find particularly funny. The laughter is not indicative of a happy or amused state. At best, there may be some one-to-one relationship between expression and state in two conditions: (1) for the primary emotions, since, as Ekman and Izard (1971) have shown, the primary facial expressions, such as fear, anger, and disgust, are present in most cultures and seem to have universal meaning, and (2) in early infancy, since an elicitor may produce a synchronous or nondifferentiated expression and state. However, for other emotions, those considered derived rather than primary (Tomkins, 1962, 1963), and for later ages, the concordance of expression and state may be less viable theoretically and has been unproved empirically (see the Introduction of this volume for a more thorough discussion of these issues).

James (1890) defined emotions as "the bodily changes [that] follow directly the perception of the exciting fact and our feeling of the same changes as they occur is the emotion" (p. 449). In James's view, in order for one to experience an emotion, a precipitating event (exciting fact) must occur and is an event which causes a bodily change. The conscious experience of that bodily change is the emotional feeling. Thus, emotion is not the precipitating event, nor the bodily change associated with that event, but is the conscious feeling of that bodily change. While the nature of the bodily change has been questioned [for example, James believed more in the importance of muscular changes, while Bard (1934) stressed neurophysiological changes, in particular activation through discharge from the hypothalamus to the cerebral cortex], the James–Lange theory and its derivatives have all maintained that the conscious feeling of bodily change is as central to the concept of emotion as the bodily change itself.

The conscious feeling of James has become, at least for some (see Schacter & Singer, 1962), a cognitive evaluative process that determines what to call or consider the somatic change. Schacter and Singer follow a long tradition of investigators who have maintained that the soma change is not specific for any particular emotional experience but rather is a general arousal state (see, for example, Lindsley, 1951). This conclusion was, in part, due to the fact that sets of physiological responses that covary with any given emotional experience have not been found. The nature of any specific emotion is thought to be in part determined by the organism's evaluation of its aroused condition. This evaluation may involve contextual cues, past experience, and individual differences. The Schacter and Singer and the James–Lange models are similar in that the elicitor produces a bodily change that is experienced by the organism. The experience of the organism, defined as a conscious feeling by James or a cognitive evaluative feeling by Schacter and Singer, *is* the feeling or emotion.

As Lewis, Brooks, and Haviland (this volume) have suggested, such a model can be used to explicate the acquisition of emotions ontogenetically. In this case, contextual cues are being determined by the infant's interaction with and knowledge about its social world, the caregiver providing the bulk of both the early knowledge and the interaction. The infant's experience is determined initially both by the elicitor, which produces a bodily change (including facial expression), and by the behavior (both verbal and nonverbal) of the caregiver in response to that bodily change. The synchrony between a facial expression of fear (mouth muscles back and down, eyes wide, body moving backward) and the emotional feeling of fear may be mediated by the caregiver's verbal labeling ("Don't be frightened") and the caregiver's responses (holding the child and comforting it). Synchrony would be acquired from the interaction and would be indicative of socialization practices. If the emotional experience is the consequence of an evaluation (whether cognitive or not) of some bodily change, then for most emotional experiences, two processes are necessary: first, the knowledge that the bodily change is uniquely different from other changes (that is, internal rather than external) and second, the evaluation process itself. Each needs to be considered.

Internal and External Stimuli

Stimuli may be classified into two groups: internal and external. External stimuli are usually verifiable by others in the sense that others can easily share them, even though experiences may differ. For example, one can say "look at that tree over there," and others are able to look at and experience that tree, even though each person's experience is different.

The second class of stimuli that impinge on an organism is internal. Internal stimuli are not externally verifiable since they cannot be shared or directly experienced by any other. Thus, for example, one could not say, "look at me thinking" or "look at me feeling sad." One would say, "I am thinking" or "I am sad." Thinking or cognitive experiences and feeling experiences have in common the fact that they both belong to the class of stimuli that are internal and not easily verified by others. Thus, both thinking and feeling experiences can be verified only if one asks the organism who is experiencing these stimuli to tell what he is thinking and feeling. The study of facial or nonverbal expression and physiological correlates of emotional experiences are attempts to explore these internal states without the use of introspection. Unfortunately, introspection has been discredited as a form of inquiry for the study of both thinking and feeling even though there is no easily demonstrated one-to-one relationship between external and internal events.

The internal–external distinction is also relevant to the concept of self. Internal stimuli have a location inside ourselves, external stimuli outside ourselves. Interestingly, this distinction appears to have a historical development (Jaynes, 1977) and is also likely to have an ontogenetic development. Historically, it appears that at some point in time people were reluctant to consider all internal stimuli as emanating from themselves. For example, while a certain stimuli emitted from the stomach region meant that a person was hungry, a set of stimuli emitted from the head (for example, an angry wish) was a God-figure's way of telling a person something. Today, both would be seen as internal. Thus, a historical change in the internal–external distinction has taken place—one that was certainly facilitated by Freud's view of the unconscious as part of the self—in which a greater set of internal stimuli have been given the self label. Nonetheless, the distinction between stimuli out there and stimuli in here implies both a concept of self and its location within the body.

The ontogenetic development of the internal–external dimension is explored in the following section. However, one might reasonably assume that the knowledge of stimuli taking place out there and verifiable with others and stimuli taking place within and with limited verifiability develops ontogenetically and is related to self awareness.[1]

Evaluation of Stimuli

The evaluation of internal stimuli or bodily changes has been conceptualized as a perceptual-cognitive process similar to information processing of other stimuli, the only difference being that the information to be processed is located within the body. The distinction between processing information emanating from inside and processing information from outside the body may not be minor. That is, although Schacter and Singer assume the process to be the same, this may not be the case. Certainly, information emanating from inside the body is more immediate and impinges directly on the person. Whether or not such differences result in different processes associated with processing internal and external information is unknown and difficult to determine.

Such evaluation involves the concept of self-awareness. Self-awareness as an information-processing and decision-making process, having to do with internal stimuli, would logically require an active organism and an organism possessing the notion of an agent or agency. *Agency* refers to that aspect of action that makes reference to the cause of the action, that is, not only who or what is causing this stimuli change but who is evaluating it. It would seem reasonable to assume that stimulus change itself has the effect of both alerting the organism and forcing it to make some type of evaluation.

The evaluation process should have similarities to other cognitive processes, such as the learning of efficacy, for which models have been articulated. The ability of the organism to cause events to occur would seem to require some, although as yet an undefined, notion of self. If the infant can cause an outcome to occur repeatedly through a behavior, as by secondary circular reactions (Piaget, 1954), then he has learned some

---

[1] Verification of internal stimuli is possible through the use of empathy. By having experienced internal stimuli, one is able to understand/appreciate the description of another's internal stimuli. The importance of empathy is that it connects people's internal experiences (Hoffman, 1975).

of the causes and consequences of that behavior. For certain associations between events, the infant has learned the notion of his own agency; that is, "he" causes something to happen. Although it is difficult to define the "he," there is a "he" that is different from other. "He" has a location even though "he" moves in space, two processes underlying the sense of permanence. This "he," different from other, having an internal and external location and permanence, is the first stage in the adult form of the concept of self. Thus, in the same way as the infant learns to affect his world, the infant also learns to evaluate himself.

In brief, the definition of an emotional experience requires a set of stimuli changes that are located in the body and that are evaluated by the infant himself. Both location and evaluation assume that a notion of self exists. Somatic changes are those internal stimulus changes located only within one's own body, a location synonymous with "me." Evaluation of these changes assumes consciousness or self-awareness as well as cognitive ability. In addition, the evaluation process itself requires an agent of evaluation. It is most difficult to construct a sentence of evaluation of internal stimuli that does not use a self-referent. The phrase "I am experiencing some internal changes 'X,'" means I am feeling "X." The source of the stimuli and the agent evaluating the stimuli are the same; this interface we call *self*. Therefore, to understand the development of emotional states, it is necessary to understand the development of self.

THE DEVELOPMENT OF SELF

A 2-year-old child grabs a toy from a peer, pulls the toy toward herself, and says, "Mine." Another 2-year-old child sees a picture of himself, smiles at it, and says, "Me." Most would agree that these 2-year-olds have an awareness of themselves or what has been termed *self*. Self-referents are produced early in relation to other nouns, begin to appear in the second half of the second year (Bloom, Lightbrown, & Hood, 1975; Brooks & Lewis, 1975b), and are common by 2 years of age in verbal children (Brown, 1973). Clearly, then, a concept of self exists by the end of the second year, although it probably exists earlier. Like other types of social knowledge, self-knowledge needs to be studied prior to the onset of speech.

There are at least two lines of argument that converge on an early self-knowledge. First, the child's knowledge of others cannot occur without some knowledge of self, for as Mead (1934), Merleau-Ponty (1964), and Lewis and Brooks (1975) have argued, knowledge of others is developed through one's interaction with these others. Without interaction with the social world, there would be little knowledge about it. Such transactions involve the infant himself, who must at least know that he is different from the person with whom he has interactions. Thus, one of the first observations of the social world has to involve the differentiation between self and others. In addition, through interaction the infant gains knowledge about self as well as knowledge about others. As Merleau-Ponty (1964) stated, "If I am a consciousness turned toward things, I can meet in things the actions of another and find in them a meaning, because they are themes of possible activity for my own body" (p. 113). Such a view has also been taken by Hamlyn (1974). In this way, the infant is an active agent since through transactions with others, he gains knowledge both of the other and of himself.

The second argument is related more to basic cognitive knowledge. By 6–8 months of age, the infant begins to understand that objects have an existence of their own (Piaget, 1937/1954). If an infant knows that objects exist, he must also know that he exists separate from objects. It would be reasonable to assume that knowledge of others, self, and objects develops at the same time.

Most psychologists, phenomenologists, and philosophers have emphasized the duality of the self and have distinguished between the self as subject and the self as object (Wylie, 1961). The first aspect is what we have called the existential self or the self as subject. James termed the self as subject *I*. Freud termed it *ego*. The self as object is the second aspect of the self. The composite of knowledge, attitudes, abilities, values, and feelings constitute oneself. James's empirical self or me (1890) and Cooley's social self (1912) are examples of self as object. Self-concept and self as object are often considered to be identical (Coller, 1971; Wylie, 1961). These two aspects of self have been considered separately both empirically and philosophically.

Origins of Self

This duality of self is useful for the study of the origins of self. The self as subject or the existential self involves learning that the self is distinct from others and that the self has a location (i. e., the body or inside the body). The self as object or the categorical self involves the self as defined in relation to others and has two components, a knowledge and a feeling component.

Existential Self

The basic notion of existence separate from other (both animate and inanimate) is developed from the interaction of the infant with its environment and is developed from the regularity and interaction of the infant's action and its outcome. The mechanism of feedback provides the basic contingency information for the child; kinesthetic feedback produced by the infant's own actions forms the basis for the development of self. For example, each time a certain set of muscles operates (eyes close), it becomes black (cannot see). The action of touching the hot stove and the immediacy of the pain inform the organism that it is its hand that is on the stove. The self is further reinforced if, when the hand is removed, the pain ceases. Such contingent feedback is also provided by the inanimate world.

Piaget has stressed the importance of contingency in the inanimate world. Circular reactions develop as the infant notices, for example, that an object's movement is a consequence of his own movement. The infant demonstrates his knowledge of relationship as well as his intent of reproducing it by repeating his own movement that leads to the desired action. While such situations occur in the inanimate world, the social world provides even more opportunities for contingent behavior since the adult has intention that the inanimate world does not have and creates more contingency situations. The adult's intention of responding to the infant has the important feature of providing both the initial contingency relationship before the infant can successfully manipulate objects and, at the same time, providing the large number of contingent sequences necessary to teach the infant about action–outcome pairing. Not only can the infant act on social objects, but social objects, unlike inanimate ones, also act on the infant. The infant's introduction to the world is interactive, as the infant both responds to and initiates behavior with others from the first days of life (Stern, 1974; Lewis & Freedle, 1973). Only later does he produce the contingent patterns with inanimate objects. Thus, having acquired circular reactions with the social world, the intention residing originally with the adults, the infant can proceed to intentionally manipulating its inanimate world so as to cause new events to occur. Intentional, instrumental behavior develops from intentional social contingencies rather than from accidental discoveries of contingency in the inanimate world. Thus, the existential self develops from the division between self and other—a division necessitated by the organism's interaction in the social world.

Categorical Self

The *self as object* refers to the knowledge and feelings about oneself. The *categorical self* refers to the categories (both knowledge and feelings) by which the infant defines itself vis-à-vis the external world. The categorical self is subject to many changes. Ontogenetically, self categories change as a function of the child's other cognitive capacities as well as with its changing social relationships. Historically and culturally, they may differ as the importance of and the need for different categories vary. Some categories are almost always invariant (e. g., gender), some vary systematically as a function of ontogeny (e.g., size), and some may depend on a multitude of factors (e.g., self-esteem). Some categories develop very early, while others may not be functional until much later. Some may operate throughout the life span while others may be salient during a relatively short time period. Within the period of infancy, three of the most salient social categories are probably age, sex, and familiarity; these categories possibly develop very early and are used throughout life (see Lewis & Brooks, in press).

As with existential knowledge, early categorical development probably involves the knowledge of both the self and other. The infant must identify himself as well as other members of a category or possessors of a category attribute. For example, gender identity seems to develop quite early. Money's work on hermaphrodites suggests that if attempts are made to alter the sexual identity assigned at birth, serious disturbances arise in children as young as 2 years of age. This finding suggests that children this young have already categorized themselves by gender (Money, Hampson, & Hampson, 1957). Likewise, as soon as infants begin to talk, they use gender-related words (e. g., *mommy, daddy, boy, girl*), indicating that they can categorize others by gender. Age identity is also alluded to by the verbal infant. One of the infant's first social words is *baby,* which is used in reference to themselves and to pictures of themselves. In addition, infants under a year of age are able to differentiate between children and adults (Brooks & Lewis, 1976a; Greenberg, Hillman, & Grice, 1973; Lewis & Brooks, 1974); by the time infants are 2 years old, they are using age-appropriate labels for adults, infants, and children (Brooks & Lewis, 1975b). These data suggest that gender and age are salient categories for the infant and that they are utilized for knowledge of both self and other.

Our discussion of the categorical self has usually been restricted to knowledge about ourselves, although the categorical self also refers to feelings about ourselves. In fact, most self categories have both features. Take, for example, gender. Gender as a category of self contains a knowledge and a feeling component. Kohlberg, (1966) and others (e. g., Emmerich, Goldman, Kirsh, & Sharabany, 1977) have shown the knowledge and the cognitive component of gender, where Green (1974) has argued for a feeling state component. Transsexuals "know" for example that they are males but they "feel" like females. This disorder might be characterized as a mismatch between feeling and knowledge.

The feeling components of categorical self are not typically studied in infancy and early childhood. It is our belief that both knowledge of and feelings about self develop from interactions with others.

Research on the Development of Self-Knowledge

The development of self-knowledge has been explored through the study of visual self-recognition. Visual self-recognition is probably the most clear-cut aspect of self, in terms of both observation and measurement. Being able to recognize oneself visually implies that the self is seen as distinct from others. It also implies an organism who perceives that he occupies a space that others do not occupy. This space is self and can be referred to by such discrete actions as visually and tactually exploring oneself and verbally labeling oneself. The self is commonly visually experienced in two representational forms: pictures and mirrors. Almost all societies have reflective surfaces available for looking at oneself, while not all societies have pictorial representations. Interestingly, the advent of videotape and moving pictures has added a third possible representation. One might hypothesize that visual self-recognition would be more difficult in some representations than in others, with the most difficult in some being a still picture of oneself.

Until recently, there have been no systematic investigations in any of the representational forms; the one interesting exception is Zazzo's (1948) study, in which he studied his son's responses to movie, picture, and mirror representations of himself from 18 to 36 months of age. Zazzo used the verbal self-referent as his measure of recognition and did not find self-recognition until 30 months of age. The recent literature has concentrated on infants' responses to mirrors, with the most systematic work being done by ourselves (Brooks & Lewis, 1975a; Lewis & Brooks, in press) and by Amsterdam (1968, 1972). Infants from 6 to 24 months of age have been observed in front of a mirror with a mark of rouge on their faces. In our studies, infants' responses to this marked condition were compared to responses to a preceding no-mark or control condition, and self-recognition was inferred from the use of self-directed rather than mirror-directed behavior. Two self-directed behaviors were observed—mark-directed and more general body-directed behavior—both of which were much more likely to occur in the marked than in the unmarked condition. In our first study of 96 infants ranging in age from 9 to 24 months, mark-directed behavior was exhibited by one-third of our sample and was highly age-specific: none of the 9–12-month-olds, one-quarter of the 15–18-month-olds, and three-quarters of the 21–24-month-olds noticed the mark. Body-directed behavior was exhibited by 40% of our sample and was seen in all age groups, even in the 9–12-month-olds. Thus, even the youngest infants responded to the rouge application in terms of increased self-directed behavior, although they did not specifically touch the mark; whether because of lack of motor coordination or less awareness of the mirror image as self was not clear.

Pictorial self-recognition exhibits the same age trends as found in mirror self-recognition (Lewis & Brooks, 1974; Brooks & Lewis, 1975b). When infants were presented with pictures of themselves and same-age peers, they did not differentiate between the two (in terms of differential fixation and affect) until 21–24 months of age. When infants were asked to verbally label pictures of themselves and other babies, the use of one's own name for one's pictures first occurred at 15 months of age and became the prevalent response between 21 and 24 months of age. In terms of a sample of 37 infants representing three age groups (15, 19, and 22 months of age), one-third of all the subjects used self-referents for their own pictures: 7% of the 15-month-olds, 27% of the 19-month-olds, and 67% of the 22-month-olds. In addition, self-referents were rarely used (by only 2 infants) to identify other baby pictures. Thus, the majority of 21–24-month-olds were clearly able to recognize their own picture and to distinguish between it and another baby picture, while a minority of the 15–19-month-olds were able to do so.

Videotape representations are the most recent addition to the study of visual self-recognition (Papousek & Papousek, 1974; Brooks & Lewis, 1976ab,). In our studies, the infants' ability to differentiate between contingent and noncontingent representations of self and between noncontingent representations of self and others was examined. In brief, 9- to 24-month-old infants were given a large number (i. e., 20–25) of trials divided among three conditions: contingent self (which was in effect a mirror condition), noncontingent self (a videotape made a week earlier in the same situation), and noncontingent other (a videotape of same-sex, same-age peer in the same situation). One of our measures was contingent play, where infants attempted to play contingently with the monitor (the most prevalent behavior was playing peekaboo with the monitor). Infants were much more likely to attempt to play contingently in the contingent than in the noncontingent trials and, within the noncontingent trials, in the self than in the other trials. The percentage of trials in which contingent play occurred for the three conditions was as follows: 24% of the contingent self, 7% of the noncontingent self, and 4% of the noncontingent other trials. Age trends were also evident, as all of the age groups (including the 9–12-month-olds) differentiated between contingent and noncontingent conditions, while only the oldest age group (21–24-month-olds) differentiated between the non-contingent self and other conditions.

These findings indicate that the awareness of self in a visual form begins to develop at the end of the first year, although this awareness is not highly differentiated at this time. By the middle of the second year, however, visual self-recognition is clearly demonstrated in some of the infants. By the end of the second year, visual self-recognition is seen in almost all of the infants.

KNOWLEDGE AND EMOTION

We have earlier suggested that without consciousness and cognitive evaluation, an emotion would not be experienced. Both are dependent upon knowing where the bodily change is located, and both imply an awareness of self, since one must know that the bodily change has a location (the self) and that the change is being experienced or evaluated by the self. In short, the organizing principle of knowledge of the self is necessary for the experiencing of emotions.

The preceding section demonstrated the acquisition of one aspect of self-knowledge—visual self-recognition—in the first two years of life. The ontogenetic changes in self-directed behavior suggest that the infant gradually learns that his body is distinct from others, that the self is located inside, not outside, his body. This knowledge may also be used to locate emotional states inside the body. The ontogenetic changes in differentiation of videotapes and pictures of self and other suggest that the infant is learning that some features are unique to himself and that the self may be defined vis-à-vis these features. Such knowledge may allow the infant to evaluate his or her own bodily changes, labeling them as "I am sad," just as he or she labels himself or herself as "I am small" or "I am female." We would hypothesize that emotional states could not be experienced without some knowledge of self. By constructing the ontogenesis of emotional experience with the help of self-knowledge and incorporating the elements of location and evaluation, the expression and development of different emotions may be better understood.

Ontogenesis of Emotional Experiences

The evaluative (Schacter & Singer, 1962), the conscious feeling (James, 1890), and the self-awareness (Brooks & Lewis, 1975a) aspects of emotion need further elaboration in terms of the ontogenesis of particular emotional experiences. Thus, emotional experiences can occur only after appropriate cognitive and social underpinnings are present. Over the first three years of life, the infant acquires these faculties and with them the ability to experience emotions. While emotional elicitors may produce specific emotional states and expressions, it is not until self-awareness exists that we can speak of the infant as having certain emotional experiences. Given this perspective, it is, of course, impossible to assign emotional experiences to the newborn or to the very young infant. The newborn or the young infant has, but does not experience, a set of stimuli changes. Not until conscious feeling emerges (self-awareness and evaluation) can we speak of the child as experiencing emotions.

This type of formulation at first appears to fly in the face of common sense; a 1-week-old who cries when a loud noise goes off must certainly be experiencing fright. It is our hypothesis that there exists an emotional elicitor, a loud noise in this case, that produces an emotional state but not an emotional experience. Thus, the newborn is in a fearful state but is not necessarily experiencing fear.

Not only are there developmental changes in the relationship between experience and state—increased synchrony with increasing age—but some emotional experiences require more of a conscious feeling and an evaluative process than others. Thus, some emotional experiences emerge developmentally earlier than others; for example, it seems clear that the emergence of fear precedes shame since the former requires less evaluative processing than the latter. That such verbal reflections of emotional states as "I am frightened" precede "I am ashamed" indicates a different development course, one that is tied to the development of self-knowledge and cognitive evaluation. The utilization of the child's growing cognitive abilities, including the acquisition of self, needs to be used in conjunction with emotional expression to obtain the sequence of emerging emotional experiences. Thus, not until the infant can incorporate the standards of others can we speak of such emotional states as shame or guilt. Even so, as our discussion on the role of self-knowledge should make clear, the emergence of self needs to precede the emergence of emotional experiences. Given our data on the origins of self, emotional experiences should not emerge prior to 8–9 months of age.

Some emotional experiences may require less evaluative ability than others and would therefore emerge first. These experiences may then serve to facilitate the development of other experiences, since they may serve both the development of self and the production of structures needed for the subsequent emotional experiences. The earlier experiences may be those that others have labeled the *primary emotions*, while the latter may be those labeled *derived emotions* (Tomkins, 1962, 1963). Such a notion of derived versus primary emotions need not imply that one set is any more biologically rooted than another, merely that one set requires less evaluative ability. A model stressing amount of evaluation rather than biological determination should be open to experimental verification, since cognitive evaluation and consciousness, as well as emotional experience, can be measured in the young.

While we have hypothesized that different emotional experiences may have different developmental sequences, it is possible that a similar distinction can be made within a particular emotional experience. Lewis (1975) discussed a variety of situations in which fear is reportedly elicited in an infant. For example, a year-old infant shows fearful behavior—and presumably experiences fear—either when a loud noise sounds behind him or when his mother, dressing for the evening, puts on a new hair wig.

These examples illustrate two points. First, expressions of fear have different elicitors and a different developmental course; the loud noise would elicit fearful expressions even at 1 week of age, while the wig would have no effect until much later. Thus, some elicitors need no cognitive structures to produce the fearful expression. These elicitors may be no more basic than the latter ones, those resting on cognitive structures, since both elicitors may be biologically rooted to produce specific responses (expressions). Second, that emotional expression of fear may occur more readily (at younger ages) for the loud noise than for the wig may be owing to the fact that the infant has acquired enough cognitive facility to experience some emotions for some elicitors but not enough for others. Thus, there may be some relationship between the onset of fearful expressions and the onset of fearful experiences, so that early elicitors of fearful expressions are likely to be early elicitors of fearful experiences.

Emotional Experiences, Cognitive Growth, and Self-Knowledge

Emotional experiences, cognitive growth, and self-knowledge appear to be related, and in order to understand the development of one, it is necessary to understand the commonalities underlying all three. We believe that all three follow a parallel developmental sequence.

Table I presents a summary of the development of self and emotional and cognitive knowing. Four major periods in the first two years of life illustrate the commonalities of this development.

Period One

The 0–3 month period is characterized by biological determinism and is primarily reflexive in nature. In terms of self-knowledge the distinction between self and other, possibly on the basis of perceptual rather than cognitive cues, is being made. At the same time emotional experience as such does not exist, as emotional expressions and states

TABLE I. Development of Self-Knowledge, Emotional Experience, and Cognitive Growth

Age (in months)	Self-knowledge	Emotional experience	Cognitive growth
0–3	Emergence of self–other distinction	Unconditioned responses to stimulus events (loud noise, hunger, etc.)	Reflexive period and primary circular reactions.
4–8	Consolidation of self–other permanence	Conditioned responses (strangers, incongruity)	Primary and secondary circular reactions
9–12	Emergence of self categories	Specific emotional experiences (fear, happiness, love, attachment)	Object permanence, means–ends, imitation
12–24	Consolidation of basis of self categories (age, gender, emergence of efficacy)	Development of empathy, guilt, embarrassment	Language growth, more complex means–ends, symbolic representations

are usually produced by strong stimuli changes and can be characterized as unconditional responses. Cognitive growth is also characterized by reflexive responses to stimuli changes. These unlearned reflexive responses appear to be both simple and complex.

Period Two

The 4–8 month period can be characterized by the emergence of social activity and the establishment of social as well as biological control of behavior. The self–other distinction is consolidated and self-permanence emerges. The self now has a location in space. Emotional experience begins to emerge as learned associations and past experiences begin to effect the expression of emotion. Cognitive growth is rapid, primary and secondary circular reactions are developed, and the child learns of its effect on the object and social world.

Period Three

The 9–12 month period can be characterized by the emergence of a truly social organism, one that knows about itself as well as others. This period is highlighted by the emergence of social categories that the infant uses to evaluate himself and others. It is a period of simultaneous comparison between different stimuli and between self and other. Emotional experiences are firmly established and their elaborate differentiation begins to emerge. Within the cognitive sphere, this period is characterized by the appearance of object permanence, reflexive imitation, and means–ends. The infant's agency emerges and, through the use of comparison, the beginning of intention and planning.

Period Four

The period between 12 and 24 months is best characterized as the beginning of representational behavior, including social representation and the representation of self. Within self-knowledge, self-recognition and the categorical self become clearly viable. Several features of the categorical self become more or less fixed (e.g., gender). More complex emotional expression, dependent on more complex cognitive skills, emerges (e.g., empathy). In terms of cognition, language development, complex means–ends, and symbolic representations emerge, facilitating self-knowledge and emotional experience.

The foregoing is only a brief mapping of developmental sequences. Nevertheless, this outline should make clear both the parallel developmental course of these three spheres and their interdependence.

Empirical Relationship between Self-Knowledge and Emotion

The preceding theoretical discussion has hypothesized a relationship between the acquisition of emotional experiences and self-awareness. We have argued that although emotional states and expression might precede self-awareness, emotional experiences are dependent on or interrelated with self-knowledge. Unfortunately, a direct comparison between the two is not possible since without verbal ability and introspection, emotional experiences are difficult to assess. As a first approximation, we observed infants' emotional expressions in an emotion-inducing situation and also observed their responses to visual representations of themselves.

In order to observe infants' awareness of themselves, we examined infants' responses to seeing themselves in a mirror after their faces were marked with rouge (see Brooks & Lewis, 1975a; Lewis & Brooks, in press). Three behaviors were of interest: mark-directed behavior (touching the marked nose), body-directed behavior (touching the torso, face, or mouth, but not the marked nose), and imitative behavior (acting silly, acting coy, or making faces in the mirror). The absence or presence of these three behaviors was coded. As in our previous mirror studies, interobserver reliabilities were high, and all were greater than 85%.

Infants' responses to the approach of a female adult stranger were also observed. Each infant, with his mother seated next to him, watched as the stranger slowly walked toward him. The entire sequence was

TABLE II. PERCENTAGE OF SUBJECTS EXHIBITING SELF-DIRECTED BEHAVIORS AND FACIAL
EXPRESSIONS

Self-directed behaviors	Age (in months)			Total
	9–12	15–18	21–24	
Mark-directed	0	45%	75%	37%
Body-directed	27%	45%	38%	36%
Imitation	9%	27%	50%	27%
Facial expressions				
Positive	18%	0	0	7%
Negative	18%	45%	13%	27%
Attention	55%	55%	88%	63%

videotaped and coded by use of the system described in Lewis, Brooks, and Haviland (this volume).[2] Three different facial patterns occurred,[3] and each subject was classified in terms of his or her predominant face during the stranger approach sequence. The patterns were positive face (corners of the mouth raised, no corners lowered or lips retracted, and eyes directed up and/or ahead); negative face (corners down or lips retracted with gaze aversion); and attentive face (squared lips or relaxed mouth with eyes up and ahead).

We saw 30 infants (14 males, 16 females) representing three age groups; 11 were 9–12-month-olds (mean age 10 months, 21 days), 11 were 15–18-month-olds (mean age 16 months, 14 days), and 8 were 21–24-month-olds (mean age 22 months, 24 days).

Table II presents the percentage of subjects exhibiting self-directed behaviors and the three facial patterns by age. These self-recognition data and the age trends are similar to the results of our previous studies. The relationship between self-awareness and facial expression was examined by the use of chi-square statistics. Table III presents the number of subjects exhibiting the self-directed and imitative behaviors, excluding the 9–12-month olds, since these behaviors were rare or nonexistent in this age group. The positive face is included in only one

---

[2] Some of these subjects were those used in the Lewis, Brooks, and Haviland study (this volume).

[3] A fourth facial pattern—attentive-negative face (retracted lips up with eyes and forehead relaxed)—is discussed in the Lewis et al. study in this volume. Interestingly, this pattern was not seen in any of the present sample, partly because in the Lewis et al. study, a majority of the attentive-negative faces were exhibited by the 6–8-month-olds, an age group not represented in the present study.

TABLE III. NUMBER OF SUBJECTS EXHIBITING SELF-DIRECTED BEHAVIORS AND FACIAL EXPRESSIONS

Facial expression	Self-directed behaviors	Yes	No	Total
	15–24 - month-olds			
	Mark-directed behavior			
Negative		5	1	6
Attentive		6	7	13
		11	8	19
	Imitation			
Negative		3	3	6
Attentive		4	9	13
		7	12	19
	Body-directed			
Negative		5	1	6
Attentive		3	10	13
		8	11	19
Facial expression	9–24-month-olds			
	Body-directed			
Positive		0	2	
Negative		6	2	
Attentive		5	14	
		11	18	

analysis, since it occurred only in the youngest age group. As can be seen, self-awareness was related to facial expression. Body-directed behavior and facial expression exhibited the strongest relationship, so that the presence of body-directed behavior was likely to be related to negative facial expressions and the absence of body-directed behavior to attentive facial expressions. This was true for the total sample ($\chi^2 = 6.99$, $p < .05$) and for those age groups that exhibited more differentiated forms of mark-directed behavior (15–24 months, $\chi^2 = 3.89$, $p < .05$). Interestingly, the two instances of positive faces occurred in the youngest infants, infants who did not touch their bodies in the mirror condition. The absence or presence of mark-directed behavior was related to facial expression, but to a much lesser degree. The absence of mark-directed behavior was related to an attentive face (88% of those not noticing the rouge exhibited an attentive face, 13% exhibited a negative face: binomial test, $p < .05$), but the presence of mark-directed behavior was not related to facial expression.

In short, the results of this study support our hypothesis that self-awareness and emotion are related when self-awareness is inferred through visual self-recognition and when emotion is inferred through facial expressions exhibited during an emotion-inducing situation. Interestingly, not all self-recognition measures were related to facial expression. Only those that involved directing body movement toward the self, measures that may be indicative of self-location, were related. These results also speak to the existence of emotional experiences. If we are correct in assuming that emotional experiences are dependent on self-awareness and cognitive evaluation, then the presence of self-awareness and facial expression may be used to infer the presence of emotion as we have defined it.

IMPLICATIONS FOR DEVELOPMENTAL RESEARCH

In this paper, we have defined emotional experiences in such a way as to understand their ontogenesis better. To reiterate, we believe that emotion is elicited by "an exciting event" that causes a somatic change. Having the capacity to reflect on the self and having other cognitive structures enables the child to have an emotional experience. Such a definition has several implications for the study of emotion in infancy.

First, facial expression does not necessarily have a one-to-one correspondence with either emotional state or experience. Although this view is certainly not unique to us, it is uncommon in the infancy literature. Indeed, a synchronous relationship between expression and state and expression and experience is implicitly assumed in most infancy studies. Our example of the fearful neonate clearly illustrates this point. Adults assume that an infant who exhibits facial response in a situation commonly thought to induce an emotion is experiencing that emotion. We must be cautious in interpreting an infant's behavior in terms of emotional experience.

Second, if the experience of emotional state is heavily dependent on self-awareness, as we have suggested, then we need to study the origins of self-awareness more systematically. Explanations of certain developmental shifts in expressive behaviors might be better formulated if the development of self-awareness was better understood. For example, the literature on stranger fear has suggested that there is a peak in "fear" behavior around 8–9 months, the same age at which body-directed behavior and exploration of the properties of mirror images become prevalent.

Third, our definition of emotion also stresses the necessity of cognitive evaluation, a process that might be closely related to information processing. Therefore, the relationship of cognitive ability and facial expression needs to be explicated in the same manner as that between self-awareness and facial expression. For example, infants' responses to discrepancies such as a wig on the mother do not seem to occur until the infant is able to process discrepant information in terms of familiar schemas and expectations about the familiar.

Fourth, our definition of emotion suggests that the interaction of the infant with the social world heavily influences his emotional experiences, first by affecting self-worth and efficacy and second by labeling his emotional responses in terms of emotional experiences. An example from one of our ongoing studies illustrates this point. Infants and their mothers have been observed in a free play setting and during a separation and reunion at 12 and at 24 months of age. Take, for example, one mother–infant dyad's response to reunion at the two ages. When the child is 1 year of age, the mother, upon returning to her infant, says, "You were crying because you were angry at me." At 2 years of age, the child, upon his mother's return, acts quite angry at her mother. Thus, the mother's labeling of the child's behavior has affected the child's subsequent experience of emotional states.

Without the *I* in "I am . . . " the verbal phrase and the emotional experience implied by it have no meaning for the Western mind.

ACKNOWLEDGMENT

We wish to thank Steven Grossman for his help in data analysis.

REFERENCES

Amsterdam, B. K. Mirror behavior in children under two years of age. Unpublished doctoral dissertation. Chapel Hill: University of North Carolina, 1968.

Amsterdam, B. K. Mirror self-image reactions before age two. *Developmental Psychology*, 1972, *5*, 297–305.

Bard, P. Emotion I. The neuro-hormonal basis of emotional reactions. In C. Murchison (Ed.), *Handbook of general experimental psychology*. Worcester, Mass.: Clark University Press, 1934, pp. 264–311.

Bloom, L., Lightbrown, P., & Hood, L. Structure and variation in child language. *Monographs of the Society for Research in Child Development*, 1975, *40*(2, serial no. 160).

Brooks, J., & Lewis, M. Mirror-image stimulation and self recognition in infancy. Paper presented at the Society for Research in Child Development meetings, Denver, April 1975 (a).

Brooks, J., & Lewis, M. Person perception and verbal labeling: The development of social labels. A version of this paper was presented at both the Society for Research in Child Development meetings, Denver, April 1975, and the Eastern Psychological Association meetings, New York City, April 1975. (b)

Brooks, J., & Lewis, M. Infants' responses to strangers: Midget, adult and child. *Child Development*, 1976, 47, 323–332. (a).

Brooks, J., & Lewis, M. Visual self recognition in different representational forms. Paper presented at the 21st International Congress, Paris, July 1976. (b)

Brooks, J., & Lewis, M. Visual self recognition in infancy: Contingency and the self–other distinction. Paper presented at the Southeastern Conference on Human Development meetings, Nashville, April 1976. (c)

Brown, R. *A first language*. Cambridge, Mass.: Harvard University Press, 1973.

Coller, A. R. The assessment of "self-concept" in early childhood education. ERIC Clearinghouse on Early Childhood Education. Urbana: University of Illinois, 1971.

Cooley, C. H. *Human nature and the social order*. New York: Scribner's, 1912.

Darwin, C. *The expression of emotions in man and animals*. London: John Murray, 1872.

Ekman, P. Universals and cultural differences in facial expressions of emotion. In J. K. Cole (Ed.), *Nebraska Symposium on Motivation* (Vol. 19). Lincoln: University of Nebraska Press, 1971.

Emmerich, W., Goldman, K. S., Kirsh, B., & Sharabany, R. Evidence for a transitional phase in the development of gender constancy. *Child Development*, 1977, 48, 930–936.

Green, R. *Sexual identity conflict in children and adults*. New York: Basic Books, 1974.

Greenberg, D. J., Hillman, D., & Grice, D. Infant and stranger variables related to stranger anxiety in the first year of life. *Developmental Psychology*, 1973, 9, 207–212.

Hamlyn, D. W. Person-perception, our understanding of others. In T. Mischel (Ed.), *Understanding other persons*. Totowa, N.J.: Rowman & Littlefield, 1974.

Hoffman, M. L. Developmental synthesis of affect and cognition and its implications for altruistic motivation. *Developmental Psychology*, 1975, 11(5).

Izard, C. E. *The face of emotion*. New York: Appleton-Century-Crofts, 1971.

James, W. *Principles of psychology*. New York: Henry Holt, 1890.

Jaynes, J. *The origin of consciousness in the breakdown of the bicameral mind*. New York: Houghton, Mifflin, 1977.

Kohlberg, L. A cognitive developmental analysis of children's sex-role concepts and attitudes. In E. Maccoby (Ed.), *The development of sex differences*. Stanford, Calif.: Stanford University Press, 1966.

Lewis, M. The meaning of fear. Paper presented at a symposium, The Origins of Joy and Fear: The Development of Affect Systems in Infancy, at the Society for Research in Child Development meetings, Denver, April 1975.

Lewis, M. The origins of self competence. Paper presented at the NIMH Conference on Mood Development, Washington, D. C., November 1976.

Lewis, M., & Brooks, J. Self, other, and fear: Infants' reactions to people. In M. Lewis & L. Rosenblum (Eds.), *The origins of fear: The origins of behavior* (Vol. 2). New York: Wiley, 1974, pp. 195–227.

Lewis, M., & Brooks, J. Infants' social perception: A constructivist view. In L. Cohen & P. Salapatek (Eds.), *Infant perception: From sensation to cognition* (Vol. 2). New York: Academic Press, 1975, pp. 101–143.

Lewis, M., & Brooks, J. *The origins of the concept of self*. New York: Plenum, in press.

Lewis, M., & Freedle, R. Mother-infant dyad: The cradle of meaning. In P. Pliner, L. Krames, & T. Alloway (Eds.), *Communication and affect: Language and thought*. New York: Academic Press, 1973, pp. 127–155.

Lewis, M., Haviland, J., & Brooks, J. Hearts and faces: A study in the measurement of emotion. Paper presented at a conference, The Origins of Behavior: Affect Development, Princeton, N. J., February 1977.

Lindsley, D. B. Emotion. In S. S. Stevens (Ed.), *Handbook of experimental psychology*. New York: Wiley, 1951.

Mead, G. H. *Mind, self, and society*. Chicago: University of Chicago Press, 1934.

Merleau-Ponty, M. *Primacy of perception* (J. Eddie, Ed., & W. Cobb, trans.). Evanston, Ill.: Northwestern University Press, 1964.

Money, J., Hampson, J. G., & Hampson, J. L. Imprinting and the establishment of gender role. A. M. A., *Archives of Neurology and Psychology*, 1957, *77*, 333–336.

Papousek, H., & Papousek, M. Mirror image and self-recognition in young human infants: I. A new method of experimental analysis. *Developmental Psychology*, 1974, *7*(3), 149–157.

Piaget, J. *The construction of reality in the child* (M. Cook, trans.). New York: Basic Books, 1954. (Originally published, 1937.)

Schacter, S., & Singer, J. E. Cognitive, social and physiological determinants of emotional state. *Psychological Review*, 1962, *69*, 379–399.

Stern, D. N. The goal and structure of mother–infant play. *Journal of the American Academy of Child Psychiatry*, 1974, *13*, 402–421.

Tomkins, S. S. *Affect, imagery, consciousness* (Vol. 1). *The positive affects*. New York: Springer, 1962.

Tomkins, S. S. *Affect, imagery, consciousness* (Vol. 2), *The negative affects*. New York: Springer, 1963.

Wylie, R. C. *The self concept*. Lincoln: University of Nebraska Press, 1961.

Zazzo, R. Images du corp et conscience du soi. *Enfance*, 1948, *1*, 29–43.

8

Toward a Theory of Empathic Arousal and Development

Martin L. Hoffman

Empathy has long been a topic of interest in psychology, but its nature and development have not been systematically treated. I have for some time been working on a comprehensive theoretical model for empathy, and in this paper, I present the most recent version of this model.

Empathy is defined here as a largely involuntary, vicarious response to affective cues from another person or from his situation. The paper includes a discussion of certain definitional issues, followed by a delineation of several different modes of empathic affect arousal. These modes vary in the degree of perceptual and cognitive involvement, the type of stimulus that sets them off (e. g., facial expression, situational cues), the degree to which they are involuntary or subject to conscious control, and the amount and kind of past experiences required. They may also be presumed to become viable and operative at different times developmentally. Empathy is also viewed as having a social-cognitive component arising from the fact that the affect is aroused in one person in response to someone else's situation. The social-cognitive processes, moreover, are assumed to produce a partial transformation of empathy into the related affects of sympathy and guilt. Finally, the motivational component of empathy and the possible role of empathic arousal in prosocial action are discussed. The main focus is on the type of arousal that seems most pertinent to prosocial motivation, the empathic arousal of distress, although I assume that many of my remarks have a bearing on the empathic arousal of other affects as well.

MARTIN L. HOFFMAN · University of Michigan, Ann Arbor, Michigan.

Definition of Empathy

Though several writers define empathy as a vicarious affective response, definitional issues still abound. Before discussing these issues, I should note that there is agreement on one point: it cannot automatically be assumed that an affective response to another person signifies empathic arousal. An increase in skin conductance, for example, when one is observing someone else being exposed to a highly noxious stimulus may usually signify an empathic reaction. It has been suggested by Berger (1962) and others, however, that some subjects may be enjoying the other person's pain (e. g., "I was rather embarrassed to see that I was grinning when my partner got shocked" [Bandura & Rosenthal, 1966]). The observer's physiological response may also reflect a startle reaction to the victim's bodily movements, an emotional response to the noxious stimulus or to the sound of the victim's scream, or even the fear that what is happening to the other person might also happen to him. In the latter case, the victim's response serves merely as a source of information about the observer's own probable fate. Examples of these "pseudo-vicarious affects" (Berger, 1962) are responding with fear to the sound of someone's crying or to the sight of a sibling being spanked for no apparent reason. A less obvious example is that of a child who responds with sadness to his mother's sadness, not out of empathy but out of a concern based on past experience that when his mother is sad, she is less likely to satisfy his emotional and other needs. Finally, it has been suggested that one's physiological response when observing someone engaged in a pleasurable activity may reflect annoyance that someone else, and not the self, is experiencing pleasure (Stotland, 1969). .

There also appears to be agreement that some degree of match between the affect experienced by the observer and that experienced directly by the model is necessary for the response to be designated as empathic. There is no agreement, however, as to how exact the match must be. One approach is suggested by the scoring system for empathy used by Feshbach and Roe (1968). If a subject looks at a picture of a child who is fearful and is asked how he (the subject) feels, he does not receive full credit for an empathic response unless he indicates that looking at the picture makes him feel fearful. Feeling sad, for example, would not be sufficient. Stotland (1969), on the other hand, appears to be more impressed with the intensity of arousal and less with the veridicality of the observer's response, just so long as the observer's response is in general accord with the positive or negative affective tone of the model's. It is obvious that two such divergent definitions often lead to different interpretations of the results, and some resolution is necessary. Since we are dealing with a person's empathic response to another, the issue of veridicality cannot be ignored. I would suggest, however, that if veridicality is made part of the definition of empathy, we will create the difficult, perhaps insurmountable problem of assessing just how exact the match must be. Furthermore, insisting on a high degree of veridicality may contribute further to the confusion that already exists between the cognitive and the affective processes in empathic arousal, and it may obscure certain fundamental issues in the development of empathic responsiveness in childhood. These views will become clear as we proceed.

A second definitional issue pertains to the nature of the cues or stimuli that evoke the empathic response in the observer. For the observer's response to be designated as empathic, must the observer be responding to direct (e. g., facial) cues reflecting the model's affective experience? Or, should it still be considered empathic if the observer responds only to situational cues? Most writers ignore this issue, and in the measuring of empathy, both facial and situational cues are typically available to the subject. In one recent instance, however, the facial and situational cues are incongrous: a boy frowns at his birthday party and the subjects, all young children, must respond in terms of the facial cues for their responses to be scored as empathic (Iannotti, 1974). One question that might be raised is the ecological one: Do people generally respond empathically to facial or situational cues or to both? The answer is not known, since the research, as just noted, provides both facial and situational cues. It seems clear, however, that limiting empathy to a response to facial cues may be too restricting because it rules out those instances in which we respond vicariously on the basis of a person's verbal or writtten communication about his affective experience or on the basis of information we may receive about his situation in his absence.

As stated earlier, the one thing on which everyone agrees is that empathy is a vicarious affective response; that is, the observer responds as if he were experiencing the same affect as the model. I suggest that this point of agreement is all we need for an adequate and useful definition of empathy. Empathy may thus be defined simply in terms of the arousal of affect in the observer that is not a reaction to his own situation but a vicarious response to another person's situation. The focus is then on the *process* of empathic arousal—the process by which a person responds affectively to another as if he were experiencing the same affect as the other. The "as if" part is important because it highlights both the emphasis on process and the fact that an exact match is not a necessary part of the definition. A certain amount of veridicality is to be expected, of course. Since all humans have essentially the same nervous system and have been exposed to many similar affect-producing experiences during the long period of socialization, facial or situational cues very likely tend to evoke the same affect in the observer as in the model. Furthermore, the actual degree of match of which an individual is capable, as well as the range of emotions with which he can empathize, may be expected to increase with age because of perceptual and cognitive development and the increasing variety of affects one experiences directly. Degree of match is, then, a variable aspect of empathy rather than part of the definition. Similarly, the nature of the stimulus that evokes the observer's affective response is also not part of the definition. As will soon be clear, certain modes of empathic arousal may require facial cues and others may require situational cues. To summarize, the focus of our definition is on process rather than on veridicality or type of eliciting cue.

EMPATHIC AROUSAL AND CONTROL

There are at least four distinct modes of empathic arousal: conditioning, motor mimicry, reflexive crying, and imagining oneself in the other's place. These will now be described, followed by a discussion of processes of self-regulation and control of the intensity of empathically aroused affect.

Conditioned Affect Arousal

The mode of empathic arousal most in keeping with mainstream American psychology, at least until recently, stems from various learning explanations that boil down to four variants of the classical conditioning paradigm.

1. According to the simplest paradigm, if an observer experiences pain or pleasure at the same time that pain or pleasure is administered to someone else, then the cues of the other person's affective state will subsequently create a similar affective state in the observer (Aronfreed, 1970).

2. In a second paradigm, empathy is seen as developing early in infancy as the result of the bodily transfer of the caretaker's affective state to the infant through physical handling (Hoffman, 1973). For example, when the mother experiences distress, her body may stiffen, with the result that the child (if he is being handled at that time) also experiences distress. Subsequently, the facial and verbal expressions that initially accompanied the mother's distress can serve as conditioned stimuli that evoke the distress response in the child. Furthermore,

through stimulus generalization, similar expressions by other persons become capable of evoking distress in the child. This mechanism has been advanced to explain the behaviors fitting Sullivan's (1940) definition of empathy as a form of "nonverbal contagion and communion" between mother and infant (e. g., the infant is viewed by Sullivan as automatically empathizing with the mother, feeling euphoric when she does and anxious when she does).

3. A third, more general paradigm holds that cues of pain or pleasure from another person or from his situation evoke associations with the observer's own past pain or pleasure, resulting in an empathic affective reaction (Humphrey, 1922). A simple example is the child who cuts himself, feels the pain, and cries. Later, when he sees another child cut himself and cry, the sight of blood, the sound of the cry, or any other distress cue or aspect of the situation having elements in common with his own prior pain experience can now elicit the unpleasant affect initially associated with that experience. This paradigm, unlike the first mentioned, does not require direct pairing of affect by the observer and the other person. Nor is it, like the second paradigm, confined to early infancy or limited to distress originating in physically communicated tensions. It therefore leaves open the possibility of a multiplicity of distress experiences with which the child can empathize, and it can potentially explain a greater variety of empathic experiences than the other two paradigms.

4. In a fourth variant of the conditioning paradigm, really an extension of the third, the connection between the other person's affective state and the observer's empathic response is symbolically mediated. That is, with language and cognitive development, a person can respond on the basis of the meaning of stimuli as well as their physical attributes. Thus, he can be empathically aroused not only by direct cues of another's affect but also by the other's verbal or written communication about his feelings or about the affectively relevant environmental events impinging on him, or even by information obtained about him from someone else. Any of these symbolic cues may evoke associations with the observer's own past experience of the same emotion.

Motor Mimicry and Afferent Feedback

A very different explanation of empathy was advanced some time ago by Lipps (1906). Lipps suggested that empathy is due to an isomorphic, presumably unlearned "motor mimicry" response to another person's expression of affect. This conception is reminiscent of McDougall's (1908) "primitive passive sympathy," wherein the expression of emotion in one individual is viewed as the innate adequate stimulus for the same emotion in the observer. Lipps was more explicit than McDougall, however, as to the actual mechanism involved. That is, according to Lipps, the observer automatically imitates the other person with slight movements in posture and facial expression ("objective motor mimicry"), thus creating in himself inner cues that contribute, through afferent feedback, to his understanding and experiencing of the other person's affect. Lipps appears to have shared with James (1890) and Tomkins (1962) the view that the experience of an emotion is the result of situationally induced bodily processes, mainly the activity of visceral and facial muscles. According to James, for example, if a situation calls for running we run, and the running, together with other skeletal and visceral responses, causes the conscious experience of fear. And in Tomkin's view, feedback from the activity of the facial muscula-ture, when transformed to conscious form, constitutes the experience or awareness of emotion. All three writers make the assumption that the inner cues are different for each emotion and that by perceiving these cues the person becomes aware of just what emotion he is experiencing. The unique feature of Lipp's theory is, of course, that the inner bodily processes are produced not by the person's own situation but by cues indicating the affective state of someone else.

Though Lipps's explanation has been ignored over the years, there appears to be some recent, modest support for it. First, the evidence for motor mimicry comes from studies showing that people engage in increased lip activity and increased frequency of eye-blink responses when observing models who stutter or blink their eyes (Berger & Hadley, 1975; Bernal & Berger, 1976). Second, the evidence for afferent feedback is that though visceral activity has long been known to lack specificity, it appears that various emotions may be accompanied by widely different degrees of tone in the skeletal muscles (e. g., the loss in muscle tone that accompanies sadness is associated with characteristic postures that are diametrically opposed to those seen in a happy mood) and different patterns of facial muscle activity (e. g., Gelhorn, 1964; Izard, 1971). There is also recent evidence to suggest that cues from one's facial musculature may contribute to the actual experience of an emotion. In a series of remarkable experiments by Laird (1974), subjects who were instructed to arrange their facial muscles, one at a time, into positions that correspond to "smiles" or "frowns" without knowing that their faces were set in smile or frown positions (e. g., by touching between the subject's eyebrows lightly with an electrode and saying "Pull your eyes down and together . . . good, now hold it like that") reported feeling more angry when "frowning" and more happy when "smiling." They also reported that cartoons viewed when their faces were set in the smile position were more humorous than cartoons viewed when their faces were set in the frown position.

Further research is needed on Lipps's theory. For example, we need to know if motor mimicry occurs not only for eye-blink and stuttering responses but also for the type of facial muscle patterning associated with different emotions. (Such patterning may also occur not through mimicry but in response to the *situational* cues pertinent to the other person's affect. That is, the perception of the other's situation may elicit the pertinent facial responses in the observer, which in turn may produce the appropriate affect.) And if such motor mimicry of facial responses does occur, it may be necessary to replicate Laird's findings, to show that facial muscle patterning may bring about particular emotional responses. Clearly, the research thus far permits us only to consider motor mimicry as a possible mechanism of empathic arousal.

From a developmental standpoint, conditioning and mimicry have certain things in common. They have few developmental prerequisites, requiring only enough perceptual discrimination ability to detect the relevant cues from the other person's face or his situation. Once the cues are detected, an empathic response is virtually automatic. The remaining two modes of empathic arousal are at opposite ends of the developmental continuum.

Reflexive Crying

There is evidence that 1- and 2-day-old infants cry in response to the sound of another infant's cry (Sagi & Hoffman, 1976; Simner, 1971). Furthermore, this reactive cry is not merely a response to a noxious stimulus, since the infants react in a more subdued manner to the sound of equally loud nonhuman cries, including computer-simulated infant cries. Nor is it merely a simple imitative vocal response lacking an affective component. Rather, it is vigorous and intense and in all observable respects resembles a spontaneous cry (Sagi & Hoffman, 1976). It thus appears that exposure to a sound that reflects another infant's affective distress results in affective distress in the newborn infant. Although this reflexive cry is not a full empathic response, since it lacks a cognitive component, it must at least be considered as a possible early precursor of empathic arousal.

It is difficult to tell whether the cry is an innate, biologically based isomorphic response to another's cry or whether it can be explained by simple conditioning principles. There is evidence that conditioning of the heart rate is possible in 2-day-olds (Crowell, Blurton, Kobayashi, McFarland, & Yang, 1976), and it seems likely that a response so natural and frequent in newborns as crying can also be conditioned. If so, this phenomenon would lend credence to a classical conditioning explanation of the newborn's reflexive cry. That is, the cry may be a conditioned distress response to cues (the sound of the other's cry) that resemble the cues associated with the infant's own past cries of distress. Both hypotheses—that the reactive cry is innate and that it is learned—would then remain tenable. The final test may require further research, preferably in the delivery room before the infant has had his own distress experiences. Even then, of course, the birth cry and the pain of the birth process might provide the necessary conditions for explanations based on conditioning principles to apply. Should we have to go back to the birth cry for an explanation, however, it would indicate that the reflexive cry is for all practical purposes constitutionally based.

Imagining Oneself in the Other's Place

The final mode of empathic arousal is that of imagining how it would feel if the stimuli inpinging on another person were impinging on oneself. In a study by Mathews and Stotland (1973), nursing students watched a training film in which a severely ill patient, followed from the time of entry into the hospital, finally dies. The students who had indicated previously that they often try to imagine themselves in the other person's place (in the movies, for example) showed more palmar sweat if they imagined themselves in the place of the dying woman. In another study (Stotland, 1969), subjects instructed to imagine themselves in another person's position ("imagine how you yourself would feel if you were subject to the diathermy treatment . . . think about what your reactions would be and the sensations you would receive in your hand") when that person appeared to be undergoing a painful heat treatment showed more palmar sweat and more verbal indications that watching the other was a painful experience than subjects instructed to attend closely to the other person's physical movements while he was experiencing the pain. It is also interesting that the instructions to imagine oneself in the other's situation resulted in more palmar sweat and verbally reported indications that it was a painful experience than a third condition, in which the subjects were instructed to imagine how the *other* person felt when he was undergoing the treatment. This last finding suggests that imagining oneself in the other's place may often produce an empathic affective response because it reflects processes generated from within the observer (rather than an outward orientation), processes in which connections are presumably made between the stimuli impinging on the other person and similar stimulus events in the observer's own past. That is, the process of imagining that these stimuli are impinging on the self has the power to evoke associations with real events in one's own past, events in which one actually did experience the pertinent affect. The process, then, has much in common with the fourth type of classical conditioning mentioned earlier, the conditioned stimulus being the mental representation of oneself in the other's situation. The important difference is, of course, that here the conditioning is the result of a complex mental operation.

In this type of empathic arousal, cognitive processes are obviously dominant since the whole process is triggered by one's imagination. There is also Stotland's (1969) interesting finding that the palmar sweat response of subjects instructed to imagine themselves in the other's place did not begin to increase until as much as 30 seconds after the experimenter announced that the painful heat was being applied to the victim. The affect aroused by imagining oneself in the other's place, then, appears to be somewhat independent, at least temporally, of the stimuli producing the affect in the other person.

As in the conditioning mode, in imagining oneself in the other's place the observer may be responding to direct cues of the model's affective state or his situation, or to symbolically mediated cues emanating from the model or from some other source.

Developmental Ordering and Integration of Arousal Modes

These modes of empathic arousal obviously make quite different perceptual and cognitive demands on the observer. First, the reflexive cry of the newborn makes virtually no such demands. Mimicry, too (if it does indeed occur), is a relatively noncognitive process, but it does require the ability to make perceptual discriminations between different facial expressions and the prior development of certain afferent neural pathways. Conditioning allows for a far wider range of possibilities than mimicry, which can presumably occur only when the model is present and his facial expression is visible. As noted earlier, conditioning allows for a simple form of empathic arousal that is mediated by the caretaker's handling of the infant, a form of arousal that probably has few neural requisites. And at the other extreme, conditioning also allows the individual to be empathically aroused through verbal and other forms of symbolic mediation, hence to empathize with a host of increasingly sophisticated and complex affects as he progresses through the life cycle. Symbolically mediated empathic arousal is obviously more demanding cognitively than nonmediated arousal, since it requires the person to respond on the basis of the meaning of stimuli rather than their physical attributes. Imagining oneself in the other's place should generally demand a higher level of cognitive functioning than conditioning, since the person is required both to register the stimuli to which he is exposed and to reconstruct it in his imagination. Of course, in comparing this mode to conditioning, we assume that other things are equal, notably the particular affect in question and the direct or symbolic nature of the available cues. The most developmentally advanced type of arousal, then, consists of imagining oneself in the other's place when the only available cues are symbolic.

Aside from the degree of cognitive involvement, but clearly related to it, the various modes of empathic arousal differ in the extent to which they are involuntary or under the observer's conscious control. The more primitive modes—reflexive crying, nonmediated conditioning, early mimicry—would seem to be largely involuntary. Given the necessary constitutional prerequisites and past experience, exposure to the necessary cues should ordinarily lead to empathic arousal. Arousal through symbolically mediated conditioning and through imagining oneself in the other's place, whether symbolically mediated or not, on the other hand, is very likely more subject to conscious control. The voluntary aspect of imagining oneself in the other's place should not be overdrawn, however. Informal discussion with friends, students, and colleagues has convinced me that adults often feel a compulsion to imagine themselves in the other's place, especially when it is distress that the other person is experiencing.

In view of these considerations, the developmental sequence of the appearance of the various modes of empathic arousal would seem to be roughly as follows: reflexive crying; conditioning mediated by direct caretaker handling; mimicry; conditioning through direct cues of the model's affect or his situation; symbolically mediated conditioning; imagining oneself in the model's place. This should not be construed as a stage sequence in the sense of each stage's superseding the previous ones. Except for the first two modes, which are probably operative only in infancy, they all may continue to operate throughout life. Furthermore, it seems likely that all the modes of which a person is capable may function in any arousal situation. Thus, it may be useful to think of empathic arousal in older children and adults as having two components. The first, relatively involuntary component, based mainly on conditioning and possibly mimicry, may account for the compelling nature of the empathic response, which is indicated by the fact that regardless of age and the empathy measure used, most research subjects have been found to give evidence of responding empathically (see review by Hoffman, in press,a). The second, more reflective arousal component, based mainly on the tendency to imagine oneself in the other's place, is more likely to be voluntary and subject to influence by the observer's past socialization, which may play an important role in determining whether or not he brings such a tendency to the situation.

It may also provide the primary basis for empathizing with certain complex emotions like disappointment. Both components may generally be expected to function in harmony with each other. For example, if the observer has an initial set to imagine himself in the other's place, doing so may direct his attention more closely to the other person's facial expression or to his situation, which may activate, or reactivate, the less voluntary component. The two components may not always operate in harmony, however. For example, if the observer has a determined set to imagine himself in the other's place, it may sometimes interfere with the operation of the less voluntary component, as suggested by the finding mentioned earlier that subjects instructed to adopt such a set showed a substantial delay in empathic arousal.

Self-Regulation of the Empathic Response

Although there may be an involuntary quality to the empathic response to distress, as argued above, empathic distress is, after all, an aversive state, and we may therefore expect to find variations in people's thresholds of tolerance for it, as well as mechanisms for avoiding it. There is suggestive evidence for these conjectures. First, the involuntary element in empathic arousal is indicated in the finding by Stotland, Sherman, and Shaver (1971) that instructing subjects "to avoid experiencing the same type of emotion as the person experiencing the heat treatment" did not result in a reduction in their level of physiological arousal. Second, there is evidence that some people may avoid the pain of empathic distress by avoiding contact with people in a severe state of distress. Mathews and Stotland (1973) found that student nurses who were high empathizers in general and who felt strong compassion for their patients experienced a need to avoid spending time in the same room with patients who were severely ill. The experimental research also indicates quite clearly that if subjects are instructed to take a detached view of the victim (e. g., to attend carefully to his leg, arm, hand, foot, or head movements or his bearing and posture or simply to "observe his emotional state closely and watch for cues indicating his state of arousal"), their level of empathic arousal is diminished (Lerner & Simmons, 1966; Aderman, Brehm & Katz, 1974; Stotland, Sherman, & Shaver, 1971; Speisman, Lazarus, Mordkoff, & Davison, 1964). These findings suggest that if the observer's set is such as to fragment the victim or make him an object of intellectual scrutiny, this set will put distance between him and the victim or at least distract him from the victim's affective state, thereby reducing the observer's empathic response. Finally, there is evidence in a study by Bandura and Rosenthal (1966) that some individuals may spontaneously adopt such empathy-inhibiting perceptual and cognitive strategies as focusing their eyes on irrelevant stimuli, such as a spot distant from the victim's face and hands; looking across the room or out the window; thinking about academic problems; planning a trip; or concentrating on a love affair. Here are illustrative quotes given by two subjects after having observed a peer who was ostensibly receiving high levels of electric shock:

> The first three or four shocks, I thought about the amount of pain for the other guy. Then I began to think, to minimize my own discomfort. I recall looking at my watch, looking out the window, and checking things about the room. I recall that the victim received a shock when I was thinking about the seminar, and that I didn't seem to notice the discomfort as much in this instance. (p. 60)

> I tried to think of other topics; general elections in Britain, will Wilson become a Prime Minister, academic problems, planned trip to New York. I was not able to keep thinking on any topic too consistently and my thoughts rather broke down after a while. (p. 60)

These quotes illustrate at once the natural tendency to empathize with the victim, the discomfort produced in the observer, and the utilization of defensive strategies to reduce this discomfort. Also illustrated is a case in which the strategy seemed to work (first quote) and one in which the victim's distress cues appear to have been so insistent as to render the observer's intensive efforts to defend against them ineffective (second quote). To place this study in proper perspective, it must be noted that only a few such instances of defensive strategies were reported, and all of them were concentrated among a group of subjects who had been given a dose of epinephrine capable of producing substantial arousal of the sympathetic nervous system. There is also no indication in this and the forementioned studies as to whether the defensive strategies actually eliminate the observer's discomfort or just reduce it slightly.

To summarize, it appears that there may be an involuntary tendency to empathize with another's distress, but there may also be a limit to how aversive a response people will tolerate before resorting to strategies designed to eliminate their own aversive state or reduce it to a more tolerable level.

The Cognitive Component of Empathy

Though cognitive processes were involved in our discussion of empathic arousal, it was only because cognition mediates between the facial and situational cues of the model and the affect aroused in the observer. The role of cognitive mediation is even more apparent when the observer is empathically aroused by someone's verbal or written communication about his feelings or situation or by information about the model supplied by a third person. What I mean by the *cognitive component*, however, is something more fundamental to empathy.

Since empathy is a response to another person's situation, the mature empathic response must include awareness of the fact that the source of one's affect is something happening to someone else, as well as some sense of what the other is feeling. (There is evidence for an attentional component in empathic, as opposed to direct, distress: when a person watches someone receiving an electric shock, the observer's skin conductance increases, as it does when he is shocked himself. The observer's heart rate decelerates, however, whereas it accelerates when he is shocked directly. Heart rate deceleration is usually associated with attentional processes, and acceleration with stress.)

The young child who lacks a self–other distinction may be incapable of these cognitions. It thus appears that how a person experiences his empathically, as opposed to directly, aroused affect depends in part on the level at which he is aware of other people as entities separate from himself. There is considerable research that suggests that this cognitive sense of the other undergoes dramatic changes developmentally. I have reviewed this research (Hoffman, 1975), which falls under the general headings of "object permanence," role or perspective taking, and personal identity, and I have come up with four broad stages, which may be summarized briefly as follows.

First, for most of the first year, the child appears to experience a fusion between self and other. Second, at about 11–12 months, he attains "person permanence" and becomes aware of others as physical entities distinct from the self. Third, at about 2 or 3 years, he acquires a rudimentary sense of others not only as being physical entities but as having inner states, thoughts, perceptions, and feelings that are independent of his own. This third stage is the initial step in role taking, which continues to develop over the years into increasingly complex forms. Finally, by late childhood or perhaps sooner (the research is unclear here), he becomes aware of others as having personal identities and life experiences that extend beyond the immediate situation.

As the child passes through these four stages, the experience of empathy may be expected to include, in addition to a purely affective component, an increasing awareness of the source of the affect as lying in someone else's situation and a more veridical awareness of the other's feelings. I will now describe the four hypothetical levels of empathic response that result from this coalescence of empathic affect and the cognitive sense of the other, as exemplified by one type of empathy— that resulting from observing another person in distress.

1. At the first level—that is, for most of the first year before the child has acquired "person permanence"—distress cues from others may be expected to elicit a global empathic distress response, presumably a fusion of unpleasant feelings and stimuli that come from the infant's own body (through conditioning, motor mimicry, or possibly some innate mechanism), stimuli from the dimly perceived "other," and stimuli from the situation. The infant cannot yet differentiate himself from the other or from the situation. Consequently, he must often be unclear as to who is experiencing any distress that he witnesses, and he may at times behave as though what happened to the other person was happening to him. Consider a colleague's 11-month-old daughter, who, on seeing another child fall and cry, first stared at the victim, appearing to be about to cry herself, and then put her thumb in her mouth and buried her head in her mother's lap—her typical response when she has hurt herself and seeks comfort. This first stage of empathic distress may be described as a primitive, involuntary response based mainly on the "pull" of surface cues and minimally on higher cognitive processes.

2. In considering the processes involved in the transition to the second stage, it seems reasonable to suppose that along with the gradual emergence of a sense of the other as distinct from the self, the affective portion of the child's empathic distress is extended to the separate "self" and "other" that emerge. Early in this process, the child may only vaguely and momentarily be aware of the other as distinct from the self, and the image of the other, being transitory, may often slip in and out of focus. Consequently, the child probably reacts to another's distress as though his dimly perceived self-and-other were somehow simultaneously, or alternately, in distress. As an example, consider a child I know whose typical response to his own distress, beginning late in the first year, was to suck this thumb with one hand and pull his ear with the other. At 12 months, on seeing a sad look on his father's face, he proceeded to look sad and suck his thumb, while pulling his *father's* ear. The co-occurrence of distress in the emerging self and in the emerging "other" may be an important factor in the transition from the first stage to the second. And it is in the second stage that the child's empathic affective arousal first occurs in combination with an awareness of the fact that another person is the victim.

The child at the second stage knows that the other is a separate physical entity and that the other is the victim. He cannot yet distinguish between his own and the other's inner states (thoughts, perceptions, feelings), however, and tends to assume that they are identical to his own. The effect of this projective attribution of the child's inner states to another person is most clearly seen in the child's efforts to help, which consist chiefly of giving the other what he himself finds most comforting. Examples are a 13-month-old child who responded with a distressed look to an adult who looked sad and then offered the adult his beloved doll, and another child who ran to fetch his own mother to comfort a crying friend even though the friend's mother was equally available. Despite the limitation of this second level of empathic distress, it is a significant advance, since for the first time the child empathizes with another person who is perceived as distinct from the self. It is also likely at this second level that the child may for the first time become capable of being aroused not only through conditioning and mimicry but also through imagining himself in the other's place. This observation does not mean that his sense of how the other feels is necessarily more accurate, however, since this assessment continues to be based on projective attribution of his own empathically aroused feelings.[1]

3. At about 2–3 years of age, as noted earlier, the child begins to acquire a sense of others not only as physical entities but also as sources of feelings and thoughts in their own right. He is no longer certain that the real world and his perception of it are the same thing, and although he may not know what other people are thinking and feeling, he is becoming aware that their inner states may at times differ from his own and their perspectives may be based on their own needs and interpretations of events. He may still have tendencies to project his own feelings to others, but knowing that their inner states are independent of his makes him cautious and tentative in his inferences, as well as more alert and responsive to additional cues that may reflect their feelings. Thus, his sense of what the other is feeling begins to be based on more veridical, role-taking processes. By about 4 years of age, most children do respond with appropriate affect and can recognize signs of happiness or sadness in others in simple situations (e. g., Borke, 1971; Feshbach & Roe, 1968). And we may assume that as role-taking ability continues to develop, they become capable of detecting more subtle cues, for example, those reflecting complex emotions like disappointment, as well as feelings of ambivalence toward persons and events. Finally, with further advances in role-taking competence, the child becomes capable, for the first time, of being empathically aroused by imagining himself in the other's place.

4. Sometime during late childhood, owing to the emerging conception of self and other as continuous persons, each with his own history and identity, the child becomes aware that others feel pleasure and pain not only in particular situations but also in the context of their larger

---

[1] I should note as a caution that although projective attribution is not a veridical process, it may often result in an accurate assessment of the other's feelings. Sharing the same nervous system, people may generally be expected to respond with similar affect to the same situation; hence, projective attribution should usually result in a fairly accurate assessment. Thus, despite the errors in certain details in the examples cited above, the children were generally correct in their assumptions about how the other person felt.

pattern of life experiences. Consequently, though he may continue to react to their immediate situational distress, his concern is intensified when he knows it reflects a chronic condition. That is, being aware that others have inner states and a separate existence beyond the situation enables him to respond empathically not only to their transitory, situation-specific distress but also to what he imagines to be their general condition. This fourth level, then, consists of empathically aroused affect together with a mental representation of the other's general plight—his typical day-to-day level of distress or deprivation, the opportunities available or denied to him, his future prospects, and the like. If this representation falls short of what the observer conceives to be a minimally acceptable standard of well-being, an empathic distress response may result even if contradicted by the other's apparent momentary state. That is, the observer's mental representation may at times override contradictory situational cues.

To summarize, the individual who progresses through these four stages becomes capable of a high level of empathic distress. He can process various types of information—that gained from his own vicarious affective reaction, from the immediate situational cues, and from his general knowledge about the other's life. He can act out in his mind the emotions and experiences suggested by this information and introspect on all of this. He may thus gain an understanding and respond affectively in terms of the circumstances, feelings, and wishes of the other—while maintaining the sense that this is a separate person from himself. (This mature type of empathy is often cited in the clinical literature as essential in a good therapist.)

It also seems likely that with further cognitive development, the person may be able to comprehend the plight not only of an individual but also of an entire group or class of people—such as people who are economically impoverished, politically oppressed, socially outcast, victims of war, or mentally retarded. Because of his different background, his own specific distress experiences may differ from theirs. All distress experiences probably have a common affective core, however, and this common core together with the individual's high cognitive level at this age provides the requisites for a generalized empathic distress capability. The combination of empathic affect and the perceived plight of an unfortunate group would seem to be developmentally the most advanced form of empathic distress.

Sympathetic Distress

Thus far, it appears that the observer's experience of empathic distress includes both the aroused affect and a cognitive component derived from his cognitive sense of the other and his awareness that the other's state is the source of his own affect. Many affect theorists, notably Schachter and Singer (1962) and more recently Mandler (1975), have advanced the view that how a person labels or experiences an affect is heavily influenced by certain pertinent cognitions ["One labels, interprets, and identifies this stirred-up state in terms of the characteristics of the situation and one's apperceptive mass" (Schachter & Singer, 1962).] These writers are talking about how we distinguish between different affects (e. g., anger, joy, fear) aroused directly. Quite apart from the issue of whether directly aroused affects are differentiated in this manner (Izard, Tomkins, and others have argued persuasively that the differentiation of affects has a neural rather than a cognitive basis), the cognitive sense of others appears to be so intrinsic to *empathically* aroused affect that it not only accompanies but actually alters the very quality of the experience of any particular affect. Specifically, I would suggest that the observer's empathic distress, which is a parallel response—that is, a more or less exact replication of the victim's actual feelings of distress—may at least in part be transformed into a more reciprocal feeling of concern for the victim. The observer may continue to respond in a purely empathic manner, to feel uncomfortable and highly distressed himself, but he may also have a feeling of compassion, or what I call *sympathetic distress*, for the victim. This partial transformation of empathic distress into sympathetic distress is in keeping with how people report they feel when observing someone in distress. They continue to respond in a purely empathic manner, to feel uncomfortable and highly distressed themselves, but they also report a feeling of compassion for the victim, which is often accompanied by a felt desire to help him because they feel sorry, not, or at least not only, because they want to relieve their own empathic distress. It is, of course, true that we feel good after helping someone, but this does not mean that we help him in order to feel good.

The signs of the transformation of empathic into sympathetic distress should initially appear developmentally when the child begins to be aware of others as physically distinct from the self—at about 1 year of age, as discussed earlier. At first, only a small portion of the child's empathic distress may be transformed. As the child develops, the transformation should become more complete, although Stotland's report that nurses sometimes experience conflict between sympathetic feelings, including a desire to help their very ill patients, and their own empathic distress, which makes it difficult to stay in the same room with them, suggests that an element of pure empathic distress may always remain even in adulthood. The last three stages of empathic distress may then be viewed as stages in the development of sympathetic distress as well. In the description of stages, the affective component was presented as exisiting alongside the cognitive. Insofar as empathic distress is transformed into sympathetic distress, this formulation should be modified to stress the interaction between the affective and cognitive components and the important change in feeling tone that results.

Guilt

Other transformations of empathic distress can also occur. For example, the burgeoning research on casual attribution suggests that young children as well as adults may have a natural tendency to make inferences about the causes of behavior and events. Since empathic distress is a response to someone else's plight, any cues about what led to that plight, if salient enough, may serve as cognitive inputs—in addition to those deriving from the observer's sense of the other—that help shape the observer's affective experience. Once the child has acquired the cognitive capacity to recognize the consequences of his actions for others and to be aware that he has choice and control over his own behavior, he then has the necessary requisites for a self-critical or self-blaming response to his own actions. If the cues in a situation in which he responds empathically to someone in distress indicate that he is the cause of that distress, his response may then have both the affectively unpleasant and cognitive self-blaming component of the guilt experience, and his empathic distress may be transformed by the attribution of self-blame into a feeling of guilt, as I have discussed elsewhere (Hoffman, 1976, in press b).

The earliest guilt experience of this type probably occurs when the child's empathic response and his awareness of harming another person occur together or at least when the awareness follows soon after the empathic response, as when the parent points out the harmful effect of the child's act (Hoffman, 1977b), since this type of situation is the least demanding cognitively. A second type of guilt, guilt over inaction, becomes a possibility once the person acquires the additional capacity to construct a mental representation of an event that might have occurred but did not (e. g., a representation of how he might have acted to help another person whose distress he did not cause). The observer's realization that he did not act to reduce the other's distress when he might have, that he may therefore be to blame for the continuation though not the cause of the other's distress, may then be expected to transform his empathic distress into guilt. A similar analysis can be made for anticipatory guilt, which is highly demanding cognitively since the person must have the capacity to visualize not only an act that he has not performed (but may be contemplating) but the other person's probable distress response as well. Still another type of guilt is illustrated by the well-known phenomenon of survivor guilt in natural disasters and wars, as well as other examples cited elsewhere (Hoffman, 1976), in which the person has neither done nor contemplated doing anything wrong but feels somehow to blame because of circumstances beyond his control, specifically because his life condition happens to be far better than that of the distressed person he has encountered. This sense of blame may then transform his empathic response to the other's distress into feelings of guilt.

Developmentally, these different types of guilt should be related to the levels of empathic and sympathetic distress discussed earlier. Thus, at the second level of empathic distress, in which the child is especially responsive to the other person's inner states in the situation, he experiences sympathetic distress when not responsible for the other's distress, but when his actions have caused that distress, he experiences guilt. With further cognitive development, but still within the second level of empathic distress, the transformation of empathic distress into guilt may result from the awareness of not helping when he might reasonably have been expected to help. And with the capability of foreseeing the consequences of action and of inaction, anticipatory guilt also becomes possible. Similarly, at the highest level of empathic distress, when the observer is particularly sensitive to the other's general plight outside the immediate situation, if the focus of the observer's concern shifts from the other's plight to the contrast between it and the observer's own relatively advantaged life style, empathic distress may also be transformed into feelings of guilt.

Thus, I am suggesting that there may be one basic prosocial affect, empathic distress, which may be transformed into sympathetic distress or guilt, depending on the causal attributions made by the observer. It also seems reasonable to suppose that if the cues in the situation point to the individual's being responsible for his own plight, the observer's empathic distress might be transformed into some sort of derogatory feeling toward the other.

THE MOTIVATIONAL COMPONENT OF EMPATHY

Although many writers past and present have assumed that empathy provides a motivational base for prosocial behavior, a comprehensive explanation has not yet been offered, nor has the empirical research been systematically examined.

To begin, an argument both for a biologically based empathic tendency in humans and for the contribution of empathy to prosocial action can be made on the grounds of natural selection. I have presented such an argument elsewhere (Hoffman, 1977c). It has two parts: one deals with the evolutionary grounds for assuming an altruistic motive tendency in man and other attempts to explain why empathy is a likely basis for that motivation. The second is pertinent here and will be summarized. First, assuming that there is a constitutional basis for altruistic behavior, what criteria would it have to meet? It is not likely to be an automatic helping response, what ethologists call a *fixed action pattern*, because this would not take account of man's egoistic needs and would thus not allow the flexibility needed for survival. Furthermore, as Campbell (1972) noted, fixed altruistic action patterns can exist in certain insect societies because the individuals who are genetically programmed to sacrifice themselves for the group are not the same as those who are programmed to carry out the reproductive functions. This genetic separation of the altruistic and reproductive functions does not exist in man, however. What therefore may be assumed to have survived through natural selection in man is not a fixed action pattern but a *predisposition* or motive to act altruistically. Furthermore, this predisposition must be amenable to influence by perceptual and cognitive processes. Following Trivers's (1971) model, for example, the person may be motivated to help another in distress, but a judgmental process must intervene wherein he weighs the risk to himself and the gain to the other of helping or not helping. In other words, natural selection would require that a motive to help others in need is reliably aroused but that it is also subject to some degree of perceptual and cognitive control.

Empathy appears to fulfill all these criteria. First, the research indicates that it is a prevalent human response, although as yet, cross-cultural evidence is lacking (Hoffman, in press, a). Second, as we shall see, it appears to be accompanied by a predisposition to help, though not necessarily by actual helping behavior. Third, as suggested by the work of MacLean (1958, 1962, 1967, 1973), there appears to be a neural basis, mainly in the limbic system of the brain, for an early primitive empathic response, and the connections between the limbic system and the cortex indicate that a neural basis exists for cognitive intervention between empathic arousal and overt action. Fourth, empathy, like other emotions, is tied to visceral arousal, and there is evidence that visceral arousal does not occur until 1–2 seconds after the person attends to the precipitating stimulus. This lag between attention and arousal allows time for cognitive appraisal to occur. Finally, there is evidence that cognition may be an inherent part of empathic arousal, namely, the research mentioned earlier in which a person observing someone receiving an electric shock showed a deceleration of the heart rate. In short, empathy appears to fulfill the usual evolutionary criteria: it is reliably aroused; it predisposes one toward helping behavior (as will be seen); and there is a physiological basis for its cognitive control.

As for the psychological processes involved, I agree with most writers that empathic distress often functions as a prosocial motive because it is an aversive state that one can often best alleviate by giving help to the victim. I do not regard empathic distress as an egoistic motive, however, because unlike the usual egoistic motives (e. g., sensual pleasure, material gain, social approval, economic success), it is aroused by another person's misfortune, not one's own, a major goal of the ensuing behavior is to help the other, not just oneself, and the potential for gratification in the observer is contingent on his acting to reduce the other's distress. Furthermore, with the transformation of empathic into sympathetic distress, the conscious aim of the helper's act is presumably changed, at least in part, from relieving his own empathic discomfort into a genuine desire to relieve the distress perceived in the other.

Developmentally, in the earliest stages of the transformation of empathic into sympathetic distress, it seems reasonable to assume that as the infant's self–other fusion gives way to a sense of the other as distinct from the self, the motivational component of the child's empathic distress is extended to the separate "self" and "other" that emerge, in much the same manner used to describe the affective component earlier (see page 240). The first anecdote cited in that discussion (about the child who sucked his thumb and pulled his father's ear) illustrates the motivational property of empathic distress, as reflected in action designed to alleviate it. It illustrates too how the child's quasi-egoistic concern for his "own" discomfort may gradually begin to give way, at least in part, to a feeling of genuine concern for the victim. That is, in the shift from empathic to sympathetic distress, the aim of the child's action is changed from relieving his "own" (empathic) discomfort to relieving the distress perceived in another person. The examples cited later and others cited elsewhere (Hoffman, 1975) demonstrate that with the further development of the self–other distinction and the emergence of a more complete sympathetic response capability, the child's action seems more clearly designed to help the other person, although his initial efforts may still often be misguided because of limited understanding of the precise nature of the other's distress and the type of action needed to relieve it. Finally, with the consolidation of the self–other distinction (Stages 2 and 3), more veridical reality-testing procedures may be employed, including trial and error, response to corrective feedback, and eventually the utilization of information about the other's general life condition, and the child's efforts to help then become more appropriate.

I have recently reviewed the research on empathy and prosocial behavior (Hoffman, in press, a). What follows is a brief summary, with only some of the more recent, interesting findings given in detail. The correlational research, most of which has been done with children, is inconclusive. In preschool samples, for example, empathic children have been found more likely to comfort others, but then in this same age group, no correlation was obtained between empathy and cooperation, and a positive one was obtained between empathy and aggression in boys. And in a recent, rather elaborate study of 5-year-olds (Kameya, 1976), a lack of correlation between empathy and any of several measures of prosocial behavior was obtained. A possible explanation for these weak results is suggested by the introspective reports given by the subjects in a study by Levine and Hoffman (1975), from which it appears that the empathic capability of very young children may often not be engaged because their attention is easily captured by other, more or less irrelevant situational demands, such as the experimental instructions.

A finding worthy of special note was obtained by Kameya with one of his altruism measures. Among the subjects who volunteered to color pictures for hospitalized children, those who actually took the pictures with them and showed signs of following through on their promise had scored higher on an independent empathy measure than those who showed no signs of following through. This follow-through behavior is the only altruism index in that study—and in any of the research on children thus far—that involves considerable self-sacrifice over a pro-longed period (the subjects were told that they would have to do the coloring during two successive recess periods while the other children were out playing). A possible limitation of this index is that since the actions involved in following through were not anonymous, they might have been engaged in by the children desirous of gaining adult approval. There is evidence against this interpretation, namely, the rather considerable body of research indicating that children who lack social approval and who therefore may be presumed to be especially motivated to attain it are *less* likely to help others (e. g., Murphy, 1937; Staub & Sherk, 1970). We may therefore tentatively interpret Kameya's finding as suggesting that though empathy may not often be engaged at that young age, when it is engaged it often serves as a prosocial motive that is effective beyond the immediate situation.

The experimental research, all done with adults, provides far more consistent support than the correlational data for the view of empathic or sympathetic arousal as a prosocial motive. It may be useful first to state what kind of evidence is needed. If empathic distress does motivate altruistic behavior, three things should follow. First, there should be evidence of an association between empathic distress and a tendency to help the victim. Second, there should be evidence that the observer's empathic distress preceded and contributed to the helpful act. Third, as with any motive, there should be a relationship between the state of arousal and the occurrence of the consummatory act; that is, when the observer acts to help, the intensity of his empathic affect should diminish, and when he does not act to help, the arousal should continue at a high level. The evidence is supportive on all three counts.

1. There are many studies, too numerous to list, showing that when a person is exposed to another in distress, he responds either empathically or with an overt helping act, whichever is being investigated, and when data on both empathy and helping are obtained in the same study, subjects typically show both responses. Furthermore, as the magnitude of the pain cues from the victim increases, the latency of the helping act decreases (the subject acts more quickly). Clearly, people tend to be empathic and help others in need.

2. The question remains as to whether the empathic (or sympathetic) distress merely accompanies or actually motivates the act of helping. Several experimental studies involving collection of data on overt helping behavior, physiological arousal in response to another in distress, and, in some instances, verbal reports of the observer's feelings provide consistent support for the important role of empathic arousal in prosocial action (Krebs, 1975; Weiss, Buchanan, Alstatt, & Lombardo, 1971; Weiss, Boyer, Lombardo, & Stich, 1973). Without repeating the detailed analysis of the findings that led me to this conclusion (see Hoffman, in press a), let me simply state that the findings taken together not only show an association between empathic or sympathetic distress and altruistic behavior but also provide modest support for the view that empathic arousal may often motivate the altruistic act.

3. There is also evidence that the observer's empathic state diminishes in intensity after he engages in a helpful act and does not diminish if he does not act. Darley and Latane (1968), for example, report exactly this pattern in adults who heard sounds from someone who seemed to be having an epileptic fit. Those who did not respond overtly continued to be emotionally aroused and upset, as indicated by trembling hands and sweaty palms, whereas those who did respond showed fewer signs of continued upset. A similar finding was obtained in Murphy's (1937) nursery-school study: when children overtly helped others, their affective response appeared to diminish; when they did not help, the affect was prolonged.

A developmental line of argument can also be applied here. The acquisition of a motive often precedes the development of the cognitive and coping skills necessary for consummatory action appropriate to that motive. It follows that when a motive is aroused early in life, it may be followed by inappropriate action or no action, but as the person grows older, it should increasingly be accompanied by appropriate action. This developmental pattern appears to characterize the relation between empathy and altruistic action. For example, the younger children in the nursery-school observations reported by Bridges (1931) and Murphy (1937) were found to react to another's distress with a worried, anxious look but to do nothing, whereas the older children typically appeared upset but nevertheless did engage in an overt helpful act.

These findings as a group make up a package that is consistent with what we would expect with any motive. It therefore seems reasonable in the absence of a more convincing alternative explanation of the association between empathy and altruism to conclude tentatively that empathy does serve as a motive for altruistic behavior. There is no evidence, of course, that empathy is the sole motive, since this would require demonstrating that people do not help others in the absence of empathic distress. Nor does empathic arousal guarantee that altruistic action will follow, any more than any motive can guarantee a particular action. Competing egoistic motives, for example, may often override altruistic motives. Perhaps the best-known example is Milgram's (1963) finding that adults administered high levels of shock on instruction from the experimenter, despite strong feelings of compassion for the victim. It should be noted, however, that in a partial replication of that study, Tilker (1970) found that when the subject was placed in the role of observer, he not only showed an increasing empathic distress response as the shock levels to the victim were increased but often intervened to stop the experiment, despite specific instructions to the contrary and continuing opposition from the person administering the shock.

Empathic Overarousal

There is evidence that altruistic action may require a certain amount of need fulfillment in the observer, so as to reduce his self-preoccupation and thus leave him open and responsive to cues signifying the other's need for help. For example, the arousal of deprived need states such as concerns about failure, social approval, and even physical discomfort due to noise has been found to interfere with altruistic action (e. g., Murphy, 1937; Staub & Sherk, 1970; Moore, Underwood, & Rosenhan, 1973; Wine, 1975; Matthews & Canon, 1975). Since the experience of empathic distress itself may also at times involve extreme discomfort for the observer, under certain conditions it, too, might be expected to increase the observer's self-preoccupation and thus actually diminish the likelihood of altruistic behavior.

There is some recent evidence for such a backfire effect in children. Kameya (1976) found, as I mentioned earlier, no relation between kindergarten children's empathy scores and various helping behaviors. However, among a group of subjects given intensive role-taking training, a *negative* relation was obtained between empathy and one of the helping behaviors. The role-taking training consisted of presenting the subjects with several stories, each involving two or more children, in which one was ill, lonely, deprived, in physical pain, or a combination of these. The subjects played one role, then another, and finally participated in a discussion about the feelings of the children in the stories. Though the training was designed to improve the subjects' role-taking skills, Kameya suggested that the training may have actually evoked extreme empathic distress, especially in the high-empathy subjects. Consequently, there may have been an excess of arousal, with the result that their own emotional state became salient and claimed their total attention, thus interfering with the recognition of the other person's needs and the problem-solving orientation that might otherwise have led to efforts to alleviate the others' distress.

Perhaps there is an optimal range of empathic arousal—determined by the individual's level of distress tolerance—within which the subject is most responsive to the other's needs and most likely to help. When the arousal is much in excess of the optimal, the observer may become preoccupied with his own aversive state and consequently may not help the other. Another possible interpretation of Kameya's finding is that those subjects may not have been aroused in the first place, like those mentioned earlier in this paper who, once over their threshold of distress tolerance, employed various perceptual and cognitive strategies to avoid being aroused empathically. This is an obviously important problem that needs further, more systematic work at all ages.

Guilt and Prosocial Action

Most of the subjects (10- and 12-year-olds and adults) in our own moral development research gave clear guilt responses to projective story-completion items in which transgressions were committed by the central figure. In most cases, the guilt feelings described were followed immediately by the attribution to the story character of some sort of reparative behavior that functioned to reduce his guilt. The central figures in the story were also often portrayed by our subjects as resolving to become less selfish and more considerate of others in the future. This response suggests that one mechanism by which guilt may contribute to prosocial behavior is to trigger a process of self-examination and restructuring of values that may help strengthen one's prosocial motives.

Experimental evidence that guilt contributes to altruism has been obtained in numerous studies in which adults who were led to believe that they had harmed someone showed a heightened willingness to help others—and not just to help the people to whom they had done wrong. Thus they engaged in various altruistic deeds, such as volunteering to participate in a research project (Freedman, Wallington, & Bless, 1967), contributing to a charitable fund (Regan, 1971), and spontaneously offering to help a passerby whose grocery bag had broken (Regan, Williams, & Sparling, 1972). These findings are limited since they show only short-run effects (the altruistic deed immediately followed the guilt induction) and the subjects were college students. Together with the story-completion data, however, they support the view that guilt may result in a generalized motive for altruistic action beyond immediate reparation to the victim.

Summary

The rudiments of a theoretical model of empathic arousal, its cognitive transformations, and its possible implications for prosocial action were presented. Empathy was defined in terms of the vicarious arousal of affect without regard to the degree of match between the observer and the model or the nature of the cues eliciting the empathic response. The experience of empathic distress consists of an affective component, a cognitive component derived from the observer's cognitive sense of the other person, and, in the case of some affects, a motivational component. The focus was on empathic distress, although many of the issues raised may also pertain to other affects.

Several modes of empathic arousal—based on reflexive action, motor mimicry, conditioning, and imagination and differing as to perceptual and cognitive requisites as well as the extent to which they are under conscious control—were presented and a rough developmental ordering of their appearance was suggested. The development of a cognitive sense of the other was discussed, and stages in the development of empathic distress in relation to this sense of the other were delineated.

Once the child begins to acquire a cognitive sense of the other as distinct from the self, his empathic distress is assumed to be transformed in part into a more reciprocal concern for the other, called *sympathetic distress*. If, on the other hand, the observer blames himself for the other's distress, this attribution transforms his empathic distress into feelings of guilt. Several types of guilt—guilt over commission, inaction, anticipated action, and relative advantage—were discussed and their probable developmental order of appearance indicated. Theoretical considerations and empirical findings were brought to bear in support of the notion that empathic and sympathetic distress as well as guilt may serve as motives for prosocial action.

In conclusion, the theoretical model offered is as yet loose and tentative. Though consistent with the available data, its confirmation or disconfirmation awaits the test of hypotheses derived specifically from it. For example, is empathic distress transformed into sympathetic distress as the child begins to acquire a sense of the other as distinct from the self? Does empathic arousal lead to an increase in guilt feelings after one has harmed another? Does the frequent use of child-rearing practices that direct the child's attention to other people's inner states (e.g., inductive discipline) contribute to sympathetic distress and prosocial behavior, or is it more likely to contribute to a tendency to be empathically overaroused and to use strategies designed to reduce the resulting aversive state?

Should the model survive the empirical test, it would be worthwhile to see if it can be extended to the empathic arousal of other affects besides distress. It might also be applicable in a general way to directly experienced affects. In this case, the arousal modes would be different because the person is responding to stimulus events that are impinging on him, and there is evidence for a difference in direct and empathic arousal: the difference in physiological response to being given electric shock and watching someone else be shocked. The cognitive component of directly experienced affect would presumably be linked to the cognitive awareness of the self rather than cognitive awareness of others, although the development of self-awareness and awareness of the other is undoubtedly highly intertwined. Finally, the motivational component of direct affect may be expected to operate in much the same manner as the motivational component of empathic affect, with the possible exception of overarousal, in which the distinction between a vicarious response to another and a direct response to stimuli impinging on the self is blurred.

References

Aderman, D., Brehm, S. S., & Katz, L. B. Empathic observation of an innocent victim: The just world revisited. *Journal of Personality and Social Psychology*, 1974, *29*, 342–347.

Aronfreed, J. The socialization of altruistic and sympathetic behavior: Some theoretical and experimental analyses. In J. Macaulay & L. Berkowitz (Eds.), *Altruism and helping behavior*. New York: Academic Press, 1970, pp. 103–126.

Bandura, H., & Rosenthal, L. Vicarious classical conditioning as a function of arousal level. *Journal of Personality and Social Psychology*, 1966, *3*, 54–62.

Berger, S. M. Conditioning through vicarious instigation. *Psychological Review*, 1962, *69*, 450–466.

Berger, S. M., & Hadley, S. W. Some effects of a model's performance on observer electromyographic activity. *American Journal of Psychology*, 1975, *88*, 263–276.

Bernal, G. & Berger, S. M. Vicarious eyelid conditioning. *Journal of Personality and Social Psychology*, 1976, *34*, 62–68.

Borke, H. Interpersonal perception of young children: Egocentricism or empathy. *Developmental Psychology*, 1971, *5*, 263–269.

Bridges, K. M. B. *The social and emotional development of the preschool child*. London: Kegan Paul, 1931.

Campbell, D. T. On the genetics of altruism and the counter-hedonic components in human culture. *The Journal of Social Issues*, 1972, *28*, 21–38.

Crowell, D. H., Blurton, L. B., Kobayashi, L. R., McFarland, J. L., & Yang, R. K. Studies in early infant learning: Classical conditioning of the neonatal heart rate. *Developmental Psychology*, 1976, *12*, 373–397.

Darley, J. M., & Latane, B. Bystander intervention in emergencies: Diffusion of responsibility. *Journal of Personality and Social Psychology*, 1968, *8*, 377–383.

Feshbach, N. D., & Roe, K. Empathy in six- and seven-year-olds. *Child Development*, 1968, *39*, 133–145.

Freedman, J. L., Wallington, S. A., & Bless, E. Compliance without pressure: The effect of guilt. *Journal of Personality and Social Psychology*, 1967, *7*, 117–124.

Gelhorn, E. Motion and emotion: The role of proprioception in the physiology and pathology of the emotions. *Psychological Review*, 1964, *71*, 457–472.

Hoffman, M. L. Empathy, role-taking, guilt and the development of altruistic motives. Developmental Psychology Report No. 30, University of Michigan, 1973.

Hoffman, M. L. Developmental synthesis of affect and cognition and its implications for altruistic motivation. *Developmental Psychology*, 1975, *11*, 607–622.

Hoffman, M. L. Empathy, role-taking, guilt, and development of altruistic motives. In T. Likona (Ed.), *Moral development: Current theory and research*. New York: Holt, 1976.

Hoffman, M. L. Sex differences in empathy and related behaviors. *Psychological Bulletin*, 1977, *84*, 712–722. (a)

Hoffman, M. L. Moral internalization: Current theory and research. In L. Berkowitz (Ed.), *Advances in experimental social psychology* (Vol. 10). New York: Academic Press, 1977, pp. 86–135. (b)

Hoffman, M. L. Is altruism part of human nature? Unpublished manuscript. University of Michigan, Ann Arbor, 1977. (c)

Hoffman, M. L. Empathy, its development and prosocial implications. In B. Keasy (Ed.), *Nebraska symposium on motivation* (Vol. 26). Lincoln: University of Nebraska Press, in press. (a)

Hoffman, M. L. Adolescent morality in developmental perspective. In J. Adelson (Ed.), *Handbook of adolescent psychology*. New York: Wiley Interscience, in press. (b)

Humphrey, G. The conditioned reflex and the elementary social reaction. *Journal of Abnormal and Social Psychology*, 1922, *17*, 113–119.

Iannotti, R. J. Empathy as a motivator of altruistic behavior. Paper presented at the meeting of the American Psychological Association, New Orleans, August 1974.

Izard, C. E. *The face of emotion*. New York: Appleton-Century Crofts, 1971.

James, W. *The principles of psychology*. New York: Holt, 1890.

Kameya, L. I. The effect of empathy level and role-taking training upon prosocial behavior. Unpublished doctoral dissertation, University of Michigan, 1976.

Krebs, D. Empathy and altruism. *Journal of Personality and Social Psychology*, 1975, *32*, 1124–1146.

Laird, J. D. Self-attribution of emotion: The effects of expressive behavior on the quality of emotional experience. *Journal of Personality and Social Psychology*, 1974, *29*, 475–486.

Lerner, M. J., & Simmons, C. Observer's reaction to the innocent victim: Compassion or rejection? *Journal of Personality and Social Psychology*, 1966, *4*, 203–210.

Levine, L. E., & Hoffman, M. L. Empathy and cooperation in 4-year-olds. *Developmental Psychology*, 1975, *11*, 533–534.

Lipps, T. Das Wissen von fremden Ichen. *Psychologische Untersuchnung*, 1906, *1*, 694–722.

MacLean, P. D. The limbic system with respect to self-preservation and the preservation of the species. *Journal of Nervous Mental Disease*, 1958, *127*, 1–11.

MacLean, P. D. New findings relevant to the evolution of psychosexual functions of the brain. *Journal of Nervous Mental Disease*, 1962, *135*, 289–301.

MacLean, P. D. The brain in relation to empathy and medical education. *Journal of Nervous Mental Disease*, 1967, *144*, 374–382.

MacLean, P. D. *A triune concept of the brain and behavior*. Toronto: University of Toronto Press, 1973.

Mandler, G. *Mind and emotion*. New York: Wiley, 1975.

Mathews, K. E., & Canon, L. K. Environmental noise level as a determinant of helping behavior. *Journal of Personality and Social Psychology*, 1975, *32*, 571–577.

Mathews, K., & Stotland, E. Empathy and nursing students' contact with patients. University of Washington, Spokane, 1973. (Mimeo)

McDougall, W. *An introduction to social psychology*. London: Methuen, 1908.

Milgram, S. Behavioral study of obedience. *Journal of Abnormal & Social Psychology*, 1963, *67*, 371–378.

Moore, B. S., Underwood, B., & Rosenhan, D. L. Affect and altruism. *Developmental Psychology*, 1973, *8*, 99–104.

Murphy, L. B. *Social behavior and child personality*. New York: Columbia University Press, 1937.

Regan, J. W. Guilt, perceived injustice, and altruistic behavior. *Journal of Personality and Social Psychology*, 19, *18*, 124–132.

Regan, D. T., Williams, M., & Sparling, S. Voluntary expiation of guilt: A field experiment. *Journal of Personality and Social Psychology*, 1972, *24*, 42–45.

Sagi, A., & Hoffman, M. L. Empathic distress in newborns. *Developmental Psychology*, 1976, *12*, 175–176.

Schachter, S., & Singer, J. E. Cognitive, social and physiological determinants of emotional state. *Psychological Review*, 1962, *69*, 379–399.

Simner, M. L. Newborn's response to the cry of another infant. *Developmental Psychology*, 1971, *5*, 136–150.

Speisman, J. C., Lazarus, R. C., Mordkoff, A., & Davison, L. Experimental reduction of stress based on ego-defense theory. *Journal of Personality and Social Psychology*, 1964, *68*, 367–380.

Staub, E., & Sherk, L. Need for approval, children's sharing behavior, and reciprocity in sharing. *Child Development*, 1970, *41*, 243–253.

Stotland, E. Exploratory investigations of empathy. In L. Berkowitz (Ed.), *Advances in experimental social psychology* (Vol. 4). New York: Academic Press, 1969.

Stotland, E., Sherman, S. E., & Shaver, K. G. *Empathy and birth order*. Lincoln: University of Nebraska Press, 1971.

Sullivan, H. S. *Conceptions of modern psychiatry*. London: Tavistock Press, 1940.

Tilker, H. A. Socially responsible behavior as a function of observer responsibility and victim feedback. *Journal of Personality and Social Psychology*, 1970, *14*, 95–100.

Tomkins, S. S. *Affect, imagery, conciousness*. New York: Springer, 1962.

Trivers, R. L. The evolution of reciprocal altruism. *Quarterly Review of Biology*, 1971, 46, 35–57.

Weiss, R. F., Boyer, J. L., Lombardo, J. P., & Stich, M. H. Altruistic drive and altruistic reinforcement. *Journal of Personality and Social Psychology*, 1973, 25, 390–400.

Weiss, R. F., Buchanan, W., Alstatt, L., & Lombardo, J. P. Altruism is rewarding. *Science*, 1971, 171, 1262–1263.

Wine, J. D. Test anxiety and helping behavior. *Canadian Journal of Behavioral Science*, 1975, 7, 216–222.

9

The Nature of Complex, Unlearned Responses

Harry F. Harlow and Clara Mears

We are very fond of the title of our chapter "The Nature of Complex, Unlearned Responses," because it illustrates one of our violent aversions. Let us try to expiate sin.

Everyone knows that nature abhors a vacuum, but there is one thing that nature abhors more than a vaccum, and that is a logical *dichotomy*. Yet, when people speak and try to think, they automatically think in such dichotomies: hot and cold, day and night, black and white, men and women, God and the Devil, heaven and hell, and, above all, learned and innate or heredity and environment. Fortunately, the pituitary gland escaped. Everyone knows that all behaviors, both learned and unlearned, are localized in the pituitary!

In the title of our chapter, we unwittingly created two dichotomies in the two successive words, *complex* and *unlearned*. *Complex* infers its opposite, simple, and *unlearned* its opposite, learned.

After choosing our topic, we prepared to research its history at the University of Arizona libraries, but the University of Arizona apparently heard about our intentions and immediately closed the libraries for 45 days. Fortunately, the senior author had taught comparative psychology for 30 years, from 1930 to 1960, and knew most of the history of the theories of unlearned, innate, or unconditioned responses. We also were aware that for the past quarter of a century these terms had been religiously avoided as thoroughly as scientists can act religiously.

HARRY F. HARLOW and CLARA MEARS · University of Arizona, Tucson, Arizona.

The first facts and theories about unlearned responses existed under the rubric of *tropisms*, defined as differential responses to unequal stimulation of the two sides of bilaterally symmetrical animals. Tropisms were supposedly the unlearned responses made by organisms ranging from mealworms to man. Almost 100 years ago, biological scientists who were interested in converting the simplest behaviors to complicated mathematics studied tropisms. Even psychologists recognize that tropisms are not important forms of mammalian behaviors until they themselves fall victim to the mathematical compulsion to thus express the meaningless. Tropisms were obviously scientific data since they could be described in terms of mathematical formulas, whether the stimuli were external or internal or both. For example, stimulation of the right side of the slug *tenebrio* is followed by head turning to the left, and this act can be simplified and described by a mathematical equation.

Note, for example, the beauty of this mathematical formula (Crozier, 1929):

$$- \frac{ds}{dt} = k_1 S_0 - K_1 x - K_2 S_0 x^2 + K_2 x^3$$

Of course, the responses being measured, the genuflection of the anterior segments of mealworms, were maudlin and meaningless movements, but maudlin movements acquire mysterious meaning if they can be expressed mathematically. Furthermore, men have tropisms if they are blindfolded and left to ice skate on frozen vastnesses in northern Minnesota. These responses are called circus responses and they are a form of tropism. Human tropistic circus responses can also be produced by having blindfolded men ride motorcycles over the white sand dunes of the Sahara.

Even sighted men engage in circus responses if they are totally lost in forest vastness. These responses can also be elicited in dogs and other normal animals by removal of either the left or the right hemisphere of the brain. Remove the right hemisphere and the animal circles to the left, and remove the left hemisphere and the animal circles to the right (Loeb, 1918).

The origin of theories of complex, unlearned behaviors trace back to instinct theory. Instinct theory was described and observed in detail by Fabre (1918) with various species of wasps, especially the giant wasp, *Specius speciosus*. Fabre doubted that these responses could be explained in terms of evolution, and even though Eisele (1975) believes that they can be traced back to evolution, he doubts that this will ever be accomplished by any living human being.

The early psychologists, including James, McDougall, and Watson, properly accepted instincts as the basis for all of its present misconnotations. J. B. Watson, one of the most ardent of the instinct theorists and also one of the most ingenious instinct investigators, defined instinct as "a series of concatenated movements unfolding serially to appropriate stimulation" (1914). With Lashley, Watson conducted two long and detailed researches on the noddy and sooty tern on the island of the Dry Tortugas. Watson, in his own comment, described his personal level of scholarship, saying, "I do not read books. I write them" Lashley once told the senior author that had Watson and he not exhausted their supply of cigarettes and whiskey while on the Dry Tortugas, they would probably not only have remained on the island, but they also might have remained instinct theorists.

Being an instinctivist came instinctively to Watson because for almost 15 years of his academic life, he had no inkling of the real significance of Pavlovian conditioned responses. In his 1914 writings, he thought of conditioned responses as just one of four different techniques for measuring sensory limens in subhuman animals. By 1919, Watson had still not abandoned instinct theory, nor had he entirely escaped from any of the fabled 13. There were no detailed accounts of conditioning and no references to conditioning or conditioned reflexes in his 1919 book. He was still far more impressed by Bechterev than by Pavlov.

By 1919, Watson had discovered a new category of unlearned behavior, the emotions. At that time, he thought of emotions and instincts as being very similar, save for the fact that emotions were more related to visceral and instincts to skeletal muscle responses. Watson's emotions were not complex unlearned responses as instincts had been. He described his three new instinct allies, fear, anger, and love, as relatively discrete, limited, and almost reflexlike responses. Fear was produced by loud sounds and loss of support, rage by hampering of bodily movements, and love by stimulation of the erogenous zones. Watson and Raynor, for whom he did feel some emotion, not fear, succeeded in conditioning little Albert, an 11-month-old infant, to the fear of a rat. Neither Albert nor Watson was ever quite the same again.

As scientifically expressed, neither Watson's emotions nor his instincts could be clearly considered complex, unlearned responses. Complex instincts were espoused by William James, Thorndike, and McDougall. McDougall believed, in addition, that every instinct carried with it some emotional aura.

In the early 1920s, Watson began to bite the hand that fed him and to deny and deride instinct theory. This was the beginning of the great black-and-white era. What was innate could not be tainted by learning, and upon innate rudiments of behavior, monolithic superstructures of learning were amassed. Instinctivists, whose instincts covered the waterfront, were just as exclusive as were the extreme behaviorists. Black was black and white was white.

Three unconditioned response theorists dominated psychological thinking on unlearned responses and these three were Pavlov, Guthrie, and Skinner. Pavlov's contributions to complex unlearned behaviors were nil. Guthrie was more broadminded and finally realized that the unconditional stimuli underlying complex learning were more than simple reflexes. Guthrie was well ahead of his time and was the first psychologist to turn down an academic offer from Harvard, which has since become one of the three greatest universities in Massachusetts.

Any survey of the nature of complex unlearned responses would be more or less incomplete if one did not mention Fred Skinner. Although Skinner never mentions unconditioned stimuli, it is clear that he conceives of unlearned responses as any responses that any animal naturally makes, the theory of "doing what comes naturally." Thus, Skinner discovered that a peck of pigeons makes a bushel of research.

Actually, Skinner's research would have destroyed the Japanese navy had the American navy not already destroyed it. Skinner had the ingenious idea of having pigeons guide guided missiles by differential pecking. Skinner approached this problem a peck at a time while hiding his light under a bushel.

After World War II ended, the navy continued these researches, and after Harlow joined the army as a civilian in 1949–1950, they generously offered to give him all of the million dollars worth of equipment as well as both pigeons and to ship everything out to the University of Wisconsin. He had no interest in keeping the navy shipshape and therefore declined the offer. Besides, Harlow had decided that Skinner's research on guided missiles was misguided. Fortunately, Skinner subsequently went farther and with greater accuracy.

When Skinner discovered some animals that didn't do naturally what he wanted them to do, he conveniently discovered the technique of "shaping," which took care of his problem. The fact that shaping by other names was just as sweet did not alter the fact that it had been previously discovered by a series of psychologists during the last half-century. It was even independently discovered by Tinbergen, whose wife used it as a therapeutic technique not yet adopted by psychiatrists. Guthrie and Horton (1946) did an original and brilliant experimental study incorporating the shaping principle as early as 1946. They created a puzzle box whose door opening was activated by a bar hung from the ceiling. When the cat in the box brushed any part of its body against the bar, the door obligingly opened. Guthrie and Horton traced the progress of the cats, watching the aimless characteristic of the behavior gradually disappear. Eventually, the cat purposefully and immediately approached and activated the bar.

In Skinner's recently evolved theories relating to unlearned behavior, one of his categories is that of "precise, fixed, but persistent" reflex-type behavior. These are not the Pavlovian acute and transient unconditioned responses. They are not only precise and repetitive but, what is more important, they are persistent behaviors. The classic example is pigeon pecking, which has a long and honorable history. Pigeons will persistently peck at any bright and precise object, and if all bright and precise objects are removed, the pigeons will persistently peck anyway. They apparently realize that a single peck does not provide a peck of pickled peppers. Just as the pigeon's peck paid off, so did Skinner's persistent research.

The other and more important type of Skinnerian unconditioned responses is that designed to serve an experimenter's predestined destiny. The classic example is lever pressing. Just as Archimedes planned to move the world with a lever, so did Skinner plan to move psychology. Since rats and some very stupid primates do not automatically make *persistent* lever-pressing responses, Skinner used his technique of shaping according to the naval doctrine of "shape up or ship out."

Although conditioning became the learning byword for the neobehaviorists of the 1950s and 1960s, their learning apparatus changed from the unconditioned response to maze manipulations. The original maze was the Hampton Court maze, but since rats did not shape readily to the HC maze, new and simpler mazes came into use, particularly the multiple T mazes and Y mazes (Hull, 1952). Having started, however, the shaping process ran its inevitable course, and the multiple T and Y mazes shrank down to single T and single Y units. Eventually, these single T and Y units were simplified into straight-alley mazes, which enabled Logan to measure incentives (Logan, 1960). Previously, Tolman and Miles learned to "shape" elevated maze learning by running rats on straight-alley mazes, and most maze runners ran rats on a straight-alley maze to shape subsequent multiple blind-alley maze performance.

"It matters not how straight the gate." Both Hull and Spence became so enchanted with their "shaping" straight-alley techniques that they subsequently abandoned attempts to study the real learning of mazes by rats. Not only were the rats shaped up, but so were the experimenters. This was beautifully illustrated by the demise of maze learning. Psychologists shaped their animals by running them down straight alleys for shaping purposes. Eventually, psychologists found that running the animals down straight alleys enabled them to measure such variables as speed of running from one end of the straight alley to the other and also equally unimportant *complicated* motivational variables such as food and water deprivation. However, there was a real advantage and probably a real tragedy produced by these shaping procedures. Hull and Spence made the unfortunate discovery that the variables underlying meaningless straight-alley learning could be reduced, and we really mean reduced to mathematical formulas (Spence, 1956):

$$_sH_R = ICO(1 - e^{-kw})e^{-jT'}(1 - lc^{-lN})$$

A description of one weekly colloquium of the Harvard psychology department in a biographical sketch of von Bekesy, a Nobel Prize winner, aptly sums up the importance of reducing pseudolearning to mathematical formulas. The guest colloquium speaker was desperately dull in discussing his mathematical theory of behavior. At the conclusion of his lay lecture, the audience responded at equally great length and with equally fatuous comments.

> When at long last it was all over, Bekesy led me directly to the blackboard in his office, picked up a piece of chalk and said, 'This is the most important but least known equation in all of the social sciences. Always remember it, for, as you have just seen, it completely describes a great deal of human behavior.' And then—summing up the whole afternoon neatly—he wrote: $0 + 0 = 0$. (Ratliff, 1976)

While giving due credit to the futile and foolish theories of the famous behavior theorists, we must accept the fact that none of these men even approached a study of the mechanisms underlying complex unlearned behaviors. By *complex behaviors*, we mean such behaviors as play, aggression, love in its many faceted forms, language, and thinking.

There are three criteria useful in the determination of complex, unlearned responses:

1. *In orderly fashion, they follow developmental maturation stages.* Complex unlearned behavior may start early or late, but the completion of maturation is always relatively late. If you study the developmental stages and sequences, it will be obvious that none of them could possibly have escaped the taint and tar brush of limited or even unlimited learning. Learning is inescapable at all times after the very start of complex unlearned behaviors.

2. *They are complex in nature, based as they are upon multiple variables.* Complex unlearned behaviors are not conglomerates of many innate elements, but there will be more than one variable, since primate behavior is by nature not simple enough to explain by only one factor. No matter how many or how few the unlearned variables, there may be countless learned ways of expressing these unlearned behaviors.

3. *Complex, unlearned behaviors are extremely persistent over long periods of time or even through life itself.*

Of complex unlearned behaviors, the love systems and especially the infant–mother relationships most readily illustrate these three criteria, probably because the surrogate mother experiments lent themselves to extensive, definitive findings. The love of the infant for the mother and the maternal love for the infant each pass through developmental stages based primarily upon the gradual maturation of the child, both in mastering its physical environment and in understanding its cultural environment. Research with the surrogate mother established the complexity of these loves based on the multiple variables of contact comfort, warmth, rocking motion, and nursing (Harlow, 1958). Numerous recent studies have found that mothers respond lovingly in their own fashion to these same variables and that, in addition, communication plays an important part in the loves of both. Communication adds to the complexity of the maternal–infant affectional system, based as it also is on multiple variables that include eye contact, smiling, touch, and gesture, plus varied auditory stimulation even before spoken language becomes added to the list. Research on these variables formed the bases for many of the presentations in the present symposium.

Maternal and infant love have been found to be very persistent in the face of many odds, including the commercialism of Mother's Day. Oddly enough, infant love in many cases proves to be even more persistent than the long belabored maternal love. It persists even when the infant is completely ignored or actually battered by the abnormal motherless mother (Harlow, Harlow, Dodsworth, & Arling, 1966).

Peer love and heterosexual love form a progression in the maturation of the first four of the love systems. The basic mechanism of peer love is social play, though peer bonds may form even before social play burgeons (Harlow & Harlow, 1969). Peer love depends also upon adequate, antecedent maternal affection. To this requirement heterosexual love adds adequate, antecedent peer relations. This trilogy is bound together by the contact comfort provided originally by the mother. The appreciation and acceptance of bodily contact through maternal love bonds prepares the young for enjoyment of the physical contact attendant upon peer play. Peer play is the proving ground for social and sexual roles that encompass preparation for heterosexual love. Without pleasant prior peer play and affection, the blushing bride or nonblushing unmarried is likely to insist upon physical privacy, which has drawbacks in promoting happy, heterosexual hugs.

The persistence of peer love is obvious from the long-lived friendships between peers of the same or opposite sexes. These friendships often outlast one, two, or even three heterosexual loves. Whether or not one accepts the persistence of heterosexual love depends entirely upon whether or not one demands the legalization of same.

There is one love, that of the forgotten man, the father, which deserves individual attention because most paternal behavior has been presumed to be largely learned. The father has been quietly accumulating attention in his own experimental right. Of course, the father has for decades been recognized for his protection of family and friends, especially of feral family and friends. The more successfully the father protects, the more likely he is to have successors, and this is one good argument for the unlearned nature of paternal protective behavior. It seems, however, that many human fathers feel more than just protective affection for their offspring, as Lamb (1975) has been proving first while at Yale and now at Wisconsin. Fathers may even play with their young ones more frequently and in a different fatherly fashion than does the ever-loving mother.

Psychological theories concerning the complex responses of many other behaviors, particularly those of play, aggression, and language, have remained troubled and muddled. Since evidence is being compiled from two primate species, and the macaque does not possess verbal apparatus anatomically adequate for spoken language, we are in this paper considering just the first two of these behaviors, play and aggression.

Just as the love of the infant for the mother was for years liquefied in maternal libations, so was play, the delight of childhood, engulfed in obscurity along with its prerequisite, childhood. Accurate records of the developmental childhood years were nonexistent during the Middle Ages, but we do know that during the 18th and 19th centuries the Industrial Revolution forced countless children, as well as their parents, into not very gainful employment. Even before the height of the industrial developments, England began to feel the force of the Puritan religious movement, which then moved, along with the Puritans, to the American continent. The Puritan fathers, who slept sanctimoniously in their straight and narrow beds, gave religious sanction to the work ethic and discouraged play along with pleasure. The development of play and games went into not a recess but a long recession.

In the United States, the first child labor laws, with New York State taking the lead, were passed at the beginning of the 20th century, but for many more years, the theories of play reflected the need to justify the very existence of childhood and play. There is still some acceptance of Groos' (1898) theory that play provides exercise for direct training for adulthood. There is even more discussion of the psychoanalytic concept of play as a receptacle for either disguising or acting out emotional conflicts. Play for pleasure and for play's sake have been tacitly recognized in studies of game preferences, but the pith of play has remained a mystery.

Harlow became interested in social play as the underlying mechanism in peer love and the proving ground for social and sexual roles. In his search for an antecedent to social play, he postulated that curiosity and exploration might form the unlearned basis but was never experimentally convinced. This theory is so obviously wrong and so hopelessly inept that it gained ready acceptance from a number of psychologists. However, as Hutt (1966) pointed out, there may have been chaos added to confusion because two different types of exploration have been considered as one.

Mears had for a number of years been interested in the role of physical activity in maintaining positive personal adjustment. She had also noted that few studies of play in young children had been conducted outdoors where the child has freedom physically and permission parentally to run and to jump, to climb and to swing, with pervasive pleasure. The element of pleasure in animal play has long been recognized and described in human play by Blurton-Jones (1967) in the rough-and-tumble play of nursery-school children.

Mears (see Mears & Harlow, 1975) proposed that exploration of one type, comparable to the "specific" form of Hutt, was connected with play but just as much with many other behaviors, since it was responsible for the initiation of new behaviors. She also postulated, however, that the fundamental play form, primary and basic to social play, was a group of behaviors termed *self-motion play* or *peragration*, the motion of a body through space. We suspect that the term *peragration* was originally used to refer to the motion of heavenly bodies through heavenly space, but as many bodies have been referred to as heavenly, prosaic license has been exercised. Rosenblum (1961), in his categories of feedback object play and activity play among rhesus monkeys, presented the picture most nearly resembling self-motion play but with some fundamental differences (Mears, in press).

Mears and Harlow (1975) conducted a three-month developmental study of the play of eight rhesus macaques from the average ages of 90 to 180 days. All behaviors were recorded with the exception of basic intake and output of food and drink. Five categories of peragration were specifically investigated, and three of these proved to be of significance. These were self-motion play, individual or nonsocial, both with and without the use of apparatus. Social self-motion play developed significantly only when apparatus was involved. Peragration is best illustrated by the activities of swinging, rocking, water or snow skiing, leaping, running, and jumping. A total list of appropriate behaviors would be extensive, but all would be dependent upon the motion of the whole body.

Self-motion play was found to exist as an entity separate from ordinary locomotion and from visual and tactile exploration, both of which started at different levels of frequency than peragration and then maintained an almost level plateau of frequency, whereas self-motion play spiraled upward at an amazingly significant rate to a level of frequency more than six times as great.

Peragration could be either a social or an individual behavior, but it developed earlier and to a greater extent as a solitary, nonsocial activity, a play form basic and primary in the maturational heirarchy. Both with and without the use of extensive motion apparatus in the playroom, self-motion individual play held significant sway, whereas social play required apparatus to raise the developmental rate to a significant level.

The pervasive and powerful persistence of self-motion play in human life is evidenced by the progressive stages of rocking behavior from rocking in mother's arms, in the cradle, and on the rocking horse to the merry-go-round, rock and roll, and the rocking chair with the approaching glimpse of the Rock of Ages.

Experimentally we also had confirmation of the persistence of peragration (Mears, in press). Two matched groups of rhesus were separated after the developmental study, four to remain in the original equipped playroom with ladders, platforms of different heights, swinging rings, bars, and revolving apparatus to encourage peragration. The other four shared a playroom with all of the motion equipment removed except for the long bar with the swinging rings. This bar was moved to within 5 cm of the ceiling, which was approximately 260 cm above the floor. The chains of the swinging rings were wound tight around the bar, immobilizing the rings.

During the 90 days of this experiment, not only the persistence but the extent of the preference for self-motion play was evident. Peragration without the use of any apparatus, leaping and jumping in the air, running, somersaulting, and tumbling significantly increased in the deprived playroom, both in individual and in social play. This increase was significant both in comparison with their own prior play and with the play of the four matched rhesus still playing in the original playroom. These two groups had shown no signficant difference in performance on any self-motion behaviors before, during, or at the end of the original developmental experiment.

An unexpected jackpot was won when one of the infant male monkeys in the deprived playroom literally reached motivational heights, as illustrated in the series of Figures 1–6. For days and weeks,

FIG. 1. Aiming high.

he sat in the pictorially documented pose, on his surrogate, looking longingly at the bar and rings no longer accessible by way of platforms, ladders, and leaps as shown in Figure 1. He also gazed at a 2-cm projection, two-thirds of the distance up the wall, on which one end of the long bar had rested. This tiny knob was some 160 cm up the sidewall and only 1 cm wide. Day after day, the infant made leaps at the wall, going higher and higher, until he finally caught hold of the little knob (Figures 2 and 3). From there on, he climbed the walls, both sideways and up, around the corner, most of the time with his back to the wall (see Figures 4 and 5). First, his finger was on the bar, then his feet and his body above it, as shown in Figure 6. He had won and sat scrunched against the ceiling but lord of all he surveyed. This act he repeated many times during the remaining weeks, in spite of the fact that the bar and the rings did not have the same end result as before. The mastery mechanism that had been suggestively evident during the play of the eight infants now received an experimental stamp of approval.

As a bonus, the liveliest female of the group proceeded to follow the master in a slow repeat performance. If two could look smug with their backs tight to a ceiling, these two did. The performance reminded an onlooker of the face of a human child taking, with every effort of every muscle of her body, the first few tottering but exhilarating steps. The

Fig. 2. Practice leap.

monkeys gave the testers an experimentally corroborated vision of early self-actualization in their physical mastery of the environment.

Knowing the appeal and the augmentation of apparatus, as well as the persistence of self-motion play, we decided to test further the relationship between individual and social peragration. In the very same playroom that had been the scene of lively play, we put each monkey, one hour at a time, once a week, all alone, to test its prowess with the lovely apparatus at its disposal. Did they take advantage of their opportunities? Not at all. They acted like miserable urchins, just sat all by themselves and screeched, then just moped and screeched some more. The rhesus would just as soon and even sooner play all alone when all of the fine, furry friends were around, but would it play without them around? No. There was a possibility that they were suffering from the separation syndrome, but each rhesus had its surrogate present when alone in the playroom and also had spent the major part of most days alone in the quadrant of the quad cage for over a year. Not being loris or lemur, they had not been able to see the other members of the quadrant at night either.

The intensity of the behavior when they were placed alone in the playroom would suggest that the monkeys were very much aware of the presence of their peers even when not playing with them, and although they did not regularly choose to play with them, they were not about to play without them. Through self-motion play, these primates learned through the primarily individual patterns of peragration to accommodate themselves to the physical environment and to discover their relation to it. At the same time, the presence of others was not an extraneous fact. The young animal was becoming agreeably accustomed to the presence of conspecifics even before social play became prevalent, and we name this phenomenon *social support*. Those individuals, both monkey and human, who gain self-confidence in the physical environment have made vital progress toward social role readiness. The individual without this background is often faced with the simultaneous demands and challenges of both the physical and the social environments, with resultant confusion and feelings of inadequacy.

The development of lively self-motion play well illustrates the course of development of complex, unlearned behaviors and the increas-

Fig. 3. Halfway house.

FIG. 4. Climbing the walls.

ing complexity of these behaviors through both learning and maturation. Early peragration permits not only exploration of the different
facets of the environment but, primarily and most potently, the understanding of one's own body in relation to the many elements of air,
water, and land, the capabilities and limitations of oneself. Because the
individual gains confidence in learning what the body can and cannot
accomplish in space, with proper experience and reinforcement, as the
physical capabilities mature, pleasure in accomplishment becomes not
only possible but probable and more prevalent.

The only key to the analysis of these complex responses is that of
tracing them developmentally, both ontogenetically and phylogeneti-
cally. One can understand the maturational meaning of one kind or class
of involved behaviors only if one also knows the maturational meaning
of different but related behavior.

Unfortunately, adequate data on the ontogenetic development of
affection, aggression, and play exist on only two animal species: man
and macaque monkeys. However, these two reinforce each other

because of the striking similarity in the order of maturational development of many complex behaviors of both. Of course, one must allow for the fact that the monkey at birth has a human anatomical age of 1 year as measured by carpal bone development, and the macaque monkey matures four to five times as fast as the human child on such diverse measures as intelligence and sexual maturity.

Take, for example, the maturation of aggression. The control of aggression is basically dependent on the fact that the primary love or affectional systems mature before aggression rears or raises its ugly head. Maternal love and infant–mother love in the macaque monkey are present at parturition or very shortly after parturition. Even agemate affection is firmly founded at 6 months of age. Contrariwise, aggression toward external objects is not firmly established until the second year of life in normal, socially raised monkeys. Self-aggression does not mature until age 4. Love is an early-maturing behavior and aggression a late-maturing behavior.

When love does not have a chance to operate with its protective power—for example, in monkeys raised in social isolation—aggression

FIG. 5. Goal gradient.

FIG. 6. Lord of all.

may, under the circumstances, take advantage of the opportunity presented and fill the void. This fact was dramatically illustrated in the case of rhesus infants raised in complete social isolation for six months, without either maternal or peer affection. Mitchell (Harlow, Dodsworth, & Harlow, 1965) found that these isolates, when tested at 2–3½ years of age, displayed aggression even to 1-year-old infants, as no self-respecting socially raised rhesus would.

Failure to recognize the importance of the relative times of the maturation of aggression and love and the appearance of the protective mechanisms resulting from antecedent love led Lorenz (1966) to create his almost remarkably inadequate theory of aggression, with concomitant recommendations of ineffective techniques of aggression control. Lorenz recognized the great difference between predation (aggression against members of other species,) and conspecific aggression between members of the same species. He believed that intraspecific aggression was minimized by "appeasement gestures or ritual submission," but the thought never crossed his mind to search for the developmental variables, the very mechanism that in reality held introspecies aggression to a minimum. One cannot research the mother–infant relationships of the macaque without seeing the mother teach the baby, through her own behavior, the use of threat gestures toward the stranger as opposed to the friendly behavior to conspecific members of the nuclear family.

Berkowitz (1962) has successfully challenged Lorenz's hydraulic drive theory, which puts a lot of water behind the dam without knowing from whence the damn water came. He has also refuted the effectiveness of releasing the energy of aggression through general release of energy as a catharsis. Lorenz (1966) suggested release through channelized sports and educated laughter. If aggression is to have a sporting chance of being controlled, it should not be laughed away. Lorenz's theory of aggression and its control beautifully illustrates the futility of theories of either learned or unlearned complex behavior without adequate ontogenetic or phylogenetic information. In a happy burst of delayed insight, Lorenz stated in the final paragraph of his famous book, *On Aggression*, that "the bond of personal love and friendship was the epochmaking invention . . . [enabling] two or more members of an aggressive species to live peacefully together and to work for a common end." Too little and too late.

Knowledge of the maturation of the primary and basic forms of self-motion play show how early and in what fashion peer love may gain ascendancy. The way is paved for social play and the development of positive and pleasant social relationships. When added to the positive affect of effective maternal love, aggression does not have a chance among conspecifics.

In early study of innate behaviors, investigators insisted that unlearned behavior must be simple to be free of learning. This inexorable and inevitable demand for simplicity caused decades of confusion even though the study of single-alley mazes did reduce the need for complex thinking.

The self-defeating theories of all-black unlearned and all-white learned behaviors have gradually been replaced, not by a dull gray merging of the two theories but by a realistic theory of interaction between the unlearned and the learned, a theory with which complex unlearned responses come easily to terms. Such behaviors were long thought to be inaccessible to experimentation, but the wealth of scientific research on the early years of primate infancy, both human and subhuman, vitiates this negative stance.

REFERENCES

Berkowitz, L. *Aggression*. New York: McGraw-Hill, 1962.
Blurton-Jones, N. G. In D. Morris (Ed.), *Primate ethology*. Chicago: Aldine, 1967, pp. 347–368.

Crozier, W. J. The study of living organisms. In C. Murchison, (Ed.), *The foundations of experimental psychology.*, London: Oxford University Press, 1929, Chapter 2.

Eisele, L. *All the strange hours: The excavation of a life.* New York: Scribner's, 1975.

Fabre, J. H. *The wonders of instinct.* London: T. Fisher University, 1918.

Groos, K. *The play of animals: Play and instinct.* New York: Appleton, 1898.

Guthrie, E. R., & Horton, R. *Cats in a puzzle box.* New York: Rinehart, 1946.

Harlow, H. F. The nature of love. *American Psychologist*, 1958, *13*, 673–685.

Harlow, H., Dodsworth, R., & Harlow, M. Total isolation in monkeys. *Proceedings of the National Academy of Science*, 1965, *54(1)*, 90–97.

Harlow, H. F., & Harlow, M. K. The affectional systems. In A. M. Schrier, H. F., Harlow, & F. Stollnitz (Eds.), *Behavior of non-human primates* (Vol. 1 and 2,) New York: Academic Press, 1965, 287–334.

Harlow, H. F., & Harlow, M. K. Age mate or peer affectional system. In P. S. Lehrman, R. A. Hinde, & E. Shaw (Eds.), *Advances in the study of behavior* (Vol. 2). New York: Academic Press, 1969.

Harlow, H. F., Harlow, M. K., Dodsworth R. S., & Arling, G. L. Maternal behavior of rhesus monkeys deprived of mothering and peer associations in infancy. *Proceedings of the American Philosophical Society*, 1966, *40*, 58–66.

Hull, C. L. *A behavior system.* New Haven: Yale University Press, 1952.

Hutt, C. Exploration and play in children. *Symposium Zoological Society London*, 1966, *18*, 61–81.

James, W. *The principles of psychology*, New York: Holt, 1890.

Lamb, M. E. Fathers: Forgotten contributors to child development. *Human Development*, 1975, *18*, 245–265.

Loeb, J. *Forced movements, tropisms, and animal conduct.* Philadelphia: Lippincott, 1918.

Logan, F. *Incentive.* New Haven: Yale University Press, 1960.

Lorenz, K. *On aggression.* New York: Harcourt Brace & World, 1966.

McDougald, W. *Introduction to social psychology.* London: Methuen, 1908.

Mears, C. E., & Harlow, H. F. Play: Early & Eternal, *Proceedings National Academy Sciences*, May 1975, *72(5)*, 1878–1882.

Mears, C., Play and development of cosmic competence. *Developmental Psychology*, in press.

Miles, W. R. The narrow path elevated maze for studying rats. *Proceedings Society Experimental Biology and Medicine*, 1927, *24*, 454–456.

Pavlov, I. *Conditioned responses: An investigation of the physiological activity of the cerebral cortex.* London: Oxford University Press, 1927.

Ratliff, F., & Von Bekesy, G. *Bibliographic memoirs* (Vol. 48). Washington, D.C.: National Academy of Sciences, 1976.

Rosenblum, L. Unpublished doctoral thesis, University of Wisconsin, 1961.

Spence, K. W. *Behavior theory and conditioning*, New Haven: Yale University Press, 1956.

Watson, J. B. *Behavior: An introduction to comparative psychology*, New York: Holt, 1914.

Watson, J. B. *Psychology from the standpoint of a behaviorist.* Philadelphia: Lippincott Co., 1919.

Watson, J. B. *Behaviorism.* New York: Norton, 1924.

10

Affective Maturation and the Mother–Infant Relationship

Leonard A. Rosenblum

God could not be everywhere, and therefore he made mothers. (Old Jewish Saying)

Survival of the infant primate is a complex affair. It must meet the necessary metabolic demands for the support of its basic biology. But, in addition, its broad cognitive potential and the complexity of the social milieu into which it ultimately must move as an independent individual require the development of a rather immense array of selective behavioral responses. Unlike the survival of their more primitive phyletic antecedents and contemporaries, the survival of the infant primate to reproductive maturity reflects an intricate blend of genetic endowments and experiential formants in determining the range of stimuli, social and inanimate, that will be sought and approached, accommodated to or "ignored," circumvented or actively avoided.

Since, indeed, God (or His/Her modern counterpart, genetic determinism) could not "be everywhere" nor prepare the infant for the major exigencies of primate development, until sufficient experience ensues and later maturing systems of response emerge, others must serve to bridge the gaps in the infants' maturing repertoire of behaviors necessary to survival.

With the higher primates at least, the full range of emotional response of which the organism may one day be capable and their evocation by specific stimuli or classes of stimuli are not present at birth.

LEONARD A. ROSENBLUM · State University of New York, Downstate Medical Center, Brooklyn, New York. This research was supported by HEW grants #MH15965 and #MH22640.

Depending upon the species involved and the nature of their general social and infant-rearing structure, siblings, peers, aunts, and males may play an important role in carrying the infant through periods when its own emotional response apparatus is incomplete and may help to shape the form of its subsequent development. However, regardless of which elements of the social network may operate, it is "nature's loving proxy, the watchful mother" who plays the primary role in supporting the infant's survival until its own response capabilities and emotional maturation afford a good chance of autonomous survival.

Whatever its neurophysiological or neurochemical concomitants, it is the maturation of emotional response that mediates the expression of the most fundamental elements of primate existence. With regard to the development of affiliative bonds between specific individuals of a troop or within consanguinal family units; the coordinated responses to group assaults; the choice of preferred sleeping, play, or foraging areas; or the sustained preferences for or avoidance of many animate and inanimate environmental stimuli, no attempts to displace the evanescent role of emotionality in influencing and sustaining these and similar elements of the strategy of survival have been successful.

At birth, the infant primate crawls or is brought to close contact with the mother's body, where it maintains itself through a series of fairly specific reflexive adjustments (Mowbray & Cadell, 1962). Generally—in macaques, for example—this close, ventral–ventral contact with interspersed rooting-initiated nursing contacts is maintained rather uninterruptedly for the first several weeks of life. During this period, as thereafter, maternal responses to the infant complement the reflexive patterns of the infant. There is relatively little redundancy in maternal and infant response patterns. Normal, healthy infants cling ventrally with sufficient strength to allow all forms of maternal locomotion, and physical support of the macaque infant by the mother disappears quite rapidly after birth. Squirrel monkey infants climb onto and cling to the mother's back, and mothers virtually never support their healthy infants, although significantly, disabled infants may be manually carried for brief periods (Rosenblum, 1968; Rosenblum & Youngstein, 1974). In fact, even nursing is reflexively initiated by the infant itself and mothers are never seen "offering the breast" to an infant. So well defined is the complementarity of normal mother and infant patterns that an injured infant, unable to root or to right itself, may starve to death while clinging to the mother, without any effective alteration in maternal response (see Figure 1).

However, these initial responses of the infant are rather nondiscriminitive; that is, they will be directed toward any member of a somewhat broad class of stimuli (see Sackett, 1970). Under appropriate circumstances, infants respond readily to foster mothering figures,

FIG. 1. A bonnet mother holding her newborn dead infant. Similar disorientation may be seen with sick or injured infants, who cannot survive in these positions.

whether other conspecific aunts (Figure 2), congeneric foster mothers of another species (Figure 3), or even inanimate mother surrogates, as H. F. Harlow and his colleagues have dramatically demonstrated. The macaque (*Macaca memestrina* and *M. radiata*) and squirrel monkey (*Saimiri sciureus*) infants that we have studied for the last 20 years fail to show the emotional concomitants of selective attachment to the mother or other caregivers until about the third month of life. Nonetheless, it is these early relationships (Hinde, 1976) that underwrite much of their early socialization and establishment of their subsequent place in the social structure of their group (Rowell, 1972).

Some years ago, we attempted to determine whether infants of one of our macaque species could be foster-reared by mothers of the other species. Pigtail and bonnet macaque infants approximately 1 month, 4 months, and 7 months of age were first housed with and then fostered by mothers of the other species. Each species dyad was housed with its opposite-species counterpart for several weeks prior to an attempt to switch the infants.

The response of the youngest infant, a 3-week-old bonnet, illustrated the relatively nonselective filial responses of young monkey infants. Removed from its mother and returned to the pen in which it

Fig. 2. A squirrel monkey aunt retrieving the infant of another mother by assuming the crouch-retrieval posture.

had lived since birth, which now contained only the pigtail mother (whose infant had also been removed), the infant immediately ran to and clung to the pigtail female. Moments later, when this female "noticed" the strange appearance of the clinging infant and rejected and violently removed him, the infant made repeated attempts to return to contact. So persistent were the infant's attempts to cling to the foreign female over the next several days that eventually she allowed the infant the privilege of clinging to her leg throughout the day and evening! When, however, after one month of living as a single dyad, this pigtail mother and her bonnet infant were placed in a group with two other pigtails and their bonnet foster infants, the young infant rapidly shifted his attachment responses to another, more placidly accepting pigtail female. Figure 3 shows that infant at about 4 months clinging to its new (second) foster pigtail mother. It is interesting to note that over the course of the next six months, this bonnet infant's relationship with this pigtail female essentially paralleled similar scores for bonnet–bonnet dyads. Neither of the two older bonnets nor the two older pigtails showed any sustained ventral contact with their foster mothers. The youngest pigtail—actually 6 weeks of age—showed some intermittent contact with its bonnet foster mother, but no sustained attachment.

Other reflections of the potential maleability of such filial foci have been observed in other species. In squirrel monkeys, for example, infants generally receive complementary maternal care from adult females other than their mother, beginning by about 2–3 weeks of age (Rosenblum, 1968). These aunt–infant relationships are usually initiated when a close associate or older offspring of the mother begins vocalizing into the ear of the clinging infant (see Figure 2). After several attempts, the "retrieval" call of the aunt stimulates the infant to climb onto the aunt's back, where it will then cling until retrieved by the biological mother. Similarly, when that infant is beginning to climb about on its own, either the mother or the aunt may run to it and assume the retrieval posture and get the baby to climb onto its back. Since neither mothers nor aunts under normal circumstances are contentious regarding their polymatric rearing system, the infant moves freely from mother to aunt and back again and responds fully to either one in the other's absence (Rosenblum, 1971a). These aunt–infant relations, once established, continue in effect until at least 6 months of age, but none are ever initially established after the infant is 8 weeks old.

These observations fit with the basic data on the development of infants' visual recognition and preference for the mother as compared with a conspecific stranger. We have been studying the development of these patterns for the last several years. Studies have now been completed on bonnet and pigtail macaques and squirrel monkeys for

FIG. 3. A pigtail foster mother with her 3-month-old bonnet infant. Two older bonnet infants, with whom cross-fostering did not succeed, cling to one another.

most of the first year of life (see Rosenblum & Alpert, 1974, 1977). In these studies, infant subjects are placed in the center of an 8-foot-long chamber. At either end is a one-way glass window that allows the infant to see a stimulus animal in the outside compartment. Because of the one-way glass and the differential lighting that is used, the stimulus animal cannot see the infant. After a brief interval, the infant is released into the box and allowed to approach either its mother at one end of the chamber or a female stranger of the same species at the other end. Prior to about 8–10 weeks of age, group-reared, socially experienced infants in each of these three species fail to show any consistent preferences for their own mother as compared to the stranger! There are the usual individual differences and significant effects of species, sex, and rearing conditions on the age at which strong specific attachment emerges in these tests. Nonetheless, these and other studies suggest that prior to about 2 months of age, these infant monkeys generally fail to show any sustained emotional disturbance in the absence of a specific caregiver, so long as a suitable substitute is available.

An examination of the unfolding pattern of protective maternal behavior demonstrates the changing role the mother plays as the infant matures during its first year. Under laboratory conditions, at least, infant monkeys generally make their first attempts to break contact with the mother at 1–2 weeks of age. In most instances, mothers restrain their infants from departing. This restraint pattern at first increases in frequency as the infant grows stronger and more determined to leave periodically, but then it is rapidly replaced by a pattern we have termed *guarding*, in which the mother walks closely beside the infant, lightly contacting its body. Finally, the mother no longer attempts to maintain continuous contact with the infant and allows an increasing freedom of movement. In this phase, her only protection pattern is her intermittent retrieval of the departed infant. Each of these patterns, in one form or another, appears in each of the three species we have studied. In each of these species, maternal protective patterns approach baseline levels of frequency by the third to fourth month of life. Again, at the point at which the infant can not only recognize the mother at a distance but has developed the emotional bond that leads him to avoid others and seek her when in danger, the maternal role of constant protector rapidly slips away.

That something different from the establishment of a reinforcement-conditioning relationship with the mother has been established by this time is further attested to when punitive maternal behavior emerges. When their infants are about 4 months old, mothers begin the act of weaning and prevention of even nonnutritive nipple contacts as well as the intermittent physical removal of their infants from them; and finally they begin restrained biting of the infant's hands, arms, and shoulders in attempts to force them to break contact. The infants' responses to these rejection patterns are generally redoubled efforts to maintain or reattain contact. Total daylight hours in contact with the mother gradually decrease after the fourth month, although in macaques, at least, the rate of decline in contact after month 4 is half of what it was in the previous months. Nonetheless, infants habitually sleep in ventral contact with the mother until a next baby is born, 8–12 months later. Moreover, all evidence from the field and laboratory (e.g., Sade, 1968; Rosenblum, 1971b) indicates that despite this period of active maternal punishment and rejection, the emotional bond between infant and mother, once established by the third or fourth month, is behaviorally demonstrable throughout life.

Before we leave this note on the role of punishment in maternal behavior, it is worth noting in passing that punishment is virtually never used to deter early departures. Mothers do not punish their infant's early and perhaps inopportune attempts to leave them; they simply prevent them. They hold the infant's body, limbs, and tail until he ceases his attempts to leave. They may even groom the young infant, which calms and placates him and serves further to deter the departure. One might suggest that extinguishing the infant's early attempts at leaving might create much trouble later on! Similarly, a recent computer analysis of sequential behavior in pigtail macaque dyads carried out by Dr. Joel Stutman and myself revealed that punishment most frequently occurred in periods of rising addyadic (i.e., positive) interaction, not at the initiation of contact. Thus, mothers do not generally punish "returning," they punish unusually high levels of positive interaction—their punishment has the effect of modulating, not terminating, the emotional bond once it has been formed.

Perhaps the most dramatic demonstration of the intense emotional attachment that many monkeys achieve toward their mothers by about 3–4 months of life has been the studies of mother–infant separation (e.g. Seay, Hansen, & Harlow, 1962; Rosenblum & Kaufman, 1968). These studies on rhesus and pigtail macaques indicate that toward the end of the first half-year infants are severely disturbed to the point of almost complete disruption of ongoing behavioral development when mothers are removed for a week or more. In fact, a behavioral syndrome that has been likened to anaclitic depression in children is not an infrequent sequela of separation. At reunion, there is generally a tremendous intensification and, in a sense, regression in the dyadic interaction pattern. For example, following one month of separation, infant pigtails of 6–8 months remain in contact with and proximity to their mothers at rates more typical of the 3- or 4-month-olds (Kaufman & Rosenblum, 1967).

One study of separation carried out in our laboratory is particularly pointed in demonstrating the impact of the mother on the emotional status of her infant in this age range (i.e., after 3–4 months). For this study, the subjects were five pigtail infants, 17–28 months of age (four females, one male), living in two groups. We separated each infant from its mother by removing the mother and leaving the infant in the home pen and group. The separations lasted eight weeks. During the separation, the infants were observed by the use of standard check-sheet sampling methods three to four times each week. In addition, however, two to three times per week, the mother of each infant was individually introduced to the pen for 30 minutes, while restrained in an open wire-mesh cage. Each infant was observed while its own mother was returned and also when any other infant's mother was similarly returned. Of the five infants, three exhibited marked depressions, one had a brief depressive period, and one showed no depressive affective response to separation. These responses followed the usual time course: the marked depression and the lack of interaction and locomotion that occurred began gradually to lift after about a week of separation and were increasingly replaced by more normal infant affective and interactive patterns.

As reflected in Figure 4, when an infant's mother was returned to the pen, the infant rarely went to the mother on the floor in the first several weeks but rather remained on one of the higher levels of the pen. Even more dramatic, however, was the fact that even after the original separation depression had lifted and the infants were less immobile and rarely assumed the hunched, "down" posture of the depressed infant, most of the depression pattern reemerged when the mother was placed in the pen (see Figure 5). Not only did the infants show frequent and sustained periods of depressed posture and immobility, but even when they did move in the presence of the mother, they moved more slowly, with the hesitant, hunched gait of the depressed infant (see Figure 6). In one case, even eight weeks after the original separation, this now active, playful infant would be cast into an immobile, cooing, hunched-over, depressed ball by the sight of the returned (caged) mother (Figure 7). Again and again, for varying periods of weeks, the returned mother, and only she, would reevoke the depressive pattern in the otherwise recovered infant. By any measure, the entire emotional status of the infants shifted dramatically in immediate response to the mother's return; ironically, in this case, the infants were quite buoyant in her absence and depressed upon her return! Again, it is difficult to consider such a pattern of response in the absence of the development of a complex emotional bond to the mother at this age.

In the normal course of events, the mother's behavior changes and her role in regulating the infant's behavior and affective state shifts dramatically during the first year of life (e.g., Hinde, 1976). The maturing infant is autonomously reacting to the world around him in an

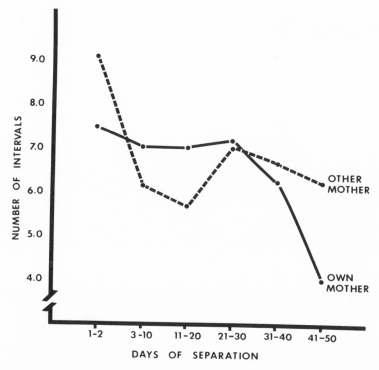

FIG. 4. The number of intervals in which separated infants remained on other levels of the pen than with their own or other mothers during the return tests.

increasingly differentiated manner, both with regard to the specific stimuli that are responded to and in the pattern of responses displayed toward them. As Welker (1971) has suggested, "the repertoires of play and explorations are conceived to develop out of a shifting spatiotemporal mosaic of progressively expanding assemblies of behavioral sequences of various types, durations, and degrees of complexity" (p. 202).

The interplay of changing maternal roles and the growing differentiation of response in the infant's discriminative behavioral repertoire are reflected in a recent study of squirrel monkey development. This study, carried out by my student Ms. Jane Rouder, was based on some earlier work that showed that under certain conditions, when environmental complexity was increased male squirrel monkey infants developed earlier and manifested independence from mother more strongly than did females (Rosenblum, 1974). For the present study, male and female squirrel monkey newborns and their mothers were housed in a double-pen enclosure. Each pen measured about 2.5 cubic meters, and contained three elevated shelves. The two pens were

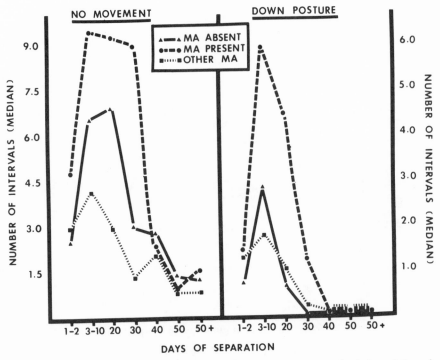

FIG. 5. The number of intervals in which separated infants were completely immobile and showed the down posture when mothers were absent, when their own mothers were present, and when another infant's mother was present at the floor of the pen.

separated by an opaque wall, which contained a 13 cm × 13 cm passageway at shelf height. Both pens contained masonry floors covered with bedding, and had overhead lighting and automatic watering systems. All observations of these animals were made through large one-way vision screens that fronted each pen. Each infant was observed three times per week with a 30-second time-sampling technique.

The special purpose of this study was to determine the responses of mothers and infants to potentially threatening and presumptively salient stimuli in their living area. In the wild, of course, these largely arboreal primates have ready opportunity to flee such threats and essentially remove them from the stimulus field. In this study, the adjoining pens were an attempt to allow for the use of psychological space in lieu of broad physical space. An animal could, by passing through the readily accessible opening, remove itself from ongoing activity or any particular stimulus present in one pen. Hence, in this study, one of three stimulus conditions was instituted one day each week, in one of the two adjoining pens. For these tests, either three brown-and-white guinea pigs were released to the floor of one pen, or three garter snakes, 1–2 feet long were released in one pen, or no stimulus was introduced (control). As in previous studies of squirrel monkey development (e.g., Rosenblum, 1968), there was a rapid overall decline in the attachment behavior of infants of both sexes regardless of stimulus condition (Figure 8). As reflected in Figure 9, after 10 weeks, the infants spent relatively few intervals in continuous contact with the mother even when in the pen containing the snakes. Although the males tended toward a more rapid decline in contact under these conditions, the two sexes showed substantially equivalent declines. The

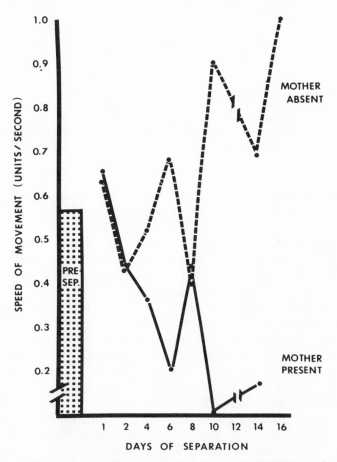

FIG. 6. The speed of movement of separated infants during the first 16 days of separation when their own mothers were present as compared to the periods when they were absent. Speed of movement was calculated by division of the number of 4-foot units of the pen traversed by the number of seconds spent in motion.

FIG. 7. Repetitive depression pattern in an infant seven weeks postseparation in response to the mother's placement at the front of the pen. Note the eye closure and down posture of the infant on the left as compared to the separated infant seated next to him, whose mother is not present.

generally increasing repertoire of autonomous behavior by the infants was similarly reflected in their readiness to move from one pen to another, leaving their mothers behind them (Figure 10).

There was little indication before 10 weeks that the infants responded very differently under the three stimulus conditions. Indeed, in terms of their readiness to make brief movements between pens without the mother, no differentiation in response levels appeared in the full 20 weeks of observation. However, the frequency with which the infants were able to spend a full 30-second interval in the absence of the mother showed some important changes. Although at 10 weeks when either snakes or guinea pigs were present, the infants spent equally low number of intervals alone in the stimulus pen, this undifferentiated pattern rapidly changed in the weeks afterward. By 15–20 weeks, the infants were "alone" without the mother in the pen containing the guinea pigs substantially more often than when snakes were present. (Figure 11). After about three months, the infants seemed to us to be less able to tolerate long periods in the snake pen when intermittent contact with the mother was not possible.

Unfortunately, with only behavioral observation measures and the limited behavioral repertoire of the young infant, it was impossible to determine with any assuredness what emotional reactions the infants

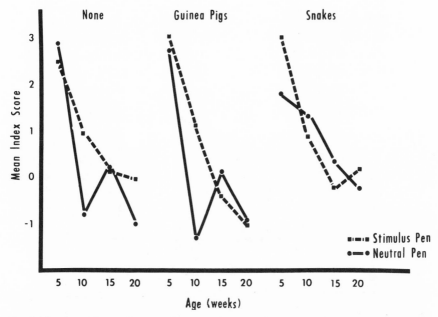

FIG. 8. The change in attachment index scores for squirrel monkeys infants during the first 20 weeks of life under the three stimulus conditions. 3 = Continuous contact; 1 = partial contact; 0 = no contact; −1 = other level; −3 = alone.

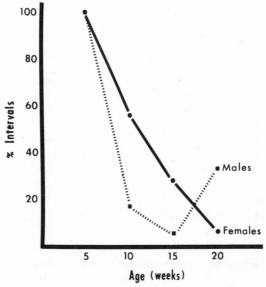

FIG. 9. The decline in intervals of continuous contact between male and female squirrel monkey infants and their mothers in the pen containing the snakes.

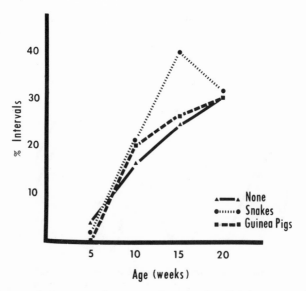

FIG. 10. The increase in frequency of movement between the adjoining pens under the three stimulus conditions.

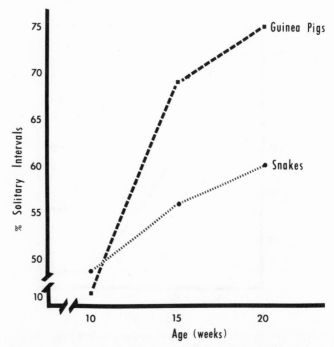

FIG. 11. The development of the infants' readiness to spend solitary intervals in the stimulus pens containing guinea pigs or snakes.

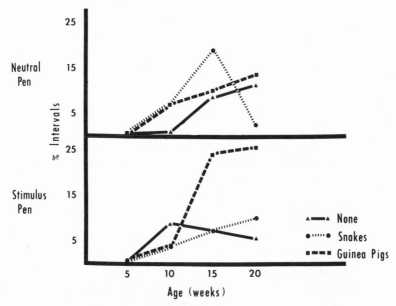

FIG. 12. The frequency with which squirrel monkey infants moved by themselves to the pen floor as a function of stimulus conditions.

were having to the stimuli during the period in which clinging was almost continuous at all times. However, a further indication of changing emotional response to the stimulus after 10 weeks is reflected in Figures 12 and 13. After 10 weeks, the infants showed much greater readiness to move by themselves to the floor of the pen when guinea pigs were there, and the infants played in the guinea pig pens more than twice as often as they did in the snake pen. In light of the similarity of some quantitiative patterns between the snake and no-stimulus conditions, one could suggest only that play and exploratory excursions to the floor were facilitated by the guinea pig stimulus rather than that snakes inhibited or frightened the 3–5-month-old subjects. Nonetheless, Figure 13 and our notes suggest that inhibition may well have played a role. All observations indicated that throughout the study, the infants were constantly aware of the snakes, would often stop and peer at them as they passed through the opening into the pen, or spent long periods looking down from the upper shelves. Were the snakes simply less "interesting" than the guinea pigs? Was the snake condition simply not different from the no-stimulus condition? This seems unlikely to say the least. It is our view that although the infants were aware of the snakes and were indeed "interested" in them, often at about 3 months they became somewhat wary of them and tense in their presence.

I suggest that the emerging differentiation of infant emotional patterns after about 3 months mediated this difference in response to the stimuli. This growing articulation of emotional patterns results in increasing degrees of autonomous infant regulation of response just at the time that the primary maternal regulatory patterns are approaching baseline. Figure 14 is an attempt to represent graphically the interplay of maternal regulation and the growth of infant regulation in a very general sense. The baseline in this case reflects a rough chronology for the squirrel monkey—and to a large degree for macaques as well. It is assumed that in other species, the scale would be shifted but the sequence would be about the same. In essence, this model suggests that maternal regulatory behaviors are initially high and then decline during the period of rapidly growing infant interest in the environment. Generalized, relatively undifferentiated response by the infant rises rapidly as the mother restricts less and less. However, as affective responses develop, they begin to effect the overall rates of infant responsiveness. Somewhere after about 3–4 months, maternal regulation is negligible, and the infant's own emotional reactions result in response differentiation and a general decline in overall environmental response rates. The relatively precise interdigitation of these unfolding maternal and infant regulatory patterns is critical to survival, and severe

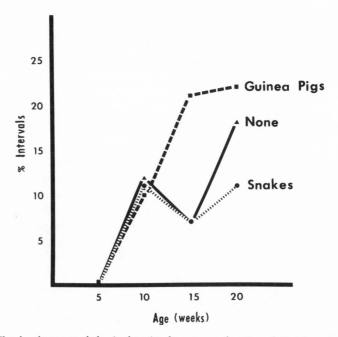

FIG. 13. The development of play in the stimulus pen as a function of stimulus conditions.

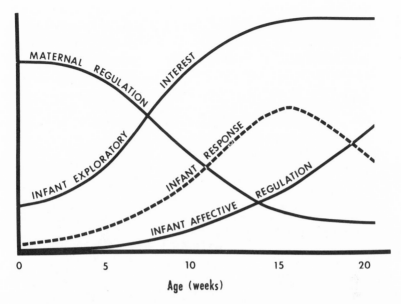

FIG. 14. The theoretical model for the interplay of maternal regulation of infant response and the increasing development of autonomous infant affective regulation of behavior. The age dimension approximates that hypothesized for squirrel monkeys and somewhat more roughly for macaques.

disruption ensues when the sequence is grossly tampered with, as in nonmaternal rearing situations. (Sackett, 1968).

These studies and many others on nonhuman primates lead us to agree strongly with Lehrman and Rosenblatt (1971)

> that synchrony between the changing psychobiological states of mother and young, based in part on preparturitional (or prehatching) changes in the parent, partly on growth changes in the young, partly on cyclically endogenous postparturitional changes in the mother, and partly on mutual influences of the two on each other, is a critically important conception for the analysis of the development of social behavior in higher animals. (p. 21)

REFERENCES

Hinde, R. A. On describing relationships. *Journal of Child Psychology and Psychiatry*, 1976, *17*, 1–19.

Kaufman, I. C., & Rosenblum, L. A. The reaction to separation in infant monkeys: Anaclitic depression and conservation-withdrawal. *Psychometric Medicine*, 1967, *29*, 648–675.

Lehrman, D. S., & Rosenblatt, J. S. The study of behavioral development. In H. Moltz (Ed.), *The ontogeny of vertebrate behavior*. New York: Academic Press, 1971, pp. 2–27.

Mowbray, J. B., & Cadell, T. E. Early behavior patterns in rhesus monkeys. *Journal of Comparative Physiology and Psychology*, 1962, *55*, 350–357.

Rosenblum, L. A. Mother–infant relations and early behavioral development in the squirrel monkey. In L. A. Rosenblum & R. W. Cooper (Eds.), *The squirrel monkey*, New York: Academic Press, 1968, pp. 207–233.

Rosenblum, L. A. Infant attachment in monkeys. In R. Schaeffer, (Ed.), *The Origins of Human Social Relations*. New York: Academic Press, 1971, pp. 85–113. (a)

Rosenblum, L. A. Kinship interaction patterns in pigtail and bonnet macaques. *Proceedings of the 3rd International Congress of Primatology*, 1971, *3*, 79–84. (b)

Rosenblum, L. A. Sex differences, environmental complexity and mother–infant relations. *Archives of Sexual Behavior*, 1974, *3*(2), 117–128.

Rosenblum, L. A., & Alpert, S. Fear of strangers and specificity of attachment in monkeys. In M. Lewis & L. A. Rosenblum (Eds.), *Origins of fear*. New York: Wiley, 1974, pp. 165–193.

Rosenblum, L. A., & Alpert, S. Response to mother and stranger: A first step in socialization. In S. Chevalier-Skolnikoff & F. F. Poirier (Eds.), *Primate bio-social development*. New York: Garland, 1977, pp. 463–478.

Rosenblum, L. A., & Kaufman, I. C. Variations in infant development and response to maternal loss in monkeys. *American Journal of Orthopsychiatry*, 1968, *38*, 418–426.

Rosenblum, L. A., & Youngstein, K. P. Developmental changes in compensatory dyadic response in mother and infant monkeys. In M. Lewis & L. A. Rosenblum (Eds.), *The origins of behavior: The influence of the infant on its caregiver*. New York: Wiley, 1974, pp. 141–161.

Rowell, T. E. *The social behavior of monkeys*. Baltimore: Penguin, 1972.

Sackett, G. P. Abnormal behavior in laboratory reared rhesus monkeys. In M. W. Fox (Ed.), *Abnormal behavior in animals*. Philadelphia: Saunders, 1968, pp. 293–331.

Sackett, G. P. Unlearned responses, differential rearing experiences, and the development of social attachments by rhesus monkeys. In L. A. Rosenblum (Ed.), *Primate behavior: Developments in field and laboratory research*. New York: Academic Press, 1970, pp. 112–140.

Sade, D. S. Inhibition of son–mother mating among free-ranging rhesus monkeys. *Science and Psychoanalysis*. 1968, *12*, 18–38.

Seay, B., Hansen, E., & Harlow, H. F. Mother–infant separation in monkeys. *Journal of Child Psychology and Psychiatry*, 1962, *3*, 123.

Welker, W. I. Ontogeny of play and exploratory behaviors: A definitive of problems and a search for new conceptual solutions. In H. Moltz (Ed.), *The ontogeny of vertebrate behavior*. New York: Academic Press, 1971, pp. 171–228.

11

A Clinician's View of Affect Development in Infancy

SALLY PROVENCE

Freud's first theory of neurosis was an affect theory. It developed into an instinct theory that, in the minds of many, superseded it. Jacobson, who pointed this out in a paper in 1954, believes that this occurrence greatly delayed efforts to clarify the concept of affects and their relationships to other aspects of development. Much that Freud formulated originally in terms of emotions has been shifted and rephrased into instinct theory, but pieces of affect theory have persisted as isolated fragments. Benjamin wrote in 1961, "we do not have [in psychoanalysis] an adequate theory of affects in general and of anxiety in particular, in spite of the significant contributions of Rapaport and others."

Bertram Lewin's (1965) scholarly paper discusses some of the historical influences on the current situation in regard to the place of affects in psychoanalytic theory and clinical practice. He reminds us that Galen's four body fluids had each their separate emotion, temperament, and illness. The word *affect* itself is old, antedating St. Augustine, who, according to Baldwin (1940), wrote, "those mental states which the Greeks call *pathe* and Cicero calls *perturbationes* are called by some *affectus*, or *affectiones* by others, keeping to the literal meaning of the Greek *passione*." Philosophers' attempts to classify mental processes, including the old academic or faculty psychology, which anatomizes the brain into the so-called faculties (perception, cognition, emotion, volition, etc.), have interplayed with the nosologies. Well into

---

SALLY PROVENCE · Child Study Center, Yale University, New Haven, Connecticut.

the 19th century, doctors in all branches of medicine, says Lewin (1965), did not distinguish between symptom and disease process, and there was equal confusion in defining and characterizing the relation of emotion and illness. For example, melancholia seemed both a mood and a disease. The divisions of the mind and corresponding classifications of mental illness persisted down through Kahlbaum and Kraepelin, and even today they appear disguised in such terms as *affective psychosis*. Psychoanalysts' efforts to think about affects are colored by this tradition: our naming of affects in psychiatry and psychoanalysis has been pragmatic and arbitrary; we use such words as *anxiety, depression, elation, love, rage*, etc., because we have found them useful. Such designations, whether used by psychiatrists or by the man on the street, come from observations and depend upon empirical common sense. We all tend to assume in the field of emotions that we know elements or mental states that need no further dissection because they are irreducible. Rage, fear, joy, and sadness impress us as self-evident and basic.

Lewin also noted that the early Greeks did not clearly distinguish semantically among perception, knowledge, feeling, and action. The word that later meant "to fear" originally meant "to be put to flight"; the word for "I know" originally meant "I have seen"—or rather, there was no semantic distinction between flight and fear, sight and knowledge. The distinctions among idea, emotion, and action, many think, are the result of human culture and social development and, in the individual, of education. If there were no concept of the independent observing cognitive self, we should have no corresponding concept of independent feeling or of independent action.

Some aspects of psychoanalytic theory of affects included below are of particular relevance to our discussion. It is by no means a comprehensive summary. Freud said that affects are always conscious. Moreover, since by definition an affect is a feeling state experienced by the ego, identifying an affect in the infant implies at least some ego development. Affective development of the child is viewed as developing out of an undifferentiated state—just as is proposed for the development of the instinctual drives and the ego. Most infancy researchers who have been interested in affect development, it appears, have gone through a similar experience. Namely, we find that we are willing to label many more and different affects in an infant of 9 months than in an infant of 3 months. Not only the number, which implies differentiation and structuration, but also nuances of feeling, which suggest control over excitation and discharge, demonstrate the direction and increasing complexity of affective development.

One of the problems for psychoanalytic investigators doing infancy studies is that the theory is a complex and demanding one. The study of the child's affects cannot be separated from the study of his human relationships nor from the study of ego development and of psychosexual development. The interrelatedness of these aspects of development has been amply demonstrated in clinical and research work. Such ego functions as motility, perception, speech, and intelligence are known to be enhanced or impeded according to the adequacy of the child's human relationships; attitudes toward reality are deeply influenced by these relationships; trouble in the human relationships often interferes with another important function of the ego, the formation of stable defenses. In regard to the instinctual drives (libidinal and aggressive), the object (human) relations are crucial codeterminants of their development, organization, and behavioral expression. On the other hand, all of the above ego and instinctual factors participate in the process of development of the child's relationships to others. For example, the infant's ability first to recognize the mother and later to "read" her nonverbal cues or understand her speech is influenced by his cognitive development. Similarly, it is believed that the infant's drive endowment, differentiation, and organization, among other congenital characteristics, determine in part his individual needs and his developmental tendencies, including the character of his object relations.

Psychoanalytic theory also points out that visible affects are expressive of internal events and of the relationships to important others. They are often in the service of the socialization process in general. Some affects, moreover, have a particular role in helping the child with the long process of self-regulation. For example, the experience of feelings of shame or embarrassment may mobilize adaptive responses that assist the child in the control of his impulses. Similarly, the pleasure and pride he feels when approved of by someone he loves or when he approves of himself strengthen his ability to regulate and control his impulses. Thus, they are important contributors both to adaptation and to defense. Psychoanalytic theory in regard to affects also includes the idea of "affect charge." Rapaport's (1942) definition of *affect charge* is that it is the energy source of which feeling and emotion (peripheral discharge) are manifestations. This energetic or economic construct has considerable practical value in the understanding of clinical data and the data of infant observations.

There are, we can safely say, affective concomitants of activities—motoric, verbal, cognitive, social, perceptual—and there are actions that themselves express the feelings experienced by the child. In practice, it is not always easy to distinguish them, but it is an important theoretical distinction.

What psychoanalytic infancy researchers do, of course—because the task is so mind-boggling—is to take one or a few aspects of development as the focus of attention, try to look at them carefully, and hope to integrate what has been learned with other aspects of psychoanalytic developmental psychology. The understanding of affective development to which this conference is devoted will depend both upon studies of undisturbed development and of disturbed functioning and upon all of those states of development somewhere in between.

In regard to the infancy period, as some psychoanalytic investigators have pointed out, we have become much more careful in recent years about the way in which we view research data of the preverbal years. Our group at Yale has been interested in how we can use research data to examine existing psychoanalytic propositions and formulate new ones. We expect that through such a process some of the gaps in developmental theory might be filled in and that many of the propositions can be refined. Such an intent has implications not only for theory building but also for clinical practice.

One of the considerations is the nurturing of the young, which is also a developmental variable in the parents—a process marked by varied and complex adaptive tasks that "average" parents meet with varying degrees of success (Benedek, 1959; Erikson, 1950; Naylor, 1970). "Good enough" nurturing usually falls short of optimally adaptive nurturing, and we need to keep that in mind, as we do the fact that on the infant side of the parent–infant partnership, there are variations in congenital characteristics that are codeterminants of development.

Correlations of aspects of affectivity with such developments—to name only a few—as recognition of the mother as distinct from other persons and things in the external environment, awareness of separation of the self from the other, and the steps in the development of the concept of object permanence in Piaget's terms as Décarie (1965) has shown are among the exciting opportunities for enriching and elaborating developmental psychology.

Various psychoanalytic writers have commented on relationships between early ego and drive development and affect development. Hoffer (1949) put forward the concept that the appearance of pleasure in the functioning of hand to mouth movements is one of the criteria for beginning ego formation at a mental level. Greenacre (1959) has written about the feelings of pleasure (later also of pride and self-esteem) that accompany the practicing of an emerging function for its own sake; that is, it does not necessarily have to be goal-directed, though it may be. Analysts have elaborated on Karl Buehler's (Waelder, 1933) term "functional pleasure" in regard to the play of infants and young children, a designation congenial with observations. The studies of Spitz (1946, 1965) and Benjamin (1961, 1963) on the development of anxiety taking off from Freud's 1926 essay have influenced several generations of infant researchers of varying theoretical preferences. Object loss and depression in infancy and early childhood have also been a focus of attention (Spitz, 1946; Spitz & Wolf, 1946; Bowlby, 1973; Freud & Burlingham, 1944; Provence & Lipton, 1962; Jacobson, 1954; Anthony, 1975).

The formulations of Margaret Mahler and her colleagues (1975) about what they term the psychological birth of the human infant are among the more stimulating of recently published studies. They describe the separation–individuation process and delineate several subphases that both reflect and depend upon the child's object relations. It is not possible in this discussion to do justice to Mahler's sophisticated formulations about the separation–individuation process, which she has dated from about age 4–5 months. But some of her thoughts about the affective life of the child beginning at about the end of the first year are of particular relevance to our discussion. Mahler noted, as others have, that concomitantly with learning to walk and his rapidly increasing awareness of his separateness and possibilities for mastery, the toddler appears to be intoxicated with his own faculties and with the greatness of his own world. Mahler has suggested that *elation* is the phase-specific characteristic or dominant mood of this approximately 6-month period, which she has correlated with the second subphase of the separation–individuation process. She has also suggested that from about 18 to 24 months, the toddler experiences more or less keenly and more or less gradually the obstacles to his "conquest of the world." His growing cognitive abilities make him begin to relinquish some of his feelings of omnipotence and his belief in the magic of his wishes and fantasies: "It dawns on him that [some of the time at least] . . . he is a small, relatively helpless and lonesomely separate individual". Verbal communication and secondary process thinking come increasingly into play, and increasingly the child recognizes his parents both as sources of comfort, security, and approval and as sources of frustration, prohibition, and disapproval, and at this stage he views them as omnipotent. (Only later does he come to know that they are not omnipotent either.)

Winnicott (1965) has said that one of the characteristics of good parents is that they can disillusion the child in a loving and gradual manner, avoiding the disturbance that might occur either if he should be unable to give up his omnipotence or if he should lose more or less completely his feelings of self-worth, self-esteem, and mastery. Mahler has suggested that if, during this period, the child is uncertain of the emotional availability of his parents, his feelings of helplessness may be dominant, and a basic mood of depression may ensue that is the basis of later negative mood swings and depressive illness. The "depressive mood" of the toddler may be represented in behavior by severe separation reactions, temper tantrums, and continual attempts to woo the mother and then giving up in despair for a while, or the mood may be revealed in impotent resignation and surrender. The quantitative factor—that is, the intensity of the feelings—is of special relevance when one is trying to determine whether the toddler's reactions are beyond the limits of reasonably healthy, phase-specific behavior. It should be said that there is no doubt that at this age, and even somewhat earlier, sadness has an ideational content as well as an affective component.

In writing about the feelings of shame and disgust that also emerge conspicuously during the second year, Jacobson (1954) has emphasized that these feelings and others reflect the child's awareness of himself as a thinking, acting, and feeling person. The appearance of reactions that suggest feelings of shame or disgust implies that the child begins to take over—that is, to internalize—parental standards for his behavior and, as it were, to react to his behavior with judgments about his own goodness, naughtiness, dirtiness, etc. These feelings, as is mentioned earlier, are not only phase characteristics in their emergence and not only expressive of psychological distress or intrapsychic conflict. They also ask for adaptive responses that, among other things, assist the child in dealing with those internal conflicts and are likely to gain him the approval of his parents and others.

The study of anxiety and the vicissitudes of its development is the best example in psychoanalytic theory of how the child's affective development and his ego development, object relations, and psychosexual development are correlated and intertwined. Though, it too is incomplete, this line of development is clearer than is true of other affects. Among the current problems being posed is how to understand more clearly the depressive affect—how to reduce the confusion between the term *depression* as a description of a mood and as a statement of a complex dynamic psychological structure.

Piaget and Inhelder (1969) provided another view of affectivity that has clinical applications. In some respects, it is congenial with psychoanalysis. They said:

> . . . when behavior is studied in its cognitive aspects, we are concerned with its structures; when behavior is considered in its affective aspect, we are concerned with its energetics. While these two aspects cannot be reduced to a single aspect, they are nevertheless inseparable and complementary. . . .
> The cognitive schemes which are initially centered upon the child's own action become the means by which the child constructs an objective and "decentered" universe; similarly, and at the same sensorimotor levels, affectivity proceeds from a lack of differentiation between the self and the physical and human environment toward the construction of a group of exchanges or emotional investments which attach the differentiated self to other persons through interpersonal feelings or things (through interests at

various levels). Insofar as the self remains undifferentiated, and thus unconscious of itself, all affectivity is centered on the child's own body and action, since only with the dissociation of the self from the other or nonself does the decentration, whether affective or cognitive, become possible. The affects observable in this earliest period are at first dependent upon general rhythms corresponding to the rhythms of the spontaneous global activities of the organism; namely, alternations between states of tension and relaxation and so on. These rhythms are differentiated into a search for agreeable stimuli and a tendency to avoid disagreeable stimuli. . . . Even before the formation of the self complementary to and interacting with others we witness the elaboration of a whole system of exchanges through imitation and the reading of gestural signs. From this time on the child begins to react to persons in a more and more specific manner because they behave differently from things and because they behave according to schemes which bear some relation to the schemes of the child's own action. Sooner or later there is established a kind of causality whose source is others, inasmuch as they produce pleasure, comfort, pacification, security, etc. However, it is essential to understand that the totality of these affective events is inseparable from the general structuration of behavior. (pp. 21–25)

Here Piaget referred to Escalona (1963), who wrote:

My data suggest the possibility that what Piaget proposes for cognition is true of all adaptive aspects of mental functioning: namely that the emergence of such functions as communication, *modulation of affect* [my italics], control over excitation, delay and aspects of object relation, and hence identification, are all the result of a developmental sequence in sensorimotor terms before they can emerge as ego function in a narrower sense. (p. 198)

Piaget and Inhelder continued "We have assumed that affective decentering is a correlate of cognitive decentering, not because one dominates the other, but because both occur as a result of a single integrative process".

I turn now to pose a question that I can answer in part: Of what assistance to the clinician working with infants are these theoretical and conceptual statements? Do they assist in the diagnosis and treatment of infants with developmental delays or deviations? My answer is yes, and I shall illustrate with case examples a little later. First, however, a brief description is given as orientation to the choice of the examples I will bring.

In the clincial setting for infants and very young children at Yale Child Study Center, we see many and varied aspects of development. We run a diagnostic and treatment program for infants and children up to age 5 years. We accept referrals of children and parents for any kind of developmental or behavioral problem in the age group with which we are concerned. Conspicuous in our case load are a number of types of disturbance of the infant's experience in receiving adequate nurturance that have an impact on affective development and behavior. These may arise from a variety of sources, among them:

1. Life events that result in considerable inconsistency and/or discontinuity of affectionate care (loss of the nurturing adults, multiple and indifferent caregivers, multiple foster home placements, etc.).

2. Disturbances in the capacity of the parent figures to nurture the infant adequately. Gross disturbances most commonly seen in our setting are parents with infantile personalities who are unable to meet the normal needs of an infant, depressed parents who are unable to mobilize themselves to respond adequately to the infant, psychotic parents who create a confusing or chaotic environment, and neglectful and/or abusing parents.

3. Less severe but nonetheless significant problems may arise between infants and parents in whom the disturbance is less overwhelming than the above. For example, there are mother–child couples who are not a good "match," who have been unable to achieve the mutual adaptation that gets development off to a good start. A mother may be unable to adapt her attitudes and child care to the kind of baby she has; the infant may have certain congenital characteristics that make him less adaptable than another infant might be to a mother's style of care. Problems in the mother–infant relationship leading to disturbances in affective development may occur in a relationship that has been heretofore a good one (an example would be separation), or they may develop in an already stressed relationship. Some of the former may be considered as slight or temporarily intense exaggerations of what would be considered normal difficulties. Often, with only a little help, these can be promptly alleviated. Many of the latter—that is, the symptoms that herald a new complication in an already far less than good relationship—both are more difficult and take longer to treat.

Some illustrative vignettes follow:

TEDDY AND LARRY

The descriptions of the following two infants are included to show some of the contrasts between a child whose affective development is proceeding well and one whose affective development—among other things—is not proceeding well. These descriptions are condensed from longer descriptions published in *Infants in Institutions* (Provence & Lipton, 1962).

Teddy

Teddy, who was transferred from the hospital to the foundling home at age 10 days, was first examined by us at age 20 days. At that time, he was a well-nourished, husky-looking baby who was taking adequate amounts of formula feeding. It was felt that his neuromuscular maturation was somewhat advanced; he gave the impression of particularly good maturation as judged especially by the good organization of reflex patterns, by the beginning replacement of some of the neonatal reflex patterns by more mature forms of behavior, and by his visual alertness. Moreover, he was robust and vigorous-looking, and had a good loud cry, and his physical growth was proceeding well.

For several months, while his development showed the same kind of retardation that characterized the other infants in this setting, Teddy's performance on the tests and his general behavior and reactivity were not as severely impaired as those of the others. It has never been clear why Teddy did relatively better than the other institutionalized infants. However, we suggest that there are two good possibilities: (1) his inherent biological endowment may have been quite good, as is suggested by the signs of good maturational progress in the earliest months; (2) he posed a problem in regard to feeding in that he frequently lost the nipple of his propped bottle and cried. Since he had a loud voice that punctured the usual quiet of the nursery, he had much more attention from the attendants. While they were not always happy with him and considered this protest something of a nuisance, it did have the result of providing more contacts with adults than other babies had in the first seven to eight months.

At the time of the examination at 26 weeks, Teddy was still doing reasonably well. He was a husky, attractive infant with a moderately strong drive toward motor activity. He was able to direct his interest toward the test materials as long as the examiner was careful not to compete with the toys for his attention. His interest in the test materials at that time was greater than we encountered in the other institutionalized infants, and he functioned at a higher level. There was no sign of anxiety to the stranger. He accepted the examiners with a friendly, amiable smile and at times was active in initiating a contact by smiling or reaching toward one of us. The attendant reported that she was unable to prop his bottle as he tended to lose it from his mouth and that when he did so, he would yell so loudly that she had to go to him often and hold it for a few minutes. He was often placed in the small canvas bouncing chair so that he would be less noisy.

The impression of Teddy at 26 weeks (six months) was that he was doing well when compared with others in the group. However, along with the signs of favorable development, one could see beginning impairment of certain functions, which was more dramatic in the last half of the first year. He was examined subsequently at 32 weeks, 38 weeks, 45 weeks, and 55 weeks, and there was a greater retardation at each examination. His decline was gradual but progressive. He became less active in his approaches to people and was not as responsive to them. His investment in toys diminished markedly, and he had little or no interest in solving the problems that are appropriate to babies of his age. He was lacking in playfulness, and the impoverishment of his affective expressions was increasingly apparent. He looked less vigorous, robust, and active while maintaining an adequate weight gain. At age 45 weeks, he was solemn-faced, unsmiling, and miserable-looking. His nose was being wiped as the examiner approached, a measure about which he cried woefully. However, he made no effort to avoid it or to push away the nurse's hand. He was still considered by the staff a "smart little boy" compared to the others in his nursery, but he looked strikingly different from an infant in his own family. A few excerpts from a detailed observation recorded at the time are given:

> As the massed cubes are presented he looks at them, leans forward, and approaches them with his right hand. He tentatively grasps one and quickly releases it. As he fails to approach them for a time, a cube is placed in his hand which he accepts readily. He next accepts a cube from my hand and looks at me as though suspicious, and finally smiles tentatively in response to my smile and my efforts to interest him in the other cubes. He seems very inhibited motorically as though unable to move or to exploit anything vigorously. . . . The arms are often held quite still in a "frozen" position which he maintains until activated by the examiner's placement of a toy in his hand.

He could sit, pull to stand, and could creep a few steps on all fours. He did more rocking than creeping in this position, however. He could (when activated) approach and grasp the toys and had the ability to hold two simultaneously. However, he regularly discarded one, focusing his interest on a single one. He showed some displeasure when the toy was removed but accepted substitutes easily. He made no effort to recover a hidden toy. When upset, he seemed more easily comforted by being given a toy than by direct contact with the adult, including the "familiar" adult. It appeared as though having the toy in hand was more important than any attraction to the specific qualities of the toy.

His imitative responses in relation to the adult were more difficult to elicit than at the time of the last contact, and the usually playful responses to social games such as peekaboo, pat-a-cake, so-big, etc., expected in babies of this age were not seen. He showed no awareness of the meaning of the adult's gesture to pick him up, though he accepted the picking up with some evidences of enjoyment.

Outstanding were his soberness, his forlorn appearance, and his lack of animation. The interest that he showed in the toys was mainly for holding, inspecting, and rarely mouthing. When he was unhappy, he now had a cry that sounded neither demanding nor angry—just miserable—and it was usually accompanied by his beginning to rock. The capacity for protest that he had had earlier was much diminished. He did not turn to adults to relieve his distress or to involve them in a playful or pleasurable interchange. He made no demands. The active approach to the world, which had been one of the happier aspects of his earlier development, had vanished. As one made active and persistent efforts at a social interchange, he became somewhat more responsive, animated, and motorically active, but he lapsed into his depressed and energyless appearance when the adult became less active with him.

There were two descriptive comments by observers that seem to convey the impression Teddy made at this time. One was "The light in Teddy has gone out"; the other was: "If you crank his motor, you can get him to go a little; he can't start on his own."

Larry

Larry, a full-term 8-pound infant, was the second child in his family. As a newborn, he was described as an attractive husky, mature, moderately active infant, with a lusty cry. Breast-fed fully for the first six months and then gradually weaned to a cup, Larry gained weight rapidly. For the first three to four months, he was somewhat fretful at night, and his mother alleviated this by holding and nursing him.

At age 1 month, he was described as a large, well-nourished infant who was visually alert and had the beginnings of a social smile. At age 7 weeks, when first tested, he was doing well. There was some hand–mouth activity, he was visually perceptive and attentive, and he responded to the adult with much smiling, cooing, and vocalizing. While he was moderately inactive as to output of movement, his movements gave the impression of strength and good organization. He adapted well to holding and reacted to being placed in the feeding position with increased sucking. His mother held him comfortably and securely; her pleasure in him was easy to see, though she had some complaints about him.

At the 20-week test, he was socially responsive and interested in the toys. The hand-to-mouth movement was well organized and purposive. He vocalized to people and also spontaneously to toys and to himself. He played with his hands, rubbed his face, touched his body. He mouthed the toys as well as his hands. He was large, well proportioned, and moderately active.

His test performance was good, both quantitatively and qualitatively. He was smiling and attentive to the examiner but frequently turned to his mother, who sat nearby, making a visual contact and often smiling and vocalizing to her.

At 43 weeks, Larry was a robust, vigorous infant. Gross motor development was well organized at the 48-week level: he crept well, pulled to stand, and cruised. Moreover, he used his motor equipment effectively, either in pursuit of a toy or person or for avoidance of an unpleasant stimulus. Fine motor skills were also well developed. His interest in the test materials was high. He could handle two objects simultaneously with ease, showing the capacity to be interested in both and to combine objects. His general interest in inspecting and manually exploring the external world of people and things was represented in the test situation by such items as the exploratory interest in the bell, which was paralleled by similar behavior toward people and toward his own body. He was aware of the relationship between the round form and the hole in the formboard and solved the problem of finding a toy behind the solid screen. He was interested in social contact with the examiner and initiated it. He participated in such games as pat-a-cake, peekaboo, and bye-bye with interest and pleasure. He had a large repertoire of sounds, which he used to express a variety of feeling states, and used *mama* and *dada* specifically as names for his parents. He was drinking milk from a cup and was eating a variety of foods well. A brief excerpt taken from the record of Larry conveys something of the impression he made:

> He is still attractive, vigorous, and friendly, but there is a change in Larry and it is difficult to know what factors contribute to this impression. He seems more mature and less of an infant. Certainly his motor skill contributes to this as does the fact that he is less chubby and body proportions have changed somewhat. However, the predominant change is in his facial expression which is more intent, purposeful, and self-directed. . . . There is considerable mouthing and banging of toys. He bangs with large vigorous swings and seems to enjoy not only the motion but the sound. His movements are well coordinated and graceful. There is no noticeable hesitancy about approaching new objects or in giving up the old, though he looks after them and tries to retrieve them if no substitute is given. This increased interest and impression of self-directed activity is accompanied by something that makes one think he has a zest for life.

ANN

Another child, one whose affective development as well as other areas suffered within her two-parent, middle-class family, is Ann. The family participated in one of the Yale Child Study Center longitudinal developmental studies. We have a great deal of data about them, from which the following is condensed.

Ann was deprived early, by her depressed mother, of many gratifying experiences, especially around feeding. The mother's problem in giving to the child, her need to be given to, and her sadistic tendencies resulted in a noxious combination of neglect, screaming at the child, and spanking her when she cried.

The child's problem was first apparent at age 4 months on a routine developmental examination, done as part of her regular monthly visit to the center. A decrease in vocalization, a lessening of voluntary motor activity, and a slightly diminished interest in toys were the first signs. Shortly after, there was a deceleration in physical growth followed by a slowing in all sectors of development measured by the developmental tests. Language development showed the greatest delay. By age 9 months, she was a small infant who slept long hours at night, had an anxious, vigilant expression when awake, cried at the slightest disappointment or frustration, and was not playful.

At the 9-month developmental examination, gross motor development was 5 weeks below age. Ann could sit erect no longer than a minute, was making some efforts to crawl on her belly, but could not creep. Fine motor development—including all items of prehension, manipulation of small objects, and eye–hand coordination—was age-adequate. In adaptive development, there were some failures below her age level but a number of successes above her age (one as high as 5 weeks above her age). Language was 11 weeks below her age and was the area of lowest functioning. Her social contacts were weak and poorly sustained, and she often reacted negatively to the approach of another person including her mother. Her interest in toys was desultory, and they seemed to give her little satisfaction. The diagnostic impression was that of an emotionally deprived and insufficiently stimulated infant rather than of a mentally retarded infant.

During the period from 7½ to 10½ months of age, there was growing concern on the part of the staff about her prognosis for future development. Further lag in development and greater emotional disturbance seemed likely if something more could not be done to help the mother modify her care of Ann. The mother's attitude toward the developmental problems varied. Initially, she was depressed and hopeless and wondered whether or not she should "start over" with a new baby with whom she would have more success. Later, she tended to deny that she was concerned.

When Ann was 9 months of age, the mother, at the pediatrician's recommendation, saw a consultant of wide pediatric and psychiatric experience in the hope that she could be helped to obtain psychotherapy. She spoke to him of her feelings of depression and loneliness and her concern about the infant's development but expressed the opinion that psychiatrists were for people "who could not help themselves" and not for her.

Efforts by the pediatrician were continued to try to alleviate the crisis for mother and child. Pediatric contacts, which the mother always professed were helpful, were increased in frequency. She was not able to accept the suggestion that she have part-time help in the care of the baby, which would permit her to renew some of the activities outside the home that had been important to her earlier. Though she spoke wistfully of her career, she felt that she should not turn over the care of her baby to another person even for a few hours a day.

These case examples are presented not because they are unusual but because they are common occurrences in a clinic for very young children. It is hoped that the descriptions speak for themselves in illustrating disturbances of affective development and their coexistence with other developmental disturbances.

In conclusion, clinicians would generally consider an infant to be in a healthy state affectively if he reveals emotions that are in line with the average expectable development of a reasonably well-nurtured child. Though we need to know more, we have information that has proved to be of practical value in therapeutic work and parent guidance. We would generally consider the infant in a healthy state affectively if he reveals a broad spectrum of feelings, if they are vivid, if there are manifold and subtle shades of feelings, and if the tapestry of the affective life is rich and colorful. In contrast, we would be concerned if his range of expressed feelings is narrow, if they lack vividness and intensity, if they do not show up in his actions, and if he shows us only a few compared with other infants of his age. Not only the number and kind of emotions that are expressed but their intensity, range, degree of differentiation, and the infant's ability to modulate and control them would require consideration in an evaluation of affective development.

REFERENCES

Anthony, E. Childhood depression. In E. J. Anthony & T. Benedek (Eds.), *Depression and human existence*. Boston: Little, Brown, 1975, pp. 231–277.
Baldwin, J. M. (Ed.). *Dictionary of philosophy and psychology*. New York: Peter Smith, 1940.
Benedek, T. Parenthood as a developmental phase. *Journal of the American Psychoanalytic Association*, 1959, 7, 389–417.
Benjamin, J. Some developmental observations relating to the theory of anxiety. *Journal of the American Psychoanalytic Association*, 1961, 9(4), 652–688.

Benjamin, J. Further comments on some developmental aspects of anxiety. In H. Gaskill (Ed.), *Counterpoint*. New York: International Universities Press, 1963.

Bowlby, J. *Attachment and loss* (Vol. 2). New York: Basic Books, 1973.

Décarie, T. *Intelligence and affectivity in early childhood*. New York: International Universities Press, 1965.

Erikson, E. *Childhood and society*. New York: Norton, 1950.

Escalona, S. Patterns of infantile experience and the developmental process. *Psychoanalytic Study of the Child*, 1963, *18*, 197–203.

Freud, A., & Burlingham, D. *Infants without families*. New York: International Universities Press, 1944.

Greenacre, P. Play in relation to creative imagination. *Psychoanalytic Study of the Child*, 1959, *14*, 61–80.

Hoffer, W. Mouth, hand and ego-integration. *Psychoanalytic Study of the Child*, 1949, *3/4*, 49–56.

Jacobson, E. The self and the object world. *Psychoanalytic Study of the Child*, 1954, *9*, 75–87.

Lewin, B. Reflections on affect. In M. Schur (Ed.), *Drives, affects, behavior* (Vol. 2). New York: International Universities Press, 1965, pp. 23–37.

Mahler, M., Pine, F., & Bergman, A. *The psychological birth of the human infant*. New York: Basic Books, 1975.

Naylor, A. Some determinants of parent–infant relationships. In L. Dittman (Ed.), *What we can learn from infants*. Washington, D. C.: National Association for the Education of Young Children, 1970, pp. 25–47.

Piaget, J., & Inhelder, B. *The psychology of the child* (Helen Weaver, trans.). New York: Basic Books, 1969.

Provence, S., & Lipton, R. *Infants in institutions*. New York: International Universities Press, 1962.

Rapaport, D. *Emotions and memory*. Baltimore: Williams & Wilkins, 1942.

Spitz, R. Hospitalism: a follow-up report. *Psychoanalytic Study of the Child*, 1946, *2*, 113–117.

Spitz, R. *The first year of life*. New York: International Universities Press, 1965.

Spitz, R. & Wolf, K. Anaclitic depression: An inquiry into the genesis of psychiatric conditions in early childhood. *Psychoanalytic Study of the Child*, 1946, *2*, 313–342.

Waelder, R. The psychoanalytic theory of play. *Psychoanalytic Quarterly*, 1933, *2*, 208–224.

Winnicott, D. Ego distortion in terms of true and false self. In D. Winnicott (Ed.), *The maturational processes and the facilitating environment*. New York: International Universities Press, 1965, pp. 140–152.

12

An Organizational View of Affect: Illustration from the Study of Down's Syndrome Infants

DANTE CICCHETTI AND L. ALAN SROUFE

Many of the outstanding questions in the field of affective development may be put within a unified framework that can be described as an "organizational perspective" (Sroufe, in press; Sroufe & Mitchell, in press). For example, the question of age of onset of various emotions becomes subsumed under the objective of tracing the unfolding of various affect systems and their integration with cognitive and social development. The question is not whether the 3-week-old exhibits fear but rather what are the circumstances for eliciting negative reactions at this age and what is the developmental course of both the reactions and the changing conditions necessary and sufficient for eliciting them. How is earlier distress related to what might later be called wariness and later still fear (whatever terms are actually used)? What does the unfolding of the affect systems tell us about cognitive development, and how do maturational and cognitive changes impact upon the expression of affect?

Likewise, from the organizational perspective, questions about

DANTE CICCHETTI · Department of Psychology and Social Relations, Harvard University, Cambridge, Massachusetts.   L. ALAN SROUFE · Institute of Child Development, University of Minnesota, Minneapolis, Minnesota.

whether infants show negative *or* positive reactions to novel events become subsumed by questions concerning contextual and developmental factors mediating these reactions. In some circumstances, infants react positively to strangers, in others negatively (Sroufe, 1977). More generally, empirical research has shown that incongruous events (masks, strangers, unusual or highly stimulating maternal behavior) can produce the range of affective reactions from laughter and smiling to wariness and distress, depending on agent, setting, sequence of events, familiarization time, and other aspects of context (Sroufe, Waters, & Matas, 1974). A close relationship between strong positive and strong negative affect is assumed within the organizational perspective, as they are linked by degree of cognitively produced arousal. However, since the same event can produce the range of affective reactions, factors beyond information inherent in the event are seen as influencing the direction of and thresholds for affective reactions (Sroufe & Waters, 1976).

Other major questions within the organizational view concern the nature of the developmental process itself, especially the role of affect and tension constructs in understanding development. Several years ago, Stechler and Carpenter (1967) pointed out that cognitive/ informational constructs such as discrepancy could not be completely adequate in accounting for behavior. Loevinger (1976) has reiterated this position. However, with the demise of drive reduction and conservation of energy as acceptable explanatory concepts (e.g., Bowlby, 1969; Mandler, 1975; White, 1959), the role of motivation, feeling, and tension in modulating and controlling behavior has not yet become clear, although there are beginnings (Ainsworth, 1974; Sroufe & Mitchell, in press; Sroufe & Waters, 1976).

AFFECT AND COGNITION

Viewing the goal of infant research as understanding the total organization of development, it is becoming clear that emotional and cognitive aspects of behavior must be examined concurrently (Cicchetti & Sroufe, 1976b; Décarie, 1965; Emde, Gaensbauer, & Harmon, 1976; Escalona, 1968; Sroufe, in press; Stechler & Carpenter, 1967). While perceptual, cognitive, and socioemotional development may be studied independently, what is being sought is an integrated conceptualization of development, that is, an understanding of the organization of various capacities of the infant, rather than a mere cataloguing of these capacities. Perceptual, cognitive, and learning processes clearly contribute to determining which particular social-emotional response will be elicited in a given stimulus context, as well as how such responses will manifest themselves behaviorally; conversely, social and emotional factors influence cognitive development (Sroufe & Mitchell, in press; Sroufe, *et al.*, 1974).

Following Piaget (cf. Piaget, 1972; Piaget & Inhelder, 1969), infant researchers are beginning to view affect and cognition as mutually influential (reciprocally interacting) aspects of the same developmental process. As does cognition, so too does affect organize the infant's behavior. In fact, in many ways affect *is* the meaning of a transaction with the surround *for the infant*. Affect is the meaning and motivational system that cognition serves (Sroufe, in press; Sroufe & Waters, 1976; Stechler & Carpenter, 1967). Other investigators as well (Engel, 1971; Vygotsky, 1962) have theorized that all thinking and activity emanate from a background of feeling. They describe this background as a matrix that connects other experiences and is indispensable for every activity. Bleuler (1932, 1950) has adopted a similar theoretical stance in regard to psychopathology in his assertion that "affective influences play such a dominant role in psychopathology. . . . that practically everything else is incidental."

SPECIAL ADVANTAGES IN THE STUDY OF DOWN'S SYNDROME INFANTS

Despite the appeal of the theoretical propositions discussed above, there has been little systematic investigation of the interaction between affect and cognition. The present research, with infants certain to be cognitively retarded to varying degrees, was undertaken with this task specifically in mind. The study of infants with Down's syndrome also offers important opportunities for formulating a more precise organizational perspective.

Since there is evidence (Carr, 1970) that Down's syndrome infants show deficits in cognitive functioning on psychological tests at least as early as 3 months, a corresponding lag in affective development may be hypothesized. At the same time, a study of affective development in retarded infants fulfills a clear need for an understanding of the socioemotional aspects of retardation itself. As Zigler (1973) has suggested, a comprehensive understanding of retarded children requires an integration of social and emotional factors with cognitive factors. In this position, it is assumed that the developmental *process* basically is similar in retarded and normal children, that is, that there is a similar organization in the behavior and development of atypical children, though the developmental pace is slowed down (Zigler, 1969).

In addition, the slower cognitive development of infants with Down's syndrome allows a separation of the early prototypes of what will later be affective expression from genuine emotional reactions that are dependent on psychological processes. Their developmental heterogeneity allows specification of the interdependence between affect and cognition (Cicchetti & Sroufe, 1976b). And the obvious autonomic deficiencies, especially of some Down's syndrome infants, enables beginning statements about the role of tension and affect in promoting development. To date, most investigations of Down's syndrome children have paid perfunctory attention to developmental processes and instead have been concerned with biochemical and cytogenetic analyses, with the hope that these inquiries would reduce the hiatus between the chromosomal anomalies and the ultimate biopsychological outcomes (Richards, 1973).

Finally, an examination of individuals with an extra autosomal chromosome may provide a clear test of the hypothesis that abnormal chromosomal material may be used as an independent variable to study behavioral differences. Generally, genetic flooding (e.g., excessive DNA) has such a deleterious effect upon the copying process that the surviving phenotype is not sufficiently rich to warrant study (Cavalli-Sforza & Bodmer, 1971; Gibson, 1975; Stern, 1973). Very few autosomal trisomies are viable, nor are they frequent enough to be tested for behavioral phenotypes; Down's syndrome is a notable exception. For example, it possesses a suitable complexity and intactness of phenotypic expression, is detectable early so that it can be charted developmentally, and occurs with sufficient frequency to allow for meaningful developmental analysis. Moreover, it exhibits several cytogenetic forms that permit intrasample comparisons (Gibson, 1975), has a genetically transmittable subtype (Jarvik, Filek, & Pierson, 1964), and manifests apparently distinctive cognitive and other psychological characteristics (Belmont, 1971; Cicchetti & Serafica, 1977; Gibson, 1975).

METHODS

To promote maximal affective expression (e.g., crying and laughter), three procedures that other investigators have found to be effective were used: (1) the study of infant's responses to a visual loom (Ball & Tronick, 1971; Bower, Broughton, & Moore, 1970; Yonas, Bechtold, Frankel, Gordon, McRoberts, Norcia, & Sternfels, 1977); (2) the study of infant's responses to a "visual cliff" (Gibson & Walk, 1960; Scarr & Salapatek, 1970; Schwartz, Campos, & Baisel, 1973); and (3) the study of infant's responses to a series of repetitive, gamelike or incongruous items presented by their mothers (Cicchetti & Sroufe, 1976b; Sroufe &, Wunsch, 1972).

Assessment of Reactions to the Loom

Subjects

The sample consisted of a total of 120 Down's syndrome infants and 90 normal infants. Of the Down's syndrome infants, 30 were seen at each of four age periods: 4, 8, 12, and 16 months. A random sample of 30 of the infants seen at the 4-, 8-, and 12-month assessments were also studied at 16 months, making 60 the total number of babies who were tested at 16 months. Of the normal infants, 30 were studied at each of three age periods: 4, 8, and 12 months. For each visit, the infants were seen within one week of their monthly birth date. All infants were Caucasian, home-reared, and free from any obvious sensory or neurological defects.

The diagnosis of Down's syndrome, made on the basis of chromosomal count for all subjects, yielded the following cytogenetic subtypes: 114 trisomy-21, 3 translocations, and 3 mosaics. The names of the children were obtained from state associations for retarded children, hospitals, and Down's syndrome parent groups. Parents were first sent a letter and then contacted by telephone. Only one of the parents contacted refused to participate.

The normal infants were recruited by telephone from a volunteer pool established at the Institute of Child Development, University of Minnesota. Parents of infants born in the Twin Cities area receive a general letter inviting them to participate in infant research. Those returning a card are then called and asked to participate in specific experiments. The families contacted spanned the middle and lower-middle socioeconomic classes.

Apparatus

The apparatus used was a shadow caster of the same general type used by Ball and Tronick (1971), Bower et al. (1970), and Yonas et al. (1977) in their studies of optical expansion. A 100-watt arc point source lamp was mounted 135 cm behind the center of a 1.8 m × 1.8 m Polocoat rear projection screen. The shadow-casting occluder was a 6.5 cm × 6.5 cm red diamond with a black cross, positioned between the screen and the point source. The diamond was supported by a vertical metal rod, which in turn was attached to a motorized track and pulley system enabling the stimulus to move toward or away from the point source at a constant velocity of 27.7 cm/sec. Each trial began with the stimulus in a position 10 cm from the rear projection screen, from which it was moved 125 cm toward the point source. After remaining stationary for three seconds, it was returned to its initial position. All trials were initiated by the experimenter on the judgment of alert attention to the stimulus by the infant.

Two conditions, counterbalanced for order, were presented to each infant. In the "hit" trials, the shadow occluder presented an image of 21 visual degrees centered on the infant's line of sight, which underwent symmetrical expansion over a period of 4.5 sec, achieving a terminal size of 144 visual degrees (filling the visual field). These trials corresponded closely to an object approaching on a collision course. In the "miss" condition, the point source was moved 10 cm to the right, resulting in an asymmetrical expansion that moved from the same initial position to the infant's left, eventually disappearing off the screen. The noise generated by the shadow-casting apparatus was masked by a continuous presentation of wideband noise from a loudspeaker located on the floor behind the screen.

Behavioral responses were recorded on videotape by a camera situated 45° to the left of and above the infant. Two small lamps located above and below the camera served to illuminate the area sufficiently for videotaping. A small mirror was placed to the right and slightly behind the infant. Its position was such that it provided the camera with a reflected display of the stimulus's position relative to the infant. A digital clock was broadcast to the video monitor via a second camera and a special effects generator. The use of the clock facilitated behavioral coding, since the timing of the infant's responses could be noted with accuracy to the second. A light mounted on the face of the clock was illuminated when the stimulus began and ended its motion along the track as it contacted a microswitch. This light served to indicate both the onset and the termination (i.e., impact) of the display. A microphone suspended above the baby recorded any sounds (e.g. vocalization, crying) made by the infant. Responses were also noted concurrently by an observer standing behind a cloth-covered screen to the infant's left.

Procedure

Subjects were accompanied to the laboratory by their parents. The procedure was explained, and a sample trial of each display was presented to the parents. After parental consent was obtained, room lights were extinguished. When the infant was alert and content, the experiment was begun. All infants were placed on a cushioned backless stool and supported by their mothers 30 cm from the rear projection screen. They were held gently around the waist, allowing for freedom of movement of the head, arms, and body. *The way in which each mother supported her baby was closely monitored.* Every effort was made to ensure that the mothers did not restrict their babies' movement, since it is conceivable that inadvertent intrusiveness on the part of the mother could reduce the likelihood of a defensive reaction. In a few cases, 4-month-old Down's syndrome infants with extremely poor head control were placed in an infant seat.

When the infant was oriented to the stimulus and in an alert state, the experimenter began the trial. Each infant was presented with a maximum of 10 trials to the first condition, whereupon the point source was shifted and the second group of trials in the next condition were presented. If an infant became tired or fussy, a break was taken for feeding, changing, or soothing. An *optimal infant state* was considered to be vital to the attainment of an accurate behavioral record. Moreover, *care was taken to see that the infant remained in an upright viewing position at the proper distance and angle from the screen* (i.e., infants were kept in a perpendicular sitting position).

Coding and Analysis of Data

Responses were scored from videotape recordings for all trials in which the child was judged to attend to the stimulus. The following behaviors were coded:

1. *Blinking*. Blinking was scored as a response to the stimulus if it occurred during the interval including the second preceding and the second following impact. It was also noted whether the response was a single closing of the eyelid, a multiple closing of the eyelid (i.e., two or three rapid blinks occurring in succession), or a fluttering of the eyelid (i.e., many movements of the eyelid that occurred too rapidly to count reliably). The latter two categories of blinking were subsequently combined and are hereafter referred to as "multiple" blinks.

2. *Defensive arm movement*. *Defensive arm movement* was defined as an upward motion of one or both arms occurring in the interval following the onset of stimulus motion up until 3 sec postimpact. The gesture most often resulted in the placement of the arms or hands between the infant's head and the projection screen. In the event that the infant's hands were up at the onset of stimulus motion, the response was not coded as defensive arm movement. Moreover, in an effort to rule out the possibility that an infant's arms were raised as a result of a loss of balance, we required that the baby's head *not* be looking up to count an arm movement as defensive. Despite these stringent restrictions, it should be noted that we had very little need to employ them, since their

defining conditions occurred so rarely. Finally, in an effort to distinguish between reaching for the oncoming stimulus and a true defensive reaction, we required that the infant either remain stationary or withdraw before terming an arms-up response protective; that is, instances of upward arm movement accompanied by forward body movement were not categorized as defensive in nature.

3. *Withdrawal*. This response consisted of a backward movement of the head, with the infant's eyes remaining straight ahead. This latter stipulation was introduced to preclude the possibility that withdrawal would occur as a counterpart to upward tracking of the stimulus display.[1] It was measured with the apex of the infant's head used as the reference point, as this position is not affected by movements in the horizontal plane. It was often accompanied by a backward motion of the entire torso.

4. *Turning away*. This response was defined as an abrupt head movement in the horizontal plane during the interval including the second preceding and the second following impact.

5. *Tracking*. Tracking was defined as a continual head and eye movement in one direction. It was scored as tracking to the side when it occurred in the horizontal plane and as tracking upward when it occurred in the vertical plane.

6. *Crying*. This category was designed as a measure of the emotional state of the infant and as an index of a negative reaction.[2] It was scored whenever the infant cried audibly once a trial was initiated and up to 3 sec after impact.

Interrater Reliability. Two independent raters coded all the videotapes. The interrater reliability ratings, expressed in percentage of agreement, ranged from 88% for multiple blinks to 100% for crying. Agreement meant that the same behavior was coded similarly by both raters. The interrater reliability ratings were obtained by division of the number of agreements by the number of agreements added to the number of disagreements.

After the percentage of agreement on each response measure was computed for each infant's record, the record was reexamined. In those instances where there were discrepancies between raters, the events in question were identified on the videotapes and examined until a mutual agreement was reached by the observers. Thus, the data reported here

[1] While the implementation of such a stringent criterion may indeed have attenuated the actual incidence of withdrawal, it nonetheless removes a large degree of subjectivity in the judgment of its occurrence.

[2] Analyses of more subtle negative reactions (e.g., "fear faces") are currently being carried out.

are based on the consensus opinions of both raters for each behavioral response scored.

Assessment of Reactions to the Visual Cliff

Subjects

For this study, 70 Down's syndrome infants, diagnosed by chromosomal count, were seen on the visual cliff approximately one month after they were capable of crawling.[3] Karyotype analysis yielded the following cytogenetic subtypes: 65 trisomy-21, 2 translocations, and 3 mosaics. Since all of these infants are involved in either an intensive longitudinal or a cross-sectional study (Cicchetti & Sroufe, in preparation), and since we have a close working relationship with their families, we could reliably gauge the onset of locomotion. Down's syndrome infants are generally hypotonic to some degree (Coleman, 1973; Cowie, 1970; McIntire & Dutch, 1964), and the development of crawling is delayed compared to that of normal infants. The age range in onset of crawling was from 9 months to 26 months, with most of the sample crawling at 15 or 16 months. All but 10 of these infants were also seen on the loom at 16 months. In the event that an infant began crawling in the same month he was to be seen on the loom, the two procedures were performed on separate occasions. Generally, they were performed within one week of each other. Assessments were carried out independently so as to minimize the possibility that there would be any carry-over negative reactions from one experiment to the next.

While we did not examine a group of normal infants, we felt that age of crawling could serve as one index of a comparable developmental level between the Down's syndrome infants and their normal counterparts. However, we recognize that this is not an infallible indicator of level of cognitive competence in the Down's syndrome infants. Rather, it is a conservative estimate, since Down's syndrome infants generally have higher mental than motor scores (Carr, 1970; Cicchetti & Sroufe, 1976b).

Apparatus

The visual cliff had a 157 cm × 183 cm clear Plexiglas platform surface, surrounded by three solid and one opaque 42-cm sides. The

---

[3] Because Down's syndrome infants have neuromuscular problems and occasionally have severe heart defects (which are now surgically correctable at an early age), not all of the babies "crawl" on all fours. Our criterion for crawling was that the infant be capable of locomoting at least 4 or 5 feet forward of his own volition at a pace commensurate with that shown by other crawling infants.

visual cliff was divided equally into a 78-cm "shallow" side and a 78-cm "deep" side, separated by a 1.5 cm × 27 cm center board. On the shallow side, a navy and white 2.54 cm × 2.54 cm checkerboard material was placed directly under the Plexiglas. At the center board, the material dropped vertically to a depth of 66 cm and continued horizontally under the deep side at the same depth. The deep side was lit from underneath by hidden lights that made the surface nearly invisible to adults when no other illumination was present in the experimental room.

Procedure

Parents accompanied their infants to the laboratory and were familiarized with the visual cliff procedure. Infants were then brought into an adjoining laboratory room where heart rate electrodes were attached.[4] Heart rate (HR) was recorded on a Beckman type R polygraph, with cardiotachometer for beat-to-beat recording. In order to ensure stability of initial HR a period of 10 minutes was allowed for electrode attachment and subsequent adaptation to the visual cliff room. When the infant was in an optimal, alert state, the procedure was begun.

A female experimenter placed the infant on the visual cliff. The infant was first placed on the shallow side straddling the center board. The experimenter then disappeared behind a partition, behind which two other independent observers dictated a running narrative record of the infant's behavior on the cliff onto a cassette recorder. The events were marked on the polygraph in the adjacent room by one of the observers with a pair of hand switches. Specific predetermined signals were relayed via these switches so that the infant's behavior could be kept closely contiguous with its HR. For example, two fast clicks signaled that the infant had vocalized, while three fast clicks either denoted that an infant had crossed over the chasm or that a trial had been initiated.

Four 2-min trials were conducted with each infant. Mothers were instructed to attempt continuously to coax their infants to cross. Each mother also used one of her baby's favorite toys as an incentive to get her infant's attention and interest. Trials were alternated between shallow-to-deep and deep-to-shallow placements. For trials initiated on the deep side, the infant was placed directly atop the chasm on this side by the experimenter. A series of knocks from an experimenter in the adjacent polygraph room signaled the end of each 2-min trial. The experimenter then took the infant off the cliff. To allow HR recovery

---

[4] While detailed heart rate data are not yet analyzed, they will be reported elsewhere. Gross indicators of heart rate change are noted here.

intervals between trials were 1 min. In the event an infant had been upset, they were longer.

Response Measures

The time taken by each infant to cross from one side of the cliff to the other—that is, to move his entire body across either side—was timed by a stopwatch to the nearest second on each trial. Behaviors such as smiling, vocalizing, crying, "freezing," grabbing the sides of the cliff, and patting the Plexiglas were recorded. Interrater reliabilities, calculated as they were for the looming situation, were quite high, ranging from 90% for smiling to 100% for crying, vocalizing, and holding onto the edges of the platform surface.

Assessment of Positive Affect

For this study, 25 Down's syndrome infants (21 Trisomy-21, 2 translocations, and 2 mosaics) were administered a series of standardized stimulus presentations designed to elicit laughter (see Table I). These babies were administered the series of 30 laughter items each month (from 4 through 16 months) in their own homes with their mothers used as the stimulus agent. On each occasion, items were presented in a different random order, generally across two 45-min administrations. Items were presented until there were six trials in which the infant was attentive. If an item elicited crying, it was discontinued. Of these infants, 20 participated in the loom assessment at 16 months, while 11 of them also were seen at an additional time period (generally at 8 months). The responses of all of these infants on the visual cliff were also obtained.

An additional sample of 60 infants were administered a series of 15 of these laughter items (numbers 2, 3, 7, 9, 11, 15, 16, 17, 18, 21, 22, 25, 26, 27, and 29 in Table I) in the laboratory by their mothers *prior* to being seen on the loom. Of these babies, 15 were tested at 4, 8, 12, and 16 months, with an additional 15 returning for a 16-month visit, making 30 the final number seen at 16 months. Of these infants, 57 were trisomy-21, 2 were translocation, and 1 was mosaic.

Previous research with normal (Sroufe & Wunsch, 1972) and Down's syndrome infants (Cicchetti & Sroufe, 1976b) indicated that laughter to the auditory and tactile items began developmentally earlier and that laughter to the social and visual items was linked to cognitive development. Since earlier research had also implicated contextual factors as determinants of affective responses (Sroufe et al., 1974), for those administrations carried out in the lab an attempt was made to

TABLE I. SPECIFIC INSTRUCTIONS FOR INDIVIDUAL ITEMS[a]

Auditory

 1. Four pops in a row, then pause. Start with lips pursed, cheeks full.
 2. Say "aah," starting low, then crescendoing to a loud voice, with an abrupt cutoff. Six-second pause.
 3. Using a loud, deep voice, pronounce "BOOM, BOOM, BOOM," at one-second intervals.
 4. With a mechanical type of sound, varying voice pitch from low to high and back down again, say, "Boo-boo-boo-baa-baa-baa-boo-boo-boo."
 5. With mouth one foot from baby's ear, whisper "Hi, baby, how are you?" Avoid blowing in ear.
 6. Falsetto voice (like Mickey Mouse), say, "Hi, baby, how are you?"
 7. With lips relaxed, blow through them as a horse does when he is tired.

Tactile

 8. Blow gently at hair for three seconds. Blow from the side, across the top of the baby's head.
 9. Four quick pecks, on bare stomach.
10. Gently stroke cheek three times with soft object.
11. Place baby on knees facing away. Five vigorous bounces.
12. Hold baby waist high, horizontal, face toward floor, and jiggle vigorously three seconds.
13. Using finger, gently tickle under baby's chin for three seconds.
14. Open mouth wide, press lips on back of neck, and create a suction for two seconds. Minimize auditory aspects.
15. Lift baby slowly to position overhead, looking down back.

Social

16. Allow baby to grasp yarn, then tug three times trying not to pull it away from the infant. Pause to repeat. (Place yarn in baby's hand if this is necessary.)
17. Put cloth in mouth and lean close enough for baby to grasp. Allow baby to pull cloth out and replace it if this is his/her tendency. (Place the end of the cloth in baby's hand if this is necessary.)
18. Say lyrically, "I'm gonna get you" ("I'm" quite protracted), while leaning toward baby with hands posed to grab. Then grab baby around stomach. If laughter is achieved, do other trials *not* followed by grabbing.
19. Stand at baby's side. Cover baby's face with cloth. If baby does not uncover his face immediately, uncover for him/her. Do not drag cloth across baby's face. Emphasis is on baby's getting out from underneath.
20. Stick out tongue until baby touches it. (Make the infant's hand touch it if necessary.) Quickly pull tongue back in as soon as baby touches it.
21. Using blank cardboard, get baby's attention with face uncovered, cover face for two seconds, uncover quickly, and pause three seconds. Do *not* say "peekaboo."

Visual

22. Focus baby's attention on your fingers. Walk fingers toward baby, then give baby a poke in the ribs. If laughter is achieved, do other trials *not* followed by poking.
23. Using a white cloth, proceed as in #29 below.
24. Use one of baby's favorite toys. Focus baby's attention on it (out of reach). Cover it two seconds, and uncover it quickly.
25. First make sure that the baby is not hungry, then take bottle, bring toward lips, take three pretend sucks, lower bottle. Minimize noise of sucks.

TABLE I. (Continued)

---

26. Place baby in high chair or infant seat. Crawl *across* his field of vision, *not* toward baby. *Stand*, return to starting point.
27. Stand with arms extended to sides, walk in an exaggerated waddle, *across* baby's field of vision. Return to starting point *walking normally*.
28. Shake head vigorously at a distance of one foot from baby's face three times. Do not allow hair to touch baby.
29. Obtain baby's attention. Hold human mask up so baby can see it. Place mask in front of your face, lean slowly to within one foot of baby's face and pause two seconds. Lean back slowly and remove mask slowly.
30. To reduce peekaboo effects, move baby slowly in front of full-length mirror. Hold three seconds, remove slowly, and then pause four seconds.

---

[a] Pauses between trials are 4 sec unless otherwise noted. All items are presented to the infant by the mother.

simulate a familiar environment. Both observers were completely out of sight, and 15 min of laboratory familiarization time was granted before the stimulus presentations were initiated. Items were presented in an entirely different room than the two in which the looming and visual cliff assessments were carried out.

Two or three independent observers rated each of the sessions. Items were scored on a six-point scale (crying, distress, neutral, smile, active smile, laughter), and interrater reliabilities, calculated as above, ranged from 92% for smiling to 99% for laughter (see Cicchetti & Sroufe, 1976b, for a description of the behavior codings).

Assessment of Mental and Motor Development

Each infant who was seen either on the visual cliff, in the looming situation at 16 months, or in the laughter assessments at 16 months was administered the Bayley Scales of Mental and Motor Development at 16 months in his or her home environment. Also, four independent raters assessed the degree of hypotonia for each of the 25 Down's syndrome infants who participated in the longitudinal laughter study. Global observations, observations of resistance to passive movement (Prechtl & Beintema, 1964), palpation of the muscle mass and observations of posture (Illingworth, 1962) served as the major measures by which degree of hypotonia was determined. While nearly all Down's syndrome infants are characterized by relatively high levels of neuromuscular flaccidity, 5 infants in this sample were markedly hypotonic, being set apart from the entire group.

RESULTS

Responses to Looming in Down's Syndrome Infants

Blinking

For all ages, blinks occurred significantly more to the collision (hit) than to the noncollision (miss) trials. Of the 4-month Down's syndrome sample 100% blinked at least once to the stimulus signifying impending collision, and overall they blinked to 81% of the hit trials. The 8-month-old group responded very similarly, blinking to 75% of the hit trials, with 97% of the subjects blinking at least once to the collision displays. Again, at 12 months, the Down's syndrome infants blinked to 78% of the hit trials, as 100% of them exhibited at least one blink at stimulus impact. Finally, the 16-month-old group blinked to 48% of the collision trials, 93% of the sample responding to at least one of the trials by blinking.

Down's syndrome infants likewise often displayed multiple blinks in response to the collision stimulus. They showed multiple blinks to 21%, 30%, 28% and 15% of the trials at the ages of 4, 8, 12, and 16 months, respectively. Similarly, between the 4- and 16-month age periods, 63%, 73%, 77%, and 48% of the respective groups exhibited multiple blinks to at least one hit trial. As was the case for blinking, multiple blinks were rarely shown toward the miss displays.

Defensive Arm Movement

Across all age periods, the Down's syndrome infants exhibited defensive arm movement more frequently to the hit than to the miss condition. At 4 months, the infants brought their arms up at impact to 15% of the collision trials; 40% of the sample displayed this response to at least one hit trial. At 8 months, the Down's syndrome infants used arm movements at impact to 37% of the trials, with 77% of the sample emitting the response on at least one occasion. At 12 months, the infants responded very similarly, with defensive arm movement occurring to 30% of the hit trials; 70% of the subjects did so to at least one collision trial. Likewise, the 16-month-old group interposed their hands in front of the looming stimulus on 33% of the trials; 60% of the infants utilized this response on a minimum of one collision trial. In contrast, defensive arm movement never occurred to more than 4% of the miss trials at any age period.

Withdrawal

Again, withdrawal from the stimulus was more pronounced in collision than in noncollision trials at all ages. The 4-month-olds withdrew from 13% of the hit trials, and 27% of the sample exhibited this response at least once. It should be noted that this percentage might have been slightly attenuated because some of the infants with poor head control were tested in infant seats, which conceivably could have made it difficult to judge withdrawal in these babies. The 8-month-old group withdrew from 14% of the trials; 50% of the infants exhibited this response in at least one instance. At 12 months, the infants reacted to 21% of the collision trials with withdrawal, and 53% of the sample utilized the response on a minimum of one occasion. Finally, the 16-month-olds withdrew from 19% of the hit trials, with 60% of the sample showing at least one occurrence of this response. Withdrawal was virtually nonexistent to the miss trials at any age.

Turn Away

Turning away as a defensive response to impending collision was observed to occur significantly more often to hit than to miss conditions across all age groups. The youngest age group showed this response to 8% of the hit trials, as 24% of the infants exhibited this behavior to one collision display. The 8-month-olds turned away from 13% of the hit trials, with 30% of the sample manifesting this response to a minimum of one trial. Again the 12-month-olds exhibited this response to 13% of the trials; 40% of the infants turned away from trials specifying impending collision at least once. Finally, 16-month-old Down's syndrome infants turned away from 19% of the hit trials, as 33% utilized turning away as a defensive reaction on one occasion. In contrast, turning away never occurred to more than 1% of miss trials in any age group.

Tracking

Tracking in the vertical dimension was analyzed separately from that in the horizontal. Upward tracking was observed to occur in 25% of the collision displays in the 4-month-old infants; 46% of the Down's syndrome infants exhibited this response. At 8 months, tracking up occurred to 15% of the collision trials, as 34% of the infants utilized this behavior at least once. Tracking up continued to drop off at 12 months, as the Down's syndrome infants responded this way to 10% of the hit trials; 28% of the sample performed this response. Finally, tracking up diminished to 5% of the collision trials at 16 months, as 15% of the sample responded in such a fashion. Vertical tracking rarely occurred to the misses at any age.

For all ages, tracking the stimulus display to the side occurred with almost perfect regularity in the noncollision condition but rarely in the collision trials. The 16-month-olds tracked only 77% of the miss trials, but this diminution in tracking accuracy can be attributed to the increased frequency of negative reactions (i.e., crying) displayed toward the stimulus in this age group. Often, infants became so upset by the hit collisions, that their tracking to the misses became impaired as a result.

Crying

No 4- or 8-month-old Down's syndrome infant cried to the hit or miss conditions. At 12 months, 2 Down's syndrome infants (6%) cried to the loom. However, information of impending collision evoked significantly more negative affect in 16-month-old Down's syndrome babies, as 22 of the subjects (37%) cried at the loom.

Responses to Looming in Normal Infants

Blinking

As was true for the Down's syndrome infants, blinking occurred significantly more often to hit than to miss conditions at all age periods. The 4-month-old normal infants blinked to 68% of the collision trials, and 97% of them did so to a minimum of one display. The 8-month-old normal infants exhibited blinking as a defensive response to 58% of the hit trials, as 90% of the sample blinked on at least one occasion. Finally, at 12 months, the normal infants blinked to 50% of the trials, with 83% of the group showing this response on one hit trial.

Likewise, normal infants occasionally blinked two or three times in succession to a hit display. At 4 months, they exhibited multiple blinks to 17% of the trials. At 8 months this percentage remained fairly constant at 21%, with 14% of the trials to 12-month-olds eliciting multiple blinks. In at least one instance, 43% of 4-month-olds, 40% of 8-month-olds, and 30% of 12-month-olds responded with multiple blinks to a hit display. Multiple blinks were almost never exhibited to the asymmetrically expanding miss conditions.

Defensive Arm Movement

Normal infants, regardless of age, utilized upward arm movement much more frequently to the collision trials than to the noncollision ones. At 4 months, they responded in such a manner to 17% of the hit trials; 47% of the infants showed this response. At 8 months, upward arm movement was employed to 27% of the collision trials; 63% of the group lifted their arms as a defensive reaction. The 12-month-olds interposed their arms between themselves and the object in 42% of the collision trials, as 87% of the babies emitted this defensive response. In contradistinction, upward arm movement never occurred to more than 3% of the miss conditions.

Withdrawal

Across each age period, withdrawal of the stimulus display occurred significantly more often to the hit than to the miss conditions. The 4-month-old normal infants exhibited withdrawal to 14% of the collision trials; 40% of the group did so on one occasion. The 8-month-olds utilized this response to 24% of the hit trials, as 60% of the babies withdrew at least once. Finally, the 12-month-old normal sample used withdrawal as a defensive reaction to impending collision on 25% of the trials, with 63% of the babies emitting this response. Withdrawal occurred to 3% of the miss trials in the 4-month age sample and was virtually absent within the other age groups.

Turn Away

The age groups studied in this experiment all utilized turning away at impact as a defensive reaction. Likewise, this response was almost exclusively reserved for the collision trials. At 4 months, normal infants turned away from 11% of the hit trials, as 33% of the sample did so at least once. The 8-month-olds turned away from 17% of the hit trials, with 37% of the sample doing so. The 12-month-olds used this response to 25% of the collision trials; 47% of the infants turned away a minimum of one time.

Tracking

Vertical tracking occurred significantly more frequently to the collision displays in all age groups. The 4-month-old normal infants exhibited this behavior on 10% of the hit trials; 37% of the sample responded in such a fashion at least once. At 8 months, infants tracked up to 12% of the collision trials, with 33% of the group exhibiting this response to a minimum of one trial. The 12-month-old group exhibited this response to 8% of the impending collision trials, as 27% of the sample did so once. Tracking up never occurred to more than 1% of the noncollision trials at any age.

Horizontal tracking occurred to 100% of the miss trials in the 4-month age group; this dropped off to 90% of the noncollision trials at 8 months and to 79% of them at 12 months. Just as was the case with the Down's syndrome infants, as the normal babies began to exhibit a negative reaction to the looming stimulus on hit trials, their performance in tracking the asymmetrically expanding miss display declined in accuracy.

Crying

Only 1 (3%) 4-month-old normal infant cried at the looming stimulus. However, 10 of the 8-month-old infants (33%) and 17 of the 12-month-old babies (57%) reacted with crying to the symmetrically expanding hit condition.

A Comparison of Down's Syndrome and Normal Infants' Responses to Impending Collision

Blinking

As Table II indicates, there were no significant differences in the percentage of blinking to collision trials between the Down's syndrome and the normal infants at 4 months, although there was a trend in that direction. However, by 8 months, significant differences were obtained, as the Down's syndrome infants blinked to a significantly greater proportion of hit trials than did their normal counterparts ($z = 2.13$, $p < .05$). The Down's syndrome infants continued to exhibit a greater percentage of blinks to impending collision than the normal babies at 12 months ($z = 3.50$, $p < .01$). In addition, between 4 and 12 months, the normal infants showed a significant decrease in the percentage of hit trials in which they blinked ($z = 2.0$, $p < .05$). In contrast, the Down's syndrome infants did not reveal any statistically significant decline in the percentage of blinking exhibited to hit trials across the 4–12 month age period. However, further analysis revealed that Down's syndrome infants did manifest a signficant decrease in the amount of blinking

TABLE II. A COMPARISON OF DOWN'S SYNDROME AND NORMAL INFANTS' RESPONSES TO IMPENDING COLLISION: PERCENTAGE OF TRIALS

Response measure	Age in months						
	4		8		12		16
	DS ($N=30$)	Normal ($N=30$)	DS ($N=30$)	Normal ($N=30$)	DS ($N=30$)	Normal ($N=30$)	DS ($N=60$)
Blinking	81	68	75[a]	58	78[b]	50	48
Multiple blinking	21	17	30	21	28[a]	14	15
Defensive arm movement	15	17	37	27	30	42	33
Withdrawal	13	14	14	24	21	25	19
Turn away	8	11	13	17	13	25	19
Vertical tracking	25*	10	15	12	10	8	5

[a] $p<.05$
[b] $p<.01$

displayed to the symmetrically expanding object from 12 to 16 months ($z = 4.29, p < .01$). Moreover, a comparison of percentage of blinking to hit trials between 12-month-old normal infants and 16-month-old Down's syndrome infants revealed no statistically significant differences.

In addition, analyses were carried out on the percentage of multiple blinks emitted by the two respective samples of infants across all age periods. While no statistically significant results occurred in the 4- and 8-month comparison, at 12 months the Down's syndrome infants exhibited more multiple blinks to the impending stimulus than did their normal counterparts ($z = 2.0, p < .05$).

Table III illustrates that a greater number of 12-month-old Down's syndrome infants blinked to the collision stimulus than did their normal counterparts ($z = 3.40, p < .01$). The 4- and 8-month groups were not differentiable by this criterion. However, across all age groups, more Down's syndrome infants emitted multiple blinks to the optically expanding display than did the normal controls. A greater proportion of 4-, 8-, and 12-month-old Down's syndrome infants exhibited multiple blinks than did the normal babies ($z = 2.22, p < .05; z = 3.88, p < .01; z = 5.88, p < .01$, respectively). Moreover, a comparison between 16-month-old Down's syndrome and 12-month-old normal infants revealed that a greater percentage of the former group utilized multiple blinks as a defensive response to the looming stimulus than did the latter group ($z = 2.57, p < .05$).

TABLE III. A COMPARISON OF DOWN'S SYNDROME AND NORMAL INFANTS' RESPONSES TO
IMPENDING COLLISION: PERCENTAGE OF SUBJECTS

Response measure	Age in months						
	4		8		12		16
	DS (N=30)	Normal (N=30)	DS (N=30)	Normal (N=30)	DS (N=30)	Normal (N=30)	DS (N=60)
Blinking	100	97	97	90	100[b]	83	93
Multiple blinking	63[a]	43	73[b]	40	77[b]	30	48[a]
Defensive arm movement	40	47	77	63	70	87[a]	60
Withdrawal	27	40	50	60	53	63	60
Turn away	24	33	30	37	40	47	33
Vertical tracking	46	37	34	33	28	27	15
Crying	0	3	0	33[b]	6	57[b]	37

[a] $p<.05$
[b] $p<.01$

Defensive Arm Movement

As shown in Table II, regardless of age period sampled there were no statistically significant differences found in the degree to which defensive arm movement was employed by the Down's syndrome and normal babies.

Table III indicates that there were no significant differences in the number of Down's syndrome and normal 4-month-old infants who employed upward arm movement as a defensive reaction. Likewise, no significant differences were obtained at 8 months, although the trend showed that a greater percentage of Down's syndrome babies utilized this response ($z = 1.75, p < .10$). However, by 12 months, more normal than Down's syndrome babies responded to the impending collision display with upward arm movement ($z = 2.43, p < .05$).

Withdrawal

As was the case with defensive arm movement, no statistically significant differences emerged at any age (see Table II).

Likewise, an inspection of Table III indicates that there were no statistically significant differences between the number of Down's syndrome or normal infants who utilized withdrawal as a defensive reaction.

Turn Away

As revealed in Table II, no statistically significant differences were found between the amount of turn away shown toward the collision stimulus by either group. There was a trend favoring the normal infants at 12 months, but it failed to reach an acceptable level of statistical significance ($z = 1.71$, $p < .10$). Interestingly, a large number of the turn-away responses occurring to the hit conditions in the normal babies at this age were accompanied by crying. Infants often reached for or clutched onto their mothers as they avoided the oncoming stimulus.

As shown in Table III, no statistically significant differences emerged in the number of infants using turn away as a defensive response in any group or at any age.

Tracking Up

At 4 months, as seen in Table II, Down's syndrome infants utilized tracking up to a significantly greater percentage of the hit trials than did their normal counterparts ($z = 2.14$, $p < .05$). Since the stimulus display began its most dramatic expansion at the second prior to impact, most tracking up responses occurred concomitantly with this explosion or within the subsequent 2 sec. It could be argued that the "occasional" tracking up response that Ball and Tronick (1971) observed to occur to hit conditions in part accounted for their findings (i.e., as the infant began tracking up, he would have begun losing balance, thereby causing him to bring up his hands, giving a false impression of a defensive reaction). Since Bower et al. (1970) have also reported that young infants evidenced defensive arm movement and withdrawal in their investigation of infants' responses to collision, we required that any withdrawal and/or arm movement responses be devoid of any upward tracking. Thus, one cannot argue that the increased amount of tracking up in Down's syndrome infants accounts, in part, for there being no difference between the normal and Down's syndrome groups. In fact, such a stringent criterion could have actually attenuated the occurrence of arm movement and withdrawal in the 4-month Down's syndrome group, since they have poorer head control than normal infants.

Further age group analyses revealed no statistically significant differences between the two groups of infants. As can be seen in Table III, no statistically significant results were obtained between the number of Down's syndrome infants who tracked up versus the number of normal babies who did so.

Horizontal Tracking

No statistically significant differences emerged in the tracking of the asymmetrically expanding miss conditions at 4 months. However, the Down's syndrome infants tracked the misses with significantly more regularity at 8 months ($z = 2.50$, $p < .05$) and at 12 months ($z = 4.20$, $p < .01$) than did the normal controls. Nonetheless, an examination of the amount of distress exhibited by the 8- and 12-month normal infants suggests that the deterioration in their tracking performance can be attributed to the extreme distress that they showed during hit trials, which disrupted their tracking of the misses. This explanation receives corroboration from a comparison of Down's syndrome infants' tracking the miss display at the first age they showed substantial crying (i.e., 16 months) with the normal infants' performance at 12 months. No statistically significant differences were obtained between these two age groups.

All of the normal and all of the Down's syndrome infants, regardless of age, tracked at least one miss trial. Therefore, no statistically significant differences emerged between groups.

Crying

While there were no differences between the 4-month-old infants, the emergence of crying was strikingly greater in the normal infants in later months (see Table III). For example, at 8 months, more normal controls manifested crying to the looming stimulus than did their Down's syndrome counterparts ($z = 11.20$, $p < .01$). This difference continued to uphold at the next two age assessments. At 12 months, the normal infants exhibited more distress at the looming stimulus than did the Down's syndrome babies ($z = 7.30$, $p < .01$). Moreover a comparison between the 12-month normal and the 16-month Down's syndrome infants revealed a greater percentage of crying in the normal group ($z = 2.86$, $p < .01$).

In an attempt to determine underlying reasons for the infrequent crying shown in the Down's syndrome infants (i.e., physiological-biochemical and/or cognitive factors), a comparison of 8-month normal and 16-month Down's syndrome infants was undertaken. This analysis revealed no statistically significant differences. However, it should be noted that since the average developmental quotient of the 16-month-old Down's syndrome group was 65 (i.e., approximately 10 or 11 months), these two groups of babies were not cognitively comparable. A comparison of the 8-month normal and the 12-month Down's syndrome infants would prove to be a good test of the role played by cognitive factors. Since our 12-month-old Down's syndrome infants were as a group comparable to the 8-month-old normals, if cognitive factors alone accounted for the differences in negative reaction, then one would expect that these two groups would show a similar amount of crying to the looming stimulus. Nonetheless, a greater percentage of normal infants continued to cry at the loom ($z = 3.86$, $p < .01$). This difference implicates both physiological (e.g., higher arousal threshold, aberrant biochemistry) and cognitive factors in explaining the results.

Qualitative Aspects of Infants' Responses to a Looming Stimulus

Trial X Trial Effects

Especially with regard to the crying data, an inspection of the trial x trial effects to the looming stimulus reveals some interesting features not made apparent by our quantitative analyses. Crying was occasionally manifested on the first hit trial of a series of stimulus presentations. Normal infants generally did not cry until they were presented with two or three collision trials, while Down's syndrome infants required a few more trials before they evidenced a negative reaction. When infants cried on an initial hit trial, it occurred approximately 3 or 4 sec after impact. This time factor suggests that it took several trials for a categorical negative reaction ("fear") to develop (cf. Bronson & Pankey, 1977; Sroufe in press). Once an infant cried, he continued to do so on subsequent trials. Often, after repeated presentations, infants became so violently upset that the collision trials had to be terminated. While normal infants' crying showed a waxing and waning during the inter-trial interval between collision presentations, whenever Down's syndrome infants became sufficiently aroused to show a negative reaction, they generally remained extremely upset throughout the successive trials.

Waiting for the Stimulus to Return after Miss Trials

As we indicated earlier, on the asymmetrically expanding miss trials, the object went off the screen, disappearing for a few seconds. At 4 months, 27% of the normal infants waited for the diamond object to return, tracking it back to its original position in the center of the Polocoat screen. In contrast, only 10% of the 4-month Down's syndrome sample waited for the stimulus to reappear. This difference proved to be statistically significant at the .05 level of confidence. Subsequently, these statistically significant differences were upheld across 8- and 12-month comparisons: 83% of the normal 8-month-olds and 90% of the normal 12-month-olds waited for the object to reappear, ultimately tracking it back to its point of movement, whereas only 30%

of 8-month-old Down's syndrome babies and 60% of 12-month-old Down's syndrome babies performed in such a fashion (both significant at $p < .01$). Moreover, only 50% of the 16-month-old Down's syndrome infants waited for the stimulus display to reemerge on the screen. However, this nonsignificant improvement over their 12-month performance can be attributed to their more pronounced upset. Whenever Down's syndrome infants became upset by the looming stimulus, their reactions tended to be more prolonged and intense.

Responses of Down's Syndrome Infants on the Visual Cliff

As indicated in Table IV, of the 70 infants tested on the visual cliff, only 6 infants (9%) crossed from the shallow to the deep side. These results are congruent with the data presented by Gibson and Walk (1960) and Walk and Gibson (1961) in their studies with normal infants. All 6 of these infants were brought back into the laboratory approximately one month later. None of them moved out over the deep gradient. All of these 70 infants crawled freely on the shallow side of the cliff. Upon placement, infants generally crawled on the center board, peered down through the glass over the deep side, and then backed away onto the shallow side, often getting into a sitting position. Occasionally, infants would pat the Plexiglas with their hands, yet, despite this textual assurance of solidity, they would refuse to go out onto the deep side. Many of the infants also crawled away from the mother when she was coaxing them to cross over to the deep side. Infants would reach to their mothers, smile, or vocalize but did not attempt to cross over the apparent chasm. Only 8 babies (11%) ever cried, despite the enticement of seeing their mothers on the deep side.[5] The infants, regardless of their initial response to placement, ultimately crawled freely on the shallow side and/or sat comfortably on the platform surface while patting the Plexiglas. While other investigators have not reported exact figures on the percentage of infants who cried or exhibited other negative reactions on the shallow side, it appears that the small number of Down's syndrome infants who did so is less than the number of normal infants. For example, Scarr and Salapatek (1970) reported that their babies between 7 and 10 months and 10 and 13 months (the two age groups that best correspond with the developmental attainments of our sample the month they were seen on the visual

---

[5] It might be suggested by some that the reason the Down's syndrome infants did not cross the chasm was that they were not attached to their mothers, thus lowering their approach gradient in this seemingly approach–avoidance situation. However, data gathered in concurrent home and lab observations in this study—and by others (Cytryn, 1975)—render this assumption untenable.

TABLE IV. RESPONSES OF DOWN'S SYNDROME INFANTS ON THE VISUAL CLIFF AFTER APPROXIMATELY ONE MONTH OF CRAWLING EXPERIENCE: NUMBER OF BABIES EXHIBITING EACH BEHAVIOR

Crossed from shallow to deep	6 (9%)
Would not cross from shallow to deep	64 (91%)
Cried on shallow	8 (11%)
Escaped from deep to shallow	20 (29%)
Cried on deep	14 (20%)
Holding onto sides of cliff while on deep	8 (11%)
Behavioral freezing	5 (7%)
Complacent on deep placement	37 (53%)

cliff) showed a mean intensity of 1.75 and 2.26, respectively, on a three-point fear-rating scale. Their infants in the 13–22 month age range (which are comparable to some of our slow crawlers and our higher functioning babies) evinced a mean intensity of 2.65 on their scale. While we have not yet developed a fear scale based on our behavioral ratings, nonetheless, by employing the most obvious indices of distress (i.e., crying and distress vocalization), we attained very little fear of the shallow side.

On deep placements, 20 (29%) of the Down's syndrome infants "escaped" from the deep side to the mother's beckoning calls on the shallow side.[6] These infants typically responded with a large magnitude HR *deceleration* upon placement on the deep side. After a look over the deep, occasionally HR accelerations were observed, followed by the infant's scampering out across to mother. Of these infants, 10 (14%) also cried; however, HR accelerations *preceded* the crying in all of these instances. Most of the babies who escaped did so within 60 sec of placement on the deep side. Occasionally, an infant would vacillate between peering at the Plexiglas on the deep side and looking up at the mother, reaching to her or emitting distress vocalizations. Often 90 sec or more elapsed before these infants crawled over to the mother. In some instances, the babies would swipe at or reach for the center board, clearly being tentative about locomoting.

An additional 8 (11%) babies held onto the sides of the visual cliff, as if to prevent themselves from falling off, with 4 (6%) of these also crying, and 5 babies (7%) were observed to exhibit behavioral freezing on the deep side; that is, after being placed atop the Plexiglas, they

---

[6] Those infants who are included in this category all showed some type of negative reaction to being placed atop the clear Plexiglas on the deep side. Also, 3 other babies crossed from the deep to the shallow side but were not placed in the escape group since they were smiling and babbling as they were crawling.

either got up into a sitting position or else remained on all fours. Regardless of their response preference, these babies did not move, seemingly to avoid falling into the abyss. Interestingly, these babies often seemed leery of looking down at the chasm on the deep side. Rather, they stared straight ahead, ostensibly oblivious to their where-abouts but clearly engrossed in them. The HRs of these infants did not accelerate.

The paucity of distress on the deep side cannot be explained on the basis that Down's syndrome infants believed their tactile input as they patted and kicked the Plexiglas. While Birch and Lefford's (1967) research on intersensory processes has demonstrated that there is an increasing reliance with age on the visual rather than the tactile mode for information that directs behavior, it should be noted that while placed on the shallow side, the Down's syndrome infants received tactile input that it was "safe" to cross the chasm, yet they did not cross, relying instead on their visual information. In addition, if, as Scarr and Salapatek (1970) suggested, length of experience with a particular mode of locomotion predicted fearfulness on the cliff, with infants who were less experienced in crawling manifesting more fear of crossing the gradient, then Down's syndrome infants would have been expected to show more intense fear, since they had all been crawling for approxi-mately one month. Moreover, the number of babies who showed HR accelerations on the deep side was extremely small, although data are still being analyzed. This finding is in marked contrast with the results reported by Schwartz, Campos, and Baisel (1973) with normal 5- and 9-month-old infants, using a direct placement technique on the cliff. These investigators reported a shift in HR responsiveness to direct placement on the cliff from 5 to 9 months. While 5-month-old infants reliably decelerated to the deep side, the 9-month-olds' HR responses shifted to acceleration. These results suggest that a shift from relative fearlessness to fearfulness on the deep side occurred between these two age periods. The fact that so few of our Down's syndrome sample (who were all older and at least as cognitively competent as Schwartz *et al.*'s 9-month-old sample) exhibited HR acceleration, even in those who escaped the deep, suggests that there are indeed some deficiencies in the sympathetic nervous systems of these infants, as suggested by other investigations (Axelrod, 1974; Cicchetti & Sroufe, 1976b; Serafica & Cicchetti, 1976).

Relation between Reactions to the Loom and the Visual Cliff

Table V reveals the breakdown of subjects who cried to either or both fear situations. It is clear that there is a high degree of correspon-

TABLE V. THE RELATIONSHIP BETWEEN REACTIONS TO THE LOOM AND THE VISUAL CLIFF[a]

	Cry on loom	No cry on loom
Cry on cliff	11	3
No cry on cliff	11	35

[a] $\chi^2 = 13.82$, 1, $p < .01$

dence between reactions to the visual cliff (regardless of the babies' age at onset of locomotion) and to the loom at 16 months. We saw 60 Down's syndrome infants both on the visual cliff and on the loom at 16 months. As can be seen, of the 14 infants who cried on the visual cliff, 11 (79%) also cried on the loom. Similarly, of the 22 infants who cried at the collision stimulus, 11 (50%) also cried on the visual cliff. Thirty-five infants did not cry in either situation ($\chi^2 = 13.82$, 1, $p < .01$).

Broadening our criterion of fear of the visual cliff to include escape from the deep, behavioral freezing, distress vocalizations, and holding onto the edges of the cliff, the correspondence between the two assessments becomes even more striking (see Table V). It can be seen that of the 22 infants who cried to the stimulus of impending collision, 20 (91%) were also fearful of the visual cliff by these criteria. Analogously, of the 28 infants who exhibited fear of the cliff, 20 (71%) cried at the loom. Thirty infants did not show fear on the cliff or cry at the loom.

The Relationship between Fear and Laughter

Of the 25 Down's syndrome infants who participated in the longitudinal laughter study from 4 through 16 months, a close tie was observed between those who had the highest rankings on positive affect (e.g., total amount of laughter or smiling to the stimulus presentations; onset of affective expression) and those who ultimately became distressed in the loom or the cliff situations. Of the 20 infants seen on the loom at 16 months from this sample, 7 of those who laughed before 10 months ($N = 12$) cried to the loom at 16 months. Similarly, of the 12 infants who laughed or smiled to the most affective items, 7 likewise cried on the loom at age 16 months. Moreover, since all 25 of these infants were seen on the visual cliff, parallel comparisons can be made between positive affective expression and manifestation of fear (broadly conceived) on the visual cliff. For example, of those infants who laughed before 10 months ($N = 15$), 12 were subsequently fearful of the visual cliff. In addition, of the 15 infants who laughed or smiled to the most stimulus presentations, 12 later showed fear of the visual cliff.

Interestingly, the 5 most hypotonic babies, who were the last to laugh to any of the stimulus items and were ranked the lowest on the above indices of affective expression, did not exhibit fear of either the loom or the cliff. The 3 babies of the mosaic cytogenetic subtype, who obtained very high rankings on affectivity, all showed fear to the looming stimulus and on the visual cliff.

In the cross-sectional laughter study, 2 of the 15 infants seen at 4 months laughed; both subsequently were fearful when seen on the loom and the visual cliff. At 8 months, 3 of the 15 infants seen laughed and all exhibited fear of the loom and cliff. Of the 15 12-month-old infants, 8 laughed to the stimulus presentations, with 5 ultimately fearful of the cliff and 3 toward the loom. Finally, of the 30 infants seen at 16 months (15 of whom had been seen at one of the earlier age periods), of those infants who had the highest rank order on the affective items (e.g., total number of items smiled or laughed to) ($N = 15$), 11 subsequently cried at the loom (7 of these subjects were also seen at an earlier age in the laboratory laughter study) and 14 on the visual cliff.

The Relationship between Affective and Cognitive Development

Positive Affect

Longitudinal Study. With the 25 infants who participated in the longitudinal laughter study, a clear relationship was obtained between cognitive development and affective development. Table VI shows rank-order correlations of indices of affective expression with the Bayley mental and motor scales at 16 months. Correlations were computed separately for two samples of the 25 Down's syndrome children: the 14 reported in Cicchetti and Sroufe (1976b) and an additional 11 subjects

TABLE VI. RANK-ORDER CORRELATIONS OF COGNITIVE MEASURES WITH SELECTED INDICES OF AFFECTIVE EXPRESSION

Indices of affective expression	Bayley mental scale (16 months)		Bayley motor scale (16 months)	
	(N=14) Sample I	(N=11) Sample II	(N=14) Sample I	(N=11) Sample II
First laughter to any item	.74	.63	.70	.57
First laughter to any three social-visual items	.80	.71	.64	.56
First smiling to any three social-visual items	.92	.83	.77	.72
Total amount of laughter to all social-visual items	.88	.79	.77	.69
Total amount of smiling to all social-visual items	.89	.84	.70	.65

who served as a replication of our prior endeavor. All of the relationships between total laughter, total smiling, and the other affective indices shown in Table VI were in the expected direction for both subsamples and are quite strong, ranging from .56 to .92. While the range in developmental levels in the Down's syndrome infants accounts in part for the magnitude of the associations obtained, these results provide suggestive evidence for the mutual influence of affect and cognition. Moore, Clark, Mael, Myers, Rajotte, and Stoel-Gammon (1977) have recently found that object permanence development in Down's syndrome children is strongly associated with language development, independent of chronological or overall mental age. Kendall's rank-order correlation (tau) between the two measures was .75; with age partialled out, it was .73. This is another illustration of how the greater variations in rate of development in Down's syndrome children might allow a disentangling of the age variable in studies examining the relationship between two developing systems.

Age of first laughter to our stimulus items proved to be an early predictor of cognitive development. For example, in the original sample of 14 infants, there was no overlap between Bayley mental scales of infants who began laughing by 10 months ($N = 9$, x DQ = 72) and those laughing after 10 months ($N = 5$, x DQ = < 50). Similarly, in the second sample, for the infants who began laughing before 10 months ($N = 7$), the mean Bayley score was 79, while among those who laughed after 10 months ($N = 4$), the mean developmental quotient was < 50. The Pearson product–moment correlation between age of first laughter and Bayley scores was also significant for each of the two subsamples: $r = -.80$, (12), $p < .01$, and $r = -.72$ (9), $p < .01$, respectively.

Cross-Sectional Study. In the Down's syndrome infants assessed in our laboratory study, once again a close association was found between cognitive development and affective expression. Even though there was a diminution in laughter because of the unfamiliar context in which the items were presented (e.g., Sroufe *et al.*, 1974), nonetheless, the infants laughed or smiled first to the intrusive, physically vigorous auditory and tactile stimulation and only later to the more cognitively sophisticated social and visual items.

Negative Affect

Looming. For the 22 infants who cried to the looming stimulus, the average Bayley developmental quotient was 76. In contrast, the remaining 38 infants had an average developmental quotient of 60 ($t = 6.27, 58, p < .01$).

Visual Cliff. For the 33 infants who exhibited a negative reaction on the visual cliff (e.g., crying, escaping, holding onto the sides of the cliff), the average 16-month Bayley quotient was 74. The remaining 37 infants, who revealed no distinguishable signs of fearfulness, obtained an average Bayley score of 60 ($t = 6.48, 68 \, p < .01$). Both assessments of the Down's syndrome infants' responses to the fear situations implicate a close correspondence between negative affective expression and cognitive development.

DISCUSSION

These data illustrate several important aspects of the organizational perspective on development, as well as underscoring the role that noncognitive factors play in some of the handicaps of Down's syndrome infants. In addition, our findings are relevant to certain controversies within the developmental literature, specifically concerning the confluence of factors involved in the ontogenesis of emotions and questions about the age of onset of negative reactions to a looming stimulus and on the visual cliff.

The Affect–Cognition Interchange

Within the organizational perspective, affect and cognition are viewed as inseparable—as two aspects of the same developmental process. The present research offers clear support for the premise that affective and cognitive development proceed in an integrated manner. The expression of positive affect was closely related developmentally to negative reactions, and both positive and negative affective reactions were closely tied to measures of cognitive development.

The Development of Smiling and Laughter

Studies of infant laughter have shown that changes with age in the nature of items eliciting laughter reflect cognitive growth, that laughter illustrates the processes of arousal and assimilation, and that laughter is influenced by cognitive factors (Cicchetti & Sroufe, 1976b; Rothbart, 1973; Sroufe & Waters, 1976). In both the longitudinal and the cross-sectional portions of this study, a close association was found between affective expression and cognitive development. The Down's syndrome infants, in spite of their slowed pace of development, showed a similar progression in the expression of positive affect to that found in our earlier research with normal infants (Sroufe & Wunsch, 1972). Within the longitudinal sample, two independent subgroups of Down's syndrome infants both smiled and laughed first at auditory and tactile items and only much later at the items that contained a more explicit element of cognitive incongruity. Such an ordering suggests a tie between cognitive development and laughter at the more sophisticated items (see Cicchetti & Sroufe, 1976b). As is the case for the normal infant, with development it is the Down's syndrome infant's *effort* in processing the stimulus content or participation in the event that produces the tension necessary for smiling and laughter (Kagan, 1971; Sroufe & Waters, 1976) rather than stimulation *per se*. Likewise, there is a trend toward a *more active participation* in producing affectively effective stimulation in both Down's syndrome and normal infants.

Perhaps the most persuasive data on the affect–cognition interchange are found in the cognitive test results. For both longitudinal samples, cognitive developmental level, as assessed by performance on the Bayley scales at 16 months, closely paralleled the level of affective development as determined by the 30 laughter items. In fact, since there is much heterogeneity among Down's syndrome infants, in addition to their slowed rate of development, demonstrations of developmental convergences are more compelling with this group of babies.

The Relationship between Negative Reactions and Cognitive Development

An examination of the looming and visual cliff data reveals that negative reactions were associated with higher levels of cognitive development. This was true whether negative reactions were described as crying or were defined more broadly. These results again support an affect–cognition interchange and, in light of the fear–laughter association found both within this study and within others (e.g., Sroufe *et al.*, 1974), are not at all surprising.

In addition, an interesting relationship was obtained between waiting for the asymmetrically expanding miss object to return on the screen and cognitive development; 83% of the 8-month-old and 90% of the 12-month-old normal infants waited for at least one miss trial to return. At the same time, a noted increase in fear of the collision trials was found, suggesting that as understanding of the meaning of the stimulus became more sophisticated, more intense negative reactions were demonstrated. Moreover, as the 12- and 16-month-old Down's syndrome infants began to respond negatively to the looming stimulus, a corresponding increase in the number of babies waiting for the noncollision object to return occurred. The ability to wait for the miss object to return entails more than possessing Stage 4 object permanence, since it requires either the ability to learn that the object reappears and/or the ability to anticipate its reemergence. Results of concurrent experiments in our laboratory suggest that this is a plausible hypothesis since Down's syndrome babies tested at 13 and 16 months on the object permanence subscale of the Uzgiris–Hunt scales of infant development are generally capable of finding an object after successive visible displacements, four steps beyond uncovering a totally hidden object (Cicchetti & Sroufe, in preparation).

The Predictive Power of Affect

In the longitudinal study, cognitive development in the second year of life was predicted by laughter (and other indices of affective expression) in the first year of life. We feel that early laughter to complex events is logically an excellent predictor because it taps the motivational, attentional, affective, and cognitive capabilities (e.g., the competence) of the infant (Sroufe, in press). These results also support Haviland's (1976) ideas concerning relations of affectivity to later intelligence. Laughter and crying, positive and negative affect, are so closely tied together and so closely tied with measures of cognitive development that suggesting one system as causal seems inappropriate. Still, we point to the predictive power of affect because of the difficulty of obtaining accurate, meaningful cognitive assessments early in life. Affective measures in the first year (positive and/or negative) predict cognitive test performance at age 2 quite powerfully, perhaps better than early cognitive or mental tests (Cicchetti & Sroufe, 1976b; Cicchetti & Sroufe, in preparation; Haviland, 1976).

Cognitive and Physiological Components of Affect

The organizational perspective of development refers to relationships between systems—physiological and psychological—and to consequences of advances and lags in one system for other systems (Sroufe, in press a). Down's syndrome infants provide an important entree into the study of these relationships.

In our model of affective expression, both tension and cognitive factors play basic roles. When the infant confronts an incongruous event, there is first an affect-free orienting reaction, leading to a period of appraisal or evaluation, with affective expression the termination or outcome of the appraisal process (Arnold, 1960; Sroufe & Waters, 1976). During orienting and appraisal, tension develops. *Tension refers to cognitively produced arousal in contrast to physiological excitation, its prototype.* This tension may be expressed as positive *or* negative affect, depending on the infant's evaluation. The *magnitude*, but not the direction, of the positive or negative affect varies with degree of incongruity ("discrepancy"; Kagan, 1971) and level of prestimulus arousal. Prestimulus arousal level is more important the younger or less cognitively developed the infant. Experiential factors and level of cognitive functioning would influence the appraisal process and thereby tension production (Arnold, 1960; Kagan, 1971; Sroufe & Waters, 1976), as would setting, familiarization time, and other aspects of context (Sroufe *et al.*, 1974).

Our studies with Down's syndrome infants suggest that cognitive factors alone are not sufficient to account for the affective behavior of these babies. Although the results point to a close association between cognitive and affective development, inspection of our data illustrates that the slow cognitive development of the Down's syndrome infants only partially explains the reduced incidence of extreme forms of affect (e.g., laughter and crying). In the laughter studies, for example, even after comparing the Down's syndrome infants with normal counterparts of equivalent developmental age, we observed a diminution in laughter. This occurred even when the Down's syndrome infants were attending carefully and smiling differentially to the items, and it was especially salient when we examined the amount of laughter exhibited to the more complex social and visual presentations. Down's syndrome infants, as a group are generally *hypo*tonic; accordingly, a lag in affect expression would be predicted by our model, especially with intense affect, as in laughter. Most importantly, the five most hypotonic babies lagged most, laughing quite late and only to the most vigorous, physical stimulation. Our view is that the Down's syndrome infants could not process the incongruous stimulus presentations with sufficient speed to generate the tension ("arousal jag"; Berlyne, 1969) required for laughter.

Likewise, even when cognitive developmental level was comparable between Down's syndrome and normal infants, normal babies showed more negative reactions to the loom and the visual cliff. For example, on the visual cliff, the Down's syndrome infants (who had approximately one month of crawling experience) rarely ventured out over the deep gradient. There was no relationship found between those who crossed the apparent chasm and cognitive development, as both high-functioning and low-functioning Down's syndrome infants did so. These results are in agreement with Campos, Hiatt, Ramsay, Henderson, and Svejda (this volume), who state that locomotor experience, rather than cognitive developmental level, appears to be sufficient to account for infants' not traversing the deep side.[7] However, fewer Down's syndrome infants were fearful of being placed directly upon the Plexiglas on the deep side than their cognitive developmental level would have led us to predict. Far fewer Down's syndrome than normal infants cried, even taking developmental level into account. They would not cross the chasm, but they did not show HR acceleration and they did not cry. The Down's syndrome infants perhaps have a general arousal modulation problem. They are not readily highly aroused, and when highly aroused, they do not readily recover. Those infants who did cry on the loom, for example, had great difficulty settling again.

As powerful as concepts such as discrepancy (Kagan, 1971; McCall & McGhee, 1977, in press) and interruption (Mandler, 1975) may be, they do not seem to account fully for these data. Neither do they account well for the sequential effects we find. Laughter builds from smiling on early presentations of laughter items and fades again to smiling, and it does not seem likely that discrepancy first increases and then decreases. And negative reactions to the loom occur more rapidly with repeated trials, yet with continued exposure, discrepancy should diminish. Indeed, the rather immediate reactions of normal infants in some circumstances (especially in contrast to Down's syndrome babies) have led us to suggest that these are *categorical negative reactions* (Sroufe, in press a). For example, normal infants may show rather immediate negative reactions to the loom, or to approaching strangers in some circumstances, or to laboratory assistants in white coats following a trip to the doctor for shots. The rapid reaction suggests that the event *is assimilated*. The negative affect suggests that the category or scheme to which it is assimilated is negatively toned ("This is one of those and I don't like it"). There is no separation between cognitive structure and affect. Certain events have negative meaning. In a similar vein, the characteristic positive greetings of caregivers suggest that this special scheme is positively toned. Such greetings are not the result of a

---

[7] Research in progress in our laboratory likewise affirms Campos *et al.*'s hypothesis. The majority of Down's syndrome infants seen immediately after they began crawling (i.e., within one week) have tended to cross the deep gradient. However, when these babies subsequently were brought back approximately three or four weeks later, they did not traverse the apparent chasm.

ponderous interpretive process. The wellspring of positive affect based on the history of interaction is immediately tapped upon recognition of the caregiver.[8]

Special Handicaps in Down's Syndrome Infants

Our results suggest that Down's syndrome infants possess some special handicaps that can, in part, account for their decreased incidence of maximal affective expression. A number of investigators have previously hypothesized that Down's syndrome children are generally low in reactivity to stressful situations (Cicchetti & Serafica, 1977; Penrose & Smith, 1966; Serafica & Cicchetti, 1976). Observations within this study lend credibility to this position. Down's syndrome infants manifested not only a diminution in positive affect but also displayed a concomitant reduction in negative affect. Since a focus on cognitive factors is insufficient to explain these data, individual differences in the strength of external stimulation necessary to produce a given amount of physiological excitation must be simultaneously considered (Lipton, Steinschneider, & Richmond, 1966). Such differential responsiveness to stimuli might have its origins in physiological variables that reflect genotypic variations in the developmental pattern of the human species.

At the physiological level, dopamine-beta-hydroxylase, an enzyme necessary for the conversion of dopamine into norepinephrine, has been found to be abnormally low in the blood of infants and children with Down's syndrome (Axelrod, 1974; Weinshilbaum, Thoa, Johnson, Kopin, & Axelrod, 1971). This finding suggests that there are abnormalities in the functioning of their sympathetic nervous systems. The infrequent observations of HR acceleration in Down's syndrome infants support this proposition, although this lack of acceleration might also be due to a central rather than a peripheral deficit. An abnormality in catecholamine metabolism in Down's syndrome children has also been demonstrated by Keele, Richards, Brown, and Marshall (1969). They reported that Down's syndrome children excreted significantly less epinephrine in their urine than did a control group of retarded children without Down's syndrome. This finding, as well as the decreased dopamine-beta-hydroxylase levels mentioned above, implicates an immature adrenal system as being a possible explanation. The adrenal system is known to play a very critical role in mobilizing an organism to respond to stress and to respond fearfully. The adrenal medulla in Down's syndrome infants may not be sufficiently mature over the first few years (i.e., even

[8] At the neurophysiological level, one may speak of cortical-limbic loops being established.

less so than it is in the normal infant, who also has a relatively immature adrenal medulla) to support the full arousal of fear to nonpainful stimuli.

The blinking data suggest specific cortical deficits in Down's syndrome infants, Not only do 8- and 12-month-old Down's syndrome babies blink to a higher percentage of trials than their normal controls, but they also exhibit more multiple blinking across all age groups. It is conceivable that these data may point to problems in forebrain inhibitory control in Down's syndrome infants, especially since blinking is most likely under subcortical control. In support of this hypothesis, Cowie (1970) has shown that early neonatal reflexes come in more slowly in Down's syndrome infants and persist for an unusually long time. The dissolution of these "transient" early reflexes at around 3 months is thought to reflect the emergence of forebrain inhibitory mechanisms in the developing brain (Parmelee & Michaelis, 1971; Peiper, 1963). Perhaps the differing rates and levels of maturation of the cortex and endocrinological systems in Down's syndrome infants account, in part, for their slowed development of fear.

Focusing on the most extremely hypotonic Down's syndrome babies as well as on the mosaic babies sheds further light on some possible difficulties that Down's syndrome infants possess, as well as on the heterogeneity of their affective expression. Those diagnosed as extremely *hypotonic*—who laugh only to the most physically vigorous stimulation, who rarely show fear and have the lowest cognitive scores—may have difficulty engaging and reacting to environmental events and special problems in modulating arousal. This possibility certainly is in keeping with our many hours of observations of these infants in a variety of settings (Cicchetti & Sroufe, in preparation). Cowie (1970) also found the most markedly hypotonic Down's syndrome infants in her sample to be the most developmentally immature. In contrast, the mosaics (some of whose cells contain the normal complement of chromosomes)—who are among the highest ranking on indices of affective expression, show fear, and do very well cognitively—seem to be more affectively engaging. What is striking is how all these factors seem to converge, regardless of the extent of cognitive retardation, *suggesting the organized nature of development in Down's syndrome infants*. A major theoretical controversy within the field of mental retardation, "developmental" theorists have conceded to "difference" theorists that retarded infants and children with known genetic etiologies may not show a developmental process similar to their normal counterparts (Zigler, 1969), while maintaining that retarded children of idiopathic etiologies ("cultural-familial" retardates) do manifest a similar organization in behavior and development. Our results suggest that the behavior of Down's syndrome infants, too, is organized and integrated, in a way strikingly similar to that of normal babies.

Finally, the fact that Down's syndrome infants as a group appear to be less affectively responsive than their normal counterparts (Cicchetti & Sroufe, 1976b); with an associated lack of clarity in signaling (Cicchetti & Sroufe, 1976a; Emde, Katz, & Thorpe, this volume), might affect the caregiver–infant interaction. The communication of these results should help assuage parental anxiety and prevent parents from giving up on their babies (see Cicchetti & Sroufe, 1976a). It may be that parents of Down's syndrome infants need to extend themselves much more than the typical caregiver, since they must assume more responsibility for helping the infant to generate tension and affect and to become emotionally engaged in the situation, and they must accept greater delays in the development of fully differentiated affective expression (e.g., laughter). Helping these infants sustain attention and build excitement is especially challenging.

Prototypes and Evolving Systems versus Age of Onset

These data illustrate nicely the advantages of viewing emotional reactions as evolving systems. Too often psychologists' attempts to pin down the age of onset of various emotional reactions have led to tedious exercises in operational definition, controversies over terminology, disputed results, and, all too frequently, dismissal of the very construct under study. For example, if one asks at what age negative reactions to the loom develop, a variety of answers could be (and have been) provided. Distress (crying) appears to occur both during the newborn period (Bower et al., 1970) and in the second half-year (Cicchetti & Mans, 1976). Blinking occurs quite early. When one would say "fear" develops is a complicated matter.

Focusing on a particular response in seeking the onset of fear or "negative reactions" clearly obscures important developmental trends. The most salient matter is not that newborns may show distress under some conditions but that young infants virtually always blink (Cicchetti & Mans, 1976), that both newborns and 8-month-olds cry, that the conditions for and the quality of these crying reactions are strikingly different, that normal infants of intermediate age (e.g., 4 months) rarely cry, and that other reactions exhibit reliable developmental trends as well. With the developmental sequence established, the issue becomes specifying the relationship between early subcortical reactions (blinking and crying) and later psychological reactions. We call only the latter *fear*, but agreement on the term is not nearly so important as recognition of the developmental process. The view of the neonatal endogenous smile (cf. Emde & Harmon, 1972) as a prototype of the later exogenous (social) smile led to an important discovery concerning the meaning and function of the smile in infant development (Sroufe & Waters, 1976). Untangling the links between early distress and blinking and what we call *fear* is certain to be similarly fruitful.

The case for a process view becomes even more clearly compelling when one examines the comparative data on Down's syndrome and normal infants on the loom. If one operationally defines the negative reaction as the blink, it could be concluded that these groups do not differ in age of onset. Likewise, there would not be any difference between groups if other indices (e.g., defensive arm movement, turning away) are employed. Alternatively, there are striking differences in the crying data. But clearly, what is most important is the total picture provided by these trends. Not only can it be concluded that the early negative reactions are based on different (subcortical) neurological mechanisms than the later reactions, but clues to the complex nature of the Down's syndrome infant's handicaps are revealed. The developmental sequence is similar for the two groups, but the Down's syndrome baby's slowness becomes apparent only when extraction of meaning from the event is crucial, and its further physiological deficit is suggested by its failure to cry even when underlying cognitive prerequisites seem established.

The importance of the process view is also seen in the visual cliff data. Down's syndrome babies obviously achieve mobility late. But do they, like normal infants, show fear of the cliff soon after the onset of crawling? Since they will not crawl across the deep side on the one hand but tend not to cry or show heart rate acceleration on the other, this question could be debated endlessly. We are impressed both with the fact that they will not venture out over the deep gradient and by the fact that they still do not show distress. Others can argue over which of these reactions is the better indicator of fear. We feel both that the developmental sequence of the reaction is established and that the nature of the Down's syndrome infant's handicap is illuminated.

CONCLUSION

The comparative study of Down's syndrome infants may itself be a prototype for approaching the organization of development. The data presented here represent the most clear demonstration of the affect–cognition interchange and of the role of tension that we have been able to produce to date. Fraiberg's (e.g., Fraiberg & Freedman, 1964) work with the blind likewise has been an extremely important contribution to an organizational viewpoint. The study of other atypical populations from this perspective is also likely to be rewarding. For example, however obvious the cognitive deficits of autistic children, they are also characterized by deviations in the attachment relationship and a lack of modulated affective expressiveness. Their cognitive deficit seems to be in large part a problem of extracting meaning from their experience (Wing, 1976). To what extent this problem is reflected in, or is due to, a failure of affective engagement is a matter for speculation. What we would suggest is that attending to the affective aspects of the autistic child's handicap will help clarify the cognitive handicaps.

ACKNOWLEDGMENTS

The authors would like to extend their sincere thanks to Mary Breitenbucher, Brad Grimes, Yvonne Johnston, Linda Mans, Ruth McCaleb, Dan Nichols, Kay Olson, Rudy Rousseau, and Vicki Spiess for their great help in the collection of the data and for their dedication, which often went beyond the call of duty. We are also grateful to the many state associations for retarded children that have helped us locate the Down's syndrome infants and their families during the four years of our research. We thank the families of the Down's syndrome babies, whose great concern and cooperation helped make our research investigations pleasant and fruitful. They have enriched our lives and been a source of inspiration to us. Finally, our appreciation is extended to Barbara Bujold-Martinez for her assistance in putting together this manuscript.

REFERENCES

Ainsworth, M. Infant–mother attachment and social development: Socialization as a product of reciprocal responsiveness to signals. In M. Richards (Ed.), *The integration of the child into the social world*. Cambridge, England: Cambridge University Press, 1974, pp. 99–135.

Arnold, M. *Emotion and personality* (2 Vols). New York: Columbia University Press, 1960.

Axelrod, J. Neurotransmitters. *Scientific American*, 1974, *230*, 58–71.

Ball, W., & Tronick, E. Infant responses to impending collision: Optical and real. *Science*, 1971, *171*, 818–820.

Belmont, J. H. Medical-behavioural research in retardation. In N. R. Ellis (Ed.), *International review of research in mental retardation* (Vol. 5). New York: Academic Press, 1971.

Berlyne, D. E. Laughter, humor, and play. In G. Lindzey and E. Aronson (Eds.), *Handbook of social psychology* (2nd ed.), (Vol. 3). Boston: Addison-Wesley, 1969.

Birch, H. G., & Lefford, A. Visual differentiation, intersensory integration, and voluntary motor control. *Monographs of the Society for Research in Child Development*, 1967, 32(2, Serial No. 110).

Bleuler, E. *Naturegeschichte der Seele* (2nd Auflage), Berlin: Julius Springer, 1932.

Bleuler, E. *Dementia praecox or the group of schizophrenias*. New York: International Universities Press, 1950.

Bower, T., Broughton, J., & Moore, M. Infant responses to approaching objects. *Perception and Psychophysics*, 1970, 9, 193–196.

Bowlby, J. *Attachment and loss* (Vol. 1), *Attachment*. New York: Basic Books, 1969.

Bronson, G., & Pankey, W. On the distinction between wariness and fear. *Child Development*, 1977, in press.

Carr, V. Mental and motor development in young mongol children. *Journal of Mental Deficiency Research*, 1970, 14, 205–220.

Cavalli-Sforza, L. L., & Bodmer, W. F. *The genetics of human populations*. San Francisco: Freeman, 1971.

Cicchetti, D., & Mans, L. Down's syndrome and normal infant's responses to impending collision. Paper presented at the annual meetings of the American Psychological Association, Washington, D.C., 1976.

Cicchetti, D., & Serafica, F. C. The development of social responsiveness in Down's syndrome children. *Child Development*, 1977.

Cicchetti, D., & Sroufe, L. A. The emotional development of the infant with Down's syndrome. In J. L. Poor (Ed.), *Aim to fight low expectations of Down's syndrome children*. Forest Lake, Minn: Forest Lake Printing, 1976, pp. 37–59. (a)

Cicchetti, D., & Sroufe, L. A. The relationship between affective and cognitive development in Down's syndrome infants. *Child Development*, 1976, 47, 920–929. (b)

Cicchetti, D., & Sroufe, L. A. *The organization of development in Down's syndrome infants*, in preparation.

Coleman, M. (Ed.), *Serotonin in Down's syndrome*. New York: American Elsevier, 1973.

Cowie, V. A. *A study of the early development of mongols*. Oxford, England: Pergamon Press, 1970.

Cytryn, L. Studies of behavior in children with Down's syndrome. In E. J. Anthony (Ed.), *Explorations in child psychiatry*. New York & London: Plenum Press, 1975, pp. 271–285.

Décarie, G. *Intelligence and affectivity in early childhood*. New York: International Universities Press, 1965.

Emde, R., Gaensbauer, T., & Harmon, R. Emotional expression in infancy: A biobehavioral study. *Psychological Issues Monograph Series*, New York: International University Press, 1976.

Emde, R., & Harmon, R. Endogenous and exogenous smiling systems in early infancy. *Journal of the American Academy of Child Psychiatry*, 1972, 11, 177–200.

Engel, G. Attachment behavior, object relations and the dynamic-economic points of view: Critical review of Bowlby's *Attachment and Loss*. *International Journal of Psycho-Analysis*, 1971, 52, 183–196.

Escalona, S. *The roots of individuality*. Chicago: Aldine, 1968.

Fraiberg, S., & Freedman, D. A. Studies in the ego development of the congenitally blind child. *The Psychoanalytic Study of the Child*, 1964, 19, 112–169.

Gibson, D. Chromosomal psychology and Down's syndrome (mongolism). *Canadian Journal of Behavioral Science*, 1975, 7, 167–191.

Gibson, E. J., & Walk, R. D. The "visual cliff." *Scientific American*, 1960, 202, 2–9.

Haviland, J. Looking smart: The relationship between affect and intelligence in infancy. In M. Lewis (Ed.), *Origins of intelligence*. New York & London: Plenum Press, 1976, pp. 353–377.

Illingworth, R. S. *An introduction to developmental assessment in the first year*. Little Club Clinics, No. 3. London: National Spastic Society, 1962.

Jarvik, L. F., Falek, A., & Pierson, W. P. Down's syndrome (mongolism): The hereditable aspects. *Psychological Bulletin*, 1964, *61*, 388–398.

Kagan, J. *Change and continuity in infancy*. New York: Wiley, 1971.

Keele, D. K., Richards, C., Brown, J., & Marshall, J. Catecholamine metabolism in Down's syndrome. *American Journal of Mental Deficiency*, 1969, *74*, 125–129.

Lipton, E., Steinschneider, A., & Richmond, J. Autonomic function in the neonate: VII. Maturational changes in cardiac control. *Child Development*, 1966, *37*, 1–16.

Loevinger, J. *Ego development: Conceptions and theories*. San Francisco: Jossey-Bass, 1976.

Mandler, G. *Mind and emotion*. New York: Wiley, 1975.

McCall, R., & McGhee, P. The discrepancy hypothesis of attention and affect. In F. Weizmann & I. Uzgiris (Eds.), *The structuring of experience*. New York: Plenum Press, 1977.

McIntire, M. D., & Dutch, S. J. Monogolism and generalized hypotonia. *American Journal of Mental Deficiency*, 1964, *68*, 669–670.

Moore, M. K., Clark, D., Mael, M., Myers, G., Rajotte, P., & Stoel-Gammon, C. The relationship between language and object permanence development: A study of Down's infants and children. Paper presented at the biennial meeting of the Society for Research in Child Development, New Orleans, March 1977.

Parmelee, A. H., & Michaelis, R. Neurological examination of the newborn. In J. Hellmuth (Ed.), *Exceptional infant*. New York: Brunner/Mazel, Inc., 1971, pp. 3–24.

Peiper, A. *Cerebral function in infancy and childhood*. New York: Consultants Bureau, 1963.

Penrose, L. S., & Smith, G. F. *Down's anomaly*. Boston: Little, Brown, 1966.

Piaget, J. The relation of affectivity to intelligence in the mental development of the child. In S. Harrison & J. McDermott (Eds.), *Childhood psychopathology*. New York: International Universities Press, 1972, pp. 167–175.

Piaget, J., & Inhelder, B. *The psychology of the child*. New York: Basic Books, 1969.

Prechtl, H., & Beintema, D. *The neurological examination of the full term newborn infant*. Little Club Clinics in Developmental Medicine, No. 12. London: Heineman, 1964.

Richards, B. W. Mongols and their mothers. *British Journal of Psychiatry*, 1973, *122*, 1–14.

Rothbart, M. Laughter in young children. *Psychological Bulletin*, 1973, *80*, 247–256.

Scarr, S., & Salapatek, P. Patterns of fear development during infancy. *Merrill-Palmer Quarterly*, 1970, *16*, 53–90.

Schwartz, A., Campos, J., & Baisel, E. The visual cliff: Cardiac and behavioral correlates on the deep and shallow sides at five and nine months of age. *Journal of Experimental Child Psychology*, 1973, *15*, 85–99.

Serafica, F. C., & Cicchetti, D. Down's syndrome children in a strange situation: Attachment and exploration behaviors. *Merrill-Palmer Quarterly*, 1976, *22*, 137–150.

Sroufe, L. A. The developmental significance of the construct of wariness. *Child Development*, 1977, *48*, 731–746.

Sroufe, L. A. The ontogenesis of emotion in infancy. In J. Osofsky (Ed.), *Handbook of infant development*. New York: Wiley, in press.

Sroufe, L. A., & Mitchell, P. Emotional development. In J. Osofsky (Ed.), *Handbook of infant development*. New York: Wiley, in press.

Sroufe, L. A., & Waters, E. The ontogenesis of smiling and laughter: A perspective on the organization of development in infancy. *Psychological Review*, 1976, *83*, 173–189.

Sroufe, L. A., Waters, E., & Matas, L. Contextual determinants of infant affective response. In M. Lewis and L. Rosenblum (Eds.), *The origins of behavior* (Vol. 2) *Fear*. New York: Wiley, 1974, pp. 49–72.

Sroufe, L. A., & Wunsch, J. The development of laughter in the first year of life. *Child Development*, 1972, *43*, 1326–1344.

Stechler, G., & Carpenter, F. A viewpoint on early affective development. In J. Hellmuth (Ed.), *Exceptional Infant* (Vol. 1). Seattle: Special Child Publications, 1967, pp. 163–189.

Stern, C. *Principles of human genetics* (3rd ed.). San Francisco: Freeman, 1973.

Vygotsky, L. *Thought and language*. Boston: MIT Press, 1962.

Walk, R. D., & Gibson, E. J. A comparative and analytical study of visual depth perception. *Psychological Monographs*, 1961, *75*, No. 15 (Whole No. 519).

Weinshilbaum, R., Thoa, N., Johnson, D., Kopin, I., & Axelrod, J. Proportional release of norepinephrine and dopamine-beta-hydroxylase from sympathetic nerves. *Science*, 1971, *174*, 1349–1351.

White, R. Motivation reconsidered: The concept of competence. *Psychological Review*, 1959, *66*, 297–333.

Wing, L. *Early childhood autism*. London: Pergamon Press, 1976.

Yonas, A., Bechtold, A. G., Frankel, D., Gordon, F. R., McRoberts, G., Norcia, A., & Sternfels, S. Development of sensitivity to information for impending collision. *Perception and Psychophysics*, 1977, *21*, 97–104.

Zigler, E. Developmental versus difference theories of mental retardation and the problem of motivation. *American Journal of Mental Deficiency*, 1969, *73*, 536–556.

Zigler, E. The retarded child as a whole person. In D. K. Routh (Ed.), *The experimental study of mental retardation*. Chicago: Aldine, 1973, pp. 231–322.

13

Emotional Expression in Infancy: II. Early Deviations in Down's Syndrome

Robert N. Emde, Eva L. Katz, and Judith K. Thorpe

A previous report (Emde, Kligman, Reich, & Wade, this volume) summarized our initial studies with emotional signaling in normal infants. This report discusses an example of a deviation in such signaling.

Over the past decade, our research program on social-affective development had considered longitudinal study as central. Through such study, in the home and in the laboratory, we are able to appreciate family variables, individual differences, and relative rates of change between behavioral and physiological sectors of development. Furthermore, we can use our clinical skills to take into account the richness of context and of unforeseen events. After two short-term longitudinal studies with normal infants (Emde, Gaensbauer, & Harmon, 1976), we are now engaged in a comparative longitudinal study of infants with Down's syndrome. Such study has allowed us to appreciate a number of factors involved in the deviant early emotional expression system of these infants.

We summarize here two types of data from six Down's syndrome infants and their families. First, we present multidimensional scaling data comparing the Down's infants with normals at 3½ months of age.

Robert N. Emde, Eva L. Katz, and Judith K. Thorpe · University of Colorado Medical School, Denver, Colorado. This work was supported by NIMH Project Grant MH 28803. Dr. Emde is supported by Research Scientist Award 5 K02 MH 36808.

Then, we discuss the onset of the social smile, offering a case vignette and a photographic demonstration–experiment. In both of these, the tragic "experiment in nature" of Down's syndrome serves to highlight the enormous importance of normal smiling onset for caregivers.

Multidimensional Scaling (MDS) of Down's Syndrome Infant Expressions at 3½ Months

There are probably more individual differences among Down's syndrome infants than among normal infants with respect to developmental events, but our longitudinal study has already suggested some tentative generalizations about early social-emotional development. Early crying is sometimes muted, and social smiling, when it appears, is less intense and less engaging. Furthermore, parents commonly speak of their young Down's infants as having "lonely," "mad," or "scared" expressions. Such interpretations have been rare among parents of normal infants in our longitudinal studies. Therefore, a question arose. Would the results from our multidimensional scaling technique (Emde *et al.*, this volume) reflect what might be uncertainty or "noise" in this early affect-signaling system? If so, would this "noise" be in the sender

TABLE I. MDS from Sorting of Mothers' Verbal Responses to Pictures of Their 3½-Month-Old Infants

	Stress		Dimension label	
	Normal infants	Down's syndrome infants	Normal infants	Down's syndrome infants
Set 1				
1 Dimension	.32	.43	Hedonic	Hedonic
2 Dimensions	.14	.34	Hedonic; activation	Hedonic; activation
3 Dimensions	.11	.23	Hedonic; activiation; internal/external	Uninterpretable
Set 2				
1 Dimension	.36	.39	Hedonic	Hedonic
2 Dimensions	.23	.28	Hedonic; activation	Hedonic; state
3 Dimensions	.17	.18	Uninterpretable	Uninterpretable
Set 3				
1 Dimension	.45	.50	Hedonic	Hedonic
2 Dimensions	.18	.39	Hedonic; activation	Hedonic; activation
3 Dimensions	.10	.29	Hedonic; activation; internal/external	Uninterpretable

TABLE II. MDS FROM DIRECT SORTING OF PICTURES OF 3½-MONTH-OLDS

| | Stress | | Dimension label | |
	Normal infants	Down's syndrome infants	Normal infants	Down's syndrome infants
Set 1				
1 Dimension	.39	.62	Hedonic	Hedonic
2 Dimensions	.29	.45	Hedonic; activation	Hedonic; state
3 Dimensions	.18	.32	Hedonic; activation; internal/external	Uninterpretable
Set 2				
1 Dimension	.31	.54	Hedonic	Hedonic
2 Dimensions	.27	.37	Hedonic; state	Hedonic; state
3 Dimensions	.22	.24	Hedonic; activation; internal/external	Uninterpretable
Set 3				
1 Dimension	.38	.53	Hedonic	Hedonic
2 Dimensions	.24	.42	Hedonic; activation	Hedonic; state
3 Dimensions	.14	.31	Hedonic; activation; internal/external	Uninterpretable

or in the receiver? If mothers distorted their interpretations of neutral or positive emotional expressions, for example, this distortion might result from the special frustrations involved in early adaptive interactions with Down's syndrome infants (Emde & Brown, 1978). Table I illustrates analyses from three sets of sortings of *verbal responses of Down's syndrome mothers* to pictures of their 3½-month-old infants. As in previous studies, judges who did the sorting of these verbal responses were 25 adult women, all experienced with children. For each set of sortings, stress values are higher (i.e., "goodness of fit is lower") for the Down's group than for sortings of a comparison normal infant group. Furthermore, the stress values are higher for each dimensional solution computed by the MDS program. But more important is the fact that the dimensions are very difficult to interpret. Even the "hedonic" dimension seems to have more noise. Interpretable solutions involve only 1 or 2 dimensions for the Down's syndrome group as compared to 2 or 3 for the normal group.

Since these results are based on sortings of mothers' verbal interpretations of their own infants' pictures, such noise could come from Down's mothers as well as from their infants. Analysis of direct sorting of pictures of Down's syndrome infants (by another 25 adult women) helped to determine the origin of the noise. Table II compares the MDS analyses from sorting of normal infant pictures and Down's infant pictures. Results are strikingly similar to those from the first sets of sortings. Again, stress values were higher and interpretability of dimensions was more difficult than for the comparison groups of normal infants. Since the pool of judges who sorted the Down's and normals were comparable (adult women experienced with children), and since the pictures were the same ones for which original mothers gave their verbal interpretations used in the previous sortings, we conclude that it is unlikely that the Down's mothers were adding noise to the system. Rather than distorting the message, these mothers seemed to be responding to abnormal signal-operating characteristics of the expressions themselves.[1]

THE ONSET OF THE SOCIAL SMILE

A family's adaptation following the birth of a Down's syndrome infant is painful and difficult. Initially, the process is dominated by grieving. There must be mourning for the expected healthy child before there can be emotional investment in the defective child. This process complicates the process by which a mother comes to know her baby and might be expected to interfere with her ability to interpret the baby's needs through emotional signaling. Nonetheless, we discovered that the vicissitudes in grieving told us much about the special importance of early infant social development in general. Defects in the Down's infant's social-emotional development occurring after the newborn period, when parental grieving has become less prominent, deprived parents of an important source of reward, and disappointment resulted in a new wave of grieving in several cases (See Emde & Brown, 1978).

At this point, we would like to share with you a case vignette that will add a humanistic context to our discussion. The vignette comes from the first family in our Down's study, and we learned much from them about grieving, parental attachment processes, and early social development. Dawn resulted from the first pregnancy of Mrs. A, a 24-year-old health-care professional. Although Mrs. A had experience with younger children, she felt relatively inexperienced with babies. She had a normal pregnancy, felt good, and was optimistic about her expected child. Her delivery was "easy," without any general anes-

---

[1] For this analysis five Down's syndrome infants were used to correspond with the five normal infants whose MDS data were previously reported in our earlier paper. Details of the sampling and sorting as well as the MDS analysis can also be found in that paper (Emde *et al.*, this volume). The reader is to be reminded that each MDS analysis involved sorting of three sets of 25 stimulus items by 25 adult women and that different women were obtained for every sorting procedure.

thesia or premedication; during it, she remembered being excited and, seeing her little girl, thinking she "was really neat." She held her baby in the delivery room. Father and mother were told the presumptive diagnosis of Down's syndrome on the next day, but the mother found it "hard to believe." Although she was told that the baby's facial appearance was different from normal, she could not envision any difference. At home, she did not want to read about Down's syndrome, for she was afraid she might "think of all the worst things." With the help of her husband, Mrs. A began to have some appreciation of her baby's future limitations, but she did not seem to appreciate the discrepancy between the baby she had been expecting and the baby she actually had.

Dawn was in the hospital a total of eight days after birth because of an infection, and so her mother went home without her. Mrs. A, who had planned to breast-feed, began expressing milk with a breast pump in anticipation of when Dawn could come home, and she began nursing when Dawn arrived. At first, she felt that Dawn nursed well "on demand," even though there was seldom vigorous crying expressing such demand. After three weeks, there was no weight gain, and the pediatrician suggested that Dawn be fed more often, on a two-hour schedule during the daytime. This change resulted in immediate improvement in her nutrition and in her sleeping. Clearly, Dawn could eat well, although apparently she could not express her demand normally.

The initial grief reaction in this family was rather mild compared to our other cases. During the first three months, we saw the family twice a month, and during home visits, we listened to Mrs. A talk about herself and about her infant. She occasionally became teary and sometimes expressed loneliness as she wondered about what the future held for both of them. But overall, her husband's basic optimism and their supportive friends buoyed her spirits. Besides, she thought, Dawn did not seem so different from other babies. She was eating well and gaining weight, although there was some expressed surprise that she was so placid and did not cry more. Dawn turned over from her stomach at 2½ months. Shortly after 1 month of age, she began smiling irregularly during wakefulness, especially in the mornings and in response to looking at colorful objects and being held. Around 2½ months, she began to smile more often to a variety of objects and occasionally began to coo by herself.

On our fourth month's visit, we arrived expecting to find the social smile in full blossom and the family playfully engaged with their baby, "using wakefulness in a new way" (Dittrichova & Lapackova, 1964; Emde et al., 1976). Instead there was a heavy air of disappointment. Both parents were visibly saddened. Dawn had continued to gain weight and, in that sense, had made progress, but they had expected "too much." They now knew she was not like other babies in that she did not look like them, did not respond in the same way as other babies, and could not yet show sustained affection. In our standard social interaction filming sequence, we then experienced this same disappointment in microcosm. As we approached, Dawn would smile—but not normally. There was bilateral upturning of the corners of the mouth, but the cheeks and eyes did not crinkle or participate; there was no brightening of the eyes, and there was no "activation" or bicycling of the arms and legs as we expect from the normal 3–4-month-old. Furthermore, eye contact was poor and there were no sparkling eyes tracking our approach. Each of us who experienced this sequence felt a sense of being let down. We expected more. The smiling seemed to raise our expectation of a fun-filled social encounter, but its dampened nature seemed to discourage rather than encourage. Even more, the relative lack of eye contact seemed to "turn us off." In that respect, a subsequent motion picture study revealed that Dawn's eyes ocasionally fixated the face for a few seconds but then wandered off, as would be more characteristic of a 1-month-old.

After this experience, we were able to be more empathic. We shared our feelings with the parents and were more direct about discussing how difficult it must be for them in terms of what they had expected. Both parents seemed grateful for this overture and relieved by the subsequent opportunity to talk. They were able to say that Dawn was not as rewarding as they had imagined and hoped she would be and that in a real sense, it was obvious that she was different from other babies—that she might be retarded. Indeed, we found that Dawn's motoric slowing became manifest after this time. Her 4-month developmental testing scores on the Bayley test (1969) were 76 (mental scale) and 103 (motor scale), and her corresponding scores at 6 months fell to 62 and 80. Now, it became possible to facilitate grieving in a way that was not possible before. Mr. and Mrs. A could see that Dawn was slow.

As we mentioned before, this family was the first in our Down's study. All three members taught us a great deal about early development with Down's syndrome. We learned, first of all, that the pace of postnatal development is such that retardation in motoric and cognitive sectors does not become prominent until after the early months. The Down's infant of the first two months is "floppy" and also has irregular muscle tone with elements of "spasticity" in some muscle groups, presumably in connection with a lesser amount of forebrain inhibition. As a result, turning over can occur weeks and even months ahead of the normal timetable—a fact that is apt to be misinterpreted as advanced development in such a way as to bolster parental denial of disability and interfere with the parents' acceptance of the problem. The social smile is delayed somewhat, but it is deviant mainly because of its dampened form, without activation and without enhanced eye-to-eye contact. Rather than the expected rewards of having fun with the baby, of receiving an unambiguous glowing message that one is fun *for the baby*, an approaching adult is disappointed, occasionally even turned off. This is a dramatic developmental statement. It draws attention to disability and serves to cut through elements of denial, setting the stage for a new wave of grieving, a process that becomes highlighted by the developmental slowing, which becomes prominent soon afterward.

Our previous paper in this volume describes our procedure for photographic sampling wherein we took 20 photographs of infants in a standardized home session. The sampling included responses to social as well as to nonsocial stimulation, and since this procedure had been used for both normals and Down's infants, a simple photographic experiment suggested itself. A laboratory technician was asked to pick the "best smile" available for each infant among the set of 20 pictures available for that infant at 3½ months. Each of the six Down's syndrome infants was age-matched with a normal infant. We chose the 3½-month age as one well beyond the usual expected age for onset of social smiling (Emde & Harmon, 1972), so as not to artificially handicap the Down's syndrome infant because of a simple lag in smiling onset. (The onset of social smiling in the Down's infant seems to occur about three to four weeks after the flowering of social smiling in the normal infant.)

Figure 1 presents an array of the best-smile pictures from six normal infants, and Figure 2 is an array of best-smile pictures from the six Down's syndrome infants. The contrast is dramatic. Even still photographs illustrate the lesser intensity of the social smile in these Down's syndrome infants. Not only is the smile dampened morphologically, with a lesser upturning of the corners of the mouth, but the eyes are less bright, and it is easy to infer from the photographs in Figure 2 that there is less motoric activation in the Down's infants. Time and time again, we have been struck with this difference as we have looked at hundreds of still photographs; the young Down's infant seems less engaging. As part of our longitudinal study, we have routinely taken 16mm movie films of a standardized social interaction involving approaches of mother and stranger. A movie documentary comparing normals and Down's infants at this age confirms these impressions, and another report gives clinical details concerning these six cases (Emde & Brown, 1978).

Finally, that there may be a more general deficit in the activation of emotional expression in Down's syndrome is worthy of further study. Cicchetti and Sroufe (1976, this volume) have found a dampening of

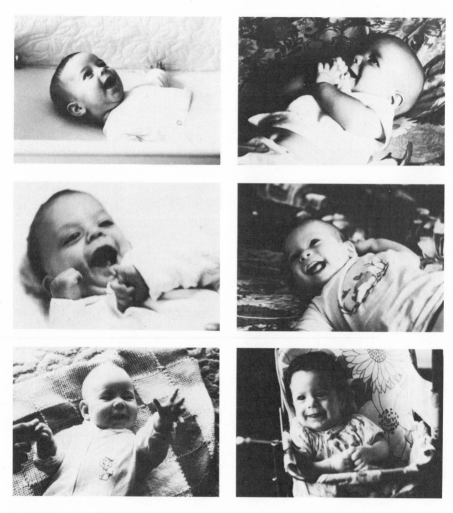

FIG. 1. Social smiles of six normal infants at 3½ months

negative as well as positive expressions during the first two years of Down's infants' development, a finding that could not be accounted for solely by cognitive deficit.

CONCLUSION

Down's syndrome serves as an unfortunate (though scientifically valuable) "experiment in nature" that highlights, by deviation, certain aspects of normal social-emotional development.

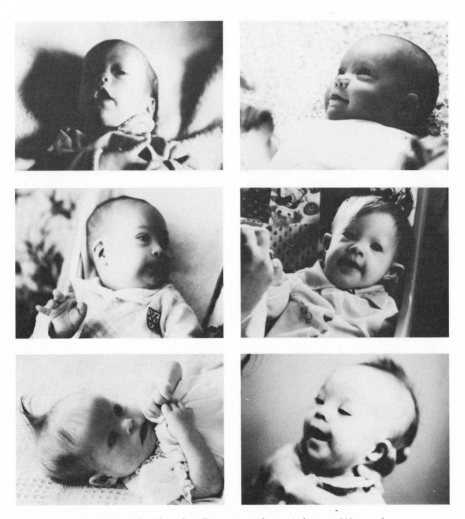

Fig. 2. Social smiles of six Down's syndrome infants at 3½ months

First, our MDS analysis suggests that there is more uncertainty or noise in the emotional signaling of the Down's infants and that this uncertainty arises from the infant rather than from the mother (although the latter undergoes a difficult adaptation of her own).

Second, the onset of the social smile in the Down's syndrome infant, although slightly delayed, is chiefly deviant by its dampened intensity, poor eye-to-eye contact, and lack of "crescendoing" activation. Instead of rewarding a social interaction, instead of engaging and "being fun," it tends to disappoint because it is so different from what is expected.

Third, our experience with the longitudinal study of six families with Down's syndrome infants highlights the importance of these phenomena in the context of social development. The parents, who have to do psychological grief work following the birth of a defective infant in the first two postnatal months, often experience renewed disappointment in the face of the dampened social smile at 4 months, and this disappointment can inaugurate a second wave of grieving for the normal infant they had expected.

References

Bayley, N. *Bayley scales of infant development*. New York: Psychological Corporation, 1969.

Cicchetti, D., & Sroufe, L. A. The relationship between affective and cognitive development in Down's syndrome. *Child Development*, 1976, *47*, 920–929.

Dittrichova, J., & Lapackova, V. Development of the waking state in young infants. *Child Development*, 1964, *35*, 365–370.

Emde, R. N., & Brown, C. Adaptation after the birth of a Down's syndrome infant: A study of 6 cases, illustrating differences in development and the counter-movement between grieving and maternal attachment. *Journal of American Academy Child Psychiatry*, 1978, in press.

Emde, R. N., Gaensbauer, T. G., & Harmon, R. J. Emotional expression in infancy: A biobehavioral study. *Psychological Issues Monograph Series*, (Vol. 10), Monograph #37. New York: International Universities Press, 1976.

14

Cognitive and Communicative Features of Emotional Experience, or Do You Show What You Think You Feel?

CAROLYN SAARNI

A continuing dilemma in the study of affect development is how to integrate several domains of emotional experience: (1) internal or somatic changes related to emotional experience; (2) the visible expression of affect; (3) the individual's cognitive comprehension of the emotion-eliciting situation; and (4) the impact of emotional expression on others. Each of these four areas has been investigated to varying degrees and, for the most part, as separate areas of research. In the current volume, extensions to infant emotional development have been made, and several integrations across domains have been attempted. (For example, Lewis, Brooks, and Haviland report on research that tries to tie together infant facial expression and internal physiological changes related to emotional experience; Décarie presents data on the expression of affect as well as on the infant's cognitive comprehension of the situation; Campos, Hiatt, Ramsay, Henderson, and Svejda discuss infants' internal physiological changes and their cognitive comprehension; and Emde, Kligman, Reich, and Wade report on infants' expression of affect as it relates to impact on others.)

CAROLYN SAARNI · New York University, New York, New York.

The least-studied problem is the interrelationship among the last three domains mentioned, namely, how the individual's thoughts about the emotion-eliciting situation are related to the visible expression of affect, and how this in turn affects the impact made on others. Hoffman's discussion (this volume) of the development of empathy comes closest to pursuing the elusive connection between what one thinks, what one feels, and what one expresses in a social context. However, his discussion does not directly consider the communicative impact of experiencing empathy on the other (empathy-eliciting) person. Clinical observation suggests that observing that one's emotional experience elicits empathy in others frequently serves to modify one's original emotional experience; that is, as a result one feels less distressed, more hopeful, etc.

For the present discussion, I would like to outline several ways of looking at emotional communication and present a brief sketch of a preliminary model of affect differentiation. Basically, the rest of this paper discusses the relation among "faces, heads, and hearts" (see Lewis *et al.*, this volume, for the relation between "hearts and faces"), or do you show what you think you feel?

COGNITION AND AFFECT

Inseparability of Cognition and Affect

From an ontogenetic standpoint, it appears impossible to study cognitive development in the absence of affective development. This follows because the behavioral performance that we observe and infer as being the result of cognitive functioning is equally a result of affective functioning (i.e., motivation, interest, expectancy). As Piaget contends (and I concur), without affect, there would be no intelligence, from either a competence or a performance point of view. According to Piaget (1962), and as elaborated by Langer (1969), cognition provides the organizational focus in adaptive behavior, while affect is the energetic force in adaptation. However, affect is not to be conceptualized here as some sort of raw force within the individual that gets turned on or off. Rather, cognitive organization and affective energy are mutually and reciprocally interactive. As Décarie points out (this volume), as intelligence differentiates with development, so too does affect. Thus, just as an adult may have highly refined, complex cognitions, so may he or she also have highly refined, complex feelings. Interestingly, recent clinical speculations about "neurotic" social-emotional behaviors in adults have begun to appreciate the inseparability of thought and feeling (e.g., Mahoney, 1977; Ellis, 1962).

Mutual Interaction of Cognition and Affect

The connection between cognition and affect is exemplified by the following four statements:

1. What you think affects how you feel.
2. What you feel affects how you think.
3. How you think affects what you feel.
4. How you feel affects what you think.

Statements 1 and 4 refer to the same interactional relationship but in reversed order; statements 2 and 3 are also reversed variations of the same relationship. These four statements reflect the interrelationship of structure (illustrated by the word *how*) and content (the word *what*). The fact that statement 1 can be reversed into statement 4 and statement 2 into 3 illustrates the reciprocity between cognition and affect: they are not only parallel and irreducible (see Décarie, this volume) but inseparably interactive. The content of one is mediated by the structure of the other and vice versa.

Transformational Structures

Piaget does not view affect as having organizational or structural properties, a view not shared by this author. However, his position is supported by Youniss (1975) and Turner (1973), who have argued that affective experience is figurative and nonlogical. (Figurative processes include perception, language, and imagery and are essentially "copies" or representations of *states* of reality [Piaget, 1969]. In contrast, operative processes include overt or interiorized actions that *transform* reality and also take into account the transformations in reality by means of cognitive structuration, for example, as illustrated in conservation.)

I contend that affective experience does have structure, as evidenced by its transformational character. Affect, or emotion, transforms experience by the very fact that it affects *what* is thought about (i.e., the content of thought). Affect can also transform experience by influencing the pace or timing of intellectual processes (as under conditions of deprivation or fatigue). Affect can further transform experience by altering the degree of precision or, conversely, the degree of "noise" in intellectual processes (as in anxiety states). When such affect-induced transformations occur, reality is experienced (or assimilated or accommodated to) differently by the individual. For example, a young child's experience of his mother is quite transformed when he is frustrated by her, yet their formal relationship remains invariant (mother : child). In addition, affective transformations in others (e.g., as displayed by changes in facial expression) are decoded and assimilated, and as a consequence, shifts in interpersonal relationships may be differentially accounted for (for relevant research, see Saarni, 1976; Saarni & Thayer, 1976).

Such transformational capacity indicates that affect does have organizing and structuring properties, a view also shared by Cicchetti and Sroufe (this volume). Affect *systems* become an object of study, and ontogenetic relationships among motivation, emotion, and tension regulation emerge as crucial areas for research (see also Kagan, this volume).

Consciousness of Affective Experience

Piaget has described the gradual development of consciousness of overt and interiorized actions (1976). He emphasizes that consciousness of one's action is constructed and does not merely emerge full-blown or epigenetically unfold in an automatic fashion. (The reader can evaluate his or her own "consciousness level" by trying to describe exactly how to locomote across the floor on hands and knees). Likewise, one can ask how we become conscious of what we are feeling. This issue has received much attention from a variety of perspectives, which are briefly reviewed by Lewis *et al.* (this volume).

Another perspective, emphasizing the feedback between facial expression and neural activity in the brain for consciousness of emotion, is presented by Izard (this volume, also 1971). His work has received some support from Laird's (1974) research with adults on self-attribution of emotion (i.e., happy or angry) when they are induced without awareness to "smile" or "frown." In contrast, Lewis and Brooks (this volume) argue that for conscious experience of emotion to occur, there must be self-awareness and cognitive evaluation, as well as facial expressiveness. The apparent difference between Izard's and Laird's data on the one hand and Lewis and Brook's findings on the other may have to do with the different populations studied (adults versus infants). In fact, Laird's hypothesis about self-attribution of emotion does indeed rest on self-awareness and cognitive evaluation, as well as on efferent facial expression feedback, illustrated by the following quotation from one of Laird's (1974) subjects (italics mine): *"When my jaw was clenched and my brows down,* I tried not to be angry, but *it just fit the position.* I'm not in any angry mood but I found my *thoughts wandering to things that made me angry*, which is sort of silly I guess. *I knew I was in an experiment and knew I had no reason to feel that way* but I just lost control" (p. 480).

Finally, consciousness of emotional experience may at times be facilitated by communications from others through labeling and sympathetic/empathic responsivity (e.g., "You sure look sad today," while a comforting squeeze is given to the shoulders). Others may also elaborate the cognitive evaluation of the emotion-eliciting situation and thus communicatively contribute to consciousness of emotional experience (e.g., in response to a child's distress: "I know you feel both angry and sad about Daddy's moving out and not seeing you so often anymore"). However, for communication to mediate consciousness of emotional experience, something has to be encoded expressively by one person and decoded as meaningful by another. This relationship brings us to the next topic: communication and affect expression.

COMMUNICATION AND AFFECT EXPRESSION

Intentionality and Communication

Definitions of the term *communication* vary along a continuum of intentionality. At the more stringent end is MacKay (1972), who requires that certain conditions be met before the term *communication* is invoked to describe a particular interaction. His two primary conditions are (1) that the communicator, or sender, intend to affect the "internal organizing function" of the receiver by means of his or her message (vocal or nonverbal) and (2) that the receiver perceive herself or himself as the target of intended communicative behavior that is meant to effect a change in her or him. Thus, for communication in MacKay's sense to occur, both sender and receiver must perceive each other as mutual targets of goal-directed and message-carrying behavior. MacKay's model also raises intricate questions of different dynamics for intentionally communicative behavior versus socially informative behavior (the latter being more similar to what we refer to as *social perception*; see Schiff, 1977, for a review). For example, what are the developmental relationships involved when an infant progresses from crying *in such a way as to gain* attention to crying *in order to get* attention.

At the more global end of the definitional continuum is a somewhat less articulated view that assumes that virtually all social behavior is communicative behavior. In the middle is the view shared by many ethologists—and infancy researchers, in particular—that communication occurs when "the behavior of one animal is broadcast to another, who perceives it and modifies his own behavior accordingly" (Pitcairn & Eibl-Eibesfeldt, 1976, p. 81). Intentionality of signal sending is not a prerequisite for communication to occur in this conceptualization. This viewpoint is also shared by Emde *et al.* and others in this volume, and with good reason, for with infants (as well as with animals) we cannot directly observe the infant's evaluation of its intended signals upon the behavior of other individuals. To do so would seem to require verbal introspection or an unambiguous physiological measure that is currently not available.

According to this more functional definition, an infant's expressive behavior certainly affects others by modifying their behavior toward the infant. The functional value of expressive displays (available immediately after birth) is, in fact, to modify others' behavior in such a way that the infant's probability of survival is increased. Thus, this moderate definition of communication is implicated in the most fundamental of adaptations: individual and species maintenance.

Expression and Affect

While an infant's early facial expressions may be quite diverse (see Oster, this volume) and correspond in muscle-group movements to many adultlike facial expressions, we would hardly infer that the infant is feeling the same emotions as an adult. For example, an infant may be capable of producing a facial expression whose pattern may correspond to that of the adult expression associated with the emotion of contempt, yet we would not assume the infant to be capable of the cognitive evaluation that occurs with the affective experience of contempt. That very young infants do produce varied and complex facial expressions (some of which do seem to co-occur with reflexlike emotional responses, such as distress) suggests that we may be biologically programmed to produce *coherency* between facial expressions and affective experiences. How this coherency develops is a critical question addressed in many of the contributions to this volume.

I would like to suggest that one crucial step in establishing coherency of affect and expression is the role played by communication or, more specifically, by the characteristic response given back to the infant after it has signaled expressively (regardless of the infant's intentionality to communicate). In other words, the moderate definition of communication allows us to look at an interpersonal feedback system that gradually works to ground for the infant its expressive signals in the meaningfulness attributed to them by the receiver/caregiver. This meaningfulness as decoded by the receiver leads to modification in his or her behavior toward the infant. As a consequence of repeated associations, the infant comes to expect certain effects from the receiver/caregiver as a function of its producing various expressive behaviors, as when the infant learns to cry in order to get attention and have its distress relieved. This development may occur in Piaget's sensorimotor Stage 4 (see also Emde *et al.*, this volume). Interestingly, this close connection between affect expression and communicative impact on another's behavior is supported by observations of children ages 3–4, who were found to cry less after falling and injuring themselves when *no one was looking* (Blurton-Jones, 1967; Ding & Jersild, 1932).

This emphasis on the communicative effect on the receiver is similar to Osgood's contention (1966) that to apply lexical denotative labels to facial expressions may be a futile exercise. He suggested that the meaning communicated by facial expression is derived experientially from how it makes the receiver feel. His position obtains some support from Davitz and Davitz's data (1959a), which indicated that certain labels such as *annoyance, disgust, scorn, loathing,* and *contempt* are affectively synonomous from the standpoint of the receiver. Such affective labels, however, are usually associated with quite different eliciting situations for the sender. It is this eliciting context that must also be evaluated (empathically) by the receiver if she or he is to adjust his or her behavior in more distinctive and specific ways to the sender's expressive signals. For an infant's expressive signals to evoke specific and appropriate behavioral adjustments in the receiver/caregiver, the receiver/caregiver must also "read" the infant's situation for further cues as to how he or she is to respond to the infant.

Infants as Receivers of Expressive Signals

The necessity for brevity prohibits a review of infants' discrimination of different facial expressions and their characteristic responses to these expressions at different ages (see Charlesworth & Kreutzer, 1973, for a review). However, a study by Monahan (1975) illustrates the variety of adjustments an infant makes in its behavior as a function of facial and vocal expressiveness by a stranger. Monahan found that most infants responded more favorably to a stranger in their home than to their own mothers, if the stranger behaved toward the infant like a normal person, namely, with smiles, friendly vocalization, mutual visual regard, and activity. Monahan was able to identify several sequences of communicative reciprocity. However, many research studies on stranger anxiety have not used normally behaving adults. Instead, the "stranger" is typically abnormally nonreciprocal in his or her communication with the infant through nonexpressiveness and nonreactivity. Unfamiliarity *per se* may not be the cause for the young child's fearfulness toward such a stranger. Rather, such a stranger is in fact sending out very unusual and forbidding messages of nonresponsiveness toward the infant's attempts to engage in a synchronous exchange. Synchrony appears to have a very early basis, as suggested by Condon and Sander's observations (1974) of neonate movements and adult speech. Such synchrony has also been observed in the patterning of visual regard between mother and infant (Brazelton, Koslowski, & Main, 1974).

COGNITION AND COMMUNICATION

Inseparability of Cognition and Communication

Whether encoding or decoding communicative behaviors, cognitive strategies continually provide feedback and "feedforward" (MacKay, 1972) on the communicative transaction. Some of the cognitive strategies studied in adults include selection and integration of the expressive coding channels, assessment of the receiver's informational needs for the message to be effective, evaluation of social-situational constraints, evaluation of intentions and incentives, regulation of relationship variables, and choice of metacommunicative behavior (for reviews see Argyle, 1972; Ekman & Friesen, 1969; Mehrabian, 1972; Moscovici, 1967).

Early Development

There is remarkably little research on the early development of these communicative-cognitive strategies. However, by age 3–4 years, several observational studies indicate that preschoolers do appear to evaluate some situational constraints, monitor their expressive coding channels somewhat, and, on rare occasions, even appear to take listener needs into account (see Blurton-Jones, 1972, for selected studies). Clearly, older infants decode and react to discrepant or unexpected expressive signals, as demonstrated in Monahan's work (1975). However, systematic investigations of young children's responses to communication discrepancies or incongruities between channels are generally lacking, particularly in the nonverbal, expressive area. For older children, a few studies relating cognition and verbal communication adequacy have been conducted (e.g., Kraus & Glucksberg, 1969; Peterson, Danner, & Flavell, 1972; Shatz & Gelman, 1973). Peterson et al. used one nonverbal channel, facial expression, in their assessment of communication adequacy. They found that both 4- and 7-year-old children ignored facial expression cues of puzzlement on the part of the adult listener, which were intended to signal back to the child the inadequacy of his or her message. Other studies using photographs or videotapes of verbal messages with incongruous or conflicting nonverbal behaviors have typically found that younger children reinterpreted the situation to fit either the verbal message or the facial expression, but rarely were integrations of the incongruity between the two channels attempted (Deutsch, 1974; Watson, 1975). Bugenthal, Kaswan, Love, and Fox (1970) found that children attended more to vocal cues than to facial cues when judging an emotion, but other data have shown that this process is reversed for adults, who weigh facial cues more (e.g., Levitt, 1964). An interesting relationship was also shown by Bugenthal, Love, Kaswan, and April (1971) between "double-bind" messages and children who were referred for clinical treatment. Those children were more likely to have mothers who sent contradictory messages between the vocal (e.g., tone of voice) and the verbal channels. Such children probably have not developed the cognitive strategies to evaluate conflicting messages and integrate them into a more complex system for dealing with such contradictory communications.

COGNITION, AFFECT, AND COMMUNICATION

Interpersonal Processes

When these three domains of behavior co-occur, we are essentially talking about interpersonal relations and processes. Curiously, few studies on social development or interpersonal relations in adulthood explicitly integrate these three domains in studying interpersonal transactions. Mehrabian's work (1972) on dimensions of nonverbal communication comes closest to such an integration. He has contended that nonverbal behavior reflects fundamental forms of social adaptation that are correlates of basic categories in the cognition of social phenomena. He has hypothesized that interpersonal nonverbal behavior can be characterized in a three-dimensional framework that reflects these basic categories of social cognition: (1) evaluation of persons and objects in terms of positive or negative affect, resulting in approach or avoidance tendencies; (2) judgment of potency or status as related to social control (e.g., dominance, power relations); and (3) discriminative responsiveness as indicative of differential salience of others for oneself. Mehrabian's extensive research (reviewed by Mehrabian, 1972) has been largely directed toward exploring the ramifications of these three dimensions in nonverbal interpersonal processes. He has concluded that evaluation is coded through facial and vocal cues and also by several postural and positional behaviors. Potency or status is communicated through patterns of gaze direction, postural tension, and use of space. Presenting particular displays and increasing display activity (e.g., rate and frequency) in facial and vocal channnels expresses responsiveness to another.

These three basic themes—approach or avoidance evaluation, judgment of social power or control, and discriminative responsiveness—appear to emerge in the second half of the first year as an infant develops social *relationships* (as opposed to earlier social transactions). Stern's (1974) painstaking analysis of mother–infant relationships comes closest, in my opinion, to charting the matrix of these three themes as they emerge in interpersonal development.

Affect Display Rules

Display rules for expressive behavior also reflect the coordination of cognition, affect, and communication. Display rules are social norms implicitly governing our expressive behavior in various social settings, roles, and relationships. Display rules are guidelines for when to inhibit, intensify, minimize, or dissimulate our affective behavior (Ekman & Friesen, 1969). Unfortunately, the cognitive parameters of display rules (i.e., when to use which display rule and how) are essentially unresearched, and how display rules are acquired developmentally is virtually unexplored.

My own research suggests that children begin to articulate display rules for standard situations such as avoiding a scolding, placating a bully, etc., by middle childhood and can also begin to infer the motivations for using a display rule (Saarni, 1977). Informal observation suggests, however, that the performance of display rules in expressive behavior may begin much earlier. For example, I have observed a preschool-aged boy who is quite terrified of dogs, and in the company of his mother or alone, he is openly expressive of his fear through facial, vocal, and postural behavior. When in the company of his rather stern father (who has expressed concern over his son's "scaredy-cat" behavior), the little boy appears more timid-looking than actually fearful. It is unclear whether the display rule of minimization is occurring here (in order to avoid paternal disapproval?) or if the child expects more adequate protection from dogs when his father is near. Perhaps both evaluations are going on in this young child's differential response.

Empathy

This is the third area in which integrations of cognition, affect, and communication have been attempted. Hoffman's discussion (this volume) is an excellent example of such integration and, further, presents the integration from a developmental perspective. Research on the development of empathy has lately been flourishing, and Hoffman reviews the various approaches and outcomes. However, the function of empathy within a communication system is absent from all present studies. Such an analysis would have to take into account how Person A's empathic response toward Person B affects the emotional experience of Person B, who consequently sends out a second modified affective-expressive message to Person A. Presumably the cognitive evaluations by both persons, A and B, become increasingly differentiated with development, and this differentiation affects the communication sequence noted above. Hoffman speculates about the transformation of empathy into sympathy, and I would suggest that the transformation may well occur in Person A as he or she evaluates Person B's second modified expressive message.

DIFFERENTIATION OF EMOTION EXPERIENCE

Having highlighted a number of conceptual concerns for studying relationships among affect, cognition, and communication, I would like to present a brief sketch of a model for how affective experience differentiates simultaneously and interactionally with development in the individual's cognitive and communicative systems. I present the model as a series of stages, but with due caution, for the assumptions of a stage model may not be met (cf. Flavell & Wohlwill, 1969).

1. Biology of affective experience.
   A. Primary and global affects are reflexively activated. They are accompanied internally by physiological changes and are externally expressed in facial, vocal, and postural channels.
   B. These expressive channels show considerable, perhaps spontaneous, behavioral variation, which suggests a physiological competence for their expression, but the competence is not yet linked to specific affective criteria for their consistent performance.
   C. Biological synchrony with others in some expressive channels is observable.
   D. Gradually the reflexively activated affects are partitioned into an assortment of simple affects that become activated by increasingly specific situational releasers. An operant connection between expressive pattern and internal sensory feedback may also be part of this gradual partitioning.
2. Coordination of affect and expression.
   A. The infant develops self-awareness.

B. As the infant's evaluation of incentive events becomes differentiated, there is a simultaneous increase in the range and kind of affective experience.

C. As the infant becomes increasingly active in its impact on its social and physical environment, affective criteria are linked to and coordinated with encoding specific expressive patterns.

D. The infant now expressively signals his affective experience to others in order to affect their behavior toward itself.

E. Constructing, maintaining, and synchronizing communicative exchanges becomes a goal in itself.

3. Representational elicitors of affect.

A. The development of symbolic schemes allows for a fluid extension of experience forward and backward in time. Now the child can anticipate incentive events as well as store memories of past incentive events. As a result, the young child can anticipate his or her emotional experience, based on memory of how he or she responded affectively in the past.

B. The young child's fantasies (e.g., nightmares) can become the incentive events for eliciting changes in affect.

C. Representation-mediated anticipation of others' psychological and behavioral reactions toward the child can elicit affective experience (e.g., anxiety, happy excitement).

D. Representation-mediated anticipation of others' psychological and behavioral reactions begins to influence the child's expressive behavior (as with display rules).

E. Communication with others extends and elaborates the child's evaluation of incentive events.

F. Communication with others extends and elaborates the child's consciousness of what she or he is feeling.

4. Cognition about affect and affect as an elicitor of affect.

A. Deliberate manipulation of expressive behavior for social-communicative goals is now readily accomplished.

B. The child can infer that the affective experience and the expressive behavior of others are influenced by their anticipation of his or her own psychological and behavioral reactions to them.

C. The child can begin to step outside of his or her affective experience and objectively reflect on it.

D. The child begins to develop affect cycles: affective experience A becomes an incentive event for affective experience B (e.g., an individual compounds his fear of some event—for example, an important examination—with anxiety about feeling the fear, because of its possible deleterious effect on his test performance. Another example is typically found in many adults' sexual dysfunction: the individual is aware that his or her performance anxiety negatively affects his or her sexual performance. When he or she then becomes conscious of again feeling performance anxiety, he or she compounds the affective experience with a secondary anxiety about feeling the performance anxiety.)

In conclusion, as organisms, we seem to be "wired" for remarkably plastic emotional development. Such plasticity is, however, stabilized by our communications with others, leading to a culture-specific socialization of emotional experience. Further stability may be contributed by certain universal classifications of incentive events (see Kagan, this volume). However, in the final analysis, plasticity would seem an absolute prerequisite for the highly diversified social and emotional adaptations that we are required to make throughout our lives.

ACKNOWLEDGMENT

I gratefully acknowledge Stephen Thayer's contribution to this essay through his critical reading and comments on an earlier draft of this manuscript.

REFERENCES

Argyle, M. Non-verbal communication in human social interaction. In R. Hinde (Ed.), *Non-verbal communication*. New York: Cambridge University Press, 1972.

Blurton-Jones, N. An ethological study of some aspects of social behavior of children in nursery school. In D. Morris (Ed.), *Primate ethology*. London: Weidenfeld and Nicolson, 1967.

Blurton-Jones, N. (Ed.). *Ethological studies of child behavior*. New York: Cambridge University Press, 1972.

Brazelton, B., Koslowski, B., & Main, M. The origins of reciprocity: The early mother–infant interaction. In M. Lewis & L. Rosenblum (Eds.), *The origins of fear*. New York: Wiley, 1974.

Bugenthal, D., Kaswan, J., Love, L., & Fox, M. Child versus adult perception of evaluative messages in verbal, vocal, and visual channels. *Developmental Psychology*, 1970, 2, 367–375.

Bugenthal, D., Love, L., Kaswan, J., & April, C. Verbal–nonverbal conflict in parental messages to normal and disturbed children. *Journal of Abnormal Psychology*, 1971, 77, 6–10.

Charlesworth, W., & Kreutzer, M. A. Facial expressions of infants and children. In P. Ekman (Ed.), *Darwin and facial expression, a century of research in review*. New York: Academic Press, 1973.

Condon, W., & Sander, L. Neonate movement is synchronized with adult speech: Interactional participation and language acquisition. *Science*, 1974, 183, 99–101.

Davitz, J., & Davitz, L. The communication of feelings by content-free speech. *Journal of Communication*, 1959, 9, 6–13. (a)

Davitz, J., & Davitz, L. Correlates of accuracy in the communication of feelings. *Journal of Communication*, 1959, 9, 110–117. (b)

Deutsch, F. Female preschoolers' perceptions of affective responses and interpersonal behavior in videotaped episodes. *Developmental Psychology*, 1974, 10, 733–740.

Ding, G., & Jersild, A. A study of the laughing and smiling of preschool children. *Journal of Genetic Psychology*, 1932, 40, 452–472.

Ekman, P., & Friesen, W. Origin, usage, and coding: The basis for five categories of non-verbal behavior. *Semiotica*, 1969, 1, 49–98.

Ellis, A. *Reason and emotion in psychotherapy*. New York: Lyle Stuart, 1962.

Flavell, J., & Wohlwill, J. Formal and functional aspects of cognitive development. In D. Elkind & J. Flavell (Eds.), *Studies in cognitive development: Essays in honor of Jean Piaget*. New York: Oxford University Press, 1969.

Izard, C. *The face of emotion*. New York: Appleton-Century Crofts, 1971.

Kraus, R., & Glucksberg, S. The development of communication: Competence as a function of age. *Child Development*, 1969, 40, 255–266.

Laird, J. Self-attribution of emotion: The effects of experience behavior on the quality of emotional experience. *Journal of Personality and Social Psychology*, 1974, 29, 475–486.

Langer, J. *Theories of development*. New York: Holt, Rinehart, and Winston, 1969.

Levitt, E. A. The relationship between abilities to express emotional meanings vocally and facially. In J. P. Davitz (Ed.), *The Communication of Emotional Meaning*. New York: McGraw-Hill, 1964.

MacKay, D. Formal analysis of communicative processes. In R. Hinde (Ed.), *Non-verbal communication*. New York: Cambridge University Press, 1972.

Mahoney, M. Reflections on the cognitive-learning trend in psychotherapy. *American Psychologist*, 1977, 32, 5l13.

Mehrabian, A. *Nonverbal communication*. New York: Aldeno Atherton, 1972.

Monahan, L. Mother–infant and stranger–infant interaction: An ethological analysis. Unpublished doctoral dissertation, University of Indiana, 1975. Cited by R. Cairns in M. Hahn & E. Simmel (Eds.), *Communicative behavior and evolution*. New York: Academic Press, 1976.

Moscovici, S. Communication processes and the properties of language. In L. Berkowitz (Ed.), *Advances in experimental social psychology* (Vol. 3). New York: Academic Press, 1967.

Osgood, C. Dimensionality of the semantic space for communication via facial expressions. *Scandinavian Journal of Psychology*, 1966, 7, 1–30.

Peterson, C., Danner, F., & Flavell, J. Developmental changes in children's response to three indications of communication failure. *Child Development*, 1972, 43, 1463–1468.

Piaget, J. The relation of affectivity to intelligence in the mental development of the child. *Bulletin of the Menninger Clinic*, 1962, 26, 129–137.

Piaget, J. *The mechanisms of perception*. New York: Basic Books, 1969.

Piaget, J. *The grasp of consciousness: Action and concept in the young child*. Cambridge, Mass.; Harvard University Press, 1976.

Pitcairn, T., & Eibl-Eibesfeldt, I. Concerning the evolution of nonverbal communication in man. In M. Hahn & E. Simmel (Eds.), *Communicative behavior and evolution*. New York: Academic Press, 1976.

Saarni, C. *Developmental analysis of structural continuity in children's understanding of phsyical and social action*. Paper presented at the International Congress of Psychology, Paris, July 1976.

Saarni, C. *Acquisition of display rules for expressive behavior*. Unpublished manuscript, 1977. (Available from 933 Shimkin Hall, Department of Educational Psychology, New York University, New York, N. Y. 10003.)

Saarni, C., & Thayer, S. *Developmental change in children's inferential explanations of nonverbal social interaction*. Paper presented at Eastern Psychological Association, New York, April 1976.

Schiff, W. *Perceptual processes and their application*. Boston: Houghton, Mifflin, 1977.

Shatz, M., & Gelman, R. The development of communication skills: Modification in the speech of young children as a function of listener. *Monographs of the Society for Research in Child Development*, 1973, *38*(5) (Serial No. 152).

Stern, D. Mother and infant at play: The dyadic interaction involving facial, vocal, and gaze behaviors. In M. Lewis & L. Rosenblum (Eds.), *The effect of the infant on its caregiver*. New York: Wiley, 1974.

Turner, T. Piaget's structuralism. *American Anthropologist*, 1973, *75*, 351–373.

Watson, M. *A developmental study of empathy: Egocentrism to sociocentrism or simple to complex reasoning?* Paper presented at the meeting of the Society for Research in Child Development, Denver, April 1975.

Youniss, J. Another perspective on social cognition. In A. D. Pick (Ed.), *Minnesota symposia on child psychology* (Vol. 9). Minneapolis: University of Minnesota Press, 1975.

15

Prior State, Transition Reactions, and the Expression of Emotion

MARK D. STARR

The problem of how best to conceptualize and describe the emotional reactions observed in infancy and early childhood appears recurrently in both this volume and in the earlier volume on the development of fear (Lewis & Rosenblum, 1974). That a generally accepted solution to this problem has not yet been found is indicated both by the diversity of approaches taken to the study of emotion and by the fact that most discussions of emotion (including the present one) begin with an attempt to clarify the conceptual framework to which they relate. Part of the difficulty in defining emotion is that to speak of "emotional behavior" implies that there exists a category of "nonemotional be-havior" as well. However, as Duffy (1941) argued long ago, "there is no evidence for the existence of a special condition called emotion which follows different principles of action from the other conditions of the organism" (p. 292). The current work on the inseparability of cognition and affect, the affective nature of consciousness, and the relation between emotional development and the concept of self both lend support to this statement and attest to the inseparability of emotion from other modes of psychological function.

Although a workable definition of emotion has not been forthcom-ing, there is implicit agreement on certain characteristics of emotion. In a fundamental sense, emotion is regarded as a general attribute or quality of behavior. By itself, this characteristic of emotion is not particularly

MARK D. STARR · Educational Testing Service, Princeton, New Jersey.

helpful. Most would agree that there are particular conscious experiences and behavioral expressions that warrant the adjective *emotional*. We both perceive and communicate emotion categorically. Labels such as *fear*, *anger*, and *happiness* are nouns, and as Emde, Kligman, Reich, and Wade have shown (this volume), these labels can be applied consistently even to the expressions of young infants. The phenomena we label *emotional* are characterized by a second agreed-upon principle. As Kagan (this volume) discusses in detail, these phenomena appear to have a "change in state" as their central attribute. That is, underlying the experience and expression of emotion is a change in what Kagan describes as the individual's "habituated feeling tone or normal feeling state." While this attribute may not distinguish emotional behavior from other forms of behavior (logically all behavior change involves a change in state), it does provide a useful starting place for the empirical study of emotion. Much of the research reported in this volume concerns the conditions under which a change in state occurs and the variables influencing this change.

With the above as prologue, we turn now to two issues that emerge from the conceptualization of emotion as a change in an affectively toned prior state. The first concerns the infant's affective state at the time of testing or observation and the role of this variable in determining reactions to emotion-inducing events. While most researchers are cognizant of this variable, especially as it affects the variability of their data, it has received little emphasis in discussions of emotion. The second issue we look at concerns such reactions as orienting, attending, and other behaviors concomitant with changing state. These behaviors logically involve a change in state themselves and appear to mediate much of the infant's affective transactions with the environment. We will term this general class of events *transition reactions* and consider them as immediate antecendents of the target emotions that occur as outcomes of our commonly used procedures.

In discussing each of these issues, our interest is to describe possible relationships between antecedent behaviors and emotional responses and to delineate areas for further inquiry. We as yet know little about those empirical relationships that do exist, and a systematic treatment of these issues must await more information.

THE INFLUENCE OF PRIOR STATE ON EMOTIONAL EXPRESSION

The affective state or status of the child at the time of testing is known to influence his reactions to certain events. In older children, for example, both self-reward and the rewarding of others is more likely when positive affect is first induced (Moore, Underwood, & Rosenhan,

1973; Rosenhan, Underwood, & Moore, 1974). It would seem likely that the infant's ongoing affective state, when he is confronted with an event, exerts causal influences on his emotional reactions to that event as well. Indeed, in most experimental work with infants, certain "state" variables are controlled for: sleepy and irritable infants are often excluded from the population being studied.

When attempting to systematize the effect of state on reactions to new events, one immediately confronts a problem: the meaning of *state* is ambiguous, and the construct has historically proved difficult to define independently of the measures used to index it (see Lewis, 1972). For purposes of the present discussion, we leave the term *state* undefined and use it simply as a category containing a number of antecedent conditions that may be expected to influence the infant's emotional response to a stimulus event.

The infant's level of arousal prior to testing is one state variable that appears likely to influence his emotional reactions. It is part of common lore that as the infant becomes tired, he may also become fussy and irritable. In a similar vein, Wolff (1969) has noted that tickling, which normally produces smiling and laughter, is likely to induce crying in irritable infants. Does the infant's state on a sleep–wakefulness dimension influence his emotional reactions? If the wakefulness of the infant affects his irritability, does it also influence his reactions to strangers and to being separated from his mother or his father? A unified-arousal theorist might suggest that emotional reactions should be less intense as the sleep (low-arousal) end of the continuum is approached. Alternatively, one might arge that emotional response thresholds might be lowered or that competing response tendencies are less pronounced when the infant is tired, and therefore more intense emotional reactions are likely to be evinced. Similar questions may be phrased in the terms of differential emotion theory: Are emotional systems affected differentially by changes along the sleep–wakefulness dimension? For example, are negative emotions more likely when the sleep end of the continuum is approached?

A within-subject design would be appropriate to an investigation of these issues. Through the use of such a design, it should be possible to determine if individual differences in reactivity are a function of differences in baseline levels of arousal. Individual response biases, too, such as crying versus goal-directed instrumental activity during maternal separation, may in part be a function of the infant's level of arousal at the time of testing.

The issue of synchrony introduced by Lewis, Brooks, and Haviland (this volume) is relevant here. As the authors suggest, there may be competitive systems at work within the autonomic nervous system that limit the extent to which emotional response systems are engaged by stimulus events. Under conditions of high arousal, more response systems are expected to covary, and consequently greater synchrony between the components of an emotional reaction (e.g., heart rate changes and facial expression) would be observed. Conversely, at low levels of arousal, there is less covariation of responses, more "drag" in the system and thus greater variability in emotional reactions. Thus, differences in arousal level, which may vary both within and between individuals and with developmental age, may be expected to affect the emotional response to an event. Information on these questions would aid in our understanding of those individual difference variables typically classified under the heading of *temperament*.

A second type of antecedent condition is the amount and quality of social stimulation prior to the occurrence of the emotion-inducing event. Many of our procedures for studying infant affect are social in nature. To the extent that infant "state" can be defined in terms of social interaction (see Lewis, 1972), it becomes important to know if the changes in state characterizing a particular emotional response are dependent on the level of social interaction prior to the initiation of that response. Weinraub and Lewis (in press), for example, report that high levels of mother–infant interaction prior to a brief separation correlate with an increased probability of the infant's being upset when the mother is absent. Is this relationship a function of temperament variables, of the attachment bond, or of a causal connection between prior affect and subsequent reactions to separation? With regard to the latter hypothesis, Solomon and Corbit (1974) have proposed that certain negative reactions, such as separation distress, are a product of homeostatic mechanisms serving to oppose the positive affect aroused during the prior interaction with the mother. This theory predicts that an increase in interaction prior to separation would result in more intense distress reactions when the mother is absent. Conversely, less separation distress would be expected following periods of reduced mother–infant interaction.

As a further illustration of this theme, consider a stranger approach procedure where the stranger interacts with the mother before approaching the infant. One way of conceptualizing this manipulation is that it varies the affective environment (as defined in terms of social interaction) prior to asking the infant for his reactions to the stranger. Using this paradigm, we may ask: (1) Is the infant's emotional response to the stranger affected if the mother–stranger interaction is an antecedent? And (2) does the affective tone of the mother–stranger interaction influence the intensity or quality of the infant's emotional response?[1]

[1] C. Feiring is currently conducting this experiment in the Infant Laboratory at the Educational Testing Service.

A third category of antecedent conditions includes those situations in which the infant has just recently exhibited an emotional reaction to some event. This state of affairs is commonly described in discussions of sequence effects: in a series of stimulus episodes, the reaction to a given event may be influenced by what went before. Sroufe, Waters, and Matas (1974), for example, noted that when an event known to elicit positive affect in a large proportion of infants (the mother's wearing a mask) followed events evoking distress (stranger approach, maternal separation), the proportion of infants reacting positively decreased dramatically. The question of what mechanisms underlie this phenomenon is still open. It is useful to distinguish between the case in which the infant's state is changed by the first event (S1) and the reaction to the subsequent event (S2) is biased by this prior change in state, and the case in which the infant's reaction to Event S1 is associated with some element of the situation (the laboratory setting, a funny-face mask) and the reaction to S2 is affected by the prior association. In the first case, the time interval between events may well prove an important variable: if the reaction to S1 dissipates prior to the introduction to S2, the sequence effect would not be expected to be as pronounced as when S2 is introduced while the reaction to S1 still persists. In the latter case, where structural changes have occurred, the sequence effect should not be as dependent on temporal variables, and the prior experience with S1 should have relatively enduring effects. In either case, it would be interesting to know if the influence of prior experience on reactions to subsequent events is a function of such variables as the intensity of the infant's earlier response. For example, are reactions to maternal separation influenced by the intensity of prior reactions to separation? Similarly, are responses to the mother on reunion affected by the intensity of the separation reaction?

In this context, there are also a number of developmental questions to be raised. Sroufe *et al.* (1974), for example, observed that the influence of prior reactions on the infant's response to an event was not as pronounced in younger infants. Younger infants are generally known to show more variable and dramatic changes in affective state than older children and adults. There are, of course, a number of ways in which this increase in consistency over development may be achieved. Socialization, prior experience, and the articulation of cognitive appraisal processes are some of the factors that may influence consistency. Yet, on a strictly empirical level, it would be good to know if the sequential dependencies between affective states—that is, the degree to which prior state influences an emotional reaction—increase over the course of development. Perhaps the processes controlling affect undergo a temporal integration during development, increasing consistency over time and across situations.

The discussion above concerned "state" variables that are relatively short-term or phasic. Arousal, social interaction, and prior emotional responses are not maintained at constant levels for long periods of time. There are, however, affective or mood states that are more enduring and contribute to what Kagan (this volume) termed the organism's "habituated feeling tone." Anxiety and depression are two such states that may become chronic and affect the individual's emotional reactions to short-term events. Developmentally, even more subtle mood states may exist. Provence (this volume), for example, describes a number of psychoanalytic concepts relating to the affective life of the child. Among these, the suggestion that the child goes through phases in the separation–individuation process with characteristic moods is relevant here (e.g., Mahler, Pine, and Bregman, 1975). For example, if the child's dominant mood is one of elation with feelings of omnipotence and mastery, he may well react one way to an event. When he later begins to relinquish his feelings of omnipotence, he may enter a phase characterized by a more depressed mood and may well react differently to the same type of event. Illness is yet another background condition against which emotional reactions may occur. Does the infant who's feeling miserable with the flu react to events in the same way as when he is healthy and feeling fine? We do not yet know the rules governing these relationships.

Taken together, these examples illustrate that there are a number of basic questions remaining to be asked about the affective background against which emotional change occurs. It seems likely that there are sequential dependencies among affective states, that is, that the infant's response to an event may be influenced by his immediately prior affective state. The variability and lack of consistency in infants' emotional reactions are well known (see, for example, Master & Wellman, 1974). Some of this variability may be explained by the fact that individuals differ greatly in their affective state at the time of testing.

The examples we have considered may be grouped into three general classes. First, there are short-term, within-individual changes in state, keyed to such variables as sleep–wake cycles, social and affective environment (including residual effects of emotion-arousing experiences), and health-related conditions. Second, there are between-individual differences in arousal and general reactivity; these may be considered as temperament variables. Finally, there may be developmental differences in mood or feeling states. An understanding of the effects of these background conditions would be an advantage methodologically, by allowing increased control of the experimental setting, practically, by allowing better prediction of the conditions under which events may have significant affective impact, and finally, theoretically, by increasing our knowledge of the processes modulating the infant's affective life.

While it is possible to conceptualize emotional reactions as changes and modulations of affective state, a realistic description of this process must include the behaviors that mediate the infant's affective relationships with objects and events in the environment. These behaviors occur at the point of transition between states and in some sense reflect the integration of affective and other psychological processes.

TRANSITION REACTIONS

Going from one state to another involves a period of transition, and the change in affective state is accompanied by a number of overt behavioral events. However, the situations in which we involve the infant when studying affect are typically complex, social, and for obvious ethical reasons, relatively innocuous—that is, they do not evoke the extremes of emotion. These factors combine to make it difficult to describe the temporal dynamics of emotional change. It is often hard to pinpoint, for example, what elements of the stimulus situation the infant is responding to. Consider three situations: the mother stands, walks across the room, opens the door and leaves; the door knob turns, a stranger enters, pauses, and approaches the infant; the infant is lifted, is carried a few feet, and is gradually lowered onto a Plexiglas surface suspended some distance above the floor. Each of these situations involves a number of stimulus elements, each of which, both in combination with others and alone, is capable of affecting the infant's behavior and affective state.

The infant's behavior during the transition between affective states often mirrors the complexity of the stimulus event itself. We often specify a discrete behavioral reaction as indicative of an underlying emotion: crying is used to index fear, laughter is used to infer happiness, etc. While such behaviors are salient markers of emotion, they typically occur in combination with and as sequelae to other behavioral reactions, especially when the emotion-inducing event is complex and of extended duration. A number of behaviors can be described during the transition period between the prior state and the affective outcome of a complex event. A partial list of these include the orienting reflex, startle, surprise, and attention. Although it is not always easy to distinguish, either conceptually or empirically, between the various reactions, two phases in the transition between one state and another may be differentiated.

The first phase is characterized by general alerting reactions and the suppression of gross motor activity. The reactions appearing in this phase include startle, surprise, and the orienting reflexes. Generally speaking, the appearance of first-phase alerting reactions indicates that the infant has become aware of a change in the stimulus situation. As Charlesworth (1969) noted, each of these reactions appears both to disrupt and suppress ongoing activity and to arouse attentional processes and orientation to the locus of stimulus change. A knock on the window, often used as a signal for the mother to depart in studies of separation, frequently results in the infant's looking up from his toys and orienting to the source of the sound. Thus, to say that the child is playing with toys prior to the mother's departure is not entirely correct. Frequently, the child is orienting and looking around the room as the mother stands to leave. The point here is simply that the first phase of an emotional reaction is often a response to stimulus change.

The infant's response to stimulus change itself constitutes a "change in state." Startle and surprise have historically been considered emotional responses of a similar sort, differing primarily in their intensity (cf. Charlesworth, 1969; Tomkins, 1962). Orienting reflexes, too, as Sokolov (1963) has documented, entail the activation of both excitatory and inhibitory processes and therefore may be considered indicative of changes in the infant's state of arousal. Pribram (1967) and Lewis and Goldberg (1969) have advanced a similar argument, noting that stimulus change may produce a state of uncertainty in the central nervous system, a state that they suggest characterizes the physiological arousal underlying emotion. It thus appears that the infant's affective state is initially modified by his becoming aware of a change in the stimulus situation.

The second phase in the transition between states is marked by the appearance of an attention response. While orienting and alerting responses involve postural adjustments and localization of the source of stimulation, attention involves focused fixation on the stimulus object and complete suppression of gross motor activity. For example, many of the infants we have observed in maternal-separation procedures sit motionless and stare at the mother as she walks toward the door. Others have described the attention response and the conditions under which it is elicited in some detail (e.g., Kagan & Lewis, 1965; McCall, 1971), and we will not describe it again here. For the present purposes, it is sufficient to note that following the first-phase alerting responses, there is often a brief interval prior to the overt expression of emotion, or the resumption of other activities, during which the infant fixates on the source of stimulus change.

The transition reactions involve a change in state and therefore may be considered as emotional responses themselves. We have not described them as such, however, primarily because they do not appear to be related by hedonic tone to the emotional expressions that occur as their sequelae.

Although transition reactions and emotional expression are sequentially related, causal relationships between these two components of the behavioral sequence remain to be described. Orienting, surprise, and startle appear as first-phase reactions to stimulus change and are often followed by more prolonged attention responses. These reactions appear in response to different stimulus conditions: Charlesworth (1969), for example, distinguishes between unexpected and misexpected events in eliciting startle and surprise, respectively. However, as he noted, positive, negative, and neutral affect are each likely outcomes of these events. Thus, while alerting reactions are accompanied by a change in the infant's affective status, this change itself doesn't appear to determine the hedonic tone of subsequent emotion. A similar statement can be made with regard to the attention response. We know something about the stimulus conditions that affect attention: novel events, for example, produce more prolonged attention. But here again, the occurrence of an attention response does not predict subsequent affective expressions. A number of authors have argued that during attention the infant is attempting to assimilate the stimulus event and that it is the ease and outcome of this activity that determines the subsequent affective response. In this theoretical scheme, negative affective responses, such as fear or wariness, are said to result when the event is discrepant and unassimilable. However, emotions such as fear may also result when familiar events or objects are encountered, as when the infant visits his familiar, injection-giving pediatrician (see, for example, Lewis, 1975). In any event, it is clear that central processes are at work during the attention phase of emotional transitions, processes that mediate the child's affective involvement with his environment. Nonetheless, we may still ask the empirical question to what extent the outcome of the transition between states can be predicted from observable characteristic of the transition reactions themselves.

While the transition reactions appear at present to be relatively independent of the hedonic tone of subsequent affective expression, it is useful to incorporate these reactions into our descriptions of emotional change. Two advantages are gained from this strategy. The first concerns individual differences in emotional reactivity. Bronson (1971) has argued that infants have different thresholds for crying in reaction to uncertainty: some individuals cry in response to low levels of uncertainty, and others tolerate much higher levels before crying occurs. By focusing on the transition reactions prior to emotional expression, we can further explore differences of this sort. For example, are the individual differences observed a function of differential sensitivity to stimulus change as gauged by the probability of orienting reactions or the durations of attention responses, or do the differences reside in a characteristic intensity or quality of emotional expression following the transition reaction?

Second, we can inquire into the changes that occur in the transition response sequence as a function of the infant's past experience. For example, from the literature on Pavlovian conditioning, we can draw the hypothesis that the orienting response habituates as the stimulus originally eliciting it acquires affective meaning. If this is true, we would expect that as the infant gained experience with an event, the transition sequence would be abbreviated and emotional expression would occur in anticipation of the original emotion-inducing event. A similar function of decreased response duration with anticipatory responding may also be observed when we examine attention responses to repeated events. For example, the mother's putting on her hat and coat may initially elicit orienting and attending. As the infant learns that this action results in his mother's leaving him, the orienting and attending responses may decrease in duration and the infant may begin to fret prior to the mother's actually departing.

Finally, the relationship between transition reactions and emotional expression may undergo changes over the course of development. Campos, Hiatt, Ramsay, Henderson, and Svejda (this volume), for example, find that attentional responses to the visual cliff, as measured by cardiac deceleration, appear developmentally prior to fear reactions to the same stimulus. As this example indicates, it seems likely that the linking of emotional response systems to certain classes of environmental events, vis-à-vis the processes underlying the transition reactions, takes place gradually over development.

To summarize, we have suggested that the description of emotion should include three terms: the prior state or background from which the emotional expression emerges, the transition reactions or behaviors mediating the change in state, and the emotional expression that occurs as an outcome of the change. These terms were derived logically after a consideration of emotion as a change in state. We do not yet know the best way to define the terms in practice. Both physiological and psychological measures of state are available, but the construct is open to a variety of interpretations. Similarly, any number of behaviors may occur during the transition between states, and a description of these is a task in itself. We also lack a full understanding of the relationships between the three phases in the sequence of emotional change. Prior state and the processes underlying transition reactions may interact in determining subsequent emotional expression, or they may act independently, controlling different qualities of the response. In either case, the variables classed under the headings of prior state and transition reactions are immediate antecedents of emotional expression, and the role they play in mediating the infant's affective relationship with his environment merits careful consideration.

REFERENCES

Bronson, G. W. Fear of the unfamiliar in human infants. In H. R. Schaffer (Ed.), *The origins of human social relations*. London: Academic Press, 1971, pp. 59–64.

Charlesworth, W. The role of surprise in cognitive development. In D. Elkind & J. Flavell (Eds.), *Studies in cognitive development*. London: Oxford University Press, 1969, pp. 257–314.

Duffy, E. An explanation of "emotional" phenomena without the use of the concept "emotion." *Journal of Genetic Psychology*, 1941, *25*, 283–293.

Kagan, J., & Lewis, M. Studies of attention in the human infant. *Merrill-Palmer Quarterly*, 1965, *11*, 95–127.

Lewis, M. State as an infant-environment interaction: An analysis of mother–infant interaction as a function of sex. *Merrill-Palmer Quarterly*, 1972, *18*, 95–121.

Lewis, M. The meaning of fear. Paper presented at a symposium on The Origins of Joy and Fear: The Development of Affect Systems in Infancy, meetings of the Society for Research in Child Development, Denver, April 1975.

Lewis, M., & Goldberg, S. The acquisition and violation of expectancy: An experimental paradigm. *Journal of Experimental Child Psychology*, 1969, *7*, 70–80.

Lewis, M., & Rosenblum, L. A. *The origins of fear*. New York: Wiley, 1974.

Mahler, M. S., Pine, F., & Bregman, A. *The psychological birth of the human infant*. New York: Basic Books, 1975.

Masters, J. C., & Wellman, J. M. The study of infant attachment: Procedural critique. *Psychological Bulletin*, 1974, *81*, 218–237.

McCall, R. Attention in the human infant: Avenue to the study of cognitive development. In D. Walcher & D. Peters (Eds.), *Early childhood: The development of self-regulatory mechanisms*. New York: Academic Press, 1971, pp. 107–137.

Moore, B. S., Underwood, B., & Rosenhan, D. L. Affect and altruism. *Developmental Psychology*, 1973, *8*, 99–104.

Pribram, K. H. The new neurology and biology of emotion: A structural approach. Paper presented at the Eastern Psychological Association Meeting, Boston, 1967.

Rosenhan, D. L., Underwood, B., & Moore, B. Affect moderates self-gratification and altruism. *Journal of Personality and Social Psychology*, 1974, *30*, 546–552.

Sokolov, E. N. *Perception and the conditioned reflex*. New York: Macmillan, 1963.

Solomon, R. L., & Corbit, J. D. An opponent-process theory of motivation: I. Temporal dynamics of affect. *Psychological Review*, 1974, *81*, 119–145.

Sroufe, L. A., Waters, E., & Matas, L. Contextual determinants of infant affective response. In M. Lewis & L. A. Rosenblum (Eds.) *The origins of fear*. New York: Wiley, 1974, pp. 49–72.

Tomkins, S. S. *Affect, imagery, conciousness* (Vol. 1). *The positive affects*. New York: Springer, 1962.

Weinraub, M., & Lewis, M. *Departure and separation*. Monographs of the Society for Research in Child Development, in press.

Wolff, P. H. Crying and vocalization in early infancy. In B. M. Foss (Ed.), *Determinants of infant behavior* (Vol. 4). New York: Wiley, 1969, pp. 81–110.

16

On the Ontogenesis of Emotions and Emotion–Cognition Relationships in Infancy

CARROLL E. IZARD

In considering emotion development in infancy, it is important to remember that the emotions and the emotion system cannot be studied in isolation. The infant is a whole human being and the personality of the infant, like the personality of the adult, consists of an organization of a complexly interrelated set of subsystems. In a general sense, infant development can be considered as the process whereby these systems become effectively organized so that they interact and interrelate harmoniously in producing integrated behavior (Izard, 1971; Sroufe, 1977).

The genetic endowment of the human infant guarantees each subsystem a minimal set of genetically encoded programs for system interaction and for person–environment transactions. In the more traditional language of psychology, the infant is born with certain capacities to stay alive (the homeostatic system); to experience and respond to drives or biological needs (the drive system); to experience and express the emotions of distress, interest, and enjoyment (the rudiments of the emotion system); to explore nearby objects in the environment (the rudiments of the perceptual system); and to react differentially, both affectively and perceptually, to changes in stimulation or information inputs (the rudiments of the cognitive system and

---

CARROLL E. IZARD · University of Delaware, Newark, Delaware.

the basis for affective-cognitive structures). In the language of Harlow and Mears (this volume), these inborn capacities are complex, unlearned responses, and they form an important part of the basis for the development of the behavioral systems of infancy. They guarantee a minimal set of adaptive subsystem and infant–environment interactions.

All the personality subsystems are not present in equal strength at birth, nor do they mature and develop at the same rate. In the neonate, the homeostatic, drive, and emotion systems are capable of a greater number of significant functions that are the other systems. The relatively greater maturity of the homeostatic, drive, and emotion systems make them functionally the most important systems in early infancy, a period in which the infant is primarily an affective being (see Sroufe, 1976). A good example of differential rates of development among subsystems is apparent in the relatively more rapid progress in the perceptual and cognitive systems than in the motor system. For example, an infant has a fairly well-developed sense of spatial relations and depth perception before it can crawl (Campos, Hiatt, Ramsay, Henderson, & Svejda, this volume). The possibility that differential rates of development among subsystems may be seen in exaggerated form in exceptional infants (e.g., Down's syndrome babies) is suggested by pilot data reported by Cicchetti and Sroufe (this volume).

A central assumption of this paper is that the emotions emerge as they become adaptive in the life of the infant. The "life of the infant" obviously does not refer to the infant in isolation but rather to the infant-in-social-surround. Thus the adaptiveness of a given emotion has to be judged not only in terms of the individual but in terms of the infant-in-social-context and particularly in an infant–caregiver relationship.

THE CONCEPTUAL FRAMEWORK

Differential emotions theory is intended to have general application to the domain of personality and social behavior, but the detailing of the theory's application to infant and child development has just begun. I recently discussed the role of the emotions in the development of consciousness in infancy and the manner in which emotions relate to sensory, perceptual, and cognitive processes (Izard, 1978). The present paper discusses the sequence of emergence of fundamental emotions and gives some indication of the relation of each emotion to certain developmental processes. The underlying theory has been detailed elsewhere (Tomkins, 1962, 1963; Izard & Tomkins, 1966; Izard, 1959,

1971, 1972, 1977), so I present here only some of the major propositions and key definitions.

1. The human personality is a complex organization of six relatively independent though complexly interactive subsystems: the homeostatic, drive, emotion, perceptual, cognitive, and motor systems. Each of these systems has motivational properties whose salience varies at different developmental levels, in different environmental contexts, and in different self–other interactions. Under relatively normal biological and social conditions, however, the emotion system is the primary motivational system for human beings over the life span.

2. The six personality subsystems produce four types or classes of motivation: drives, emotions, affect-perception and affect–cognition interactions, and affective–cognitive structures and orientations. The term *affect* includes both emotions and drives. The drives include such phenomena as hunger, thirst, elimination needs, pain, and sex, and these assume importance for personality and social behavior as they interact with emotions. The fundamental emotions are interest, joy, surprise, distress, anger, disgust, contempt, fear, shame/shyness, and guilt. An affect–cognition interaction may be the interaction of any drive or emotion with perceptual and cognitive processes, the affect determining the selectivity and direction of these processes. Affect–cognitive structures result from recurring interactions between the same affect or pattern of affects and the same imagery or cognition. Affective–cognitive structures have traitlike characteristics, and a relatively homogeneous set of affective–cognitive structures may form a basic personality orientation described by such terms as *passive, aggressive, egotistical, skeptical, introverted, extraverted, anxious,* and *depressed*.

3. An emotion has a neurophysiological, expressive, and phenomenological component. The expressive component, particularly the facial expression, plays two important roles: it provides sensory data to the brain for the cortical-integrative activity that produces emotion experience, and it provides a set of social signals that are particularly important in infant–caregiver and other social relationships.

4. The neural mechanisms for emotion expression and emotion experience are innate, and the ontogenesis of a particular fundamental emotion is primarily a function of maturational processes and secondarily a function of learning and experience.

5. The emotions emerge as they become adaptive in the life of the infant and in the infant–caregiver and infant–environment relationship.

6. The emotions constitute the principal organizing factors in consciousness and provide the experiential/motivational conditions and cues for cognitive-interpretive processes and action.

7. Each emotion is a unique quality of consciousness and has distinct motivational characteristics that tend to instigate a broad class of responses that are generally adaptive in relation to the eliciting event.

8. Each emotion adds to the complexity of consciousness, increases the capacity for processing and responding to different types of information, and increases the individual's capacity to respond appropriately to a broader set of contingencies.

9. At the neural level, emotion experience is activated by sensory feedback from the face. Once an emotion is activated, however, it typically recruits the autonomic nervous system and the physiological systems it innervates. Subsequent hormones and neurohumors influence biochemical processes that play a role in mobilizing energy and maintaining emotions over time.

10. At the conscious level, the causes of emotion range from what Bowlby (1973) has termed "natural clues" (eliciting events that tend to act as innate releasers) to an almost infinite variety of causes that result from conditioning and social learning. Particularly after the emergence of symbolic processes, perception and cognition play a highly important role both in learning emotion-eliciting events and in learning effective ways of responding to or coping with emotion-eliciting situations.

11. A given stimulus situation or incentive event may elicit different emotions, depending on the stage of development in the perceptual, cognitive, emotion, and motor systems.

12. Each emotion helps set the stage for a particular type of learning and development. In a sense, the emergence of a particular emotion, along with correlative changes in other systems, marks the beginning of a "critical period" for certain types of experiences and for the learning of certain types of responses that are important to development at that particular stage of life.

13. The emotion process is a function of the somatosensory system, and the fact that this system is under voluntary control has important implications for the management and control of emotions, both in the socialization process and in psychotherapy and behavior modification (Izard, 1971). Although through learning and experience reafferent loops may come to be effective in emotion activation, the sensory feedback from the face is critical in the emotion process in infancy and early childhood. Recent research by Kleck, Vaughan, Colby, Cartwright-Smith, Vaughan, and Lanzetta (in press) and Lanzetta, Cartwright-Smith, and Kleck (1976) suggests that the simulation or dissimulation (intensification or deintensification) of facial expression in pain and emotion amplifies or attenuates both the physiological response and the self-report of the affect.

14. The early learning of voluntary emotion expressions through

imaginative play, imitation, and role assumption figures significantly in the acquisition of techniques for the self-regulation of emotion. The significance of this process is evident when we consider the importance of self-regulation of emotions for the larger domain of self-control.

Some of the foregoing propositions are discussed in a bit more detail in this paper. The reader is referred to the earlier sources, however, for a more complete presentation.

MILESTONES IN THE ONTOGENESIS OF EMOTIONS

Emotion ontogenesis consists mainly of processes that are a function of age-related biological changes and secondarily of developmental processes that are influenced by experience (exercise of functions and learning). The development of affective–cognitive structures and orientations is primarily a function of ecological variables and learning and secondarily a function of age-related biological processes.

In discussing the development or increasing complexity of consciousness as a function of the emergence of the various discrete emotions and their relative accessibility to awareness, I suggested three broad overlapping levels or processes in consciousness. At the first level, consciousness consists primarily of sensory–affective processes. Changes in stimulation or information processing and the differential selective and organizing functions of receptors produce different affects, the expression of which differentially influences the social surround. At level two, consciousness consists primarily of affective–perceptual processes. The differential affect-eliciting characteristics of objects differentially focuses interest and attention and facilitates the formation of percepts and affect–percept bonds. At level three consciousness consists primarily of affect–cognition interactions. These interactions ultimately result in affective–cognitive structures or sets of such structures (e.g., social attachment, need achievement, a circumscribed phobia, or a specific prejudice), and a certain organized set of such structures may constitute an affective–cognitive orientation that tends to locate the person on a dimension such as introversion–extraversion, autonomy–dependency, or passivity–aggressiveness. The idea of three types of processes in consciousness may have some relationship to the concept of distinct memory functions designated as *affective permanency*, *perceptual permanency*, and *cognitive permanency* (see Décarie, this volume).

The fact that the neonate is primarily an affective being does not mean that it is incapable of certain perceptual and motor activities. The neonate can fixate, scan, and track moving objects and even react defensively to an apparent looming object (Cicchetti & Sroufe, this

volume). The defensive reaction includes what appears to be appropriate motor responses. The preeminence of sensory–affective processes
probably begins to wane sometime around the end of the first or the
beginning of the second month.

Between the ages of approximately two and four months,
affective–perceptual processes gain in importance. During this period,
affect–percept relating is suggested by the presence of reliable visual
preferences in relation to objects or geometric patterns (Greenberg,
1977). It is also during this period that the infant obtains the prototypical
social percept, the facial gestalt (Spitz, 1965; Emde, Gaensbauer, &
Harmon, 1976). The face percept clearly demonstrates the affective
nature of early perceptual development. The face is an innate or
environmentally stable affective stimulus, and obtaining the face percept
regularly releases the smiling response at this stage of development.

The formation of affective–cognitive structures, which relies on the
ability to store and retrieve information, begins sometime in the second
half-year of life. Although all three types of processes may be present in
consciousness at any age, affective–cognitive phenomena are predominant in consciousness after the development of symbolic processes
and language make possible a virtually infinite number of affective–
cognitive bonds.

In the following paragraphs, I sometimes refer to stages or levels of
emotion development. I agree, however, with Flavell (1971) and Kagan
(1976) that a "stage" should not be interpreted as a sharply demarcated
period. The underlying processes of development are probably more
continuous than suggested by the term *stage*. I use *stage* or *level* as terms
of convenience, as a way of grouping certain related functions that
emerge together and assume relatively greater prominence than at
earlier ages. In emotion development, however, this use of the terms
does not mean that new emotions emerge and replace older ones. New
emotions emerge and older ones remain. However, if we consider the
interrelationships among incentive events, emotions, affective–
cognitive processes, and actions as a "behavioral system" (Kagan,
1976), then Kagan's apt description of development as processes
whereby new forms emerge to replace older ones can be applied to
developmental changes relating to the emotion system. For example,
the face (stimulus)-smile (response)-positive-affective-interchange
sequence in the 3-month-old will surely be replaced in certain contexts
by face-distress- or face-fear-negative response sequences sometime
after 6–8 months of age. Thus what changes developmentally is not
only the number of discrete emotions but equally importantly the
relationships between the emotion system and the other subsystems of
the personality. In the first weeks of life, a limited set of affects relate

mainly to internal sensory events and minimally to the object world and the social surround. Ultimately, a much greater variety of emotions and patterns or interactions of emotions relate minimally to biological-need signals and extensively to persons, objects, images, symbols, ideas, ideologies, and action patterns.

The following extension of differential emotions theory to infant development should be considered as a tentative outline. It will be made more precise and complete only through empirical research.

Emotions Facilitate Survival

Emotion expressions that are present in the neonate include the distress cry, the neonatal smile, interest, startlelike movements, and disgust. In terms of differential emotions theory, the presence of the expression suggests that a corresponding emotion experience is also present, at least in rudimentary form.

According to Lewis (Lewis, Brooks, & Haviland, this volume; Lewis & Brooks, this volume), emotion cannot be inferred until the infant has achieved a level of self-awareness that occurs around 8–9 months of age. While I infer the presence of some emotion experiences in at least rudimentary forms from birth, I think Lewis's position may well characterize the emotions in which a more stable self-conception or self-awareness plays some role. A relatively more stable self-image may be required for the emotions of contempt, fear, shame, and guilt. It is also possible that the phenomenological component of shame or contempt or any emotion may become less diffuse and have different effects as a result of the maturation of the underlying neural substrates of the emotion and the developmental changes in other systems, perhaps particularly in the realm of self-cognition.

Whether or not we can agree that the very young infant has emotion experiences isomorphic to its emotion expressions, we probably can agree that it is the expressive or social aspect of emotion that is most important in the early weeks of life. The caregiver behavior that is motivated by the emotion expressions of the infant is crucial to survival and healthy development.

The Distress Cry

The infant's distress cry probably does serve an elemental intraindividual function. Just as the distress cry of one neonate tends to elicit a distress cry in another (Simner, 1971; Sagi & Hoffman, 1976), so does the infant's cry tend to produce further crying in the same individual. That is, distress induces further distress until the distress cry as a social signal accomplishes its purpose. The distress experience may play some role in distress-induced distress in the neonate, but this phenomenon may be explained more parsimoniously as a function of a positive sensory-feedback loop.

While the assumption of emotion experience in early infancy is a matter of inference, the evidence for the motivational impact of the distress expression is quite clear. The distress cry is a peremptory message to the caregiver for help: "Come change what is happening" (Emde *et al.*, 1976). The caregiver's response to the infant's distress cry is the prototype of expression-motivated behavior.

Neonatal Smiling

Experts agree that neonatal smiling remains largely unexplained. We can infer a concomitant enjoyable experience only on the basis of a facial feedback hypothesis. The fact that the neonatal smile is a complex, unlearned reflex does not imply that it is without antecedent conditions or the capacity to motivate others. The expression-motivated behavior elicited by neonatal smiling is generally positive in nature; even though it typically occurs in rapid eye movement (REM) sleep and is apparently unrelated to the social surround, it has some of the same signal value as the social smile. Emde *et al.* (1976) report that it is only rarely that a mother is puzzled and mildly distressed that the neonate's smiling is not related to her or to any social stimulation. Mothers generally respond positively to the neonate's smile.

Startlelike Movements

Anyone who has observed a neonate's response to a loud sound or a pinprick is aware that the infant is capable of startlelike movement patterns. Although the facial movements involved have not been closely studied, casual observation suggests that some patterned facial activity is present. The adaptive function of the startlelike movement in the neonate may reside in part in withdrawal from the stimulus but probably more significantly in calling the attention of the caregiver to the presence of a potentially noxious or dangerous source of stimulation.

Disgust

The disgust expression facilitates the removal or rejection of distasteful substances from the mouth. It also signals the caregiver that the infant cannot tolerate the substance and may need help in removing it.

Interest

Interest in the very young infant clearly serves both the individual and the social functions of emotion motivation. In terms of individual motivation, the function of interest is to focus and maintain attention and to motivate exploratory activity. Interest is activated by novelty and change (of which movement is a prime example) and serves as the basis for the infant's first self-initiated interaction with the object world. The visual tracking that follows from movement-activated interest contributes to the development of depth perception and spatial relations.

The interest expression is also capable of motivating behavior in the perceiver. The increased alertness in the face of the infant tends to engage the caregiver's own interest in the baby and in the baby's activities.

In summary, the emotions present at birth play an important role in the survival and the well-being of the infant, primarily through the power of the emotion expressions to attract attention and motivate helping behavior and social interchange. The neonatal smile and the interest expression motivate positive social responses from the caregiver and others in the environment. Interest plays another important role by beginning to engage the infant in the object world and the physical environment.

Positive Emotions Facilitate Infant–Environment Interactions

Beginning in the second month of life, a social stimulus—a high-pitched voice—elicits a smile. At about 2½ months, the human face becomes a highly effective stimulus for eliciting the smile. As suggested by Spitz (1965) and Emde et al. (1976), the advent of the social smile signals a "biobehavioral shift," a shift to a different and more complex level of consciousness and behavior. Perhaps the principal function of the social smile is that of inviting continued social stimulation and the strengthening of interpersonal affective bonds. The social smile operates more to bond the caregiver to the infant than vice versa. The social smile functions virtually indiscriminately for a month or two, suggesting that the infant has not fully discriminated the mother from other people and hence smiles at one face as readily as another.

Strengthening the mother's emotional tie to the infant is certainly one of the adaptive functions of the social smile. The fact that the smile is not discriminatory may also be adaptive in that it invites care and attention from anyone who can attend. Also from an evolutionary-biological perspective, the positive affective interchanges initiated by the social smile help provide the infant with more opportunities for establishing an effective infant–caregiver relationship independent of any one person.

During this period, the emotion of interest increases in maturity and plays an increasingly important role in the life of the infant. The infant has longer periods of alertness, during which interest focuses and sustains attention to visual and auditory stimuli and facilitates visual, tactual, and manual exploration.

Emotions Facilitate Differentiation of Self and Others

Although the precess of self–other differentiation has beginnings in earlier periods (Lewis, 1976; Lewis & Brooks, this volume), the process is enhanced by the strengthening of interest and the emergence of two new emotions, shyness and anger, each of which relates in a particular way to the developing sense of self. Piaget and Inhelder (1969) maintain that with the differentiation between self and other, the differentiated self becomes affectively attached to things by virtue of "interest" and to other persons through "interpersonal feelings."

Shame and Shyness

As Tomkins (1963) has suggested, shame or shyness can occur at any time after the infant has the capacity to discriminate self from other and familiar person from strange person. Shyness at this level of development is a sensing or experiencing of a difference between a self–familiar-person relationship and a self–strange-person relationship. That is, an infant relates to a familiar loved one and experiences positive emotions of interest and joy, but the overture of a stranger may not provide the infant with the usual cues and thus may create in the infant some feeling of awkwardness or ineptness, the rudiments of the shame experience. The heightened consciousness of self that occurs in shame has motivational value for developing self-identify and self-esteem. Eventually, shame anticipation motivates the development of skills and competences that increase self-worth and decrease the likelihood of experiencing shame.

Anger, Disgust, and Contempt

The emergence of anger marks the transition of the baby from one who deals with troubles and frustrations primarily through use of the distress cry to obtain help from others to one who may add to a distress–anger cry a determined effort to remove or change the frustrating condition. Between 4 and 6 months, the infant is capable of experiencing and expressing anger, and the anger experience motivates efforts to deal with frustrating restraints and barriers. Thus anger increases the infant's opportunities to sense self-as-causal-agent and hence to experience self as separate, distinct, and capable. As Yarrow (1972) noted, "The differentiation of self from environment is partly dependent on the child's awareness that he can have an effect on the environment" (pp. 92–93).

During this period, the rudiments of contempt may emerge on occasions when the infant "triumphs" over a restraint or barrier. The full-blown experience and expression of contempt in relation to others come later.

During this period, the expression of disgust, which may be seen in the first days of life in response to distasteful substances, may be seen in response to other kinds of stimuli. That is, disgust becomes more of a psychological and somewhat less of a biological reaction.

In summarizing the important developments at this level, we see two quite different kinds of emotions emerging. There is shame or shyness, on the one hand, that initially motivates a turning away from the emotion-eliciting source and a turning inward on the self. On the other hand, the emergence of anger, disgust, and contempt motivates and directs and effort against the emotion-eliciting source. Shame and shyness facilitate the development of self-awareness and an increased understanding of self and its limitations, and they motivate efforts to develop skills and competences that increase the shame threshold. Anger and disgust contribute to self-development through increasing the infant's sense of self-control and self-determination in the face of frustrating or distasteful situations.

Emotions Facilitate an Expanding Sphere of Activity

Beginning around the age of 5 months, the emotion of interest–excitement begins to play an increasingly significant role in the infant's development. The neural mechanisms underlying the emotion of interest have now achieved a level of maturation that enables interest to initiate and sustain sensory and motor processes that lead to a wide variety of receptor inputs. It is during this stage that Piaget (1952) describes activity "to make interesting spectacles last" and that Hunt (1965) describes the development of intrinsic motivation, during which infants begin acting to regain perceptual contact. The infant's efforts to regain perceptual contact or to make interesting things last increase the duration of the infant's contact with persons and objects in the environment.

The increased amount of contact with specific persons and things initiated and sustained by the positive emotion of interest is a fundamental aspect of the phenomenon of emotion attachment. The processes whereby novel, strange, and undifferentiated inputs become familiar and differentiated percepts lead to "recognitive familiarity" (Hunt, 1965), and the emotion of joy that results from the recognitive familiarity adds the other important positive emotion-motivational force in the development and maintenance of emotion attachments.

During this period, healthy infant development depends upon opportunities to act on the increasingly strong motivational impact of the developing emotion of interest. Varying the infant's environment, providing a variety of playthings, and providing the opportunity for sustained face-to-face human interactions are critical. The infant now has an increased capability of initiating and sustaining sensorimotor activities, and healthy development requires that the infant be given varied opportunities to alter and change sources of stimulation (information input). As Hunt (1965) put it; "Although hunger and thirst are of the essence for survival, opportunities for such informational interaction are very likely of the essence for *interest* in objects, persons, and places" (p. 234, italics added).

Although surprise or startle as a reaction to sudden change in stimulation may be present in earlier stages, it is at this level that the infant can experience surprise as a result of violation of its own hypotheses or expectations. Charlesworth (1969) has made a strong case for the proposition that this type of incentive event–surprise sequence plays an important role in cognitive development. Surprise in this context "illuminates and reinforces" a variety of responses that contribute to changes in cognitive structures. Surprise also increases arousal, which can amplify subsequent interest in the object or the process that elicited surprise.

We now have the basis for complex emotion–perception–cognition–action sequences of a positive nature: perception of the novel activates interest, interest motivates exploration, exploration leads to surprise, surprise interacts with interest to heighten attention, and further exploration, familiarization, or mastery leads to joy. The significance of such sequences for the integration of the infant's personality subsystems is apparent.

Emotions Facilitate Self-Cognitions and Self-Control

In the early stages of development, the infant's sense of self is based on coenesthesis, the bodily sense of me (Allport, 1955). This bodily me is a function the stream of sensations arising from any neurophysiological process (e.g., drive state) capable of achieving awareness. As Allport pointed out, while this bodily sense "remains a life-long anchor for our self awareness," it provides only the biological or life-process background for the total concept of self.

It is not until some time after the infant has begun the process of differentiating self from other that noncoenesthetic self-perceptions and self-cognitions begin. Virtually all of the emotions play some role in the self-related perceptions and cognitions that lead to self-concept or self-identity and self-control. Interest and joy motivate activites that lead to a sense of positive relatedness to persons and things and to one's world. Distress provides the first opportunity for the infant to begin sensing self-as-agent. Anger and disgust provide motivation for activities that strengthen the sense of self-as-agent capable of altering the relationship of self to source of stimulation. Surprise facilitates the development of the sense of self as affected by sudden, unexpected (or misexpected) changes occurring in the environment.

Two new emotions emerge during this period and play a critical role in facilitating the development of self-cognitions and self-control. Fear begins to emerge sometime during the latter half of the first year of life, and the emotion of guilt as a distinct experience in consciousness and as cause of recognizable guilt-related behavior emerges sometime in the second year. The emotions of fear and guilt have in common the fact that both are associated with the establishing of behavioral limits. Both are associated with the learning of a complex set of prohibitions, or to put it more positively, these emotions motivate actions that contribute to the physical safety and psychological integrity of the individual.

Fear

The emergence of fear, like the emergence of each of the other emotions, marks the beginning or sets the stage for a kind of "critical period," an optimal time for a highly important set of learnings. The socialization and learning processes that occur in relation to fear dramatize the fact that socialization and learning processes have been occurring in relation to each of the other emotions.

Fear is the ultimate reminder of the vulnerability of the bodily and psychological self. Fear motivates escape from harm and danger. The escape may take the form of "flight to one another" (Eibl-Eibesfeldt, 1971) for mutual defense and protection. This flight to other is first seen in caregiver–infant separation, where fear or fear anticipation motivates proximity-maintaining behavior that serves to strengthen emotion attachment. The developmental process whereby fear comes to serve adaptive functions is aptly described by Rosenblum (this volume) as fear in the infant's taking over some of the protective functions of the mother.

The fear experience is the experience of self endangered, and fear anticipation motivates cognitions relating to self-defense or self-protection. All of these phenomena play a role in the development of self-awareness. In particular, fear generates cognitions about self as affected by dangerous or threatening situations.

Guilt

Guilt, on the other hand, motivates cognitions about self-initiated actions that cause harm to others. Guilt plays an important role in the development of self-responsibility, and it is the principal experiential motivational factor in the mature conscience.

Thus fear and guilt play distinct but complementary roles in the development of self-cognitions and self-control. Fear motivates cognition and action strategies that enable the self to navigate the world in such a way as to minimize harm and danger. Guilt, on the other hand, motivates conceptions of self and cognitive and action strategies that help maintain self-integrity and the integrity of self–other relations.

It is reasonable that a sense of self-as-causal-agent would precede the capacity to experience the emotion of guilt. Guilt involves a sense of feeling responsible for one's actions and an ability to sense that one's actions have brought psychological or physical harm to another.

Hoffman (this volume) notes that empathic distress may be transformed into a feeling of guilt by the attribution of self-blame. Hoffman's discussions of the development of empathy and sympathy and the process whereby thwarted altruistic activity may produce guilt suggest that this emotion may be experienced in some form as early as the latter part of the first year of life. Radke-Yarrow (1977) has considerable data that suggest that guilt experience occurs with some frequency during the second year of life.

Emotions and Self-Recognition

Evidence presented by Brooks and Lewis (this volume) suggests that an important new type of emotion–cognition interaction emerges at about 15–18 months of age, when the child becomes capable of visual self-recognition. Their data suggest that negative emotion often occurs when a child recognizes self in the mirror and sees a smear of rouge on the nose. Casual observation of some of these responses on videotape led me to speculate that the negative emotion was shame, which since Darwin (1872) has been described in terms of a heightened awareness of self (H. Lewis, 1971; Lynd, 1961; Tomkins, 1963).

Although the infant may experience an incipient form of shame or shyness any time after the first self–other discrimination (that between infant and primary caregiver), a more differentiated experience of shame and shyness emerges with the sharper demarcations of the boundaries of the self that begin developing around 8–9 months of age and increase rapidly in the second year.

The data of Brooks and Lewis (this volume) suggest that the emergence of visual self-recognition (an indicator of increased capacity for self-awareness) during the second year of life greatly extends the variety of shame elicitors and probably leads to an intensification of shame–shyness responses. This observation suggests that the infant's second year of life is critical for developing healthy social relationships, for differentiating various social roles, and for learning appropriate responses to each of them. It is probably the infant's "failures" or social ineptitudes during this sensitive period of social development that provide the basis for the frequent observation that shyness and timidity characterize 2-year-olds (Shirley, 1933, as cited in Kagan, 1976).

The juxtaposition of shame and the capacity to store a self-image in memory probably mark another highly important period for the development of affective–cognitive structures. This increase in the stability of the self-image facilitates the interactions of self-related emotion experiences and self-related cognitions. Such interactions lead to the network of affective–cognitive structures and orientations that produce the self-concept. As Provence (this volume) puts it, shame can also mobilize adaptive responses that assist the child in the development of impulse control, which in turn enhances the self and the self-concept.

Emotions Interact with Cognitions to Form Affective–Cognitive Structures

Although in the early days, the infant has a relatively high threshold for external stimulation, in the alert–active state the emotion of interest is capable of focusing and sustaining attention and of making a rudimentary beginning in the development of object percepts. In the first weeks of life, an important function of emotion is to amplify drive signals and communicate them to the social surround, but beginning in the second month, the emotions begin to take their place as the primary motivational system. The increasing duration of alert–active states and the further maturation of the interest emotion mark the transition from dominance of the sensory–affective processes of consciousness to a period when consciousness is more influenced by affective–perceptual processes.

Beginning about the last quarter of the first year and continuing through the second, increased differentiations of self and other, the sharpening of self-awareness and the self-concept, and the ability to form and store memories enable the infant to begin the development of affective–cognitive structures, the linking or bonding of particular affects or patterns of affects with images and symbols, including words and ideas. The type of affect or emotion associated with a particular concept or cognition determines the motivational characteristics of a given affective–cognitive structure. Each affective–cognitive structure, therefore, has motivational properties as distinct and as complex as the associated emotions.

Since there is essentially an infinite variety of emotion–symbol interactions, affective–cognitive structures are far and away the predominant motivational features in consciousness soon after the acquisition of language. What I am calling an *affective–cognitive structure* here is similar in some ways to what Kagan has defined as a *motive* and not unlike Katz and Stotland's (1959) classical definition of *attitude*. Although Kagan's concept of *motive* emphasizes the cognitive process, he has implied that there is an affective underpinning. The Katz–Stotland definition of attitude clearly includes affective and cognitive components and a behavioral tendency.

Developmental Changes in Specific Emotions and Emotion–Cognition Interactions

In discussing landmarks of emotion development and some aspects of self-awareness, self-cognition, and learning associated with them, I suggested that not only did emotions emerge at different times during the first two years of life but that a given emotion experience becomes increasingly organized and centered during the first two years of life. The experiential component of an emotion present at birth achieves considerable organizational stability and centeredness by the age of 6–9 months. Fear may be relatively centered by the end of the first year, and the last emotions to emerge—contempt, fear, shame, and guilt—reach this level of phenomenological organization toward the end of the second year.

The developmental change in emotion experience that I am describing is not a change in the quality of the phenomenon in consciousness. The invariance of the phenomenological components of the fundamental emotions provides an essential continuity in consciousness and in organism–environment interchanges. The change is one of decreasing diffuseness of the experience of a given emotion—for example, the change from diffuse distress that totally dominates the 2-month-old during acute pain following inoculation to the more organized and centered distress experience of the 6-month-old in the same situation. In general, the greater the organization and centeredness of the emotion experience, the less diffuse and dominant it is in consciousness. That is, the organized, specific emotion experience allows for concomitant cognitive processes in consciousness that increase the infant's ability to act appropriately and to cope with the situation. While the acutely pained 2-month-old can only emit the distress cry, the 6-month-old can turn from the source of pain to the mother and initiate comforting behavior.

In addition to developmental changes in phenomenological organization, numerous changes occur in the kinds of percepts, images, and cognitions that are associated with a given emotion experience. Since what we usually measure through self-report techniques is a function of the images, thoughts, and actions associated with a particular emotion, it is possible to develop relatively independent measures of different affective–cognitive structures and emotion–cognition orientations. This is what Mosher (1978) did when he developed reliable measures of three types of guilt or, more precisely, three different types of guilt–cognition orientations: guilt associated with sexual imagery, thoughts, and behavior; guilt associated with aggressive imagery, thoughts, and behavior; and guilt associated with such things as lying, cheating, and stealing. I assume that the quality of the emotion experience of guilt is the same in each of these types, although the associated cognitions and actions differ widely.

Development Changes in Joy

Since I hold that the essential prerequisite for emotion activation is sensory feedback from patterned facial movements and the subsequent integration of these data by the brain, I infer at least a rudimentary or diffuse form of enjoyment from the neonatal smile. Although the events or conditions that trigger the neonatal smile remain undetermined, the underlying neurophysiological processes seem to be consonant with positive hedonic tone (Emde, Gaensbauer, & Harmon, 1976). There is no evidence that the neonatal smile appears during high drive states, distress, or other negative emotion. Even the seemingly meaningless neonatal smile probably has a generally positive effect on parents and caregivers.

Beginning at about 4 weeks of age, a high-pitched human voice serves as an effective stimulus for a smile. In a sense, this is a social smile, in that the stimulus is social in nature. At this stage, the increased vocal and motor responses and general positive-affective animation of the infant more clearly suggest an underlying motivational experience that we can call *enjoyment*. At about 2½ months of age, the human face moving toward the face of the infant elicits the smile, and this incentive event is effective for the next couple of months. This is what has been typically called the *social smile* because the stimulus event is clearly social in nature and involves face-to-face interaction. Enjoyment, at least on the part of the parent or caregiver, is now clearly evident, and signs of enjoyment and joy in the infant are more readily and easily inferred by other observers. The smile elicited by the high-pitched human voice and the human face tends to increase the positive-affective interchanges between infant and primary caregiver and between infant and the social surround in general. The infant's need for positive-affective interchange during this stage is suggested by the fact that the infant responds with a smile to any moving face, whether of principal caregiver or stranger.

At around 4 months of age, the infant engages in true social smiling. That is, it smiles differentially at familiar and unfamiliar persons. The most outstanding motivational consequence of this development is the beginning of the infant's attachment to the mother or caregiver.

Beginning somewhere around the middle of the first year of life, the image or memory of the mother or of a familiar person may trigger enjoyment and the smile of joy. This perceptual–cognitive development along with accompanying affective–cognitive changes greatly strengthens the attachment process. The next step occurs when anticipation of the mother's presence elicits the smile of joy, and this development facilitates the growth of courage, since it increases the infant's ability to tolerate the mother's absence.

Somewhere around the last quarter of the first year of life, the sudden disappearance and reappearance of a familiar human face (the game of peekaboo) often elicits smiling and laughing. The adaptive function of laughter (as pointed out by Sroufe & Wunsch, 1972; Rothbart, 1973) is twofold. First, the infant's laughter tends to sustain the game and the interaction between mother and infant. Second, laughter games provide the infant with positive-affective experiences in relation to new or changing events in the environment.

Ultimately, sustained creative activity may lead to an insight or discovery that attenuates the underlying motivating excitement and triggers the experience of joy. The adaptive effects of joy here are to provide a recuperative phase, a momentary relief from the high excitement of sustained creativity. In addition to its recuperative function, this change of pace resulting from the joy experience also provides a change of perspective that may facilitate a new creative surge, and the cycle repeats itself.

It must be clear from this brief sketch of developmental changes in the joy-related phenomena that any attempt at a taxonomy of incentive events as suggested by Kagan (this volume) needs to be carefully linked to the developmental stage of the person. From the foregoing sketch, it can be seen that the human face as an incentive event is quite different at age 3 months and at age 6 months. The smile of the 2½-month-old at the moving human face may be the precursor of what Kagan (1971) has called the *smile of assimilation*. The true social smile that is elicited by a face-discriminated-as-mother or as-familiar-person is the result of re-cognitive familiarity. Smiling in response to a mental image of the mother and the ability to experience joy in anticipation of a parent or caregiver involves complex cognitive processes that include storage and retrieval of information.

Developmental Changes in Distress

As with joy, there is continuity in the distress experience through the life span, but the incentive events and the emotion-related be-havioral consequences change with maturation and development. In the first couple of months of life, high drive states (hunger, thirst, pain) are the principal activators of distress. Simner (1971) and Sagi and Hoffman (1976) found that the distress cry of another infant also elicits distress, and Hoffman (1975, this volume) suggests that this may be the funda-ment of empathic distress and sympathy. Somewhere around the end of the first year of life or sometime in the second, the distress expression of a playmate or a parent can elicit empathic distress in the child, and the motivational consequences may include efforts that can be interpreted as altruistic in nature (Hoffman, this volume; Radke-Yarrow, 1977).

Between 4 and 6 months of age, separation of the infant from the principal caregiver can elicit distress. The distress cry now has a different function, that of maintaining the proximity of infant and significant other. This distress cry is not simply a cry for help based on negative affect; it is more an appeal for continued positive social interaction. Sometime in the latter half of the first year of life, strange-ness (see Lewis and Rosenblum, 1974) and heights (e.g. Campos *et al.*, this volume) may elicit distress (or fear or both), and the behavioral consequence is a sort of vigilance and motivation in the infant to seek the comfort of proximity to a familiar person.

Looked at another way, "strangeness" is processed differently as maturation and experience change emotion–perception–cognition in-teractions. Strangeness may first be perceived as novelty and result in interest or surprise or both, depending upon the suddenness and intensity of the strange or novel event. Later, depending on the context and the level of development, strangeness may elicit distress or fear, depending upon how it is processed and depending upon the cognitive associations. The specific emotion elicited by strangeness varies with (1) the quantity and quality of information processed, a function of perceptual and cognitive development; (2) the maturational–developmental stage of the motor system, which helps set the limits of adaptive responses; and (3) the maturational and developmental stage of the emotion system, which limits the alternatives among emotional–motivational conditions.

Thus, as in the case of the human face, "strangeness" as an incentive event is different for the 4-, the 8-, and the 12-month-old infant. The "causes of emotion" have to be considered at four different levels.

1. At the neural level, the concern is with the effect of the incentive event on the nervous system. Tomkins (1962) has explained emotion activation in terms of changes in density of neural firing, and Singer (1974) has translated Tomkins's terms into the language of information theory and described emotion activation in terms of the relative assimilability or unassimilability of information. Both conceptualizations seem useful, as well as the idea that receptors' organizational functions and differential selectivity change with development and contribute to the activation of different emotions (Izard, 1971, 1977).

2. At the perceptual level, the concern is with what is perceived, the object–percept or image. The appraisal processes as described by Arnold (1960) and Lazarus and Averill (1972) are operative here.

3. At the cognitive–interpretive level, the concern is with the imagery and symbolizations that are associated with the emotion in consciousness.

4. At the contextual level, the concern is with the effects of context on perception and the cognitive–interpretive process, which in turn trigger neural activity that activates a specific emotion or pattern of emotions.

The processes at the neural level are unconscious and automatic. The processes at the other levels typically achieve awareness and are therefore subject to the influence of other ongoing processes in consciousness.

Developmental Changes in Responses to Acute Pain

Differential emotions theory (Izard, 1977) conceives of pain not as an emotion but as an affective process that has some of the characteristics of emotion and some of the characteristics of drives. Common observation, as well as experimental literature, shows that pain typically recruits an emotion, which in turn influences subsequent behavior.

A study of infants' responses to inoculations currently underway at a Delaware Public Health Clinic is providing an opportunity to see developmental changes in responses to acute pain. In the regular immunization program, infants are inoculated at approximately 2, 4, 6, and 15 months of age. Video–audio tape recordings are being made of the infant's as well as the mother's response to the infant's pain–emotion reactions and of the infant's response to mother, nurse, and needle.

Our preliminary observations suggest that 2-, 4-, and 6-month-old infants do not perceive the needle as a threatening object or the nurse as an agent of pain. The facial expression following the inoculation appears to be that of the emotion of distress. After the mother has calmed the baby and obtained a smiling response, the nurse has no difficulty in eliciting a smile and in taking the baby.

Possibly as early as age 4 months in some infants and at age 6 months in others, the acute pain may elicit an anger response, as well as distress. Both pain and distress can activate anger, and once activated, anger alters the infant's behavior to some extent. Anger cannot alter the infant's behavior very much at 4 or 6 months, since the infant has a limited anger-related response repertoire and because the infant cannot comprehend the situation and direct appropriate responses.

Beginning in a few infants as early as 6–8 months, and in a substantial proportion at 12 months, perceptual–cognitive processes alter the pain–emotion–behavior sequence. The preparation of the arm for the inoculation and the approaching needle may elicit fear, which may in turn amplify the pain and the subsequent distress. The needle may now be perceived as a threatening object and the nurse as an agent of harm. In some cases, the inoculation elicits a combination of fear, distress, and anger. Such infants now cringe at the sight of the needle, respond unfavorably to the nurse's effort to engage them in play, and refuse to allow the nurse to take them.

The changes in pain–emotion–behavior sequences in response to a "standard" stimulus for pain (inoculation) again illustrate the relativity of the concept of incentive event. In this case, it is quite easy to observe clear differences in pain–emotion–action sequences that are a function both of the maturation of emotion mechanisms and of developmental changes in the perceptual, cognitive, and motor systems.

SUMMARY

The emotions and the emotion system develop in relationship to the other personality subsystems, and infant development may be viewed as the process whereby the various subsystems become effectively organized and interact harmoniously to produce integrated behavior. Genetically encoded programs guarantee a minimal set of adaptive subsystem and infant–environment interactions, and many of these are mediated by the emotions. However, conditioning and social learning quickly become influential in relating subsystems to each other and the infant to the social and physical world.

The conceptual framework for this paper is differential emotions theory, and several of its key assumptions and definitions are briefly summarized. Four of these assumptions are of special importance here: (1) the emotions emerge as they become adaptive in the life of the infant and in the infant–caregiver and infant–environment relationship; (2) each emotion adds to the complexity of consciousness, increases the capacity for processing and responding to different types of information, and increases the individual's capacity to respond appropriately to a broader set of contingencies; (3) each emotion has a public aspect (facial expression), which provides social signals of great importance in the infant–caregiver relationship; and (4) each emotion helps set the stage for a particular type of learning and development.

While the ontogenesis of the emotions proper is mainly a function of age-related biological changes, the development of affective–cognitive structures is primarily a function of ecological variables and learning. The emergence of different emotions and parallel developments in the perceptual and cognitive systems foster an increasing complexity of consciousness that eventually organizes and interrelates sensory–affective, affective–perceptual, and affective–cognitive processes.

The emotions present at birth play a vital role in the survival and the healthy development of the neonate. Of particular importance are distress, whose expression is a peremptory signal for help, and interest, which motivates exploratory activity. Beginning as early as the second month, the positive emotions take on an increased capacity to facilitate infant–environment interactions and positive affective interchange.

Two contrasting groups of emotions play a special role in the differentiation of self and others. Shame and shyness, which initially motivate turning away from the emotion-eliciting source and inward upon the self, eventually facilitate the development of self-awareness, an increased understanding of self, and the development of skills and competences. Anger and disgust contribute to self-development by increasing the infant's sense of self-control and self-determination in the face of frustrating and distasteful situations.

In the second half-year of life, interest and enjoyment increase in intensity and are activated by a much wider range of incentive events. The infant is now capable of complex emotion–perception–cognition–

action sequences of a positive nature, and such sequences are highly important to the integration of the infant's personality subsystems.

New emotions emerge to play a critical role in facilitating the development of self-cognitions and self-control. Fear, which sets the stage for a highly important set of learnings, is the ultimate reminder of the vulnerability of the self. Thus, it helps set the limits or boundaries of the self and of self-initiated action. Guilt motivates cognitions about self-initiated actions that cause harm to others and plays an important role in the development of self-responsibility.

The emotions play a part in the development of self-recognition and the self-concept, and self-related cognition in turn influences emotion responses and emotion–behavior sequences. There are important relationships between self-recognition and the self-concept on the one hand and the emotions of contempt, fear, shame, and guilt on the other. Of great importance to social and emotion development and to the personality as a whole are the interactions that produce affective–cognitive structures, each of which has distinct motivational properties. After the development of memory and the capacity for symbolization, affective–cognitive structures become the predominant motivational features in consciousness.

Emotion development includes not only the emergence of different emotions but changes within a given emotion. While the experiential quality of a particular emotion is invariant over the life span, each of the emotions becomes increasingly organized and centered during the first two years of life. As an emotion reaches a higher level of phenomenological organization, emotion experience becomes less dominant in consciousness, and the resulting increase in freedom of operations in consciousness facilitates emotion–cognition interactions and the development of affective–cognitive structures.

References

Allport, G. W. *Becoming: Basic considerations for a psychology of personality*. New Haven: Yale University Press, 1955.

Arnold, M. B. *Emotion and personality: Psychological aspects* (Vol. 1). New York: Columbia University Press, 1960.

Bowlby, J. *Attachment and loss: Separation, anxiety, and anger* (Vol. 2). New York: Basic Books, 1973.

Charlesworth, W. The role of surprise in cognitive development. In D. Elkind & J. Flavell (Eds.), *Studies in cognitive development*. London: Oxford University Press, 1969.

Darwin, C. R. *The expression of emotions in man and animals*. London: John Murray, 1872.

Eibl-Eibesfeldt, I. *Love and hate: The natural history of behavior patterns*. New York: Holt, Rinehart, and Winston, 1971.

Emde, R. N., Gaensbauer, T. J., & Harmon, R. J. *Emotional expression in infancy*. New York: International Universities Press, 1976.

Flavell, J. H. Stage-related properties of cognitive development. *Cognitive Psychology*, 1971, 2, 421–453.

Greenberg, D. J. Visual attention in infancy: Processes, methods, and clinical applications. In I. C. Uzgiris & F. Weizmann (Eds.), *The structuring of experience*. New York: Plenum Press, 1977.

Hoffman, M. L. Developmental synthesis of affect and cognition and its implications for altruistic motivation. *Developmental Psychology*, 1975, 11, 607–622.

Hunt, J. McV. Intrinsic motivation and its role in development. In D. Levine (Ed.), *Nebraska Symposium on Motivation* (Vol. 13). Lincoln: University of Nebraska Press, 1965, pp. 189–282.

Izard, C. E. Positive affect and behavioral effectiveness. Unpublished manuscript, Vanderbilt University, 1959.

Izard, C. E. *The face of emotion*. New York: Appleton-Century-Crofts, 1971.

Izard, C. E. *Patterns of emotions: A new analysis of anxiety and depression*. New York: Academic Press, 1972.

Izard, C. E. *Human emotions*. New York: Plenum Press, 1977.

Izard, C. E. The emergence of emotions and the development of consciousness in infants. In J., Davidson, R. J. Davidson, & G. E. Schwartz, (Eds.), *Human consciousness and its transformations: A psychobiological perspective*. New York: Plenum Press, 1978, in press.

Izard, C. E., & Tomkins, S. S. Affect and behavior: Anxiety as a negative effect. In C. D. Spielberger (Ed.), *Anxiety and behavior*. New York: Academic Press, 1966.

Kagan, J. *Change and continuity in infancy*. New York: Wiley, 1971.

Kagan, J. Emergent themes in human development. *American Scientists*, 1976, 64, 186–196.

Katz, D., & Stotland, E. A preliminary statement to a theory of attitude structure and change. In S. Koch (Ed.), *Psychology: A study of a science* (Vol. 3). New York: McGraw-Hill, 1959.

Kleck, R. E., Vaughan, R., Colby, C., Cartwright-Smith, J. E., Vaughan, K., & Lanzetta, J. T. Effects of being observed on expressive, subjective, and physiological responses to painful stimuli. *Journal of Personality and Social Psychology*, in press.

Lanzetta, J. T., Cartwright-Smith, J. E., & Kleck, R. E. Effects of nonverbal dissimulation on emotional experience and autonomic arousal. *Journal of Personality and Social Pscyhology*, 1976, 33, 354–370.

Lazarus, R. S., & Averill, J. R. Emotion and cognition: With special reference to anxiety. In C. D. Spielberger (Ed.), *Anxiety: Contemporary theory and research*. New York: Academic Press, 1972.

Lewis, H. *Shame and guilt neurosis*. New York: International Universities Press, 1971.

Lewis, M. The origins of self competence. Paper presented at the NIMH Conference on Mood Development, Washington, D. C., November 1976.

Lewis, M. & Rosenblum, L. A. (Eds.), *The Origins of Fear*. New York: Wiley, 1974.

Lynd, H. M. *On shame and the search for identity*. New York: Science Editions, 1961.

Mosher, D. L. The meaning and measurement of guilt. In C. E. Izard (Ed.), *Emotions and psychopathology*. New York: Plenum Press, 1978.

Piaget, J. *The origins of intelligence in children*. New York: International Universities Press, 1952.

Piaget, J., & Inhelder, B. *The psychology of the child*. New York: Basic Books, 1969.

Radke-Yarrow, M. Presentation to Social Science Research Council Committee on Social and Emotional Development, Cambridge, Mass., March 1977.

Rothbart, M. K. Laughter in young children. *Psychological Bulletin*, 1973, 80, 247–256.

Sagi, A., & Hoffman, M. L. Empathic distress in the newborn. *Developmental Psychology*, 1976, 12, 175–176.

Shirley, M. M. *The first two years: A study of 25 babies* (Vol. 2). Institute of Child Welfare Monograph Series, No. 7. Minneapolis: University of Minneapolis Press, 1933. (Cited in Kagan, 1976.)

Simner, M. L. Newborn's response to the cry of another infant. *Developmental Psychology,* 1971, *5*(1), 136–150.

Singer, J. L. *Imagery and daydream methods in psychotherapy and behavior modification*. New York: Academic Press, 1974.

Spitz, R. A. *The first year of life*. New York: International Universities Press, 1965.

Sroufe, L. A. Emotional expression in infancy. Unpublished manuscript, 1976.

Sroufe, L. A., & Wunsch, J. P. The development of laughter in the first years of life. *Child Development*, 1972, *43*, 1326–1344.

Tomkins, S. S. *Affect, imagery, consciousness: The positive affects* (Vol. 1). New York: Springer, 1962.

Tomkins, S. S. *Affect, imagery, consciousness: The negative affects* (Vol. 2). New York: Springer, 1963.

Yarrow, L. J. Attachment and dependency: A developmental perspective. In J. Gewirtz (Ed.), *Attachment and dependency*. Washington, D.C.. Winston, 1972, pp. 81–96.

Author Index

Italic numbers indicate pages where complete reference citations are given.

Abelson, R. P., 136, 145
Adamson, L., 51, 73
Aderman, D., 237, 253
Ainsworth, M., 56, 73,
   149, 173, 179, 182,
   195, 198, 199, 200,
   310, 347
Albertini, B. von, 183, 203
Alcock, J., 72, 73
Allport, F. H., 49, 73
Allport, G. W., 400, 411
Alpert, S., 280, 292
Als, H., 51, 73, 80, 120
Alstatt, L., 249, 255
Altmann, S. A., 49, 73
Amatruda, C., 142, 146
Ambrose, A., 185, 200
Ambrose, J. A., 86, 120
Amsterdam, B. K., 214,
   224
Anderson, D., 154, 179
Anthony, E., 297, 306
Anthony, J., 187
Appel, M., 152, 179
April, C., 369, 373
Aquinas, T., 21, 22, 23, 26,
   40
Archimedes, 261
Argyle, M., 80, 120, 368,
   373
Aristotle, 20, 21, 23, 26,
   34, 40
Arling, G. L., 263, 274

Arnold, M. B., 141, 144,
   145, 341, 347, 408,
   411
Aronfreed, J., 230, 253
Averill, J. R., 408, 412
Ax, A., 154, 179
Axelrod, J., 334, 343, 347,
   350

Bachas, J. D., 83, 121
Bacon, F., 23, 40
Baisel, E., 88, 122, 153,
   182, 312, 334, 349
Baldwin, J. M., 190, 200,
   293, 306
Ball, W., 175, 179, 192,
   200, 312, 313, 329,
   347
Bandura, H., 228, 237, 253
Bard, P., 81, 120, 207, 224
Bateman, D. E., 81, 121
Bayley, N., 81, 120, 142,
   145, 156, 179, 356,
   360
Bechtold, A. G., 172, 182,
   312, 350
Beebe, B., 70, 75
Beebe-Center, J. C., 20, 40
Beintema, D., 321, 349
Bell, C., 56, 73
Bell, S., 56, 73, 197, 198,
   200

Belmont, J. H., 312, 347
Benedek, T., 296, 306
Benjamin, J., 293, 296, 306,
   307
Bennett, S. L., 70, 75
Berger, S. M., 228, 232,
   254
Bergstrom, R. M., 142, 145
Berkowitz, L., 273, 273
Berlyne, D. E., 341, 347
Bernal, G., 232, 254
Beveridge, W. I. B., 43, 73
Birch, H. G., 334, 347
Bless, E., 252, 254
Bleuler, E., 311, 348
Bloom, L., 210, 225
Blurton, L. B., 233, 254
Blurton-Jones, N. G., 44,
   73, 86, 93, 120, 265,
   273, 367, 368, 373
Bodmer, W. F., 312, 348
Bond, E., 152, 180
Borke, H., 241, 254
Borton, R., 197, 202
Bower, T. G. R., 153, 175,
   180, 190, 191, 192,
   193, 197, 200, 312,
   313, 329, 345, 348
Bowlby, J., 35, 40, 150,
   173, 180, 194, 200,
   297, 307, 310, 348,
   392, 411
Boyer, J. L., 249, 255

415

Brady, J. V., 154, *179*
Brannigan, C. R., 44, 45,
  46, 53, *73*
Brazelton, T. B., 51, 56, *73*,
  86, *120*, 139, *145*, 368,
  373
Bregman, A., *307*, 382, *387*
Brehm, S. S., 237, *253*
Bridges, K. M. B., 68, *73*,
  85, 86, 87, 93, *120*,
  126, 142, *146*, 172,
  180, 189, 200, 250,
  254
Bringuier, J. P., 189, *200*
Bronson, G. W., 87, *120*,
  143, *146*, 171, *180*,
  331, *348*, 385, *387*
Brooks, J., **77–123, 205–**
  226, 49, 72, 86, 87, 90,
  92, 104, 119, *120*, *122*,
  197, *201*, 207, 210,
  213, 214, 215, 216,
  220, 221, *225*, *226*,
  361, 364, 379, 395,
  398, 402, 403
Brossard, M., 185, 194,
  200
Broughton, J., 153, 175,
  180, 192, 197, *200*,
  312, *348*
Brown, C., 353, 354, 357,
  360
Brown, J., 343, *349*
Brown, R., 210, *225*
Buchanan, W., 249, *255*
Buck, R., 84, 118, *120*
Buehler, 296
Bugenthal, D., 369, *373*
Burlingham, D., 297, *307*

Cadell, T. E., 276, *292*
Callender, W. M., 194, *203*
Campbell, H., 86, 88, *122*,
  246, *254*
Campos, J. J., **149–182**, 88,
  89, 90, 91, 93, 104,
  117, *120*, *122*, 142,
  144, *146*, 149, 151,
  152, 153, 154, 155,
  170, 171, 172, 173,
  179, *180*, *181*, *182*,

Campos (*cont.*)
  197, *201*, 312, 334,
  342, *349*, 361, 386,
  390, 407
Cannon, W. B., 22, 40, 78,
  120
Canon, L. K., 250, *255*
Carlson, V., 175, *180*
Caron, A., 175, *180*
Caron, R., 175, *180*
Carpenter, G., 70, 72, 74,
  127, *147*, 310, 311,
  349
Carr, V., 311, 317, *348*
Cartwright-Smith, J. E.,
  392, *412*
Casler, L., 185, *200*
Caul, W. F., 84, 118, *120*
Cavalli-Sforza, L. L., 312,
  348
Charette, J. M., 192, 193,
  200
Charlesworth, W. B., 87,
  120, 129, *146*, 170,
  180, 190, 191, *200*,
  367, *373*, 384, 385,
  387, 400, *411*
Chevalier-Skolnikoff, S.,
  86, *120*, 142, *146*
Cheyne, J. A., 53, *74*
Cicchetti, D., **309–350**,
  172, 175, *180*, 310,
  312, 313, 317, 319,
  321, 334, 336, 339,
  340, 343, 344, 345,
  348, *349*, 357, *360*,
  364, 390, 393
Claramontius, S., 23
Clark, D., 337, *349*
Clifton, R., 151, 154, *180*
Cobliner, W. C., 187, 194,
  201, 203
Colby, C., 392, *412*
Coleman, M., 317, *348*
Coller, A. R., 211, *225*
Condon, W., 368, *373*
Cooley, C. H., 211, *225*
Coombs, C. H., 81, *123*
Corbitt, J. D., 116, *123*,
  380, *387*
Cowie, V. A., 317, 344, *348*
Cross, H., 157, *182*

Crowell, D. H., 233, *254*
Crozier, W. J., *258*, 274
Curcio, F., 173, *181*, 194,
  202
Cytryn, L., *348*

Dannel, F., 368, *374*
Darby, B. L., 197, *202*
Darley, J. M., 249, *254*
Darwin, C. R., 25, 40, 49,
  70, 71, 74, 77, 78, 79,
  84, 85, 86, *120*, 127,
  146, 189, *201*, 206,
  225, 402, *411*
Davison, L., 237, *255*
Davitz, J., 367, *373*, *374*
Davitz, L., 367, *373*, *374*
Day, R., 157, 175, *180*, *181*
Decarie, T. G., **183–204**,
  44, *75*, 155, 173, *180*,
  181, 185, 194, 195,
  197, *200*, *201*, 203,
  296, *307*, 310, *348*,
  361, 362, 363, 393
Delorme, A., 192, 193, *200*
Descartes, R., 23, 24, 27,
  28, 34, 40
Deutsch, F., 369, *374*
Diamond, R., 176, *181*
Di Franco, D., 175, *180*,
  192, *201*
Ding, G., 367, *374*
Dittrichova, J., 355, *360*
Dodsworth, R. S., 263,
  272, *274*
Dodwell, P., 175, *180*, 192,
  201
Duchenne, G. B., 56, 57,
  74
Duffy, E., 377, *387*
Durkheim, 187
Dutch, S. J., 317, *349*

Eckerman, C. O., 87, 92,
  104, *122*, 154, 156,
  182, 195, *203*
Eibl-Eibesfeldt, I., 80, *120*,
  366, *374*, 401, *411*
Eisele, L., *258*, 274
Ekman, P., 27, 40, 44, 46,

Ekman/ (cont.)
47, 48, 49, 50, 56, 67,
69, 70, 71, 74, 79, 80,
83, 86, 121, 127, 128,
129, 136, 144, 146,
172, 180, 189, 201,
206, 225, 368, 370
374
Ellis, A., 363, 374
Ellsworth, P., 40, 127, 146,
172, 180, 189, 201
Emde, R. N., 125–148,
351–360, 56, 65, 68,
72, 74, 86, 89, 120,
121, 125, 128, 130,
141, 142, 143, 144,
146, 149, 155, 172,
173, 180, 181, 195,
201, 310, 345, 346,
348, 351, 352, 353,
354, 355, 357, 360,
361, 366, 367, 378,
394, 396, 397, 405,
412
Emerson, P. E., 149, 172,
182, 194, 203
Emmerich, W., 213, 225
Engel, G., 311, 348
Engen, R., 136, 146
Erikson, E., 126, 146, 187,
296, 307
Escalona, S., 299, 307, 310,
348
Evans, W. F., 197, 201

Fabre, J. H., 258, 274
Falek, A., 312, 349
Fernberger, S. W., 80, 121
Feshbach, N. D., 228, 241,
254
Fields, J., 157, 180
Fischer, K., 173, 181, 197,
201
Flavell, J. H., 368, 371, 374,
394, 412
Fox, M., 369, 373
Fox, M. W., 142, 146
Fraiberg, S., 173, 180, 187,
201, 346, 348
Frankel, D., 172, 182, 312,
350

Freedle, R., 86, 122, 212,
225
Freedman, D., 150, 158,
180
Freedman, J. L., 252, 254
Freidman, D. A., 346, 348
Freud, A., 293, 294, 296,
297, 307
Freud, S., 126, 135, 146,
185, 187, 208, 211
Friesen, W. V., 40, 44, 46,
47, 50, 70, 74, 79, 80,
83, 121, 127, 128, 144,
146, 172, 180, 189,
201, 368, 370, 374
Frijda, N., 136, 146

Gaebelein, C., 154, 181
Gaensbauer, T. J., 65, 74,
89, 120, 125, 142, 146,
149, 155, 172, 180,
195, 201, 310, 348,
351, 360, 394, 405,
412
Galen, 293
Gall, F. J., 26, 40
Galosy, R., 154, 181
Gardiner, H. M., 20, 40
Gardner, J. K., 197, 201
Gasser, R. F., 47, 74
Gates, G. S., 80, 121
Gelhorn, E., 232, 254
Gelman, R., 368, 375
Gesell, A. L., 142, 146
Gibson, D., 312, 348
Gibson, E., 150, 151, 153,
156, 161, 162, 180,
182, 312, 332, 348,
350
Gibson, J., 152, 181
Gladstone, W. H., 136, 146
Glucksberg, S., 368, 374
Goffman, E., 80, 121
Goldberg, S., 86, 87, 115,
121, 122, 384, 387
Goldman, K. S., 213, 225
Gordon, R., 172, 182, 312,
350
Goulet, J., 194, 201
Gower, E., 181
Graham, F. K., 88, 121,

Graham, (cont.)
151, 152, 154, 181
Grant, E. C., 44, 53, 74,
86, 93, 94, 121
Gratch, G., 192, 195, 197,
201
Green, R., 213, 225
Greenacre, P., 296, 307
Greenberg, D. J., 213, 225,
394, 412
Grice, D., 213, 225
Groos, K., 264, 274
Guilford, 33, 37
Guthrie, E. R., 260, 274

Hadley, S. W., 232, 254
Haith, M., 170, 171, 181
Hamburg, B. A., 83, 121
Hamburg D. A., 83, 121
Hamlyn, D. W., 211, 225
Hampson, J. G., 213, 226
Hampson, J. L., 213, 226
Hansen, E., 281, 292
Harlow, H. F., 260, 263,
265, 272, 274, 281,
292, 390
Harlow, M. K., 257–274,
263, 272, 274
Harmon, R. J., 65, 74, 86,
121, 125, 141, 142,
146, 149, 156, 172,
180, 181, 195, 201,
310, 346, 348, 351,
357, 360, 394, 405,
412
Haviland, J., 77–123, 49,
87, 121, 189, 201, 207,
221, 226, 340, 348,
361, 379, 395
Hays, W. L., 61, 74
Hebb, D. O., 171, 181
Hein, A., 176, 177, 178,
181
Held, A., 176, 177, 178,
181
Held, R., 185, 204
Henderson, C., 149–182,
89, 120, 142, 146, 149,
180, 342, 361, 386,
390
Hetzer, H., 142, 146

Hiatt, S., **149–182**, 144,
    146, 172, 181, 342,
    361, 386, 390
Hillman, D., 213, 225
Hinde, R. A., 49, *74,* 142,
    146, 277, 282, *291*
Hobbes, T., 24, 25, *40*
Hoffer, W., 296, *307*
Hoffman, M. L., **227–255,**
    209, 230, 233, 236,
    239, 244, 245, 246,
    247, 248, 249, *254,*
    255, 362, 370, 371,
    395, 402, 407, *412*
Hood, L., 210, *225*
Hooff, J. A. R. A. M. van,
    53, *74*
Horton, R., 260, *274*
Howard, J. L., 82, *122,* 152,
    154, *181*
Hull, C. L., 116, *121,* 261,
    274
Humphries, D. A., 44, 45,
    46, 53, *73*
Humphrey, G., 231, *254*
Hunt, J. McV., 167, *182,*
    194, 204, 399, 400,
    412
Hutt, C., 265, *274*

Iannotti, R. J., 229, *254*
Illingworth, R. S., 321, *348*
Inhelder, B., 184, 188, *203,*
    298, 299, *307,* 311,
    349, 398, *412*
Izard, C. E., **389–413,** 11,
    18, 22, 27, 28, *40,* 127,
    128, 129, 131, 132,
    136, 144, *146,* 172,
    181, 189, 206, *225,*
    232, 243, *254,* 364,
    374, 390, 392, 408,
    412

Jackson, E., 173, *181,* 197,
    201
Jackson, J. C., 88, *121,* 152,
    154, *181*
Jacob, F., 48, *74*

Jacobson, E., 293, 297, 298,
    307
Jaffe, J., 70, *75*
James, W., 22, 23, 25, 27,
    34, *40,* 77, 78, 79, 84,
    115, *121,* 125, *146,*
    206, 207, 211, 216,
    225, **232,** 254, 259,
    274
Jarvik, L. F., 312, *349*
Jaynes, J., 208, *225*
Jersild, A., 367, *374*
Johnson, D., 343, *350*
Johnson, H. J., 88, *120*
Jones, H. E., 81, 84, 118,
    121

Kagan, J., **11–41,** 35, *40,*
    81, 86, 88, *121, 122,*
    171, 173, *181,* 193,
    199, 339, 341, 342,
    349, 364, 378, 382,
    384, *387,* 394, 403,
    404, 407, *412*
Kahlbaum, 294
Kalafat, J., 86, 88, *122*
Kameya, L. I., 248, 251,
    254
Kanner, L., 79, *121*
Kant, 25, 26
Kaplan, L., 187, *201*
Kaswan, J., 369, *373*
Katz, D., 404, *412*
Katz, E. L., **351–360,** 345
Katz, L. B., 237, *253*
Kaufman, I. C., 281, *291,*
    292
Kearsley, R. B., 30, *40*
Keele, D. K., 343, *349*
Kirsch, B., 213, *225*
Kleck, R. E., 392, *412*
Klein, R., 193, *201*
Kligman, D. H., **125–148,**
    351, 361, 378
Kobayashi, L. R., 233, *254*
Koenig, K. L., 56, *74*
Kohlberg, L., 188, *201,*
    213, *225*
Kopin, I., 343, *350*
Koslowski, B., 139, *145,*
    368, *373*
Kotelchuch, M., 193, *201*

Kraepelin, 294
Kraus, R., 368, *374*
Krebs, D., 249, *254*
Kreutzer, M. A., 129, *146,*
    170, *180,* 367, *373*
Krowitz, A., 88, *120,* 151,
    180
Kruskal, J. B., 133, *146*

Lacey, B. C., 81, *121*
Lacey, J. L., 81, 82, 88, 108,
    115, *121,* 154, *181*
Laird, J. D., 232, 233, *254,*
    364, *374*
Lamb, M. E., 197, *201,* 264,
    274
Landis, C., 79, *121*
Lange, C., 23, 25, 27, *40,*
    78
Langer, A., 88, *120,* 151,
    152, *180*
Langer, J., 362, *374*
Lanzetta, J., 392, *412*
Lapackova, V., 355, *360*
Lashley, 259
Latane, B., 249, *254*
Laurentius, A., 23
Lawler, J., 154, *181*
Lazarus, R. C., 237, *255*
Lazarus, R. S., 408, *412*
Lecompte, G. K., 197, *201*
Lefford, A., 334, *347*
Lehrman, D. S., 291, *291*
Lerner, M. J., 237, *254*
Lester, B., 193, *201*
Levi, L., *40,* 83, *121*
Levine, L. E., 248, *254*
Levitt, E. A., 369, *374*
Levy, N., 136, *146*
Lewin, B., 293, 294, *307*
Lewis, H., 402, *412*
Lewis, M., **1–10, 77–123,**
    205–226, *10,* 49, 72,
    81, 86, 87, 88, 89, 90,
    92, 99, 104, 115, 119,
    120, 121, 122, 123,
    189, 197, *201, 202,*
    207, 210, 212, 213,
    214, 215, 216, 218,
    220, 221, *225, 226,*
    361, 362, 364, 377,
    379, 380, 384, 385,

Lewis, M., (cont.)
387, 395, 398, 402,
403, 407, 412
Lightbrown, P., 210, 225
Lindsley, D. B., 81, 122,
142, 147, 207, 226
Lipps, T., 231, 232, 233,
254
Lipton, R., 297, 300, 307,
343, 349
Littenberg, R., 193, 202
Loeb, J., 258, 274
Loevinger, J., 310, 349
Logan, F., 261, 274
Lombardo, J. P., 249, 255
Lorenz, K., 272, 273, 274
Love, L., 369, 373
Lucas, T. C., 199, 202
Lynd, H. M., 402, 412
Lynn, R., 154, 181

MacKay, D., 365, 368, 374
MacLean, P. D., 246, 254,
255
Mael, M., 337, 349
Mahler, M., 297, 307, 382,
387
Mahoney, M., 363, 374
Main, M., 139, 145, 149,
182, 368, 373
Malmstron, E. J., 79, 80,
121
Mandler, G., 11, 27, 30,·
40, 68, 74, 82, 122,
243, 255, 310, 342,
349
Mans, L., 345, 348
Marshall, J., 343, 349
Masters, J. C., 382, 387
Matas, L., 89, 123, 149,
155, 171, 182, 310
349, 381, 387
Mathews, K., 234, 237,
255
Mathews, K. E., 250, 255
McCall, R., 342, 349, 384,
387
McCarter, R., 80, 123, 127,
148
McDougall, W., 231, 232,

McDougall (cont.)
255, 259, 274
McFarland, J. L., 233, 254
McGhee, P., 342, 349
McIntire, M. D., 317, 349
McKenzie, B., 157, 175,
180, 181
McRoberts, G., 172, 182,
312, 350
Mead, G. H., 119, 122, 210,
225
Mears, C. E., 257–274,
265, 266, 274, 390
Mehrabian, A., 368, 369,
374
Melanchthon, P., 23
Melges, F. T., 142, 137
Meltzoff, A. N., 71, 74
Merleau-Ponty, M., 210,
211, 226
Metcalf, R. C., 20, 40
Meyers, K., 154, 181
Michaelis, R., 344, 349
Miles, W. R., 261, 274
Milgram, S., 250, 255
Miller, R. E., 84, 118, 120
Mitchell, 272
Mitchell, P., 309, 310, 311,
349
Monahan, L., 367, 368,
374
Money, J., 213, 226
Moore, B. S., 250, 255,
378, 379, 387
Moore, M. K., 71, 74, 153,
175, 180, 192, 197,
200, 202, 312, 337,
348, 349
Mordkoff, A., 237, 255
Morf, A., 183, 203
Morgan, G. A., 92, 122,
156, 181, 194, 202
Moscovici, S., 368, 374
Mosher, D. L., 405, 412
Moss, H., 81, 121
Mowbray, J. B., 276, 292
Muir, D., 175, 180, 192,
201
Murphy, L. B., 248, 249,
250, 255
Mussen, P., 255
Myers, G. D., 197, 202,

Myers (cont.)
337, 349

Naylor, A., 296, 307
Norcia, A., 172, 182, 312,
350

Obrist, P. A., 82, 88, 122,
152, 154, 181
Olds, J., 142, 147
Olds, M. E., 142, 147
Osgood, C., 136, 141, 147,
367, 374
Oster, H., 43–75, 44, 47,
48, 49, 50, 56, 69, 74,
86, 87, 366

Pankey, W., 331, 348
Papousek, H., 215, 226
Papousek, M., 215, 226
Paradise, E., 173, 181, 194,
202
Parmelee, A. H., 344, 349
Patterson, E., 81, 122
Pavlov, I., 259, 260, 274
Peiper, A., 49, 74, 344, 349
Penrose, L. S., 343, 349
Perez-Reyes, M., 154, 181
Peterson, C., 368, 374
Philipszoon, E., 136, 146
Piaget, J., 143, 147, 174,
176, 178, 179, 181,
183, 184, 185, 186,
187, 188, 191, 195,
196, 197, 199, 202,
203, 209, 211, 212,
226, 298, 299, 307,
311, 349, 362, 363,
364, 367, 374, 398,
399, 412
Pick, H., 175, 182
Pierson, W. P., 312, 349
Pine, F., 307, 382, 387
Pitcairn, T., 366, 374
Plato, 20, 21, 23, 25, 26
Ploog, D., 49, 74
Plutchik, R., 11, 27, 33, 40,
189, 203
Poresky, R. H., 141, 147
Prechtl, H., 321, 349

Pribram, K. H., 142, *147*, 384, *387*
Prideaux, E., 117, *122*
Provence, S., **293–307**, 297, 300, *307*, 382, 403
Provost, M., 155, *181*

Radke-Yarrow, M., 402, 407, *412*
Rajotte, P., 337, *349*
Ramsay, D., **149–182**, 342, 361, 390
Rapaport, D., 185, *203*, 293, 295, *307*
Ratliff, F., 262, *274*
Raynor, 259
Redican, W. K., 142, 143, *147*
Regan, D. T., 252, *255*
Regan, J. W., 252, *255*
Reich, J. H., **125–148**, 155, *180*, 351, 361, 378
Reymert, M. L., 11, 25, *40*
Rheingold, H. L., 87, 92, 104, *122*, 154, 156, *182*, 195, *203*
Ricard, M., 197, *203*
Ricciuti, H. N., 92, *122*, 141, *147*, 194, *202*
Richards, B. W., 312, *349*
Richards, C., 343, *349*
Richmond, J., 343, *349*
Riss, W., 142, *147*
Roe, K., 228, 241, *254*
Rosenblatt, J. S., 291, *291*
Rosenblum, L. A., **1–10**, **275–292**, *10*, 86, *122*, 157, *182*, 189, *202*, 274, 276, 279, 280, 281, 283, 285, *291*, *292*, 377, *387*, 401, 407, *412*
Rosenhan, D. L., 250, *255*, 378, 379, *387*
Rosenthal, L., 228, 237, *253*
Rossi, M., 183, *203*
Rothbart, M. K., 339, *349*, 406, *412*
Rowell, T. E., 277, *292*

Ruriel, E., 188, *201*
Russell, B., 38, *40*
Rutherford, E., *255*
Rutter, M., 185, *203*

Saal, D., 197, *203*
Saarni, C., **361–375**, 364, 370, *374*, *375*
Sacket, G. P., 276, 291, *292*
Sade, D. S., 281, *292*
Sagi, A., 233, *255*, 395, 407, *412*
Saint-Pierre, J., 194, 197, *203*
Salapatek, P., 92, *122*, 153, 156, 170, 172, 173, *182*, 193, 194, *203*, 312, 332, 334, *349*
Sander, L., 368, *373*
Sartre, J. P., 26, *40*
Savin, V. J., 84, 118, *120*
Scalia, F., 142, *147*
Scarr, S., 92, *122*, 153, 156, 170, 172, 173, *182*, 193, 194, *203*, 312, 332, 334, *349*
Schachter, S., 22, 25, *40*, 82, 84, 118, *122*, 207, 209, 216, *226*, 243, *255*
Schaffer, H. R., 149, 171, 172, 173, *182*, 193, 194, *203*
Schiff, W., 365, *375*
Schlosberg, H., 79, 80, *122*, 135, 136, *146*
Schwartz, A., 88, *122*, 153, 154, 155, 162, *182*, 312, 334, *349*
Seay, B., 281, *292*
Sellers, S., 193, *201*
Serafica, F., 198, 199, *203*, 312, 334, 343, *348*, *349*
Sermat, V., 136, *145*
Seward, G. H., 81, *122*
Seward, J. P., 81, *122*
Sharabany, R., 213, *225*
Shatz, M., 368, *375*
Shaver, K. G., 237, *255*

Shepard, R., 133, 134, *147*
Shepherd, J. F., 81, *123*
Sherk, L., 248, 250, *255*
Sherman, M. C., 87, *123*, 126, *147*
Sherman, S. E., 237, *255*
Shirley, M. M., 403, *413*
Shock, N. W., 81, *123*
Simmons, C., 237, *254*
Simner, M. L., 233, *255*, 395, 407, *413*
Simonov, P. V., 83, 84, *123*
Singer, J. E., *40*, 82, 84, 118, *122*, 207, 209, 216, *226*, 243, *255*
Singer, J. L., 408, *413*
Skinner, B. F., 79, *123*, 260, 261
Smith, G. F., 343, *349*
Sobey, K., 192, *203*
Sokolov, E. N., 154, 384, *387*
Solomon, R. L., 116, *123*, 195, *203*, 380, *387*
Somervill, J., 170, *182*
Sparling, S., 252, *255*
Speisman, J. C., 237, *255*
Spelke, E., 193, *201*
Spence, K. W., 261, 262, *274*
Spencer, 26
Spencer, H., 135, *147*
Spinoza, 25
Spitz, R. A., 85, *123*, 126, 142, *147*, 185, 194, 195, *203*, 296, 297, *307*, 394, 397, *413*
Spurzheim, 26
Sroufe, L. A., **309–350**, 31, 39, *41*, 65, 68, 72, 74, 86, 89, *123*, 143, *147*, 149, 155, 171, 172, 173, 175, *180*, *182*, 189, 194, 195, *203*, 204, 309, 310, 311, 312, 313, 317, 319, 321, 331, 334, 336, 338, 339, 340, 341, 342, 344, 345, 346, *348*, *349*, 357, *360*, 364, 381, *387*, 390, 393, 406, *413*

Starr, M. D., **377–387**
Staub, E., 248, 250, *255*
Stayton, D., 149, *182*
Stechler, G., 70, 72, 74, 127, *147*, 310, 311, *349*
Steele, W., 81, *123*
Steinschneider, A., 343, *349*
Stern, C., 312, *350*
Stern, D. N., 51, 56, 68, 70, 72, 75, 139, *147*, 212, *226*, 370, *375*
Sternfels, S., 172, *182*, 312, *350*
Steven, R., 193, *202*
Stich, M. H., 249, *255*
Stoel-Gammon, C., 337, *349*
Stone, C. P., 274
Stotland, E., 228, 234, 235, 237, 243, *255*, 404, *412*
Stutter, J. R., 82, *122*
Sullivan, H. S., 231, *255*
Suomi, S., 274
Sutterer, J. R., 152, *181*
Svejda, M., **149–182**, 342, 361, 386, 390

Thayer, S., 364, *375*
Thoa, N., 343, *350*
Thompson, J., 80, *123*
Thorndike, 259
Thorpe, J. K., **351–360**, 345
Tilker, H. A., 250, *255*
Tinbergen, 260
Tolman, 261
Tomkins, S. S., 18, 22, 25, 27, 28, *41*, 50, 70, 72, 74, 75, 79, 80, 94, *123*, 127, *147*, *148*, 189, *204*, 206, 217, *226*, 232, 243, *255*, 384, *387*, 390, 398, 402, 408, *412*, *413*

Trivers, R. L., 246, *255*
Tronick, E., 51, *73*, 175, *179*, 192, *200*, 312, 313, 329, *347*
Tulkin, A., 193, *202*
Turner, T., 363, *375*

Underwood, B., 250, *255*, 378, 379, *387*
Uzgiris, I., 167, *182*, 191, 194, 198, 199, *202*, *203*, *204*

Van Lehn, R., 81, *121*
Vaughan, K., 392, *412*
Vaughan, R., 392, *412*
Vine, I., 87, *123*
Von Bekesy, G., 262, 274
Vygotsky, L., 311, *350*

Wade, T. D., **125–148**, 351, 361
Waelder, R., 296, *307*
Walk, R., 150, 151, 153, 156, 157, 158, 159, 160, 161, 162, 170, *180*, *182*, 312, 332, 348, *350*
Wallington, S. A., 252, *254*
Walters, C., 160, *182*
Warnberg, L., 170, *182*
Waters, E., 72, 74, 86, 89, 90, 91, 93, *123*, 149, 155, 171, *182*, 189, 195, *203*, 310, 311, 339, 341, 346, *349*, 381, *387*
Watson, J. B., 86, *123*, 126, *148*, 259, 274
Watson, J. S., 71, 75, 86, *123*, 172, *182*
Watson, M., 369, *375*
Watson, R., 86, *123*
Webb, R. A., 82, *122*, 152, *181*
Wechsler, D., 81, *121*

Weinraub, M., 86, *123*, 380, *387*
Weinshilbaum, R., 343, *350*
Weiss, R. F., 249, *255*
Welker, W. I., 283, *292*
Wellman, J. M., 382, *387*
Wenger, M. A., 78, *123*
Werner, H., 126, *148*
White, B., 185, *204*
White, R., 21, 310, *350*
Williams, M., 252, *255*
Wilson, 154, *182*
Wine, J. D., 250, *255*
Wing, L., 347, *350*
Winnicott, D., 297, *307*
Wise, S., 51, *73*
Wittig, B., 198, *200*
Wohlwill, J., 371, *374*
Wolf, K., 85, *123*, 142, *146*, *147*, 297
Wolff, P. H., 56, 72, 75, 86, *123*, 187, *204*, 379, *387*
Wood, D. M., 154, *181*
Woodworth, R. S., 135, *148*
Wundt, W., 79, *123*, 135, *148*
Wunsch, J. P., *204*, 313, 319, 339, *349*, 406, *413*
Wylie, R. C., 211, *226*

Yang, R. K., 233, *254*
Yarrow, L. J., 185, *204*, 399, *413*
Yonas, A., 172, 175, *182*, 312, 313, *350*
Young, G., 44, *75*
Youngstein, K. P., 276, *292*
Youniss, J., 363, *375*

Zazzo, R., 214, *226*
Zigler, E., 311, 312, 344, *350*

Subject Index

Affect charge, 295
Affect display rules, 370
Affective–cognitive structures, 393–394, 403, 405
Affective concomitants of activities, 295–296
  health-clinical criteria for, 306
Affective regulation (primates)
  infant, 290–291
  maternal, 290–291
Affective states
  definition of, 379
  sequential dependencies among, 378–383
Affectivity
  and egocentrism, 298–299
  and sensorimotor intelligence, 299
Affectivity and cognition, relationship between, 310–311
  functional parallelism, 185–187, 193–195
  indissociability (inseparability), 184–185, 189–193, 362
  interaction, 187–188, 195–199, 363
Affects
  psychoanalytic theory of, 294–295
  relationships to other personality factors, 295
  and self-awareness, 298
  and the socialization process, 295
Aggression in rhesus monkeys, 271–273
Alerting reactions, 384
  sequelae of, 384–385
Alienation, 33

Anger, 32, 127, 143, 398
Anxiety, developmental study of, 298
Arousal, 27, 379
Assimilation, 385
Attachment, 35, 197–199
  infant primates, 287
Attention, 384, 385

Bayley test, 356

Cognition and affect. *See* Affectivity and cognition
Cognitive growth, 219–220, 224
  circular reactions, 209, 212
Communication, 126
  expression, 366
  intentionality, 365
Communication and cognition
  early development, 368
  inseparability, 368
  interpersonal processes, 369
Consciousness, 364
  processes in, 393–394
Contempt, 25, 399
Crying, 68–69, 127
  and the visual cliff, 332, 333, 335
  and the visual loom, 324, 326, 330–331, 335

Depersonalization, 33

Depth perception, 150–151, 152, 153, 157,
        159, 165
    in locomotor infants, 153, 161, 165
    in prelocomotor infants, 152–153, 162,
        179
Developmental shift, 149, 150, 151, 153,
        156, 158, 159, 162–166, 169–178,
        179
    discrepancy explanation, 150, 170–171
    experience, 150, 158, 170, 179
    fear system, development of, 172–173
    Piagetian theory, 173–176, 179
    reafference, 150, 176–178, 179
    self-produced movement, 150, 176–
        178, 179
    separation, 149
    stranger, reactions to, 149, 154–155
Differential emotions theory
    definitions, key, 391, 393
    propositions, major, 390, 393
Disgust, 127, 396, 399
Distress, 127, 395
    developmental changes in, 407–408
Disturbances of affective development,
        examples of, 300–306
Down's syndrome infants, 351, 356
    affect development, 311–312, 319,
        335–338, 340
    cognitive development, 311–312, 336–
        340
        and affect behavior, 341–343
    cortical deficits, 344
    hypotonia, 321
    motor development, 317
    object permanence, development of,
        337, 340
    physiological responsivity, 343
    retardation, 356
    visual cliff, response to, 332–334
    visual loom, response to, 322–324
        comparison to normal infants, 326–
        332
Duality of the self, 211–214, 220
    categorical self, 212–214, 220
    existential self, 211–212

Emotion
    categories of, 127
    as a change in state, 378
    characteristics of, 377–378
    definition of, 206–207, 210, 377
    expressions, present at birth, 395, 397

Emotion (cont.)
    facial patterns of, 221–223, 224
    history of, 20–26
    and infant–environment interactions,
        397–398
    James–Lange theory, 206–207
    measurement of, 78–84, 85, 87–88
        body posturing, 79–80, 84, 93
        facial expression, 79–80, 82, 84, 86,
            87, 89–91, 93–94, 97–102, 104–
            110, 112–114
            relation of heart rate to, 88–91, 92,
                97–110, 112–114, 116
        introspection, 78–79, 82–83, 84, 88–
            89
        nonverbal expression 82–83, 84
        physiological indices, 81–82, 83, 84,
            88–91, 115
            blood pressure, 81
            galvanic skin response, 81, 82, 84
            heart rate, 81, 82, 83–84, 88,
                89–91, 94, 96, 97–107, 109, 110,
                112–114
        synchrony among affect response
            systems, 116–118
    Schacter and Singer model, 207, 209
    and self-cognitions, 400, 402
    and self-control, 400, 402
    and self-recognition, 402–403
    survival functions, 395, 397
Emotional experience, differentiation of,
        371–373
Emotional expression, 125, 127, 141
    and cognitive development, 338–340
    peak, 127, 129
Emotional signaling, 354
Emotion–cognition interactions, 403,
        405. See also Affective–cognitive
        structures
Empathic arousal
    mechanisms, 230–237
    as a prosocial motive, 245–250
Empathic distress and prosocial action,
        245–250
Empathic overarousal, 250
Empathic response, self-regulation of,
        237–238
Empathy, 370–371
    cognitive component of, 238–242
    definition of, 228–230
Expressive signals, 367–368
    synchrony, 368

Facial action coding system (FACS), 44–
    49, 50, 53–57, 58–59, 62–63, 65,
    67–69
  advantages, 46, 49
  limitations, 46–47
Facial expression, 15, 18, 28, 45–46,
    68–69, 71–73, 127, 139
  brow–forehead region, 45–46, 57, 60–
    61, 63–72
  eyes, 45–46, 63
  lower face, 69
Fear, 17, 19, 20, 31, 32, 86–87, 90–91,
    104, 127, 143, 217, 218, 259, 401
  of heights, 150, 157, 179
    absence of, 150, 152, 153, 156
    avoidance and, 150, 156, 161, 162,
      164–165, 179
    cognitive–perceptual development,
      150, 166–169
    detour behavior, 161, 162, 164–166
    differential crossing, 160, 161,
      162–166
    direct placement, 151–152, 153, 166–
      167, 168–169
    discrepancy explanation, 150,
      170–171
    experience, 150, 158, 170, 179
    and fear system, development of,
      150, 172–173
    heart rate, 151–152, 153–156, 166–
      167, 168–169
    innate sensitivity, 150
    locomotion, 150–151, 156–157,
      162–166, 179
    locomotor crossing, 156, 159–166
    placing response, 160, 161, 162, 165,
      168
    reafference, 150, 176–178, 179
    self-produced movement, 150, 176–
      178, 179
Fear stimuli, infant primates, 284
Feeling tone, 28
Foster mothering, infant primates,
    276–279
  aunt–infant, 278–279
  cross fostering, 276–278

Guilt, 17, 37, 244–245, 401–402
  and prosocial action, 251–252

Habituation, 386
Happiness, 30, 127, 128
Hate, 20
Hedonic tone, 133, 135, 141, 142
Hostility, 18

Incentives, 29, 32, 33, 36
Infant–mother relationship, 263
Instincts, 258–260
Interest, 127, 397–400
Internal vs. external stimuli, 208–209
Isolation, 33

Joy, 30
  developmental changes in, 405

Laughter, 319
  relation to cognitive development in
    Down's syndrome infants,
    337–338, 339
  relation to development of fear
    expression in Down's syndrome
    infants, 335–336
Love, 20, 21, 22, 259, 263
  for mother, 263, 264
  for peer, 263
  among rhesus monkeys, 272

Macaque monkey, 277, 279, 281, 282
Maternal protection, infant primates, 280
Maternal rejection and punishment,
    infant primates, 280–281
Mood, 37, 382
Moro response, 130
Motives, 17, 18, 19, 38
Multidimensional Scaling, 133, 136, 137,
    141, 351–353, 359

Object concept, 190–191, 194–195,
    197–199
  object permanence scales, 194–195
  virtual object experiments, 192–193
Opponent process theory, 380
Orienting response, 378–383

Pain and emotional responses, 408–409

Parental attachment processes, 354
Personality, subsystems of, 389–390
Person permanence, 197–198
Play, 264–265
  in rhesus monkeys, 265–269
  mastery in rhesus monkeys, 267–268
  in squirrel monkeys, 289
Pride, 30
Primary emotions, 189
  vs. derived emotions, 217
Psychoanalytic theory, 185, 187

Rage, 259
Recognition of mother, infant primates,
    279–280
Reflexes, infant primates, 276
Rhesus monkeys,
  aggression, 271–273
  love, 272
  mastery, 267–268
  play, 265–269

Sadness, 17, 32, 127
Self, 30–31
Self-awareness, 209, 222–223
  differentiation between self and other,
    210–211, 218, 219
Self-recognition, 214–216, 220–221, 223
  mirror, 214–215, 220–221, 223
  pictorial representations, 215
  videotape representations, 215
Separation anxiety, 29, 35
Separation from mother, 380
  primates, 281–286
    depression, 281–282
    repeated depression, 286
    return of mother, 282, 283
Separation–individuation process, 297
Sequence effects, 381
Sexuality, 25
Shame, 20, 127, 398
Shaping, 260–261
Shyness, 398
Signal-operating characteristics, 354
Smiling, 53–57, 60–61, 63–67, 68–72,
    127
  neonatal, 396
  onset of, 355, 357
  social, 71–73, 352, 354, 355, 359
Social affective development, 141, 351
Social emotional development, 352, 354,
    358
Social signaling, 125, 143–144

Squirrel monkey, 276, 277, 278–279, 283
Startle, 384, 396
Stranger, response to, 193–195, 380
  anxiety, 29
  fear, 86–87, 89–90, 91, 92, 94, 97–104,
    220–221, 224
  in primates, 280
Stress values, 353–354
Surprise, 16, 190, 127, 143, 384, 400
Sympathetic distress, 242–244
  and prosocial action, 245–250

Temperament, 380
Tension, 341
Transformational structures, 363
Transitional reactions, 383
Tropisms, 258

Unconditioned responses, 260–261

Visual cliff, 151, 152, 161, 317–319
  fear on, 150, 151–152, 153–156, 158,
    166–169, 170–171, 172–178
  discrepancy explanation, 150, 170–171
  experience, 150, 158, 170, 179
  fear system, development of, 150,
    172–173
  heart rate, 151–152, 153–156, 166–
    167, 168–169
  Piagetian cognitive–perceptual
    development, 150, 166–169
  Piagetian sensorimotor development,
    173–176, 179
  reafference, 150, 176–178, 179
  self-produced movement, 150, 176–
    178, 179
  relation to response to visual loom
    experiment, 334–335
  response by Down's syndrome infants,
    332–334
  comparison with normal infants,
    332–334
Visual loom experiment, 313–316
  relation to response to visual cliff, 334–
    335
  response
    by Down's syndrome infants,
      322–324
    comparison with normal infants,
      326–332
    by normal infants, 324–326